WITCHCRAFT MEDICINE

Witchcraft MEDICINE

HEALING ARTS, SHAMANIC PRACTICES, AND FORBIDDEN PLANTS

Claudia Müller-Ebeling
Christian Rätsch · Wolf-Dieter Storl
Translated by Annabel Lee

INNER TRADITIONS
ROCHESTER, VERMONT

Inner Traditions
One Park Street
Rochester, Vermont 05767
www.InnerTraditions.com

Originally published in German under the title *Hexenmedizin: Die Wiederentdeckung einer verbotenen Heilkunst—schamanische Traditionen in Europa*

First U.S. edition published by Inner Traditions in 2003

Library of Congress Cataloging-in-Publication Data

Müller-Ebeling, Claudia.
  [Hexenmedizin. English]
  Witchcraft medicine : healing arts, shamanic practices, and forbidden plants / Claudia Müller-Ebeling, Christian Rätsch, and Wolf-Dieter Storl ; translated by Annabel Lee.— 1st U.S. ed.
     p. cm.
Translation of: Hexenmedizin.
Includes bibliographical references and index.
  ISBN 0-89281-971-5 (pbk.)
  1. Traditional medicine—Europe. 2. Medicine, Magic, mystic, and spagiric—Europe. 3. Witchcraft—Europe. I. Rätsch, Christian, 1957- . II. Storl, Wolf-Dieter. III. Title.
  GN477.M8513 2003
  306.4'61—dc22
                              2003016591

Printed and bound in the United States at Capital City Press

10 9 8 7 6 5 4 3 2 1

This book was typeset in Janson, with Franklin Gothic as a display typeface

Contents

Introduction: Is Witchcraft Medicine Good Medicine?

Wolf-Dieter Storl

Witchcraft medicine is the medicine of the earth. It is the oldest medicine of humankind, the healing art still used by the last remaining primitive peoples. Witchcraft medicine is primordial wisdom, primordial memory, and the true *religio*. It is the legacy of our Stone Age ancestors, which has been passed down in a continually shifting form through the Neolithic agricultural period, through the Bronze Age, and through the Iron Age, into the era of the Christian Middle Ages and their belief in miracles. The Inquisition did its best to destroy this ancient wisdom. But neither the threat of torture nor that of being burned at the stake, neither the ax of the so-called rational Enlightenment nor the reductionist straitjacket of a soulless, positivistic science has been able to permanently damage nature's medicine. For this medicine not only lives on in decaying, dusty traditions, but is nourished by the clear spring of wisdom, by the immediate inspiration of the devas, and by the inspiration of the spirits of the plants, animals, stones, stars, and elements as well.

Witchcraft medicine is based on the understanding of the healing powers of our inner and outer natures. Witchcraft medicine is more than a factual knowledge of medicinal herbs, poisonous plants, psychedelic compounds, or gynecological preparations. It is the ability to converse with the animal and plant spirits and to forge friendships with them, an ability that has been suppressed in most people. It is the ability to achieve the ecstasy that makes communion with these beings possible.

While this natural medicine includes the power plants, the ones that cause intoxication and ecstasy and that humans reach for when they want to obliterate their mundane state of existence and catapult themselves into the world "beyond," it mostly emphasizes the gentle plants that capture cosmic harmonies and convey them to humans so that the people may be healed. Only when humans radiate happiness and health can nature be happy and healthy. This is why Mother Gaia has powerful herbs and roots ready at hand.

Witchcraft medicine transcends clinical medicine, which, being bound in the corset of experimental natural science, proceeds only by measuring, documenting, and blindly testing what is tangible—the superficial matter—according to the principle of trial and error. Witchcraft medicine recognizes the "inner being" of the illnesses, the "little worm without skin or bones," the worms of hate and envy that wriggle their way into us and suck out our life energy. This healing art understands the magical bullets and destructive memories that bore deeply into our physical and spiritual bodies. In order to heal the wounds caused by such etheric-astral entities and negative occult energies, the practitioners of witchcraft medicine, the shamans, call on their allies—the plants, the stones, the animals, the water, the fire, the earth. These also have a deep dimension as spirit beings, angels, and devas. You can speak with them; they can respond.

Witchcraft medicine understands the vitality of existence and knows about the souls and the spirits of all creation. Witchcraft medicine is magical, and for this reason it causes discomfort to those whose souls are dead and frightens those whose spiritual eyes are blind. It scares them because it is a reflection of their powerlessness. To the bigoted inquisitors the efficacy of this medicine was granted by the devil himself. Thus the women who guarded this ancient wisdom were considered evil seductresses. To the schoolmaster of the "Age of Enlightenment," witchcraft medicine was an annoying superstition based on erroneous thinking that had to be eradicated from the minds of the country folk. To the masters of modern ideology, witchcraft medicine, with the special powers of communication it entails, is simply not a matter important enough for discussion; it belongs to the realm of a schizophrenic, a mentally unstable person, or, at best, a hopeless romantic. But in the end it might just be witchcraft medicine that leads us out of our current ecological and spiritual crisis, for its roots reach deep into the earth and tap into the healing waters of primordial wisdom.

But the following must also be acknowledged: Evil witches do indeed exist! Asocial magicians, malicious sorceresses driven by resentment and greed, and those who use their knowledge of the occult in order to bring harm to others can be found throughout the world, from South America to East Asia, from Africa to the South Pacific. Their abilities are feared mainly in unstable societies where poverty, violence, and oppression reign. A central concern in African medicine is determining who the destructive magician is and rendering him harmless. Ethnologists have collected from exotic lands many examples of witchcraft and murder by voodoo (Lessa and Vogt, 1965: 298).

These phenomena also exist in the Western world. During the mid-1970s hippies, alternative communards, illegal immigrants, dropouts, and legions of Southern Californians fleeing violence and environmental catastrophes (such as pollution and smog) streamed north into the still-pristine forests of Oregon. The resulting unstable social climate became a breeding ground for sorcery and unhealthy occultism. I lived in Oregon at the time, and during those years bizarre occurrences were seen frequently. Again and again farmers found their horses and cows dead in the pasture, their genitals or udders cut off. Not far from my house a hitchhiker was arrested, and his pockets were found to be filled with severed human ears. One day the gas station where I usually filled my car was not in service because a biker had killed the owner and then sucked blood out of her jugular vein before driving off. The talk was of witchcraft and Satanism.

This sort of pathological behavior has nothing to do with the witchcraft medicine that we are talking about here! Nor does witchcraft medicine have anything to do with the kind of rabid, man-hating feminism that experienced a peculiar flowering during this period in Oregon. The archaic medicine we are speaking about is a holistic one, embracing both the masculine and the feminine, the sun and the moon.

The malicious witch of fairy tales, like the one in the story of Hansel and Gretel, eats small children. However, this figure is never representative of a living person; instead it represents a negative spiritual archetype that impedes the maturation of the individual soul. This witch symbolizes the fear of the light of truth. She lives in the darkness, unripened by the light. Because she is separated from the whole of herself, she is unable to shine; therefore she is, necessarily, ugly. Like the old winter witch made of straw that country people burn in the springtime so that the beautiful goddess of summer can make her entrance, the negative spiritual witch must also go through the purifying, transforming spiritual fire. Only then can the king's daughter (Anima) and the king's son (Animus) celebrate their marriage. Their wedding symbolizes the discovery of the self, the process of healing and becoming whole.

The Christian inquisitors were obsessed with the archetype of the ugly, life-hating witch. They projected their own spiritual disease, their own obsessions, onto innocent women, often poor or elderly, whom they tortured and burned at the stake. What was originally intended as an internal process of becoming whole was turned into an external practice of black magic.

In order to understand the nature of witchcraft medicine, we must look deeply into the well of remembrance. The roots of witchcraft medicine lie in our Stone Age ancestors' experience of nature. We shall now dig into this soil.

"When the strong commit violence against the weak, it means that the strong are opposing nature. That which places itself contrary to nature will very soon come to an end."

—Lao Tse, *Tao Te Ching*

Wolf-Dieter Storl

The Wild Earth and Its Children

After the glaciers receded, the Ice Age tundra where great herds of buffalo, reindeer, woolly rhinoceros, and mammoths had grazed was gradually sown with the seeds of trees. Many of the herds died out; some migrated to Siberia. The last of the nomadic hunters of large animals followed them. It was, in Eurasia, the end of the Paleolithic period.

The forest drew under its spell the small hunting tribes that remained behind. They hunted the shy wild animals that hid in small herds deep in the forest—deer, stags, and wild boars—and the somber lone wanderers, such as the bear, the badger, and the moose in the bogs. To hunt like this was laborious; it took more time than it had before and bagged less. In equal proportions to the rate at which the hunting bounty diminished, plant-gathering increased in value. Within the natural division of work of the primitive people, collecting roots, fruit, bark, and birds' eggs fell mostly to the female gender; thus the work of women gained in importance. While the meat was distributed among the community according to strict regulations, the women gathered the daily plant rations for their families. It is still like this today among hunter-gatherers: The men work at politics, securing friendships and nurturing alliances for when the time comes for the meat to be divided; the women tend to the daily aspects of survival.

The tribes would settle for a while in places where gathering was feasible. Harbors were prized as camps, for there one could find the starchy tonic roots of the cattail, the marsh woundwort, the club rush, the arrowhead, or the water chestnut. One could also use the duckweed (*Lemna*) for soup or eat the juicy shoots of the reed, and the nutritious seeds of the winnowed or flooded sweet grass (*Glyceria*) were greatly valued. In addition, harbors provided various crustaceans, mollusks, and small amphibians.

Besides making arrows for hunting birds and small animals, constructing fish traps, knotting nets, and making harpoons and hooks, the men probably spent the rest of their time—similar to the hunter-gatherers of today—loafing about and communicating with the many spirits that animated the forest, the cliffs, and the water. This era is known as the Mesolithic period.

The Mesolithic people moved with the seasons in broad circles to different hunting-and-gathering regions. They always returned to the same camps. Many of their favorite plants grew there. Spilled seeds and the disposed rinds of tubers found a suitable environment when the competitive vegetation was trampled down and the ground was fertilized with ashes, excrement, urine, and trash. The step to domestication was, therefore, but a small one. During this period some hunters in the Near East intentionally began to turn the soil, make small mounds, and sow grass seeds they had gathered previously. Young animals were tethered or fenced in, and eventually tamed. In this way the hunter-gatherer groups became settled. They built themselves permanent houses with stalls for the captured animals.

Hunter-gatherers have few possessions, and most of these are incorporeal: They are visions, fairy tales, songs, magical incantations, and medicinal knowledge. These people live from hand to mouth, in the here and now. Who wants always to be lugging heavy burdens around with them? But for sedentary tribes it makes good sense to have large jugs and containers made of clay. Grains and other food can be stored in them, and beer can be brewed. In ancient times beer—made with consciousness-expanding herbs—was a sacred drink with which the forces of the fate, the sun, the earth, and the vegetation gods were celebrated (Rätsch, 1996: 50). This cultural transformation in which the first permanent settlements developed is called the Neolithic revolution by primeval historians.

Neolithic village settlements spread out from Asia Minor and up the Danube River and its tributaries. Toward the end of the fifth century the pioneers, people of what is known as the Linear Pottery culture, settled the river valleys of central Europe. There they

Paleolithic cave painting of a mammoth.

Wild men inspired the imagination of the Middle Ages, and they remain a fascination around the world today. This woodcut is the title picture of a book that tells the story of a wild man and the lady Venus. The giantlike man, with hair over his entire body, carries a small figure of Lady Venus in his arm. The naked figure in the radiant halo is reminiscent of the Virgin Mary in the mandorla. In this context she represents the temptation to sin, because with her eyes she is urging the young knight to follow her. However, what awaits him is the "prison of love," where as a prisoner of Lady Venus he will be subject to hellish torture. The wild man serves as the guard of the prison of love. (Woodcut by Diego de San Pedro from the *Carcel de Amor*, 1493.)

farmed wheat and barley, fava beans, and flax, and for their matrilineal families they built square communal houses twenty to thirty meters long in the middle of areas that had been burned. After a decade or two, when the soil had been depleted of nutrients and the fields and meadows had lost their fertility, the first farmers moved on. Once again they cleared the next piece of the immense primordial forest, logged the huge trees using fire and hewn-stone axes, seeded the disturbed land, and provided the cattle, goats, and sheep with a new grazing area.

The Neolithic settlements were tiny islands in a sea of green leaves. Still, several thousand years later, in the early Middle Ages, the tree cover was so thick that a squirrel could have leaped from tree to tree from Denmark to southern Spain without ever touching the ground.

On the edges of the cultural islands, on the transitional ground between agricultural fields and the primordial forest, an edge-biotope developed. Thorny undergrowth such as blackberry, wild rose, sloe, gooseberry, hawthorn, buckthorn, barberry, and sea buckthorn and fast-growing hedgerow trees like rowan, black alder, hazel, and elder found a suitable ecological environment there. This natural hedge acquired a practical purpose for the Neolithic farmers: It was an effective fence for the scattered grazing animals. The more the ruminants chewed on the growth, the thicker the thorn barrier became, until a natural hedgerow was created. Posts, stakes, and rods could also be cut from the hedge, as could laths for the walls (which were then daubed with clay) and materials for basket weaving. Nutritious birds' eggs, juicy berries, and tasty nuts could be found in the hedgerow. The most potent medicinal herbs also grew in this edge-biotope.

But above all, the thick thorny hedge offered protection. It prevented the wolves and bears from penetrating, as well as the voracious deer, which had a keen eye for the emerging agricultural crops. The hedge probably also discouraged the "wild people"— the last of the fur-wearing hunter-gatherers who still roamed the forest and who were thought to steal children—from entering. (In the Middle Ages such "wild folk" were hunted and executed by the knights.)

Today the thorny shrubs, especially the hawthorn and the wild rose, symbolize protected, undisturbed sleep. Fairy tales speak of a thorny hedge of roses, and many farmers still place a rose gall (the round, mosslike growth on the stems of wild roses that is caused by the sting of the rose gall wasp, also called a rose apple or sleep rose) under the crib of newborns so that they will sleep quietly and deeply.

For Stone Age settlers the hedgerow was not only a physical barrier between the cultivated land and the wilderness; it was a metaphysical boundary as well. The wild men lived behind the hedges, and the world of ghosts, trolls, goblins, and forest monsters also began there. This was where one encountered the seductive, beautiful, and sly elves. In this place the old deities of the Paleolithic past were still at work.

The archaic hunters and gatherers had been one with the forest, and they had lived in harmony with the forest spirits. In contrast, the forested wilderness was no longer very familiar to the Neolithic farmers and was, in fact, sinister.[1]

---

[1] The forest is full of frightening things for those who do not live in it. This has always been the case. For the central African Bantu tribe, who clear the woods in order to plant their plantain and yams, the primordial forest is a dangerous place, whereas for the Ba-Twa, a forest tribe in Africa, the forest is God itself—goodness and security. Over time the Western world has distanced itself so far from nature that here too the forest has become a frightening place—but for different reasons. Western people are scared of rabid foxes, and they are afraid to eat wild raspberries or blueberries—after all, they might be contaminated with fox tapeworm eggs. And there are ticks, which can cause Lyme disease and encephalitis if they bite you. The best solution is never to go into the

The Paleolithic goddess of the cave, the protector of the animals and of the souls of the dead, increasingly came to be viewed as a fertile earth mother in the Neolithic period. As with the early Stone Age hunters, the goddess of the farmers appeared to the Neolithic people in visions and sent them their dreams. They also knew that the goddess could hear, feel, and mourn. The fertility of the soil was dependent on her benevolence. Agriculture progressed in a continuous dialogue with her. Plowing and tilling the soil were considered an act of love; impregnating Mother Earth was the religion, and those who impregnated her were the worshippers. In fact, the word *cultivate* originally meant nothing more than service to the gods, honor, sacrifice, and nurturing.

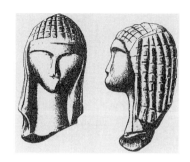

The great Paleolithic Goddess: the Venus of Brassempouy, carved in ivory.

But in spite of worship and ritual, discontent arose and the consciousness of the first farmers was seized with negativity. They defiled the forest, scorched the earth, and laid waste to the soil. The earth goddess became the lamenting mother. She mourned the countless children to whom she had given birth and who had fallen victim to the sickle, the ax, and the spade.

The creation myths of cultivators and farmers always place the violent death, murder, or sacrifice of a divine being at the beginning of their agricultural way of life. The feelings of gratitude and security that permeated the connection between the simple hunter-gatherers and the forest disappeared into feelings of guilt that had to be ameliorated with increasingly elaborate sacrifices, including gruesome, religiously institutionalized human sacrifices, head-hunting, and cannibalism.[2] Consequently, according to Mircea Eliade, the great scholar of religion, the Neolithic revolution brought about a reevaluation of all values, a "religious revolution" (Eliade, 1993: 45). The Christian concepts of the sacrifice of the innocent son of God and the *mater dolorosa* who mourned him and held him in her lap also have their roots in the myths of the sedentary Neolithic farmers. The community was increasingly guided by the priests, who ruled over the ritual calendar and who determined when to sow and harvest and when to make offerings and sacrifices according to the position of the stars, and less by the shamans, who could talk to the forest and animal spirits.

The unified world of the primitives was gradually separated into two realms: the cultivated land on one side and the wilderness behind the hedgerow on the other; the tame, working animals and the dangerous wild animals; the friendly spirits of the house and farm and the forest spirits one must be careful of. And so the era, which people remember as "golden," dims—"By the sweat of your brow / you will eat your food / until you return to the ground / since from it you were taken" (Genesis 3: 19).[3]

---

forest! (Or you can do what many do when they go hiking, and march through the forest as if through enemy territory.) When considered soberly, however, the fear of the forest reveals itself to be mere hysteria. The likelihood of catching rabies or tapeworm in the woods is less than the chance of being hit by a truck. The fear of the forest is the fear of one's own soul, of the "evil witch," of the shadows of one's own personality.

[2] Slash-and-burn farming and agriculture are heinous acts to the hunter-gatherers. When the American authorities wanted to force the Native Americans in the Northwest to become farmers, Smohalla, the dreamer of the Nez Percé tribe, expressed his anger with the following words: "You demand that I should plow the soil? Should I take a knife and slice open my mother's breast? When I die, then she will not let me rest in her lap. You want me to dig up the stones? Should I take the bones out from under her skin? When I die, she won't take my body so that I can be born again! You demand that I cut the grass and make hay and sell it like the whites! But should I dare cut the hair of my mother?"

[3] The Neolithic worldview, which separated the cultural landscape from the wilderness, peaked in the dualistic vision of Zoroaster. Thus a Satan (Ahriman) stands in opposition to the God of creation (Ahura Mazda). One is responsible for all that is evil (wild animals, poisons, weeds) and the other is responsible for good (domestic animals, medicine, cultivated plants). This schizophrenic vision still guides Western religion—Judaism as well as Islam and Christianity (Storl, 2002: 139).

The Power of the Wilderness

The hedgerow that surrounded the clearing was by no means an impenetrable wall. People were conscious of the fact that their small islands of communities, which had been carved out of the primordial forest, were in and of themselves weak and powerless. Thanks only to the boundless power of the wilderness were life and survival possible. From the wilderness came the firewood that burned in the hearth, in the heart of the farm, and with its help the meat was roasted, the soup cooked, and the cold kept at bay from body and soul. Deer, boars, and other wild animals that completed the diet came from the wilderness, as did the medicinal plants and mushrooms that the old women collected. And in a few years, after the fertility of the soil had been depleted, the community had to turn once again to the primordial forest and clear a new place and make it habitable. But the expended earth was taken back into the fold of the wilderness, was overrun with fresh green growth, and her fertility was regenerated.

From beyond the hedgerow came strength. From the wilds came fertility. The human race also renewed itself from one generation to the next through a stream of energy that the dead mediated from beyond the fence. The ancestors came from there seeking rebirth in the circle of the clan. For a long time the hazel tree, a typical hedge tree, was considered a conduit for wild fertile energy from the dimension beyond.

"To the hill I wended, deep into the wood, a magic wand to find, a magic wand found I . . ."

— *THE LAY OF SKÍRNIR*

Hazel Tree *(Corylus avellana)*

Man has always expected the hazel tree to protect him from the chaotic powers and energies of the beyond, energies such as lightning, fire, snakes, wild animals, diseases, and magic. In the last century the anthroposophists planted a "protection wall" of hazel trees around the Goetheanum* to ward off negative spirits. However, it is precisely the dimensions beyond that the small tree connects to. According to René Strassmann, if you fall asleep under a hazel, you will have prophetic dreams (Strassmann, 1994: 174). And the alchemist Dr. Max Amann advised that "contact to friendly nature spirits can be easily gained beneath hazel branches."

Hazel branches had probably already been used by Stone Age magicians to tap into the powerful energies of the world beyond and transmit them to the everyday world. It then becomes clear why the magical stave with the snake coiled around it, the caduceus of Hermes (the shamanic god of antiquity who crossed boundaries), was cut from a hazel tree. This stave became the symbol of trade, medicine, diplomacy, and the river of Plutonic energy that revealed itself in precious metals (money). When Hermes touched people with the hazel branch, they could speak for the first time.

Dowsers still consider hazel branches to be the best conductors of energy. With them dowsers can detect the sensitive water veins in the earth, as well as precious metals (silver and gold). The ancient Etruscans knew of dowsers *(aquileges)* who were able to find buried springs with hazel branches. The Chinese feng shui masters of more than five thousand years ago also knew how to use these wands in order to detect the flow of the "dragon lines" in the earth. Hazel branches still work today for this purpose, and are much faster and cheaper than technical instruments.

* The Goetheanum in Basel, Switzerland, was designed by Rudolf Steiner (1861–1925) as a place to teach the doctorines of his spiritual, mystical, and pedagogical system known as anthroposophy. (Trans.)

The ability to influence the weather is a shamanic trait recognized throughout the world. The ancient European shamans used hazel branches in order to make rain; such weather-makers still existed in the Middle Ages. A law from a seventeenth-century witch trial reads, "A devil gave a hazel branch to a witch and told her to beat a stream with it, upon which a downpour followed." It also says, "A witch-boy flogged the water with a hazel switch until a small cloud rose up from it. Not long thereafter a rainstorm began" (Bächtold-Stäubli, 1987: vol. 3, 1538).

Hazel energy can also be used to subdue nasty weather. When there is too much thunder and hail, farm women of Allgäu throw a few hazel catkins from the bunches of herbs that were blessed on Ascension Day (August 15) onto the hearth fire. And didn't Mary, when she wanted to visit her cousin Elizabeth in the mountains, seek protection from a storm under a hazel tree? People today still know that the hazel has something to do with fertility. To "go into the hazelwood" means nothing other than to copulate. "Anneli, with the red breast, come, we'll wend our way into the hazelwood," goes a Swiss folk song. "Easy" girls are given a hazel stick during the May Festival. In the symbolic language of the Middle Ages the hazel was considered to be the "tree of seduction." A Moravian song warns a virgin about the dangerous tree:

> *Protect yourself, Lady Hazel, and look all around,*
> *I have at home two brothers proud, they want to cut you down!*

The unconcerned Lady Hazel responds:

> *And if they cut me down in winter, in summer I'll green again,*
> *But when a girl loses her maidenhead, that she'll never find again!*

It is no wonder that the nun Hildegard of Bingen did not speak particularly highly of the hazel: "The hazel tree is a symbol of lasciviousness, it is rarely used for healing purposes—when, then for male impotency." In those days a hazel branch was hung over the bed of a married couple as a remedy for infertility. And as a sign that they were hoping for the best, the couple carried with them hazel branches pregnant with nuts.

"When there are hazelnuts there are also many children born out of wedlock." "When the hazelnuts prosper, so do the whores." Such sayings are found throughout Europe. Ethnologists trace them back to the fact that the youth escaped the suspicion of the guardians of public morals when they were out collecting nuts in the forest. More likely there is another explanation—people who are bound to nature determine themselves instinctively on and are part of the fertility rhythms of the forest.

Our forefathers believed that the ancestral spirits conveyed the unspent energy from the wilderness and the beyond to the living. It was the spirits who sent babies and who blessed the fields with fresh green life. Among the northern European heathens, many midwinter rituals included boys wrapped in fur pelts who raided the villages and flogged people and animals with hazel branches. The boys embodied the ancestral spirits. The Celtic god of winter, Green Man, who visited the houses, hearths, and hearts of the people during the winter solstice, also carried hazel branches, whose lash made everything fertile, prosperous, and rich with milk.

But the living could also send essential nourishment to those on the other side.

The hazel bush (*Corylus avellana* L.) has always been considered a magical tree and an important remedy in witches' medicine. The writers of antiquity already attributed magical powers and rare effects to the "pontic" (bitter) nut. Dioscorides said that "the eyes of blue children can be colored black by rubbing the oil of roasted, finely grated shells on the forehead" (*Materia medica* I.179). (Woodcut from Hieronymus Bock, *Kreütterbuch*, 1577.)

It was believed that those who found the *Haselwurm*—a creature half human, half snake—and ate its flesh would attain extraordinary powers.

Since Neolithic times hazelnuts have been "fed" to the dead by pressing a nut into their hands or between their teeth. The dead Celts, like the Chieftain of Hochdorf, Germany (from the Hallstatt period), were laid to rest on hazel branches. In November, on the ancient Celtic festival of the dead, children dressed as spirits of the dead and ghosts went begging from house to house. They were given the seeds of life—hazelnuts and apples—which lasted throughout the winter. The Germanic tribes, in particular the Alemanni, stuck sticks of hazel on grave sites.

Fertility is not the only gift from the other world. The kind of wisdom that far exceeds the boundaries of ordinary human understanding also comes from there. The hazel tree makes this knowledge available to the living; it helps them to crack the hardest "nuts" (riddles). Celtic judges carried hazel branches. The ancient heralds, who strode over borders like Hermes, also carried such staves so that their words would be intelligent and well chosen. The Germanic tribes stuck hazel branches in the ground around the *Thingstead*, the place where the tribal council was held and where duels took place. In this way the thunder-god, Thor, whose hammer symbolizes justice, was present. The hazel branches were sacred to this god of fertility and of the life-giving rain, who was the protector of the earth's treasures and the vanquisher of the snakes. The hidden treasures Thor found with his magic wand also belonged to him; presumably the handle of his hammer was made of hazelwood. The shamanic god Odin (Wodan, Wotan), lord of the bards and magicians, also made use of the hazel branch. The magical wand sacred to him was cut from the hazel tree and carved with reddened runes on Wodan's day (Wednesday). The hazel is also said to be the enemy of snakes. Saint Patrick, the patron saint of Ireland, allegedly used a hazel stick to chase all the snakes off the green island. In the Black Forest region children who had far to travel were given hazel branches so that they would be safe from snakes. And if a circle is drawn around a snake with a hazel branch, the snake cannot escape.

In addition, the *Haselwurm*, a white serpent with a golden crown, was believed to live under a very old hazel tree, one that had been invaded by a mistletoe. Eye witnesses described this snake queen as half human, half serpent. She had a head like an infant or a cat and she cried like a child. She was called the "serpent of paradise" in the Middle Ages, because she was believed to be the same snake that had seduced the humans in paradise. Nevertheless, those who find this snake and eat of her flesh will receive wondrous powers: They will have command over the spirits, they will have the ability to become invisible, and they will know all of the hidden healing powers of all herbs. Paracelsus was said to have eaten such a snake, and "that is why when he went out into the fields the herbs spoke to him and told him which evils and illnesses they were effective for." Naturally, it is not easy to capture this snake. One should go before sunrise on a new moon. And the right spells must be spoken: one that addresses the hazel branch and one that charms the snake. So that the snake will remain quiet, dried mugwort must be strewn on the magical creature.

This mysterious serpent is connected to the archaic brain stem, including the entire limbic system, which appears in the minds of those deep in meditation (the crowned snake-head). The instincts are anchored here in this most ancient part of the nervous system. Sexuality, fertility, premonitions, and emotions have their physiological basis here as well. The hazel is able to transmit subtle impulses to this center.

Divine Visitors to the Small Cultural Island

The gods also came from beyond, from deep in the forest. They came to demand tribute from the people and to bless and inspire them. For a long time into our own era, the "spirit of life," decorated with the branches of fir and holly trees, strode through the snowy winter forest on the solstice. The spirit blessed the animals in the forest and those in the barn before he made the humans happy with visions of the newly ascending light of life. This light-bringing spirit lived on in the Christ child, who came at midnight, as well as in Santa Claus. The spirit comes from far away, from the North Pole or from the dark, saturnine conifer forests. Often he flies like the shamans, with a sleigh drawn by reindeer, or rides an elk, or sometimes he even walks. A merry band of elves accompanies him. He slips down the chimney in the deep of the night to touch the sleeping people with his life-dispensing hazel wand and leave good fortune in their shoes, which have been set out.

Those from beyond, the transsensory beings, also came through the hedgerow so as to spend awhile with the humans during periods determined by the arc of the sun, the phases of the moon, and the weaving of the constellations. During the full moon of February the white virginal goddess of light left the caves with her bears and a retinue of elementary spirits. She woke up the bees and the seeds, which were still sleeping under a blanket of snow, and shook the tree trunks so that the sap would flow anew. For her appearance Stone Age people prepared themselves with a cleansing sweat lodge. Fermented birch sap sweetened with honey provided great happiness. Seized by the awakening spirit of life, stirred by the dancing and singing elemental beings, the people began to dance wildly and make faces. The disease-bringing spirits—usually crippled, knotty figures with angry expressions—were also honored and sent back into the woods with small offerings.

The Alemannic *Fastnacht* (Shrove Tuesday) celebrations, with their wild man and their witch's dance, is an echo of the ancient nature festivals. These processions of horrifying and beautiful *Perchten** who visit the human settlements during this time of year visually represent much transsensory wisdom. The first day of February, known today as Candlemas, was celebrated as the Imbolc festival in honor of the birch goddess by the insular Celts. As one of the quarter days, it is still considered to be a witch's holiday.

> ### Birch (Betula)
>
> The spirit of the birch tree appeared to the archaic humans as a virgin veiled in light, full of magical and healing powers. The original Indo-Europeans called this benevolent goddess and friend to man Bhereg, meaning "wrapped in brilliance." To this day the birch tree is called this, in different variations, throughout Germanic-, Slavic-, Baltic-, French-, Spanish-, and Celtic-speaking regions. It has always been endowed with qualities of purity, light, and new beginnings.
>
> The Celts saw Brigit, the muse of the seekers of wisdom, the healers, and the inspired bards, in the birch. She is the white virginal bearer of light who lets the days grow longer again in February. During this prespring period, the primitive people tapped the birches and collected precious sap. The sap stimulates urine and bile, purifies and cleanses the blood, and strengthens the kidneys and urinary tract.
>
> The tree of light reminded the Slavic and Siberian peoples of white-feathered

"Be joyous birch trees, be joyous green ones! The maidens are coming to you, bringing you cakes, bread, and omelets."

—OLD RUSSIAN SONG

---

* The costumed, masked participants in the Shrove Tuesday processions. (Trans.)

The birch tree (*Betula* spp.) is generally considered the tree that supplied the branches that were bound together to make witches' brooms. The "witch's broom" was originally a shamanic spirit horse, a heathen wand of life (a symbol of fertility), and was used as a magical bundle during sacred ceremonies and for the protection of the house. Parasitical growths on the branches of the Moor birch (*Betula pubescens* Ehrh.) caused by an invasion of a fungus (*Taphrina betulina*) causes deformations that are still referred to as "witch brooms" in botanical literature. (Woodcut from Hieronymus Bock, *Kreütterbuch*, 1577.)

swan maidens. Sometimes these women wed shamans and lent them their wings, which carried them into the etheric dimensions. The German peoples thought about Freya in her delightfully sparkling necklace (*Brísingamen*) when they saw this tree. They also associated the tree with Bertha, "the radiant."

In the distant Himalayas the birch (Sanskrit: *Bhurga*) is worshipped as the radiant white goddess, whose vehicle is a white swan or a goose. Saraswati—as she is called there—inspires the humans with wisdom and knowledge, with the arts of writing and oratory. She brings everything into flow, and brings the river of healing and poetic inspiration. She too appears to the people in February, when whole throngs of schoolchildren and their teachers get dressed up and carry her image through the streets. The first books in which the Vedic sages wrote their visions were made from the bark of birch trees. In Europe the birch was also considered to be a tree of learning. During antiquity children were taught the joys of learning with birch whips.

Like the white virginal goddess herself, the birch represents beginnings. She is young and fresh, like a blank page upon which the future can manifest itself. Birch green symbolizes the promise of a new spring. At the start of the agricultural year, the northern European farmers placed birch branches on their fields and buildings. The first time the cows were let out to pasture they were driven along with birch sticks or herded over birch branches. The farmers "flog," "slap," or "beat" everything that is to flourish. The virgins are not spared, and are driven from their beds with laughter. The birch stands for the beginning of love. In pre-Christian times smitten boys would place fresh green birch twigs in front of the house of the one they were courting. The young people danced merry round dances beneath the maypole, which was a decorated birch tree. And when Freya blessed love with the birth of a child, the placenta was buried beneath a birch tree as an offering to the goddess. The crib, the first bed of a new citizen of the earth, was to be made from birch wood as well.

Naturally, the druids made the birch (*Beth*) into the first letter of their tree alphabet (*Beth loius nion*) and the first month of the tree calendar. Robert Graves believed that this month went from December 24 to January 20 (Ranke-Graves, 1985). But because the Celtic calendar was a fluid moon calendar that went from new moon to new moon, such an exact calculation of time is doubtful. It is possible that the birch month commenced with the appearance of the "virgin of light" in February.

The Germanic tribes knew of a birch rune (ᛒ) that transmits the feminine growing energy of spring. At least that is what my friend Arc Redwood—an English gardener who carved this rune in wood, reddened it, and placed it in his garden like an idol—believes. He claims this has caused everything in his garden to grow better.

The birch tree is a sign of new beginnings not only in a cultural sense, but in nature as well. The cold-hardy tree was the first to seed itself on the ground after the glaciers receded. The Stone Age people were able to survive with its help. Archaeological digs show that Paleolithic hunter-gatherers used birch gum to secure their arrowheads and harpoons to the shaft. Shoes and containers were made from birch bark, and clothing was made from the bast fiber. "Ötzi," the Neolithic man who was found frozen in a glacier crevasse, also carried a bag made out of birch bark. The Native Americans and Siberians still carry birch-bark containers like our Stone Age ancestors once did. Maple syrup can be stored for a whole year in such containers. The inner bark could be eaten in an emergency, and in the springtime people tapped the sweet sap, which was occasionally left to ferment into an alcoholic drink. The birch is still the most important tree to the Ojibwa Indians. They decorate their wigwams and make everything from canoes to spoons, plates, and winnowers for wild rice from the birch bark. They even make watertight buckets and cooking pots with the bark. Glowing hot stones are placed in the sewn and resined birch-bark pots for cooking.

The birch tree stands for purity. Shrines and sacred sites were ritually swept with a birch broom to encourage evil ghosts to depart. In later times the ritual broom became the witch's broom; witches used it to fly to Blocksberg. The birch broom is occasionally used in England to fight against invisible flying astral spirits (witches) or the lice and fleas brought in by them. The old year is also swept away with a birch broom. In ancient Rome the lectors carried bundles of birch branches tied with red cord when swearing a magistrate into office. A bundle of birch branches with an ax in the middle is known as a *fascis*, and is considered the sign of the cleansing rule of the law. Italy's "Mr. Clean," Mussolini, appropriated this symbol for his fascist movement.

In the vicinity of the small farm where I live there is a "broom chapel." Like other such chapels in the Alemann region, it is dedicated to the patron saint of the plague, Rochus. If any of the inhabitants suffer from skin diseases, one of the family members takes it upon herself to make a pilgrimage to this chapel and pray for healing. A broom made from birch branches must be brought along as an offering. Just a few years ago there were still dozens of such brooms in this chapel.

Birch branches belonged to the inventory of the Stone Age sweat lodge, as they still do in saunas and Russian sweat baths. The whipping of the overheated body is considered to be healing and cleansing. The Native Americans of the Great Lakes region place birch bark, which contains volatile oils, on glowing stones to cleanse the lungs and skin during the sweat lodge ceremony.

The archaic peoples associated the birch with light and fire. They made brightly burning torches out of dried rolled birch bark. But this is not the only connection between fire and birch. The tinder polypore *(Fomes fomentarius)*, which grows mainly on birch trees, is more suited than almost any other material for making fires. For this a stick of wood, usually an ash branch, is spun so quickly that the fungus, which is used as the base, begins to glint and catch fire. In the imagistic minds of the primitive peoples, this was a sexual act in which the birch fungus represented the feminine, fire-bearing womb—another connection to the light-bearing goddess!

Healers in the New World as well as the Old place small burning pieces of coal made of tinder polypore (moxa, punk, touchwood) on painful areas. Such pieces of fungus coal are found in the archaeological digs of the settlements of the Maglemose people, who lived more than ten thousand years ago in northern Europe. Hildegard of Bingen reached back to this healing method from the Stone Age, prescribing charcoal made from birch bark for the back, limbs, and internal pain. The poison or the disease-bringing spirit was then able to exit through the resulting burn wound.

Another mushroom is symbolically associated with the birch: the psychedelic red fly agaric *(Amanita muscaria)*. With its help the shamans of the northern hemisphere climb up the inverted Tree of Life, all the way to the roots, in order to visit the gods and ghosts. (In many cultures elements of the "other world" are upside down or backward in relation to this world.) In this context the connection to light is also apparent; in Siberia fly agaric is often called "lightning mushroom." It is taken only at

Saraswati, the Indian goddess of healers, singers, and scholars, corresponds to the Celtic Brigit. Her vehicle is the swan or the wild goose.

night, and it causes entopic light phenomena that resemble lightning flashes. Thus we can understand why the northern Germanic peoples consecrated the birch not only to Freya, but to the storm god Thor as well. Manabozo, the cultural hero of the Ojibwa, found protection from the projectiles of the thunder god in a hollow birch tree; since that time these Native Americans use birch incense to soothe or scare off the lighting hurler. The farmers of Allgäu also burn birch branches left over from the *Fronleichnamumzug** when the stormy weather has lasted long enough. In the Protestant regions, on Whitsunday (Pentacost)—the day when the Holy Spirit appeared to the faithful in the form of a tongue of flame—buildings and vehicles are decorated with fresh birch leaves.

The birch is the ultimate shamanic tree. The Eurasian shamans ascend the consecrated, decorated birch when they visit the spirit world. Their masks are carved from birch bark; their familiars are cut from birch wood. The frame-drum stretched with the hide of a wild animal is made from birch wood, preferably one that was struck by lightning. The Siberians say that the cradle of the original shaman stood beneath a birch tree, and that birch sap dropped into his mouth.

The dead are also concealed and protected by the birch. The Ojibwa wrap their dead in birch bark. The Jakuten used it to surround the head of bagged bears. The Celts placed a conical birch hat on the dead, as they did, for instance, with the Chieftain of Hochdorf or the warrior of Hirschlangen. There is an old Scottish ballad about dead sons who appeared to their mothers wearing birch hats on their heads; the hats are a sign that they will not hang around as ghosts, but will return to the heavens.

---

* The procession celebrating the Feast of Corpus Christi. (Trans.)

Mugwort (*Artemisia vulgaris)* was one of the most important ritual plants of the Germanic peoples. Fresh bundles of the herb were stroked over the sick person and then burned to dispel the spirits that brought disease. Mugwort is one of the most ancient incense herbs in Europe. Mugwort is also considered to be an herb of Saint John. (Woodcut from Hieronymus Bock, *Kreütterbuch*, 1577.)

In May, when everything is blooming and budding, the radiant sun god came from the heavens to celebrate with his beautiful bride, the flower goddess. With great revelry the celebrants brought the sun god from the forest or the nearby holy mountain—later from the sacred grove or from a cavelike temple. The divine couple took tangible form in the maypole—usually a birch that has been stripped of its bark—and another one decorated with painted eggs, red ribbons dipped in sacrificial blood, flower garlands, and other votive offerings. Sometimes the gods were also embodied in the lavishly adorned May Queen and May King, the prettiest maiden and the strongest boy in the village. They were usually received with frenzy and wild orgies. How could it be any other way? The immediate presence of the divine robs humans of their reason! The heirs of the Neolithic and Bronze Age farmers continued to celebrate the May Queen, whom they decorated with flowering hawthorn.

Midsummer's Dream

During the period of the summer solstice, the days are so long that it was once believed that the sun was standing still. Again the people were nearing the divine: The sun god and the great goddess, pregnant with the powers of heaven, were seen in the ripening grains and fruits of the forest and field. The mighty thunder god, Thor, who brings the summer storms, was also there. Dancing elves and throngs of ethereal sylphs and fiery salamanders appeared as well. And as usual when the numinous nears, humans fall into ecstasy.

Elements of the archaic summer solstice customs have been retained throughout the agricultural regions, and if we reached into the deep layers of our own souls, we could paint a reasonable picture of what the celebrations were like. Like the winter solstice, the summer festival lasted a full twelve days. The people took in the fullness of the light and the power of the fire and enhanced their experience with the solstice fire, with fire-walking, with burning brooms and torches, and by rolling wheels of fire down the mountains and hills. With the fire they celebrated the apex of the year but at the same time they celebrated death, the sacrifice of the sun god, of fair Balder, as he is called in Scandinavia.

In Wales and elsewhere nine types of wood were gathered for the solstice fire.[4] Either respected elders or a young couple lit the fire. Dried mugwort, the healing and "hot" herb, which played a sacred role in midsummer festivals all across the northern hemisphere, was placed on the fire, creating a raging and high violet-colored flame (Storl, 1996a: 45). The celebrants jumped through this fire one after the other or holding hands; the goddess herself—Frau Holle, Artemis, Dea-Ana, or whichever name she was called by—was present in the mugwort. They jumped over the purifying flames wrapped only in a mugwort girth with a wreath of ground ivy in their hair and vervain in their hands, leaping from one season through to the next. The companion and paramour of the goddess, the thunder god with the mighty hammer, was represented in the ground ivy and the vervain.

The people of today, who largely shield themselves from nature, find it difficult to comprehend the ecstasy of midsummer, of being unconditionally swept along with the natural occurrences. As recently as the Middle Ages, the most incredible rumors could be heard. It was as if one had stepped into a painting by Hieronymus Bosch—the sun produced three springs, water turned into wine, elves disclosed hidden treasure, horses could talk, music sounded out of the mountain, and ghost processions, water nymphs, and fairies became visible. White maidens revealed themselves or else asked to be released from confinement, dwarfs celebrated marriage, serpents honored their king, the fern bloomed at midnight and carried seeds (which bestowed invisibility and wealth on the one who found them), crabs flew through the air, and the Bilwis* rode a fiery buck over the fields.

What kinds of visions are these? They are pictures of the inner realm of nature. Were they induced by the henbane beer that was drunk in copious amounts? Was the endless dancing, the hours upon hours without sleep responsible? Or maybe it was the hallucinogenic mushrooms, such as bell caps, haymaker's mushroom, liberty caps, fly agaric, and others, that transported the people? After all, in the Middle Ages Saint Vitus's Day (June 15) was considered the beginning of midsummer—"here the sun will go no higher!"—and Saint Vitus is the patron saint of mushrooms. The Slavs say that he is accompanied by good gnomes who help the mushroom to grow well. Saint Vitus was also invoked for fainting sickness and rabies, which occurred again and again in the Middle

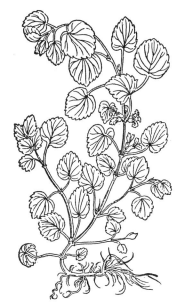

Ground ivy (*Glechoma hederacea* L., *Nepeta hederacea* [L.] Trev.) is an edible wild plant; it is particularly good in a spring salad and "Thursday's green soup." This Germanic hedgerow plant is bound into garlands that are used to detect and reveal witches on Walpurgis Day (May 1). Ground ivy is also said to have the power to protect milk from spells or free it from curses. The women of Aargau sew ground ivy into the hems of their skirts for fertility magic. The herb is used in folk medicine to stimulate the production of milk, for wounds, to chase away the "tooth worm," and as an abortifacient. (Woodcut from Hieronymus Bock, *Kreütterbuch*, 1577.)

---

[4] The country people continued to gather nine types of wood for the solstice fire for a long time. They were used as incense or as a decoction to bathe in if there was a suspicion that a spell had been cast on a human or an animal. For protection against all evil the wood is collected on the early morning of Good Friday or on Midsummer Day, and the bundle is hung on the house. In France wood is still hung on the chimney; as it dries the illness caused by the spell disappears. Ultimately it became only the "witches" who gathered such wood. On the winter solstice in order to seduce a lover a witch lit the wood at midnight and threw her dress to the door of the room as she said, "Here I am, buck naked and bare. If only my love would come and throw my dress in my lap!" During the witch trials (in Mecklenburg in the sixteenth century) the witches admitted they had used nine types of wood from "oak, birch, alder, thornbush, rowan, elder, spruce, and two kinds of thorns [probably hawthorn and blackthorn]" (Bächtold-Stäubli, 1987: vol. 6, 1061).

* Grain demon of folk belief. (Trans.)

Ferns have a long history in witches' medicine. It is said that the fern can make one invisible, and that the seeds, preferably harvested during the night of Midsummer's Eve, bring luck and magically increase one's wealth. However, the fern is also feared as a "crazy herb" and is classified in the nocturnal realm of the witches and devil. There are even different indications of the psychoactive species of ferns. (Woodcut from Otto Brunfels, *Contrafayt Kreüterbuch*, 1532.)

Saint John's wort *(Hypericum perforatum)* is one of the most important herbs of midsummer. (Woodcut from Otto Brunfels, *Contrafayt Kreüterbuch*, 1532.)

Ages.[5] During these "psychological epidemics" the people had a burning desire to form a circle and dance until they were overcome with total exhaustion.

For many years it was believed that witches picked their herbs at the summer solstice, and that they did it naked in the middle of the night. The farm women also made a bouquet of midsummer herbs, a summer solstice bundle, from one of the countless versions of nine herbs—a magic number. To increase the healing power of yarrow, wood betony, or other herbs the women peered through the bundle into the fire and spoke a charm, something like the following: "No boil shall come on my body, no break to my foot."

It is a heathen custom to strew carpets of flowers and aromatic herbs on the ground at the solstice for the gods to rest on. Love nests were also prepared in this way. With the Christian conversion this carpet of flowers became known as *Johanistreue* (Saint John's bedstraw),* the bed upon which John, the favored disciple of Jesus, lay down to rest, the intention being to mix that same loyalty into the love nest. The mugwort belt became the belt that John the Baptist was said to have carried through the desert.

The plants considered to be midsummer herbs differed from region to region, but they almost always included the following:

- Saint John's wort *(Hypericum perforatum):* This true midsummer flower is strongly influenced by the midday sun. The countless gold-yellow filaments burst out of the calyx like sun rays. They make the flowers, which open only during dry weather, look like tiny suns. The flower petals look as if they might be small airplane propellers and are reminiscent of swirling beams of light and of the light chakras. As a medicinal herb, this plant of the Sunflower family has a soothing effect on the nerves, brings light into the soul, and chases away the darkness.
- Chamomile *(Matricaria chamomilla):* The northern peoples saw the countenance of the sun god in this yellow Asteraceae with its white radiant crown (ray flowers). They called this friendly little herb Balder's brow. It is a powerful medicinal herb with anti-inflammatory, antispasmodic, antiseptic, and soothing properties. As a "mother's herb" it was used to wash and cleanse the woman during the weeks following childbirth.
- Wild thyme *(Thymus serpyllum):* Wild thyme is also anti-inflammatory, antispasmodic, digestive, and expectorant. It is a good herb for colds and lungs. Thyme is also a "woman's herb." It was sacred to Freya, and was placed in the pillows of the sickbed. The Slavs call it "little soul of the mother."
- Wolf's claw *(Lycopodium):* The mosslike wolf's claw, or common club moss, is used in folk medicine for rheumatism, lumbago, diarrhea, cramps, and disorders of the genitourinary tract. The green fronds are woven into the midsummer belt or burned in the solstice fire. The plentiful yellow spore dust known as witch's flour, lightning powder, or druid's flour is oily and explodes with a bright bolt of lightning and thunder when thrown on flames. Stone Age magicians made use of these dramatic effects, just as the theater directors of the past century did. The Celtic druids considered wolf's claw to be an important magical herb. According to Pliny, ancient people sacrificed bread and mead and then picked wolf's claw with

---

[5] In the Slavic lands the patron saint of mushrooms replaced the god Svantjevit. This god was worshipped as the protector of the fields, and he rides a white horse and carries a horn of plenty. From the foam of his horse's mouth the mushrooms grow.

* Literally, "midsummer straw"; more precisely, "midsummer bedstraw." (Trans.)

their left hands while barefoot and wearing clean white robes on the night of a new moon. They made protective amulets from the *selago*, as they called wolf's claw. During the Middle Ages wise women used it against sorcery, spells, and the evil eye.

- Mugwort *(Artemisia vulgaris):* This gray, bitter herb is considered one of the most important women's herbs. Sitz baths and teas of mugwort—depending on the strength of the dosage—help to bring on missed menses, hasten birth or afterbirth, or expel a dead fetus. The herb has also played an important role as an incense and for the blessing of shamans before entering the flight of the soul.

- Arnica *(Arnica montana):* This yellow-flowered plant in the Sunflower family is also known as leopard's bane, *Wolfsgelb* (wolf-yellow), and *Wolfsauge* (wolf-eye). It is strewn in the fields at midsummer in order to protect the crops from the grain demon, the Bilwis. In heathen times the Bilwis, which means "he with wondrous wisdom," was none other than the priest who protected the fields; that was before the missionaries demonized him. He placed "wolfwort" around the fields so that the field's vital energy, the so called grain-wolf, would not escape. If this energy vanished from the field, the grain would spoil. Later, during the harvest, the grain wolf slipped into the last sheaf. It was then decorated and carried triumphantly and with great rejoicing by the harvesters into the village.

  This herb of Freya is, as might be expected, very medicinal and should not be absent from the bundle of solstice herbs. It has antiseptic, anti-inflammatory, and regenerative properties. It is particularly good for bruises, sprains, bursitis, joint problems, and disorders of the lymphatic system. In small oral dosages it works as a vasodilator and circulatory stimulant; in strong doses it is poisonous and has an abortifacient action. Arnica was used in weather magic as an incense during storms:

Chamomile (*Chamomilla recutita* [L.] Rauschert, syn. *Matricaria chamomilla* L., *Matricaria recutita* L.) is a widespread folk remedy that is "trusted for everything." It is also one of the midsummer herbs. (Woodcut from Hieronymus Bock, *Kreütterbuch*, 1577.)

> *Arnica burn hot, that the storm might be not!*

- Calendula *(Calendula officinalis):* The golden yellow flowers, called "Marygold" or "sun-bride" in the Middle Ages, were once sacred to the Great Goddess (Freya) and were used for love magic everywhere. When a girl plants or harvests the *Niewelkblume*, the "never-wilt flower," in the footprints of her lover, he must come to her regardless of whether or not he wants to. No wonder that the Protestant priest Hieronymus Bock wrote indignantly in his *New Kreütterbuch* [New Herbal, 1539] that "many women use it superstitiously and in love potions." As a medicinal plant calendula is similar to chamomile. It is one of the best wound-healing herbs, useful for cuts, phlebitis, herpes, ulcers, and inflamed nipples. The salve, preferably cooked in goat lard, is good for burns, bruises, and sunburn. The tea is an effective remedy for cramps, gallbladder complaints, glandular disorders, intestinal inflammation, and liver problems.

- Elder *(Sambucus nigra):* The elder is a sacred tree, a ritual tree around which circle dances were performed. It was sacred to Frau Holle, the "witch goddess." At the summer solstice, when the elder bloomed, it was associated with the ecstasy of summer love.

Wild thyme (*Thymus serpyllum* L.) is said to deter "destructive earthly rays" and thus be curative. The plant is one of the more important mother's and Saint John's herbs. (Woodcut from Hieronymus Bock, *Kreütterbuch*, 1577.)

> *On midsummer when the elder blooms, then love is even greater!*

The flowers were dipped in batter and fried to make sweet elder cakes. The person who ate the most would be the best at leaping over the solstice fire. In Allgäu,

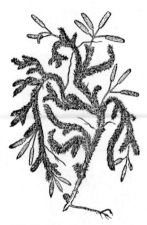

Wolf's claw (*Lycopodium clavatum* L.) is an ancient magical plant of the druids and is known in the vernacular as common club moss, *Hexenkraut* (witches' herb), *Schlangenmoos* (snake moss), *Teufelklauen* (devil's claws), and *Erdschwefel* (earth sulfur). The spores of the moss, which are used medicinally, are called druid's flour, Alp flour, witches' flour, or wood dust. The spore powder was mainly used as a wound powder in folk medicine. The plant is also one of the Saint John's and mother's herbs. (Woodcut from Hieronymus Bock, *Kreütterbuch*, 1577.)

Calendula (*Calendula officinalis* L.) was mainly used in folk medicine in Galenic preparations and salves (calendula butter) for the treatment of wounds. The yellow-flowering plant is one of the Saint John's herbs. (Woodcut from Hieronymus Bock, *Kreütterbuch*, 1577.)

Germany, the lard in which the little fritter had been fried was saved and used as a medicinal salve. In general, elder is considered the farmer's "pharmacy."

> Bark, berries, leaves, and blossoms,
> Every part is strength and goodness,
> Every part is full of blessings!

- Oxeye daisy *(Chrysanthemum leucanthemum):* This midsummer flower, also known as marguerite, was used as an oracle. Midsummer, like all sacred times when the intangible grows near, is the time of oracles. A daisy is the "star flower" of Gretchen in Goethe's *Faust:* "He loves me, he loves me not." Elsewhere the girls pluck the white raylike flowers to see whom they will marry: "Noble man, beggar man, city man, farmer, soldier, king, emperor, lawyer."

  Those who are pregnant ask: "Boy, girl; boy, girl?" A girl can also place a daisy under her pillow and her future husband will appear to her in a dream. The oxeye daisy has a medicinal action similar to that of chamomile, but much weaker.
- Vervain *(Verbena officinalis):* Like arnica, vervain was placed around the fields to prevent bad weather and to ensure a good harvest. It was sacred to the mighty hammer-god, who rules over lightning and thunder and who drenches the earth with fertile rain. The ancient smiths, protégés of the thunder-god, used vervain in a procedure for hardening steel. Thus it comes as no surprise that this herb was used to make love as hot as "burning iron." It was mixed into love potions for a man so that his member would "become as hard as iron."
- Yarrow *(Achillea millefolium):* This aromatic Asteraceae is also known as the "eyebrow of Venus" because of its small, finely feathered leaves. It is one of the most important medicinal herbs for women and for wounds.
- Wood betony *(Stachys officinalis, Betonia officinalis):* This nearly forgotten plant in the Mint family has become increasingly rare but was once considered almost a panacea. It was the most beloved of the bewitching herbs. It was boiled in water and used to bathe children and pets who were possessed or bewitched; the bathwater washed away the bad magic. In addition, betony tea was also used for chest problems, vomiting of blood, lung problems, worms, fever, jaundice, spleen problems, gout, uterine bleeding, dizziness, spiritual and emotional confusion, and many other afflictions. The esteem in which betony was held can be appreciated in the Italian saying *Venda la tonica e compra betonica* ("Sell your coat and buy betony").
- Burdock *(Arctium lappa):* Burdock, with its huge leaves and clinging fruits, was considered a true "bear" plant by the Celts and Germanic peoples, sacred to the mighty thunderer and hammer-slinging Thor. And because the "heavenly bear" (Asenbär, or Osbjorn), who scared off the giants and the *thurses* who were antagonistic to humans, reigned over the fierce summer storms, the plant was also gathered in midsummer. It was placed in the gables of houses to protect against lighting strikes and the machinations of giants. A brew of the roots was used as a shampoo to make the hair as beautiful and as full as that of the divine bushy-bearded, long-haired god. As late as the Enlightenment, farmers hung burdock over their doors and braided it into their hair or a cow's tail to ward off evil. For threadworm—the thunderer hates every kind of worm and snake—a bundle of burdock was held in one hand, a stone (representing Thor's hammer) in the other, and words like the following were spoken:

Burdock leaf, I strangle you,
burdock leaf you shall not go
'til the cow lets the threadworm go.

Many people looked for the mysterious "midsummer coal" beneath the roots of the burdock during the noon hour of the longest day of the year. (It is also alleged to be underneath a tangle of mugwort roots.) Those who dared to pick up the red-hot coal with their bare hands would be spared bad luck and sorrows.

Folklorists have given themselves a headache trying to figure out what sort of "coal" the fools had been digging up. Recently it has been thought that it was kermes lice, which contain a red pigment. The "witches" know better: This "coal" appears at certain moments in inner visions. It has to do with beings of the etheric dimension, with "salamanders" that can be connected in service to people who have a psychic relationship with nature. These fire spirits know well how to conceal themselves from the critical gaze of curious scientists.

The August Festival

During the dog days of August the grain—the staff of life—grows ready to harvest. Again the Divine draws near. As the noble matron with the horn of plenty or as the Madonna carrying a sickle, she reveals her presence in dreams and visions. Her womb produces berries, fruits, grains, and the most potent herbs. Her companion, the sun god, no longer shows his gentle, brightly radiating figure; he is now fiery, burns hotly, and is drying. The Celts called him Lugh, the smart and skillful god, the "master of all arts" (Lugh-Samildánach), the "Lion with the Quiet Hand" (Lleu Llaw Gyffes). It is he who brings everything to fullness and ripeness with his flame (*lohe*), his wisdom (*logos*). He symbolizes the receding year, the west where the sun sets in red-hot embers. Under his reign the grain grows golden, the fruit becomes sweet and red-yellow, the herbs become spicier and stronger than at midsummer. But the sun god is also the ruthless harvester, the reaper, the Terminator who finishes off the green and budding life with his heat. The northern Germanic peoples knew him as Loki, who killed the gentle Balder (who was beloved by all), ultimately provoking the utter destruction of the apocalypse. However, Loki is not the devil the Christians made him out to be.

Lugh and the goddess of the earth celebrated a wedding during the full moon of August and invited the people to celebrate with them. The festival of Lugh (Lughnasa) was a fire festival during which huge piles of wood were ignited. This tradition endured among the insular Celts for many years. During the three-day-long festival, water was taboo; washing and bathing were prohibited and fishing was not permitted (not even with nets).

Another part of the festival included the grain king (grain wolf, grain bear) being brought into the village in a festive procession and sacrificed. During the late Neolithic period and the Bronze Age it was a human sacrifice, wherein the chieftain's son, a foreigner, or a prisoner of war would take the place of the grain king. The celebrants would be blessed with the sacrificial blood. The corpse was cut into pieces and buried in the fields in order to transmit its strength to the soil. This was a kind of agricultural magic that was entirely alien to the hunter-gatherers! The Goddess, as the mother of the grain, mourned her sacrificed son, and thus turned into the mother of sorrow. She lived on into the Christian era as the Mater Dolorosa who bitterly mourns her son, the one who revealed himself by preaching, "I am the bread and I am the wine."

Tansy (*Tanacetum vulgare* L., syn. *Chrysanthemum vulgare* [L.] Bernh.) was hung by the Germanic peoples on the house as magical protection against monsters. The aromatic herb was also used as an incense. The herb is used in folk medicine for worms. The volatile oil contains the neurotoxin thujone. (Woodcut from Otto Brunfels, *Contrafayt Kreüterbuch*, 1532.)

This festival was called *Hlafmaesse* (bread mass) by the Anglo-Saxons; Lammas, the "witches' festival" celebrated on or around the first of August, derives from this word.

Lughnasa was the occasion for blessing all the herbs that would be needed during the coming year for the health and well-being of the house and stable. It also made good sense to collect the plants during the dog days of summer because the aroma, taste, and medicine precipitates in the active ingredients (mainly the volatile oil) are manifestations of the powerful light and warmth the vegetation takes in during this season. At other times of the year these characteristics are not yet fully matured or the active ingredients are decomposing.

The women made these powerful herbs of August sacred to the Goddess, who was slowly retreating from the world of appearances. In the synod of Liftinea (743 C.E.) the missionary Boniface—who had felled the sacred tree of the heathens—attempted to ban this custom. But the women did not want to abandon their herbs, and so they placed them under the dominion of the Mother Goddess and consecrated them to the dying Mary on the day of her Assumption. These plants are believed to be the flowering herbs that were found in Mary's grave instead of her corpse.

During Lughnasa nine sacred healing plants were gathered: herbs that protected against witchcraft, firestorms, and hailstorms; herbs that were good for sex; and herbs that eased births. Some of the plants were placed in graves or in coffins with the dead. Many were used as incense for sacred times (such as the "smoking nights" of the winter solstice).

Yarrow was included in the medicine bundle along with mugwort, arnica, calendula, and sage. In addition there were such well-known herbs as lovage *(Levisticum officinale)*, which was valued as a culinary spice and an aphrodisiac, and dill *(Anethum graveolens)*, which was trusted to ward off any ill-willed spirits. Dill's powerful aroma is probably also the reason that the ancient peoples, such as the Scythians, used the herb with other aromatic herbs for the embalming of their dead. Dill, a garden herb brought to central Europe by monks, not only chased off the *Buhlteufel** but also suppressed fertility (Müller, 1982: 77). And a bride who didn't want to be subjected to her husband's will could secretly bring mustard and dill seeds to her wedding and murmur, "I have you, mustard and dill. Husband, when I speak, you stay still!"

Valerian *(Valeriana officinalis)* also belonged in the bundle. The old name alone, Weyland's herb, indicates a powerful magical plant: Weyland the Smith was a great magician and a shaman with a swan's wings. Before the Industrial Age, when this witches' herb came to be used as a nervine, valerian was above all considered an aphrodisiac. Both husband and wife were supposed to drink wine in which the root had been soaking. An old recipe advises: "Take valerian in your mouth and kiss she who you desire, and she will be yours in love right away" (Beuchert, 1995: 31).

Tansy *(Tanacetum vulgare)*, with its aromatic yellow flowers, was also included in the sacred bundle. Because of its thujone-containing volatile oils it was an important vermifuge, as well as an abortifacient.

The sacred bundle was also decorated with stems of grain and flowering weeds, such as the blue cornflower (which was reminiscent of the Goddess's heavenly blue cloak) and the red corn cockle (which was sacred to the fiery Lugh). The artistic creation was then surrounded by low-growing herbs—flowering chamomile, thyme, bedstraw, feverfew. In the middle of the bundle reigned, like the Goddess herself in the middle of her retinue, tall mullein, also known *Himmelbrand* (heavenly fire) or *Königskerze* (king's candle). In the Middle Ages it was said that Mary traveled through the land during this time of year,

---

* *Buhl* = lover; *Teufel* = devil. A Buhlteufel is an incubus. (Trans.)

blessing it. An old saying relates, "Our beloved Lady goes through the land, she carries mullein in her hand!" Sometimes she touched the sick with the mullein and heals them.

The herbs for the August festival must be picked in the hours before the sun rises, while speaking the right charms. The woman should go to the plants silently, naked or at least barefoot, without being seen and without thinking any thoughts. Under no circumstance should the herbs be cut with an iron knife or dug up with an iron spade, for that would take away their power.

Yarrow *(Achillea millefolium)*

Yarrow is one of the main herbs sacred to midsummer. It is sacred to August and is a beloved medicinal plant. Yarrow tea tastes slightly bitter and spicy, and it is a mild diaphoretic; if taken as part of a treatment, it will help rid the body of toxins. Yarrow lowers the blood pressure, disinfects the urinary tract, is anti-inflammatory, and relieves cramps. Because of its bitter properties it stimulates the entire digestive system and increases bile production. In other words, it is a true health tonic. It was also taken during the Middle Ages when the plague, the black death, was making its rounds.

The scientific name of the genus is *Achillea* and refers to Achilles, the hero of the Trojan War. His mother made him invincible to wounds by holding him in the heavenly fire during the night and healing him again with ambrosia in the morning. Only at his heels, where she held him, did he remain vulnerable. It was in this unprotected spot that the poisonous and deadly arrow of Paris struck Achilles. Following the advice of Aphrodite, the goddess of this pleasant-smelling herb, Achilles placed yarrow on the wound and it healed immediately (Birmann-Dähne, 1996: 92).

As a young warrior Achilles, like Asclepius and other great men skilled in the arts of medicine, entered into an apprenticeship with the intelligent horse-man Chiron in order to learn about the wound herbs. Chiron revealed to Achilles the power of yarrow, which the horse-man had used to heal many wounded comrades. The saga suggests that yarrow is truly an excellent wound medicine. This is also indicated by the many common names for the herb: soldier's woundwort, knight's milfoil, nose bleed, carpenter's weed, bloodwort, staunchweed, *Sichelkraut* (sicklewort). In Russia it is called ax-blow herb. In France it is known as *herbe militaris* and, in honor of the patron of the carpenters, *herbe à charpentier* or *herbe de Saint-Joseph*. According to religious legend Joseph once gravely injured himself at work. Christ picked some yarrow from the meadow and laid it on him. The wound immediately stopped bleeding and miraculously closed over.

Dioscorides, the ancient Greek "father of phytotherapy," used the "thousand-leafed soldier's herb" for puncture wounds and slashes. Hildegard treasured the *Garwe*—Old German for the plant, which can be interpreted as "to make healthy"—for internal and external wounds, to quell the flow of blood and tears, and as a remedy for insomnia. The plant contains tannic acids, which are contracting and astringent, helping to dry the wound and encouraging coagulation. In other words, the tannins neutralize the poisons excreted by the wound bacteria. Yarrow also contains the anti-inflammatory volatile oil azulene, which is found in chamomile as well.

Astrologers placed the wound medicines under the dominion of the warlike Mars. But where Mars is found, his beloved Venus is never far. Names such as virgin's herb, *herbe de Notre Dame*, Margaret's herb (Saint Margaret was called on for many female illnesses), and the eyebrow of Venus *(supercilium veneris)* are testament to the role that

"When the yarrow and dandelion flourish, it is for the good of humans."
—COMMON FOLK SAYING

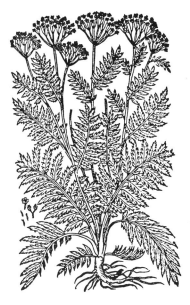

Yarrow (*Achillea millefolium* L.) is one of the most valued medicinal plants throughout the world. It contains bitters, flavonoids, and a volatile oil with cineole and proazulene. The aromatic herb is used as a bitter, as a wound medicine, and primarily as a medicinal herb for women. (Woodcut from Tabernae-montanus, *Neu vollkommen Kräuter-Buch*, 1731.)

this medicinal herb plays in women's health. "Yarrow inside the body is good for all women," goes an old farmer's saying. As a Venus plant yarrow was used for the drying and healing of venereal diseases; Venus rules problems such as these in the urogenital tract. The English herbalist Nicholas Culpeper (1616–1664) also ascribed yarrow to Venus and described its characteristics as "binding and drying, for weak kidneys in men and discharge in women." Yarrow is used in a warm sitz bath—often in combination with other relaxing and tonifying women's herbs such as melissa and lavender—to ease abdominal tension and cramps. When used in this way or as an enema or drunk as a tea, the herb regulates discharge or prolonged heavy menstrual bleeding.

Women also used this plant of Venus for oracles. If a girl wished to know what the young man who would marry her and free her from her parents' care looked like, she turned to this herb. For this the yarrow was picked from an unusual place, one where ghosts were found, such as a fork in the path or, better yet, from the grave of a dead man. The girl placed the herb under her pillow and whispered:

> *The first yarrow I found there,*
> *In the name of Christ I picked it right,*
> *And as Jesus thought of Mary with love,*
> *Let my beloved appear in my dream tonight!*

In the British Isles maidens cut the yarrow at moonlight with a black-handled knife, placed it under their beds before going to sleep, and said,

> *Thou pretty herb of Venus' tree,*
> *Thy true name it is Yarrow:*
> *Now who my bosom friend must be,*
> *Pray tell me to-morrow.* *

Yarrow oracles such as these are found in many cultures. Rudolf Steiner spoke about the "sulfur action" of this plant, which allows it to channel supernatural and future events. (According to anthroposophists, "The spirit moistens its finger with sulfur in order to work in the physical world.") In China yarrow stalks have been used with the I-Ching for thousands of years. The oracle sticks are thrown in a particular manner, thus creating a "natural connection" between the person seeking advice and the energy of the *feng shui*, which reveals the future events.[6]

---

[6] Yarrow is a power plant. It has also changed the destiny of my life. A friend I visited in a Camphill community (in the Swiss canton of Geneva) pointed out a roundish object hanging off the roof on the sunny southwest side of a garden shed. "I don't know what is going on here," he said, somewhat disturbed. "But it gives me the creeps. It's a deer bladder filled with yarrow. It's buried in the earth over the winter and then put into the compost. Is it sorcery or something?" As an ethnologist I naturally found this very interesting. I couldn't stop thinking about this yarrow wrapped in a deer's bladder. Because I assumed this could have to do with ancient magical practices that had been handed down, I took the time to conduct field research and stumbled unexpectedly upon the world of biodynamic agriculture initiated by Rudolf Steiner. It would not be exaggerating to say that yarrow, the sweet, dirty-white to pink flower of the Sunflower family with the finely feathered leaves, enjoyed the status of a quasi-sacred plant in the village community I researched. The places where yarrow grew were not permitted to be mowed, for had Steiner not said that the plant's mere presence radiated healing energy? I discovered that the herb was placed in compost because it contained a lot of sulfur, and that yarrow preparations helped the cultivated plants to better assimilate cosmic impulses because "sulfur carried the spiritual into the physical." And what is good for the humus and the garden plants is also good for the humans. So the tender leaves were picked in the springtime and added to salads. Yarrow tea was served with nearly every evening meal. The tea "brought the astral body into harmonious connection with the etheric one."

* From Halliwell's *Popular Rhymes* cited in Maude Grieve's *A Modern Herbal*, p. 864. Originally published in 1938, London: Jonathan Cape Ltd.; this edition published 1994, London: Tiger Books.

Yarrow was a sacred plant to the ancient Germanic peoples. The aromatic herb was generally dedicated to Freya as a medicine and a women's plant. The tender leaves belonged to the nine green herbs that are eaten in springtime as folk food (the so-called green nine). With this soup or little cake consecrated to the Goddess, the humans connected to the greening and rejuvenating nature. Eggs, the symbols of life, were also colorfully decorated. In those days—as is still done today—the eggs were probably wrapped in yarrow leaves and dunked into dye to create delicate patterns.

The use of yarrow leaves in love oracles is also an ancient heathen custom. In order to be sure that a distant boyfriend would stay true, a girl could speak the necessary words, which went something like: "Yarrow, yarrow, if my beloved is good, neither water nor foam comes, otherwise red blood." She would then turn a yarrow leaf three times around her nose. If she got a bloody nose, her lover was true. The fact that the tips of the feathery leaves had tiny prickers was certainly on the side of the questioner.*

Before the Benedictine monks introduced hops, the northern Europeans used yarrow and other bitter and aromatic herbs (such as ground ivy, heather, and wild rosemary) for the flavor and preservation of beer. As a brewing herb yarrow was more sacred to the mighty thunder god Thor, lord of the intoxicating drinks, than to fair Freya.

---

* A version from the British Isles uses the same method: "Yarroway, Yarroway, bear a white blow; If my love love me, my nose will bleed now." From Maude Grieve, *A Modern Herbal* (1931; reprint, London: Tiger Books, 1994), 864. (Trans.)

The Equinox

The equinoxes in spring and fall are two of the four cardinal points of the solar year. It is said that the witches gather herbs on these days as well. Frau Holle appears around the spring equinox as a gardener bringing the fresh, life-giving green herbs. Conversely, she appears as the harvest goddess at the fall equinox. This is when fruits and nuts are collected and the fall harvest is brought in, while life gradually pulls back into the chambers and the stalls. Ancient heathen harvest festivals, which celebrated the Goddess and the harvest god with banquets, feasts, recreation, and pilgrimages to the cemeteries, live on in the traditional customs of Michaelmas. The archangel Michael, leader of the heavenly legions, replaced the harvest gods such as Lugh, Jupiter, and Thor.

According to the farm calendar Michaelmas (September 29) was considered the beginning of the winter work—the feminine spinning and yarn making, the masculine weaving—which was sustained until Candlemas (February 2). It is said, "When Michael turns the light on the farmhands must start spinning!" The people sang while they industriously spun in what was known as the spinning or rocking room. The women went—or so it is said—on "rocking trips," on "women's journeys." Grandmothers told stories about their life experiences, village incidents and love relationships were discussed, and judgments were made against those who offended good morals. Thus the women spun and wove—like the Fates themselves—the future fate of the village and tribe with their thoughts and talk.

> *What remains secret throughout the year,*
> *is revealed in the sacred* Brechtelzeit.*
>
> —KÄRTNER SAYING

---

* Brechtelzeit is the time following Michaelmas when the women beat the hemp or flax fibers in preparation for spinning. (Trans.)

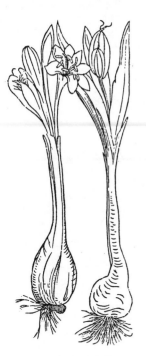

The autumn crocus (*Colchicum autumnale* L.) is an important medicinal herb in witches' medicine. Today the feared poisonous plant is used only in homeopathy (as colchicinum), for, among other uses, rheumatism, gout, and early-stage arthritis. According to Boericke *(Handbuch der homöopathischen Materia medica)* the remedy produces "dreams of mice." (Woodcut from Hieronymus Bock, *Kreütterbuch*, 1577.)

Meanwhile, the season of old woman summer is outside the door. The fine spider's webs, which glide through the air and hang from the branches, are considered the threads from the spindle of Frau Holle. The archaic goddess who spins the threads of life of all creatures and weaves their futures, Frau Holle sometimes appeared to the women during the late-night hours and helped them with their work.

Like no other plant, the autumn crocus, also called meadow saffron, *Herbstzeitlose* (fall-timelessness), *Spinnblume* (spin flower), or *Kiltblume* (Alemannic *Chilt, Kilt* = to work at night), is associated with the darkening time of year. It is the "flower of light" because with its appearance people's work had to be done by the light of the kindling, the hearth, or the lantern. Autumn crocus was considered to be a true witches' flower, and naturally belonged in the repertoire of the poison makers.

Autumn Crocus *(Colchicum autumnale)*

As the sun loses its power and the nights grow longer than the days, delicate light purple flowers suddenly appear on the grazed meadows. They are naked, with no leaves, stems, or other coverings. Like a crocus that somehow missed spring, the autumn crocus sits there in the cold fall weather and hopes for the last stiff-membered insect to pollinate it. But because the crocus doesn't put in the effort to attract insects with a seductive aroma, pollination often fails. The flower has no other choice than to become flexible like an animal: It bends its filaments over their stigma and pollinates itself.

After this pollination a few months pass until the pollen grows down the long style to the ovaries. The ovaries and ovules of the crocus are not raised up to the sun on a pedestal as in normal flowers; they are instead located in the bulb or tuber twenty centimeters deep in the dark earth. The subterranean fertilization of the ovum takes place on the winter solstice when the nights are the longest. During a time of year when other plants go dormant, resting in seeds or buds, this strange plant celebrates its apex.

Then in the springtime, when the other plants begin to bloom, the autumn crocus seed capsules grow together, and usually three blunt tuliplike leaves rise from the earth. But the leaves of the autumn crocus become yellow, wilt, and disappear entirely by May. Because of this, superstitious people once believed that the flowers had been eaten by the witches for Walpurgis Night. By early summer dry, rattling seed capsules with countless black seeds are all that remain. When the sun has reached its highest point and nature only indulges in greening and flowering, there is no trace of the strange "timeless" plant. It hides from the life-dispensing star like an evil fairy.

The many regional names demonstrate that this unusual plant of the Lily family has strongly influenced the folk imagination. Heinrich Marzell, who has made it his life's work to collect all of the plant names in the German-language regions, found no fewer than five hundred different names for the autumn crocus, all of which indicate something about its character. It is called Michael's flower, *Herbstschneeblume* (fall snow flower), and *Winterblume* (winter flower), as well as *Grummetblume* because it appears after the last haying *(Grummet)*. It is known as the gall flower not only because it is bitter and poisonous like gall, but also because it blooms on Saint Gall's day (October 16) (Marzell, 1943: 1070).

Just as the spring flowers wood sorrel and sorrel are used to protect against heat, thirst, and other summer problems, the autumn crocus is good for all of the problems that winter brings. The stamen and stalks were cooked in lard to make a salve that was said to heal frostbitten hands. As a preventive measure against frostbite, the first flower found was rubbed on the unprotected body parts. Women rubbed one of these "spin flowers" between their hands so that their hands would not become sore or stiff during the winter spinning. The people of the upper region of Zurich, the Oberlanders, rubbed the "flower of light" on their eyelids to prevent them from getting tired during the upcoming months of winter work.

Although it heralds the time of year for making yarn and fabric, the autumn crocus is known in many places as naked ladies, *Nakte Jungfer* (naked virgin), *Nakte Maid* (naked maid), or *Nakte Hur* (naked whore) because the lazy flower is "too lazy to cover her nakedness with a leaf-dress like all other upstanding flowers!" Thus in the language of flowers it became a symbol of immodesty. In Saint Gall the girls with questionable reputations had the rattling seedpods—the so-called *Hundshoden* (dog's balls) or *Pfaffensäcke* (priest's scrotum)—strewn on their doorways on the first of May.

It might be expected that a plant that deviates so drastically from the sun's rhythms is poisonous. Indeed, the autumn crocus is particularly toxic. It contains twenty different alkaloids—the bulbs, leaves, flowers, and, above all, the seeds are poisonous. The fatal dosage is five seeds! The poison works slowly, like arsenic. Only after hours or even a whole day does the victim begin to feel the scratching and burning in his mouth, which gradually turns into vomiting, bloody diarrhea, cramps, bladder pain, and cardiac rhythm disturbances. After one or two days death occurs due to paralysis of the respiratory center. The poisonous plant has been given cautionary names such as *Giftzwiebel* (poison onion), *Hennenvereck* (hen destroyer), *Ziegentod* (goat death), *Hundsblume* (dog flower), *Viehgift* (cattle poison), *Leichenblume* (corpse flower), and *Teufelswurz* (devil's spice). However, as a *Lauskraut* (licewort) for poisoning lice it was considered useful.

The Greeks called the specterlike plant *euphemeron*, the one-day killer, and the fire of the Medea of Colchis. Medea of Colchis was a disciple of the black three-headed witch-goddess Hecate. White hellebore, oleander, belladonna, poison hemlock, foxglove, and other poisonous plants grew in her garden on the Black Sea in Colchis—hence the genus name *Colchicum*. When Jason, the Greek Argonaut, reached the strand of Colchis, Medea fell passionately in love with the young sailor. With a brew of her herbs the sorceress made the dragon who guarded the golden fleece fall asleep, and then helped the Argonauts escape.

Medea's art was possible thanks to the autumn crocus. For nine days she wandered through the forests and mountains in order to gather witches' herbs to make the grizzled father of her beloved young again. She cut the old man into pieces, cooked him in a brew, and put him back together again—probably an archaic initiation. The autumn crocus sprang from drops of the brew that accidentally spilled onto the ground.

While farmers usually fear and avoid the flower, modern genetic researchers hold this flower in great esteem. These biotechnical sorcerers have discovered that colchicine, the primary poison, has a cytostatic action. It inhibits the development of the spindle during mitosis as well as the development of cell walls. Thus it is possible to arrest cell division at the metaphase, photograph the chromosomes, and establish exact chromosome maps. Although colchicine inhibits further division of the cells, it does not influence the mitotic doubling of the chromosomes.

Therefore, multiplication of the chromosome set is achieved. With colchicine-induced mutations, genotypes have already been manipulated. For example, tobacco plants with significantly larger leaves have been developed, and Swedish researchers have even achieved the creation of polyploid giant rabbits.

In other words, this poison has the ability to separate the archetypal spiritual principle form from protoplasmic life. In this way the effects are similar to radioactive rays, which also create volatile mutations. The ancient astrologers placed autumn crocus under the domain of Saturn, the dark, cold planet, the "guardian of the threshold" that stands at the edge of the world of appearances. Today this plant would more likely be categorized under the dominion of Pluto, the chaotic, cataclysmic power beyond the threshold.

Modern medicine has investigated the possibility of integrating the cytostatic action of colchicine into cancer and leukemia therapy. In folk medicine the freshly picked autumn crocus has been used for warts, corns, and even cancerous ulcers. At one time the bulb was carried in a bag or as a charm when the plague and other infectious epidemics visited the region; the reasoning was to rebuke a poison with an even stronger one.

Colchicine tincture continues to be used as a remedy for gout. The Greek doctor Galen and the Arabs used autumn crocus for particularly painful acute cases of gout. The bulb was considered to be the "signature" of a foot deformed by gout. Indeed, the tincture prohibits the uptake of uric acid crystals through the white blood cells in the gouty nodes. The pain is immediately eased, but nausea, vomiting, and diarrhea are the side effects of the treatment. Homeopaths, who understand how to remove the quills from even the most potent of poisons, prescribe it in varying dilutions for different ailments such as gout, rheumatoid arthritis, pericardial and pleural disorders, diarrhea, nausea, and dropsy.

The Time of the Dead: Samhain, Halloween

During the wet, cold, foggy days of November otherworldly beings move silently through the bare, thorny hedgerow. During the eerie nights of the full moon of the eleventh month—it is diametrically opposite of the joyous nights of May—the graves open. The dead swarm out to worship the Goddess, who now appears in the form of the frightening black goddess of death. She roams around restlessly, cloaked in shadows and fog, making the beams squeak and creak, shaking the windows, or emitting plaintive cries. The black god of the underworld, whom the Celts knew as Samhain, enters into his reign. He weds the Goddess, who is preparing to move into her underground chambers. She brings the green, the life energy, and the seeds with her into the depths. The radiant sun wastes away and dies. During Neolithic times the sun was imagined as an elk with golden antlers that the black hunter kills with a death blow. (During midwinter, deep in the earth, the black goddess gives birth once again to the light.) Because the energy of life is gone during this period, it follows that no herb, no medicine, should be gathered.

In turn the humans are affected by the events of these ghostly nights. They cleanse the hearth so that their dead ancestors and forefathers can visit. They put out apples, hazelnuts, hemp seed gruel, and other food of the dead and light candles, and the dead show their gratitude for the effort.

For the wise women it is one of the best times to go out flying. They sacrifice a goose and honor Frau Holle by rubbing mugwort on their bodies or by fumigating it. They

Halloween (Old English for "sacred night") was originally celebrated on the full moon in November. It marks the beginning of the reign of the god of death and winter. During this time ghosts swarmed and shamans (witches) went on trips. On Halloween a special beer is still brewed with pumpkins. The pumpkin on this beer label represents the full moon.

simmer the "flying herbs" in goose fat and smear the mixture on themselves or on the handle of a broom. They fly through the chimney to the dark side of the moon in order to plumb the depths of the profound mysteries of this time of year. During these sacred nights of the dead the deceased reveal the future. (The witches' moon was symbolized by a hollowed-out rutabaga with a candle burning in it. Today the hollowed-out pumpkin takes on this role.)

No one dared leave his house during these ghostly nights. But if someone needed to go somewhere, she was never to look over her shoulder, for a dead person who could then steal her away might be following. Those who dared to go out dressed as ghosts. In the lands influenced by the Celts the youth dress up as ghosts and witches and roam through the night. They knock on doors and ask for gifts. The stingy get pranks: Their doors are pelted with heads of cabbage, smoke is blown through the keyholes, peat is stuffed into the chimney, and the windows are smeared.

The alder symbolizes the Goddess in her dark aspect as ruler of the underworld. Primordial European symbolism places the Goddess in her youth as a birch, in motherhood as the hazel, and in crone-hood as the alder. The ground beneath the alder is better suited than any other for the psychic experience of the world of the dead. The witches often met here—and some still do—in order to visit the underworld and to ask questions.

This land of ghosts radiates a diminished but nonetheless pleasant light. It ripples and pools all around; gnomes, tiny moss-men and water sprites in their ever-changing shapes, and sometimes a twinkling will-o'-the-wisp reveal themselves to the visitor. When a person resurfaces he notices how cold it was there—but he also notices how the body and spirit vibrate with an exceptional energy. There is nothing else to do but jump, dance, and cheer, touching the earth and the sun, not only to warm up but also to shake off the aftereffects of this wondrous world.

Outsiders who happen upon an alder grove where the clairvoyant are taking such a trip must stop to wonder at the sight: It really looks like a witches' dance. Such an alder grove was found in Saterland—the island so deep in the impenetrable Frisian moors that it was impossible for the authorities to find—the last dance site in northern Germany where witches and sorcerers from all over Europe still went throughout the Middle Ages.

The alder (*Alnus* spp.) is called *ellerkonge* (elf king) in Danish. The *Edda* relates that the first woman came from alder. Medieval dowsers used crosses of alder wood, which is allegedly drawn to water. According to Goethe the ghostly Erl King lives in the branches. In the folk medicine of lower Austria the inner bark of alder is cooked in wine and drunk as a remedy against magic potions. (Woodcut from Hieronymus Bock, *Kreütterbuch*, 1577.)

Alder (*Alnus* spp.)

The alder—also called black alder, red alder, owler, *Eller*, or *Else*—is well suited to the ecosystem of the meadows, marshes, and streambeds. Because, like members of the Pea family, it builds nitrogen-collecting knots at its roots, it helps feed the nutrition-poor soil of the moors. The seeds from the woody "cones" are outfitted with air cushions, and float in the water until they find a suitable place to germinate.

Wetlands where the alders grow are called "alder fences." They have always been considered eerie, inhospitable places. Many a careless wanderer has been lured to his death by the ghostly will-o'-the-wisp in such places. Amphibians, otters, and saprophytes make their mischief there. The souls of suicide victims and drowned or unbaptized children float around as wafts of mist, and malicious elves dance in the moonlight. It is no wonder that an old saying postulates, "Red hair and alder don't grow on good soil."

These dark deciduous trees are just as strange as the places in which they grow.

The hawthorn (*Crataegus monogyna* Jacq.) is an ancient Germanic fence or hedgerow plant. Hawthorn is a versatile and cherished heart medicine. Even with long-term use no side effects have been observed. (Woodcut from Hieronymus Bock, *Kreütterbuch*, 1577.)

The pale wood turns red when it is struck. This red coloring—recognized today as the effects of the nitrogen—was once considered a sign that a sentient being lived inside the tree.[7]

But what sort of sentient being lived inside the alder? The perceptive peoples of the olden days believed it was an elf, the elf queen, or the daughter of the elf king who lived there. It is she who bleeds and mourns when a human strikes the trunk with an ax. In the alder fence near Tegernfeld sometimes she can still be seen combing her hair by moonlight and rubbing honey, which she scrapes from the leaves, into her locks.

A Danish folktale sees her as the daughter of the elf king. Lord Olaf rides through the green land to invite guests to his upcoming wedding. He sees elves dancing in the moors. The elf king's daughter stretches out her hand and invites him to join in:

> *Come Lord Olaf, dance a step with me,*
> *Two golden spores I shall give to thee;*
> *A shirt of silk, so white and fine,*
> *My mother bleached it in the moonshine.*

He refuses, saying, "I am not allowed to dance; I do not want to dance. Tomorrow is my wedding day." Three times she asks him, promising him another pile of gold. When he nevertheless continues to refuse her, the daughter says,

> *And if Lord Olaf shan't dance with me,*
> *Scourge and disease for him shall be!*

She hits him in the heart;

> *Oh, woe is me, full of fear and pain!*

Then she lifts the pale lord onto his horse.

> *Ride and greet your little bride!*

The groom barely makes it home. His mother is startled, and he responds to her query of what happened as he falls to the ground, dead: "Oh, mother, oh, mother, I was in the realm of the elf king, that is why I am so pale and weak."

The knight Wolfdietrich had a different experience. The elf lady, the *rauhe Ilse* (wild or rough Ilse), desired to love him. She stood before him, wild, unkempt, and covered in moss. He avoided her, and she turned him into an animal. On the next day she asked him again, but he still refused. Then she placed a sleeping spell on him and cut off two locks of his hair and two fingernails. For half a year he had to roam through the forest and feed himself with herbs and roots like a wild animal. When she appeared a third time he took the wild woman in his arms and made love to her. Afterward she transported him to a magical land where she was the queen. She bathed in a fountain of youth and

---

[7] The students of Rudolf Steiner still believe that alder wood is a resting place for *astralized* (sentient and invisible) beings. They consider the rhizobia, which greedily absorb the element nitrogen, to be the physical carrier of the astral body. Just as life incarnates by way of oxygen, so the soul incarnates through nitrogen.

appeared in front of him as Siegeminne, the most beautiful woman in the world.

Behind the figures of rauhe Ilse and the elf king's daughter hides the archaic Goddess. It is the same Great Goddess who, in her radiant youth, revealed herself in the bright birch and in the flowering hawthorn as the bride of the sun god. In the alder she is the goddess of death. Alder fences and moors have been considered places of the dead since Neolithic times. Folklorists have suggested that the ancient Germanic term for alder, *aluza* (Indo-European *alisa*), had something to do with a sacrificial cult. At the base of an alder a young man was chosen and sent to the Goddess as a bridegroom. According to Robert Graves, Alys was the name of the goddess of the burial island, similar to the Alycamps island in the Rhône River. The priestesses either buried the sacrificed on river islands such as these, which were covered in alder, or sank them in bogs. It is possible that the Elysian fields, the "islands of souls" of antiquity, were originally islands in similar rivers.

The story of the daughter of Helios, as told by Virgil in the *Aeneid*, also belongs in this context. The girl dared her brother Phaeton to hitch the sun chariot without the permission of her father, the sun god. Because Phaeton was not strong enough to control the horses, he scorched the earth and caused the world to catch fire. Zeus was furious and killed him with a bolt of lightning. When the sister mourned his death on the banks of the Po River in Italy, her tears became alder trees.

The Celtic people who invaded matriarchal, megalithic Europe identified the alder spirit not with the goddess of death but with Bran. In the Welsh "Battle of the Trees" *(Cad Goddeu)* it says:

> *The long staffs of alder on your shield,*
> *Bran you are called, after the shimmering branches . . .*
> *The long branch of alder in your hand,*
> *Bran you are, after the branch which you carry.*

Bran is a god of the dead, a god of the underworld. Carrion-eating ravens are his birds. The West, where the sun-hero sinks, bloodred, into his underworldly domain where the island of the souls lies, is under his rule. Bran is the god with the cauldron who brings the dead back to life, the one who transforms the past into the future. A dead person who is thrown into the cauldron in the evening will be alive again on the next day—returning as a "person from beyond."

Oracle flutes were cut from the bones of the sacrificed victims and from alder wood (Ranke-Graves, 1985: 125). Shamans were also cooked in Bran's cauldron and then put back together again. Thus, even though they still lived in the here and now, they were already from beyond, and like the bone and alder flutes they became an oracle giver from the dimension beyond. The cult of Bran was melded with the cult of Teutates, who also drowned humans in his cauldron in alder groves. Much later, during the Christian Middle Ages, the god was transformed into the Fisher King, the guardian of the Holy Grail who meditates on the depths of the waters.

Bran's cauldron was, above all, an attribute of the Great Goddess of Paleolithic times. It was her womb, her vagina, that bore all life-forms and then took them back again. The chosen, the shamans and the warriors, were chopped up and cooked in her cauldron. She then put the bones back together and vivified them. This cauldron is a fountain of youth. The moors and the alder breaks in which life disintegrates and rejuvenates itself are also cauldrons of the Goddess. Bran and Teutates have not suppressed the Goddess; they are only her stand-ins, her sacrificial priests, the guardians of her womb.

This background clarifies certain customs and superstitions. We can now better understand why the Irish regard cutting down an alder a heinous act, and why the alder symbolizes departure and renunciation as well as rejuvenation. When vacating a house the Germanic people broke four alder branches and threw them in different directions. In the Middle Ages the breaking of a piece of alder wood over one's head in court symbolized the complete severing of social relations with one's family.

Throughout western Europe alder branches were placed on the doorsteps of unpopular girls whom people avoided. And in Mecklenburg it was said of the dead, *Hei is bie'n leiwen Gott, in't Ellenbrauk* ("He is with his beloved God in the alder break").

As a sacred and sacrificial tree that combines the element of fire (the red color) and water, the alder has not fallen into complete obscurity. Pious mothers see the red wood as an indication that this was the tree that the Savior bled on for our sins. In contrast, farmers believe that the wood turns red when peeled because the devil beat his grandmother with an alder branch until she bled.

In the wake of the Christian conversion of the European peoples, the image of the great alder goddess was distorted into that of a mean witch and the tree itself became a witches' tree. In Thuringia the alder was called Walper tree (Walpurgis tree) because the witches ate the buds during their flight and used its branches to influence the weather. The people of the Allgäu region believed storms occurred when red-haired witches shook the alder bushes. But this superstition is a displaced memory of the abilities of the woman who found rebirth in the cauldron of the Goddess: Like all shamans, she had the power to influence the weather.

A fairy tale from southern Tirol also contains a similar primordial memory. Deep in the forest a boy accidentally came across a witches' gathering. He hid behind a bush and watched as the witches chopped up an elder companion and cooked her in a cauldron until the flesh fell from her bones. When they tried to put the bones together again they realized a rib was missing. Because they could not find the rib they replaced it with an alder branch and they brought the witch back to life again as a young and beautiful woman. But she warned her sisters that she would have to die if anyone accused her of being an alder-wood witch. The next day the boy met the witch by chance on the path. She tried to bewitch him and made seductive eyes at him. But he recognized her and called her an alder-wood witch. At that she fell dead on the ground.

Folk medicine has found little use for the alder, probably because of its reputation as a witches' tree. The Welsh physicians of Myddfai, heirs of the druids, prescribed an infusion of the leaves for dropsy and as a footbath for cold tired feet. To Saint Hildegard the tree was the symbol of uselessness. Nevertheless it was used to protect against witchcraft—*similia similibus curantur* ("like cures like"). The crushed leaves were strewn to protect against fleas, bugs, mice, and other bewitched or "alderlike" animals. The branches were quickly placed around the house on Walpurgis Night (April 30). The poor burned coal from the wood. Husbands carved wooden shoes out of it. The bark was used to tan leather black, and pigment was made from the cones. When mothers weaned their children they would place a wreath of alder leaves on their breasts and say that the witches had stolen their milk. Because the wood does not rot, the Neolithic people used it as stilts for their buildings. Venice was also built on alder posts.

Rites of Initiation

In the previous pages we have seen how divine beings break through the barrier of civilization and affect the destiny of humans at specific magical times during the year. But not only do the gods approach the humans; the humans approach the gods as well. They go into the wilderness, into the numinous magical world behind the hedgerow, in order to accumulate energy that can be found nowhere else. They go exhilarated, expectantly, but also full of respect and modesty.

Above all, those who are loaded with magical energy—hunters, herb-gathering women, shamans, and fools—go into the woods. They decorate themselves with the feathers and furs of the wild animals they have encountered in their visions or those they have befriended. They scent their bodies with the smoke of aromatic herbs, color their faces white with chalk, red with ocher, and black with soot. They wear flower wreaths and green branches in their hair. In this way they come into harmony with the creatures of the forest, the spirits of the animals, and those of the plants. They not only bring medicinal and magical plants, mushrooms, antlers, hunting bounty, and other delicacies when they return home, but they also tell tales of wondrous encounters, dangers withstood, and victories achieved.

The stories that were once told by such people to a rapt audience by the crackling fire have been partially passed down to us in fairy tales and legends. These boundary walkers were initiates, not parroting believers like the throng of churchgoers and sect members of today. Nor were they initiates in the sense of our modern scientists, who train their eyes only on the external data of the senses, painstakingly measuring, weighing, and numbering them. No, the people we are talking about combined an astute, precise observation of nature with an ear toward its internal workings. In the mirrors of their souls they looked into the soul of the forest. This forest soul appeared to them in the form of fairies and moss-beings, who instructed them about the medicinal powers of the roots and crystals and also revealed the entrances to the realm of Frau Holle. The soul of the forest appeared as tree elves, fire spirits, grim trolls, talking birds, and radiant virgins, and had conversations with the people.

Nearly all primitive peoples send their pubescent boys into the wilderness, to the source of power and wisdom, for initiatory rites. For only deep in the woods, in the caves, or in another place far removed from the village, beyond human time and its sorry efforts, beyond motherly protection, can the boys set aside their childhood and experience their own true natures and the meaning of their existence. Under the guidance of older men, with the help of poisonous herbs and empowered by fasting, pain, and deprivation, the boys' everyday consciousness dies. Themselves having become spirits, they encounter beings from beyond that will be their teachers. They meet their totem animals, they learn to recognize their animal helpers and befriend their own primordial, wild nature that has been untouched by society. Through this animal—the natives of Central America call it the *nagual*—they experience a power they have never imagined: It awakens the instinct of the jaguar, the sacred rage of the warrior, the intuition of the healer, the enthusiasm of the singer, or the spiritual energy of the thinker. It lets them dive into the depths or fly into the bright heavens, where they encounter gods. An unshakable self-confidence emerges through this experience in the regions beyond the thorny hedgerow.

The experience of initiation is one of death and rebirth: Like wild game, the initiates are killed, chopped up, and cooked in the cauldron of the Great Goddess. They are reborn with a new personality, a new name, and a more mature outlook. They are born twice: the first time from their human mother and then again from the Great Mother. Only in this way can they truly become men, able to take over responsibility for the women and children, for the old and infirm, for the clan and the whole tribe.

The initiation has been different for girls and usually not as dramatic. The most important secrets of womanhood were passed on through the course of the daily work with the grandmothers, sisters, aunts, and other female blood relations while gathering wild plants, sowing, hoeing, weeding, spinning, sewing, and cooking. The actual initiation was, and still is among many peoples, the first menstruation. Many Native Americans send the women to a menstrual hut outside the village where they learn the mysteries of the female body and fertility. As the fairy tale of Rapunzel suggests, we once had menstrual huts for girls in puberty under the care of an old "witch" (Diederichs, 1995: 267). Marriage and the birth of the first child were further initiations.

Methods using psychedelic plants and traumatic pain (wounding, hunger, pulling teeth, tattooing and scarification, cutting), which catapult the soul into the beyond, play a less important role in the feminine mysteries because, according to the anthropologist Felicitas Goodman, the female human is closer to her instincts and intuition by nature. However, the female shamans and prophets, the "flying women," especially in the European cultural regions, did know the most about entheogenic plants.

Wolf-Dieter Storl

The Old Woman in the Hedgerow

The old woman by the fire was an important adviser to the community, for she had a wealth of experience and wisdom that had been passed down over the generations.

The women in the archaic hunter-gatherer groups who roamed through the forest with their children and female relatives gathering useful and edible roots, berries, nuts, and medicinal plants gained intimate knowledge of the plants over the centuries. Just as the men gained knowledge about the animals they hunted, the women developed a confident understanding about the location, growth patterns, pharmacological characteristics, and transsensory aspects of the vegetation. Of course, in the first Neolithic villages the women tended to the domesticated vegetation, the preparation of the beds and fields, the plants, the sowing, and the harvesting. All evidence indicates that the fields belonged to matrilineal clans and were worked communally by women of blood relation, as the Iroquois and other horticultural tribes have historically done. In such societies the men were responsible for the heavy work of clearing and cultivating the fields, as well as hunting, making magic, communicating with nature spirits, and taking care of the domestic animals—if there were any. With the exception of psychoactive botanicals, such as tobacco among the Indians, which played a role in the house of the men and in vision quests, the knowledge of the secret of the plants and plant spirits fell mainly to the women.

On account of their long years of experience and as carriers of traditional knowledge, grandmothers enjoyed great respect and their advice was considered valuable. It is still like this today among primitive people: Since their children are grown, they can retreat from the necessary daily work and have the time and leisure to ponder. They are concerned with the health and well-being of the people in the house and of the animals in the barn. When someone gets cut, the grandmothers know which herbs are styptic. They know where the root grows that stops diarrhea in calves. They collect calming tea herbs for teething infants. They know the birthing herbs, love herbs, herbs of youth, and also the right sayings so that the plants release their full effectiveness.

Every settlement, every clan, had a white-haired old woman to whom the ancestors and forest spirits or the Goddess whispered many a secret. These women cooked salves—carefully stirring while murmuring magical words—in the lard of bear, badger, wild goose, or pig with herbs they gathered when the moon was right. The grandmothers knew how to brew healing and intoxicating herbal beer, to bake herbal cakes, to bind magical plant amulets, and whatever else would bring health and relief to the sick. Sometimes the touch of an old woman's wrinkled hand and a good word was enough.

The old woman also tended to the fire that lived in the heart of the house. Before sunrise she stoked the coals, prayed for friendship and protection, and told the fire the dreams the previous night had given her. Native Americans still do this.

In the winter the old woman usually sat by the fire, listened to the crackling and popping sounds, and occasionally heard therein the voices of the ancestors and the spirits. And when she sometimes fell into a trance—the word comes from the Latin *transire*, "to go over"—her soul, pulled upward with the swirling smoke, slipped up the chimney, through the opening, and into other dimensions.

The Chimney

The campfire has been in the center of social life since the beginning of the time of man. Primordial man *(Homo erectus)* was already warming his body by the fire a good million years ago. Fire not only gave warmth and light, dried wet clothing, and cooked meat, but was also sacred and healing. It was the sun spirit or the heavenly fire that had taken up residence among the people. The ring of boulders that were placed around the fire were the original medicine wheel. The stone circle became the focus (in Latin, *focus* means "hearth" or "fireplace") of the sacred. (Later, in the High Neolithic period, stone circles such as Stonehenge took on gigantic proportions.)

During the winter nights people sat around the fire in the tent, yurt, or tepee and listened to the stories of the shamans. In the flickering lights, in the dancing shadows on the tent wall, in the glowing and fading of the coals, in the ascending smoke, the spirits, the inhabitants of other dimensions, could briefly be incarnated. Sometimes it was an ancestor, sometimes an animal spirit from the forest.

There in the fire the ancestors could be given scraps from the meal so that they remained in good spirits. The Chinese still burn colorful resplendent clothing made from silk paper, money, and cloth in order to please the ancestors on the other side. For a long time Scandinavian housewives continued to sacrifice a little butter, a little bread, and such to Loki, the fire spirit. Bowls with milk and porridge were set out for the "poor souls" and the underworldly all the way into the Middle Ages, especially on Christmas, Easter, Whitsuntide, and other sacred days.

Sacred is the hearth. When a new bride (for instance, in Indo-European settlement areas, in eastern Asia, and in Mexico) enters the house she must first walk around the hearth and greet the fire. Newborn babies are also carried clockwise around the fire to honor the ancestors.

Many people, including prehistoric Europeans, buried the bones of their dead under the fireplace or by the hearth. Celtic headhunters smoked their trophies, the heads of slain enemies, in the chimney. In many places, such as China, figurines of the house spirit are placed on the hearth.

The opening for the smoke, the "wind eye" (window), as the Germanic peoples called it, was the door through which the ghosts entered and exited. So that no evil ghost could slip through, the wind eye was protected with magical symbols. Germanic peoples hung the heads of sacrificed horses on it—horses that, like Falada in the fairy tale of the goose maiden, made prophecies and whose words were understood by the wise old woman. The Scandinavians carved dragons and serpent motifs—typical protectors of the threshold— on the roof beams where they cross above this opening.

As early as the Paleolithic period the smoke hole in the peak of the tent must have been a ghost door and gateway to the transsensory worlds. Siberian shamans make notched birch trunks that reach to the smoke hole. They climb up the "shamanic tree" when they enter the spirit world during the ritual. (Just as the tent has a wind eye at the top through which the spirits enter and exit, the tent of the heavens that covers the earth has a hole: the North Star on the top of the world "tree." The gods of the heavens enter and exit through it.) The smoke hole is thus also a kind of hedge, a threshold to the regions beyond. The image of the witch that flies out of the chimney remained in public consciousness for a long time.

In the winter the old woman sat at the hearth, but in the summer she went to the grove, to the thorny hedgerow at the edge of the settlement. Throughout most of the world it was the duty of the white-haired woman to collect dry brushwood and kindling. She knew the nine kinds of wood. She knew which wood gave warmth when burned, which one healed sick children, with which one evil ghosts could be smoked

The witch flying out of the chimney. (From Thomas Erastus, *Dialogues touchant le pouvoir des sorcières et de la punition qu'elles méritent*, 1579.)

out.[8] She had learned how to use the wood from her grandmother, who in turn had learned it from hers, and so on, until the chain of tradition was lost in the campfires of the ancient Stone Age, in the Dreamtime, when the gods were still visible and wandered the earth. She also found nine herbs, which she used for seasoning, spells, and medicine. And when she rested on her favorite spot in the hedgerow, underneath the elder, the hawthorn, or the hazel tree, the Dreamtime came tangibly nearer. A spirit would approach her in the form of a speaking bird, a beetle, a fox, or a little gray manikin and whisper secrets to her. Sometimes it was even Frau Holle herself who stood before the woman as a beautiful sorceress or as a wrinkled troll-wife with big frightening teeth and eyes that glowed like red coals. The grandmother showed her gratitude with a small offering—a little porridge or a bowl of milk—which she brought the next day to the hedge. Maybe she also blessed the stone or the tree where she had received the vision with some blood or some red ocher, or she burned aromatic mugwort or juniper. Witches' ceremonies!

Because the grandmother frequently visited the hedge and spent a long time there, it follows that the other inhabitants of the village described her as a "hedge-sitter." *Hagadise* or *Hagezusse* means "the woman *(Zussa)* or the spirit *(Dise)* in the hedge *(Hage)*," so eventually the different Germanic peoples called her something similar. In English she is called the old hag. Clan mothers, the female ancestors who still weave the fate of the tribe and who stand by them with advice and protection, were described as the *disir*. The disir* give the warriors courage, the poets inspiration. They are present at birth as the "mothers of fate" when the umbilical cord is severed. For the dying they sever the threads of life and help them on their journey to the other side. Frau Holle is the ruler of the disir. Lovely Freya, the dispenser of love and sexuality, is known as Vanadis (Lady [Dis] of the Vanir) (Sigruna, 1996: 17). The Vanir are the gods of growth, of joy, of fertility, and of the woods.

The old woman in the grove and at the hearth represents the connection to the disir, the mothers of the tribe. The wise woman is herself an incarnation in an earthly chain who binds the past with the future generations. She was honored not only as a grandmother but also as the Goddess herself. She was the Freya (literally "lady") of the house, the *housewife* in the original sense of the word. It was she who brought harmony among the house, ancestors, and hedge spirits, who kept up the communication with the animals and plants. With this she became the guardian of the local ecosystem.

Out of the word *Hagezusse* came the word *Hexe* (witch). The ancient Scandinavians call this woman *Tunritha*, "the fence rider." *Zunrite* is her name in the upper German dialect; she is *Walriderske* in low German. This name was not given to the wise women because they flew through the air riding fence posts, as some etymologists have suggested,

---

[8] The knowledge of the different qualities of the different species of wood is still known in a few places. The farmer-philosopher Arthur Hermes (1890–1986), who used a different kind of wood in his hearth for every day of the week, explained to me, "It is really primitive to only reduce heat to what the thermometer says! Each species of wood has its own unique qualities. Essentially, they could be classified into seven groups because trees also correspond to the seven planets. Beech burns long; fir burns hot. So when you want to cook a little soup with the warmth of Saturn, you should heat the oven with beech or fir. You get the warmth of Jupiter from the maple and also from the oak, which also contains the warmth of Mars. Ash wood radiates the sun but Mercury is also there. Cherry, poplar, and willow give off a pleasant, cooler moon warmth. Birch and linden contain a very healing Venus warmth. I am lucky to live here in the forest and can find my planets for the oven myself. The city folks can't do that. Nevertheless, they should know that the different types of firewood are healing. Now and then they should make a fire for themselves and let the heat work on them. Many problems are healed this way— everyone has experienced how relaxing it is to gaze into a lively wood fire. If the rays are caught in a cooking pot it is even better" (Storl, 1989: 32).

* The *disir* (singular *dis*) are divine female guardian spirits in Old Norse sagas. *Dis* also means "woman" or "lady." (Trans.)

but because they sat in the hedgerow, on the threshold between nature and culture, between the world of the spirits and that of the humans.

The wise woman, who understood best how to mediate between the two worlds, and whose knowledge and spiritual range were great, could be called a shaman in an ethnological sense (Duerr, 1978). *Angenga* was the Anglo-Saxon name for the *Haegtesse*; it means "the lone one who slips around." *Wicca*, from the Germanic *weiha* and Old Norse *vigja* ("sacred," "worshipped," "numinous"), was another name, which means something like "dedicated to the gods." In medieval ecclesiastical Latin she was called, among other things, a *lamina* (little wood mother) and *herbaria* (little herbal mother).

Naturally there were also male magicians, sorcerers, and "sacred men" who knew how to negotiate the world of the spirit and the Divine. There were also hunters, shepherds, and forest visitors who knew their way around the realm beyond the hedgerow. In addition there were powerful shamans who could climb up and down the World Treeas nimble as a squirrel, or could fly like eagles. There were shamanic healers who, with the help of their animal allies, were able to sniff out the disease demon that had nestled deep inside the body. Some men could tell where the game was hiding in the forest by the rips and skips made by a stag's shoulder blade as it smoldered in the fire.

But when it came to the secrets of the plants, the women mainly were responsible. According to the elder Tsistsistas medicine man Bill Tallbull, the women usually inspired the plant shamans in their relationship to the plants. While we were walking together in the Bighorn Mountains he explained to me, "If a plant radiates a blue light, it is a sign that the plant spirit wants to make contact with you. If you don't understand it, then wait until it appears to you in a dream. If you still don't understand it, then ask your grandmother. She will know."

It is said that the ancient Knight Wate, the weapons master of the Gothic king Dietreich of Bern, that a "wild woman" had initiated him into the arts of medicinal roots:

> *She had a long time ago taken note,*
> *That Wate was doctored by a wild woman!*
>
> —Song of Gudrun

Odin/Wotan, the great shamanic god, was said to be able to heal with magical spells—and could do so better than the divine women of medicine. In the Merseburg charm,* written down by an unknown monk in the tenth century, the author says:

> *Phol (Balder) and Wodan rode to the wood,*
> *then Balder's filly sprained its foot.*
> *Then Sinthgunt sang over it and Sunna her sister,*
> *then Frija sang over it and Volla her sister*
> *then Wodan sang over it, as well he knew how:*
> *"like the leg-sprain, the blood-sprain,*
> *thus the limb contorts:*
> *Leg to leg—blood to blood!*
> *Limb to limb, such as they belong together!"*

---

* Such charms or spells were usually used for medicinal purposes in folk practices and often contained remnants of heathen beliefs. (Trans.)

But Woden also heals with herbs, as we know from a collection of eleventh-century Anglo Saxon herb charms:

> *Nine healing plants against nine horrible poisons.*
> *A worm [a disease-demon] came slithering,*
> *to strike and to kill.*
> *Then Woden took nine wonderful twigs,*
> *he smote the worm until it flew apart in nine shredded parts.*

But when he gathers his roots and herbs and uses them to heal, Odin dresses as a woman (Grimm, 1877: 333).

Often it was forest women, swan maidens, and fairies that revealed the right medicinal herbs to the herbalist. In the time of the plague the wood-maiden called from the forest, "Eat anise and valerian and the plague can't touch you!" (Meyer, 1903: 195).

Male shamans in Eurasia often have wives in the other worlds who inspire them, but female shamans can also be married to someone from the other world. Sometimes it is the Goddess herself—the grandmother earth, the tree-green Jörd, Holda, Freya, the threefold Brigit—who appears to the herbal shamans.

That women have particularly easy access to the secrets of the plants did not escape unnoticed by the first Latin Church scribe, Tertullian (c. C.E. 160–220). The Church father was convinced that not only could the women seduce men, but also they could enchant angels. In exchange for the indecency they had committed with the fallen angel, Lucifer had given women the knowledge of herbs and cosmetics as a sort of whore's payment. (*De anima* LVII).

Not every witch was an old crone; naturally, there were also young ones. There were girls whose uniqueness was demonstrated very early through signs and wonders or through obvious clairvoyant abilities. Perhaps it was a child that was abducted by a predator animal and miraculously returned home unharmed. Those who had been struck by lightning and survived were also considered special. It might be a young woman who unwittingly prophesied future occurrences, who fell very easily into a trance without being confused, or who could let her spirit soar with the birds. Hildegard of Bingen is said to have been able to describe exactly the appearance, color, and pattern of a calf even though the animal was still in its mother's belly. Only when it was born did everyone know that her description had been accurate. During the Middle Ages a child as unusual as this was placed in the care of the convent under the protection of the Church; today the concerned parents would bring her to a therapist. Primitive people often give up these children for adoption to shamans, or they go to the shamans as apprentices. The Native Americans of Arizona and New Mexico know that they need people with such unusual gifts, and that is why they hide these children from school officials and don't allow them to cut their hair.

Even when they are still young, girls with special gifts are respectfully referred to as "old," for their wisdom is ancient and archetypal. Thus it is said in a Chinese legend that at his birth Lao Tse, whom we have to thank for the *Tao Te Ching*, came out of his mother as a "white-haired old man." Particularly powerful *sadhus* (wandering holy men) and yoga masters are often said to be hundreds, sometimes thousands, of years old, although they are still in the prime of their lives.

Before the Christian era the witches enjoyed great respect among northern Europeans as magicians, healers, and prophets. Tacitus, the Roman "expert on Germania," found it remarkable that the barbarians were convinced that "there was something sacred and prophetic about women, and they neither neglect their advice nor their answers" (Tacitus, *Germania* 8). These women were called *Seidhkona* (woman who knows magic) or *Volva* (seeress) in the far North. They carried a magical wand, sang themselves into ecstasy with magical songs, and prophesied (Ström, 1975: 259). But they also liked to bring bad luck to their enemies. They could call the hidden creatures by name, and knew words and runes that worked in the depths. Their words and their magical herbs could work as a blessing or a curse. Therefore they were—like the shamans and medicine men—not only respected everywhere, but also feared.

The ability to ward off black magic and to kill enemies without any visible weapons was grist for the mill of the Christian missionaries, who sought to convince the Celtic, Germanic, and Slavic tribes of the superiority of their dogma. Right from the beginning of their missionary work, during the time of the European migrations, the missionaries tried to defame the wise herbalist women. Along with the berserkers and the heathen priests, the women represented the primary hindrance to conversion. They were rivals in the battle over the rule of the souls.

Sacred trees were felled, gods were degraded into demons, the heathen religion became a cult of the demon (*cultus daemonum*) and its practice was severely punished, the wise women were depicted as weather-witches and poison-mixers. Instructions for the missionaries, such as the eighth-century *Indiculus superstitionum et pagarum* [Declaration on the Superstitions and the Countryfolk], listed the prohibitions forced upon the heathens (Daxelmüller, 1996: 102–105). The following was forbidden:

processions through the countryside carrying images of the gods

idol worship at grave sites, grave sacrifices, the meal of the dead, and the singing of songs of the dead

invocation of the dead, or the questioning of the dead

rituals and sacrifice in the forests, groves, on trees, stones, springs, and crossroads

the spring festival in February

singing magical words

moon magic of the women

oracle, prophecy, and divination from sneezing, smoke, ashes from the hearth, and the behavior of birds, horses, and other animals

The *Penitentia*, or penance books, laid down the punishment for prophesying, invoking the gods, the interpretation of dreams, herbal knowledge, love potions, and going about with animal masks on. The representatives of the Christian faith did not bother with the actual contents of the indigenous, nature-oriented religion of the heathens when restricting their customs—it would have been sinful to deal any closer with such horrible idolatry. For the monks and the missionaries it was of no consequence whether or not the devil and demons were called Wotan, Woden, Odin, Pan, Frau Holle, Diana, or Artemis. The disir, *idisi*,* and wise women were all thrown in one pot along with the kidnapping, bloodsucking witches and lamia of the Romans, with the poisonous python of classical antiquity, and with the witch of Endor and other evil daughters of the darkness from the Old Testament.

Nevertheless, as herbalists and midwives the wise women were indispensable to the

Mezereon (*Daphne mezereum* L.), also called dwarf bay, spurge laurel, *Waldlorbeer* (wood laurel), or *Giftbeere* (poison berry), was categorized by the father of botany, Linnaeus, as one of the "shit laurels" because the plant was used as a powerful laxative. Mezereon contains the glycoside daphnin and the very poisonous daphne toxin. Ten to fifteen of the red berries can be fatal. Mezereon is used in homeopathy, usually at strengths greater than D6, for skin diseases, shingles, toothaches, and stomach problems, among other uses. Today the plant is rare and has been placed under protection. (Woodcut from Tabernaemontanus, *Neu vollkommen Kräuter-Buch*, 1731.)

---

* The *idisi* are female beings mentioned in the first Merseburg charm. They are a kind of Valkyrie. *Idis* is the Old Saxon word for a respected woman. It is possible that the idisi are related to the Old Norse disir. From Karl Simrock, *Dictionary of Northern Mythology* (Cambridge, England: Brewer, 1993), p. 171. (Trans.)

villagers. Although they were relegated to the shadows of the Christian Church, they remained carriers of ancient spirituality until the Middle Ages, albeit under the guise of folk Christianity. The herbs dedicated to Freya were collected in the name of the Holy Mother or the Trinity. Some of the herbs of Woden were dedicated to Rochus, patron saint of the plague, for he was a wanderer with a stave like Woden's, and he wore a cloak and a floppy hat and had a wolf (or dog) at his side. The plants of Thor, who protected the treasure seekers or root diggers from serpents and lindworms, were attributed to Saint George, the dragon slayer Michael, or Christopher the "giant." Mezereon *(Daphne mezereum)*, which once was dedicated to the sky god Tyr (Ziu, Tius), the tamer of the Fenris wolf, was transformed into a devil's plant like many other poisonous plants. As long as the people went to Mass and made their contributions, no one bothered the rural healers and magicians, or the foolish and "superstitious" people who worked with such plants.

But then in the late Middle Ages, as the plague grew worse and worse, as increased feudal oppression stirred a general anxiety about life, and as fanatical Cathari accused the Church of spiritual laxness, the state of the culture changed again. From then on superstition was a sin against God, as defined by the Church scholar Thomas Aquinas. Eager academics began the work of constructing a demonology in which the devil took on terrifying proportions as the mighty Lord of Darkness and a dangerous opponent to God. No longer was he "Hans-jump-in-the-fields" who sometimes appeared in the midday hour when people were resting from the heavy field work, nor was he the poor devil who had to haul stones to build a church or a bridge in order to be repaid for his service by being pelted with stones. No longer was he the wild hunter, the Green Man who made gold from lead, the black stranger who turned the heads of the young women but who could be chased off with spicy herbs. No, from this point on he was the very embodiment of evil itself.

In the minds of the clerics, a satanic oppositional church developed that forbade everything that was right and good. Midwives, herbalists, and superstitious farm wives eventually fell under suspicion of being servants in this temple of Satan. But only from about 1480 on were witches identified as negative by the laws of Church and state.

The Wrath of Venus

With the discovery of the New World (1492), the Christian worldview based on the Bible began to falter. Many problems arose for which the "word of God" had no answer: Was the earth round after all? Who were the Indians? The question of whether or not the native inhabitants even had human souls was only first given an affirmative answer in 1512. Surely they were not ancestors of Noah, whose three sons—Japheth, Shem, and Ham—were considered to be the primordial fathers of the Europeans, Asians, and Africans. Were these native people—as certain classical scholars dared to suggest— survivors of the drowned island of Atlantis, whom Plato had spoken about in his works *Timaeus* and *Critias*? Were they antipodes who, like flies on the ceiling, crawled on the underside of the earth's disk with their heads down? Were they the pre-Adamites, creations of a previous God, as Paracelsus conjectured? Were they the ancestors of the lost tribes of Israel?

But it was not only epistemological devils that eroded the foundations of Christian self-understanding. One year after the return of Columbus, a new plague broke out among the mercenary troops of the French king and spread rapidly throughout the entire Old World. It was called the "French disease" *(Morbus gallicus)*, or "syphilis," after the frivolous shepherd Syphilos, who brought shame to the temple of the sun and was punished for it by Apollo with a festering pestilence. Rubbing the sick person with vinegar liniments containing angelica, rosemary, and other herbs or essential oils and using elaborate fumigations with expensive resins—methods that had been helpful with the first plague—proved ineffective. Neither mastic gum nor goose fat, honey, mallow roots, or other softening and cooling herbs could prevent the wet, noxious-smelling pustules, the infections of the mucous membranes in the throat, gums, and nose, the perpetual runny nose, and the proliferating figlike growths on the intimate parts. Nor were the "Mars plants," such as narcissus root and nettles, able to stop the "wrath of Venus." No herb seemed suited for this disease! And the patron saint of syphilis sufferers, Saint Fiacrus (otherwise known as the patron saint of hemorrhoids), offered by the Church really wasn't able to do anything either.

The guaiacum resin imported from America, in which so much hope had been placed, as well as sarsaparilla, sassafras, and other plants with which the Indians had successfully treated syphilis, proved useless in Europe. They were useless mainly because the European doctors ignored the cultural and ritual contexts in which the successful cure took place in the New World, including strict fasting, sweat lodges, total abstinence, and chastity. This was all too elaborate, too heathen. It is now known that the phenol derivative guajacol found in the resin, when combined with the daily sweat lodges (wherein the body reached a temperature of at least 42°C), thoroughly kills the syphilis spirochetes in the organism (Griggs, 1982: 40).

Many levels of society were infected, but the disease mostly affected the ruling classes. It affected Church leaders as well as monarchs: Pope Julius II, whose feet had been eaten away by the disease, could no longer allow anyone to kiss his feet. Despite his having six wives, all of the British king Henry VIII's children were either born dead or proved inviable—they had already been infected in the womb. The king believed that his wives were to blame, and so that he could legally divorce them he joined the Reformation and declared himself head of the British Church. Ivan the Terrible terrorized his people in Moscow, murdering his own son and wife after syphilis had infected his brain.

The only treatment that seemed to help was the highly poisonous quicksilver (mercury) salve borrowed from the Arabian alchemists. For the pain there was the opium preparation laudanum. The medicinally induced quicksilver poisoning left the patients sweating, shaking, and foaming at the mouth; they got diarrhea, became apathetic, and lost their appetite. Sores appeared on their teeth and gums, their skin turned yellow because of liver damage, their hair and teeth fell out, their kidneys became inflamed, and they suffered serious disturbances of the intestinal tract. But because this "quacksilver" alleviated the symptoms of syphilis a little, it was considered successful and was prescribed—the "miracle drug" of the times—for practically all other diseases, from asthma to colds. The result was an iatrogenic catastrophe: Modern chemical medicine was born! "Heroic medicines"—heavy metals, mineral poisons (antimony, vitriol, and so forth), and strong purgatives for the intestines, which had been destroyed by therapy—were considered advanced. The herbalists and their wisdom were no longer needed!

The horror this plague ushered in ran deep. The malicious disease, which was passed through sexual intercourse, sowed mistrust between the sexes. Brief sexual contact, no matter how tempting, could bring pain and death. The Puritans had a new impetus, and they preached against unchastity and impure sexual relations. The culture of the bathhouses, with their sensuous, carefree interaction between the sexes, succumbed. The joyous May and midsummer festivals, with their dancing and trees of love, found themselves in dangerously close proximity to the witches' sabbat. Typical

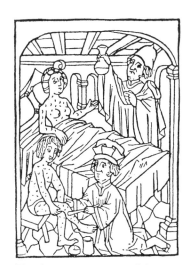

Two doctors treating a syphilis patient with quicksilver (mercury). (From Bartholomeo Steber, *A Malo françozo morbo Gallorum praeservatio ac cura*, 16th century.)

of this new attitude was the writing of the Puritan Phillip Stubbes, who called the maypole a "stinking idol" and identified the Lord of the May Festival and Dance as Satan, Lord of Hell. He also warned that "of the maidens who go into the forest on May night, barely a third returns immaculate."[9]

Indeed, nature was no longer understood to be the Bride of God, as "the realm of earth in which God sowed the sacred grain" (according to Hildegard of Bingen). No longer was it the good wise soul of the world, full of the signs and wonders of God, but it was instead a dangerous witch that had to be brought under control. It is symbolic that the worst phase of the syphilis epidemic—between 1550 and 1650—was crowned by the Inquisition, and that during this time the fundamental principles of modern experimental science, whose goal is to control nature, were formulated. The dialogue with the souls of the world, the conversation with the plants and animals that had been sustained since the Stone Age and had still been cared for within the frame of the traditional Christianity, came to a standstill. Over many centuries celibate, misogynistic priests led a campaign of destruction against the carriers of the ancient tradition of shamanic culture in the form of the Inquisition. And this happened not only in Europe but also with the same brutality against the idol and devil worshippers in the New World and other colonies.

We all know the gruesome stories about "witches" that were spread by men of the Church—for example, how they caused harvests to go bad and brought about pestilence, how they slaughtered babies so they could use the fat for their witches' salve, how they made a pact with the devil by letting a drop of their blood fall into the fire in which bones burned, how they fornicated with the adversary, kissing his stinking rear end. Yes, the ruling power, the Inquisition, had to make a powerful intervention, for Satan, he who severely threatened the divine order of things, was at work. The "henchmen of evil"— usually poor farmers, herbalists, and midwives—averred their innocence, but under torture they confessed almost every time. And if they did not confess, then that was double the proof of witchcraft, for what mortal could have withstood the torture without the help of the devil's power?

The New Science

While the Inquisition murdered the carriers of an intuitive and visionary understanding of nature, academics fiddled around with new methods of obtaining knowledge and power over nature. Francis Bacon (1561–1626), who functioned as state attorney under King James I during the witch trials, was considered one of the fathers of experimental natural science. In his writings nature appears as a revolting witch who had to be "stretched on the torture rack in order to squeeze her secrets out of her" (Merchant, 1987: 177). Man, he wrote, should exploit her with the help of mechanical manipulation and make her into a slave for the "good of humanity."

---

[9] "In May, at Whitsunday or at other times, all young boys and girls, old men and women walk in the woods, groves, hills, and mountains at night, where they spend a pleasant night of leisure. In the morning they return with birch trees and branches in order to brighten their gatherings. It is no wonder as a great lord is amongst them and rules over their pleasure and games, namely Satan, Lord of Hell. But the greatest treasure which they bring back with them is the May apple, which they carry home with them with great respect in the following manner: They have twenty or forty yoked oxen, each of which has a sweet smelling bundle of flowers tied to their horns. The oxen pull the maypole, or better said, this stinking idol which is decorated top to bottom with herbs and grasses, wrapped with ribbons and sometimes painted in different colors, home. Two to three hundred men, women, and children follow in deep respect. They set it up, ribbons and cloths flutter off the end, and they strew the ground, bound green branches around and place summer leaves and bows of leaves next to it. And then they begin to dance around it, just as the heathens did when an idol was consecrated" (Phillip Stubbes, *Anatomie der Mißbräuche* [The Anatomy of Abuses], London, 1583).

For René Descartes (1596–1650), who was also a priest, nature was only a machine without consciousness, without feelings. Plants and animals were mechanical objects that could be mathematically (quantitatively) described and manipulated like all mechanisms. Finally, with Newton (1642–1727) the planets themselves were no longer gods but lifeless satellites in an empty space. An approachable nature, full of elemental spirits, fairies, elves, and deities, ceased to exist; these were foolish superstitions. Today if these subjective delusions present themselves, we have, in our humanitarian age, psychiatric remedies that are paid for by medical insurance.

The preachers of the Christian faith took the first step toward the demythologizing of nature, in which the old gods were banned and degraded (Storl, 1997a: 121). Natural science, which was formulated in the wake of the torture of the witches, removed the soul from nature entirely. This reductionist science also left behind a dead landscape of the soul, for when nature has been desacralized and emptied the pictures, scents, and colors of the soul are taken as well. It too becomes empty, alienating, joyless—a "wasteland," as the poet T. S. Eliot called it.

Thus the hedgerow, in which the witch once sat and talked to the animals, plants, and spirits, turned—as noted by Hans Peter Duerr in his important book *Dreamtime*—into an impenetrable wall. The forest was already a frightening place for the Church scholar Augustine. It was profane, a *sylvus daemonicum* full of unclean demons. The heavenly city of Jerusalem—a citadel surrounded by reinforced walls, protected from the devil and his fallen angels, where the only "true" God ruled—was offered as an alternative for those seeking redemption. This citadel god increasingly revealed himself as the personification of the human ego. And this ego always felt threatened by the "devil," by the irrational, the uncontrollable, by the immeasurable magical fullness and the indescribable magic of being. The Inquisition found an effective weapon in the ego's fear, or *Angst* (from the Old High German *angust*, meaning "narrow, clamped"), of dissolving into the transcendental being. The people most affected by the Inquisition were the simple nature-bound people. Ultimately the windows of this prison were barred shut with grates made of Cartesian coordinates and walled over with abstract theories during the rational Age of Enlightenment.

Those who had a clairvoyant relationship with nature disappeared; the people were blinded in their souls. The new science was the blind man's walking stick, with which he tapped around in the dark. Because the natural spirits disappeared from human consciousness, the animals became sad and silent and the banned gods grew increasingly wrathful and more threatening. Beloved Freya revealed herself more and more as Hel; as Hecate, who brings insanity and destruction; as the black, bloodthirsty Kali. The green earth became a desert. Heaven, the etheric heights on which the gods once wandered, became an empty space, filled with black holes and chaos.

Contrary to current propaganda, witchcraft medicine is not based on ideological grounds, on the knowledge of how to poison the unwanted unborn in the womb, on how best to combine drugs in order to take a "trip," or on making amulets to protect against existential angst. Witchcraft medicine is the practice of becoming whole. It heralds the reestablishment of the wonders and magic in internal and external nature: the resettlement of the meadows, forests, and souls with the delightful and colorful elves, with the nature spirits of Pan, with the radiant angels. It also brings the ability to enjoy these places and souls and to understand their healing songs, words, and advice.

The time has come to rip down the walls and plant hedges.

The Witch

As

Shaman

Wolf-Dieter Storl

The great cultural anthropologist Bronislaw Malinowski spoke of the basic needs of humans that must be satisfied by each society in order for it to function. They are:

1. food and shelter
2. gratification of physical urges and reproduction
3. physical and spiritual health
4. social security
5. meaning (religion, art)

The witch's familiar is a shamanic helping spirit. (Woodcut from Matthew Hopkins, *The Discovery of Witches*, c. 1645.)

Power and authority within a society are given to those who prove their ability to address these needs successfully. When conquest, colonization, or unrest makes it impossible to ensure the satisfaction of these basic needs, then the former functionaries, priests, and authorities are deprived of their power, reviled, persecuted, tortured, or arrested. From then on a new paradigm, a new concept of meaning, regulates the satisfaction of the basic needs.

A transformation such as this, a reversal of values, took place after the Great Migration, and then again with renewed elan in the fifteenth century. The elders—those who were closest to shamanic heathendom, such as the wise women and the priests—were stripped of their power. They were accused of hindering the satisfaction of human needs on all levels. With black magic they threatened the food supply and the overall survival by conjuring up bad weather, invoking plagues of mice and rats, and secretly milking animals. The *Bilwis* ("he who knows about magical power"), formerly a priest who blessed the growth of the grain, was degraded into a malicious grain demon. The wise women, protectors of the life of the tribe, were identified as witches who destroyed the fertility and health of the tribe. The rituals that provided meaning and festivities throughout the year's holidays were replaced by others, and ancient forms of worship were condemned as devil worship.

The accusations of the Inquisition can be understood more clearly against this backdrop. They reveal themselves to be part of an ideological campaign of destruction against the last bearers of archaic shamanic consciousness in the Western world. We shall look at the points of their accusations a little more closely from this perspective.

Devil worship: The witches were said to have rejected the true God and made a pact with the devil. On the witches' sabbat *(Synagoga diabolica)* practitioners worshipped the devil, who held court as a black goat. On certain witches' holidays the witches attended gatherings that usually took place on the moors or on a mountain. They flew there on animals (dogs, goats) or objects (brooms, fireplace shovels, pitchforks) with Diana, the "forest devil woman."

Sex magic: Witches had sex with the horned one and with the *Buhlteufel* ("lover devil") as well. As *succubi* ("those who lie underneath")—erotic spirits of the night—the witches sucked semen and created demonic beings on their own. In their world the witches slept with *incubi* ("those who lie on top") and gave birth to demon children and ugly changelings. Some even had a long-standing, almost marriagelike relationship to demonic lovers (Biedermann, 1989: 114).

Supposedly, witches could bewilder innocents and seduce them with false love using spells and philters, which were made with a combination of aphrodisiac magical herbs such as mandrake and henbane, or even menstrual blood. Conversely, they could make men impotent by binding knots into their laces and make the women frigid and insensitive, or destroy the fruits of love by "closing their womb."

Black magic: Witches destroyed the crops by conjuring hailstorms, tornadoes, and floods. They usually brewed the bad weather in their "witches' cauldron." They lamed,

In the early modern era the apple tree was considered the "tree of knowledge," as is made clear by this book illustration. (Woodcut from Lonicerus, *Kreüterbuch*, 1679.)

In Europe the apple tree was associated with the fall of man. The skull behind the apples represents those expelled from paradise and the first mortal man, Adam. Mandrake fruits are still called "Adam's apple" in Turkey. (Woodcut from Hieronymus Bock, *Kreütterbuch*, 1577.)

made infertile, or in some other way harmed the cows and other domestic animals. They secretly stole milk from cows. They knew the poisonous herbs and used them to poison people. They sent diseases to people.

Devil Worship

For the native people who have converted to a civilized religion—whether Christianity or Islam—the immediate surroundings become increasingly less familiar. They can no longer synchronize their existence with the local mountains and forest, but instead must look to a faraway desert land brought closer to them by a priest who refers to a book written in an incomprehensible foreign language. His religion is based on an abstract belief instead of on personal direct experience and vision. Folk Christianity moved the sacred occurrences back to their immediate surroundings: The Christ child was born in a manger, which looked just like the mangers in their village. Mary dried the swaddling cloth on the elder bush that grew next to the manger. And if the congregation wanted to believe that the Savior and his disciples walked through cornfields and meadows, well, the village priest could live with that.

But the so-called witch went further. She was still connected to the wilderness behind the fence. She still had access to "inner" nature. She knew the depth of the forest as well as the depth of her soul. She knew both inside and outside—after all, they are one and the same. The same ancient deities who had appeared to her Paleolithic ancestors many thousands of years before came to her deep in the forest, in the depths of her soul. She was still aware of the Great Mother, the Earth Mother. All ancient peoples knew her. The traditional peoples, such as the Native Americans, still know her as the grandmother who lives in a realm of light beneath the earth. She is the guardian of the souls of humans and animals. She takes in the dead, and after a period of time gives them a new birth. She helps the dying and those who are about to be born over the threshold.

The ancient Stone Age hunters—possibly already Neanderthals—worshipped her in caves deep in the earth. On the walls of the cave they drew the outlines of the buffalo, woolly mammoths, horses, and reindeer that ripened in her womb in order to be born on earth, where the hunters could encounter them. In the darkness of these caves the shamans traveled to her, sometimes dressed as an elk—like the sorcerer in the Trois Frères caves—and prayed or gave thanks for the game. Here in the womb of the Earth Mother the youth were initiated into the spiritual mysteries. The Venus statues carved out of soapstone and ivory that archaeologists have found in many such caves were probably depictions of this primordial Goddess.

We still know the Great Goddess from the Grimm fairy tale about Frau Holle. She captures the souls of those who have lost the thread of their lives and have fallen into the depth of the well shaft. The shamans of many different peoples tell of the underworldly realm through which the soul wanders. It is a bright land with golden green meadows and apple trees—it is the Avalon (apple lane) of the Celts. The Goddess has large teeth like a dragon's and wild hair; thus many who behold her are frightened. But to friendly souls she shows herself in a sweeter, kinder figure. When she shakes her feather bed it snows and bestows fertility on the fields. Often she visits the world of the humans—as a wise virgin with a growling bear in the spring, as a beautiful forest goddess riding on a stag, as the flower-bedecked May bride of the sun god, as a dancer during the midsummer round dance, as a fat farmer's wife with pears and apples at harvesttime, as an old gray witch in the November fog. She frequently flies through the stormy weather as Mother Goose on her gander, with the accompaniment of her companions. The wild goose, the swan, and the baby-bringing stork have been symbols of the flight of the soul—the shamanic flight—since the Stone Age (Campbell, 1969: 1679). When she is Parvati, the mountain woman, she delicately caresses the feathers of the wild geese—they are the masters of yoga—when she rests after her long flight on the mirror-clear Manasa Sea beneath Kailash, the world mountain. She fills the geese's souls with the light of inspiration and sends them back into the world of humans. As goddess of the wild animals, the wilderness, the springs, and the caves, and as a birth assistant, Frau Holle appears to the Mediterranean peoples in the form of Artemis or Diana. The Neolithic Chinese knew her as Mother of the Valley, who created heaven and earth. She found her place in folk Christianity, transfigured into Mary of the grotto.

However, to the Church leaders and inquisitors struggling for power, these Goddess manifestations revealed themselves—reflecting the state of their own souls—as evil, dangerous witches who deserved to be destroyed. In Christian fairy tales Frau Holle eventually became the "the devil's grandmother" or a witch with the poisonous apple; the apple was once considered a symbol of life and happiness. Her underworldly realm of light became a hot cave stinking of sulfur and pitch. In Russia she mutated into the frightening Baba Yaga with an iron leg; her magical house in the middle of the forest is built on a chicken leg and turns endlessly in a circle. She lies on the oven, her nose has grown into the ceiling, her snot pours over the threshold, her breasts hang over a hook, and she grinds her teeth (Diederichs, 1995: 37).

The elder bush (*Sambucus nigra* L.) was considered by the Germanic peoples sacred to the Great Goddess, who was also called Frau Holle or Holda. It was believed that the house spirits lived in the bush that grew near the house. It was considered the "farmer's pharmacy." (Woodcut from Otto Brunfels, *Contrafayt Kreüterbuch*, 1532.)

Elder *(Sambucus nigra)*

The names Hölderlin and Hollabiru are old German folk names for the devil, and are connected to the German name for the elder bush, *Holunder*. But linguists vehemently argue over whether the Holunder has anything to do with Frau Holle, the devil's grandmother—that would be too romantic, too tacky. They derive the prefix *hol* from *kal* (black) and the suffix *der* from *tro* (tree); thus *Holunder* would be the black tree. However, those who have been able to retain a minimum amount of clairvoyance find the elder to be a kind of threshold, a gateway to the sort of transsensory, underworldly realm that has been traditionally associated with Frau Holle.

The Swiss plant esotericist René Strassmann is of the opinion that elder protects those living on earth from being attacked by the beings that live below the earth. Thus elder defines the boundary between the underworld and the middle world. Strassmann uses the wood, bark, roots, and flowers as incense for making direct contact with the shadow world (Strassmann, 1994: 153). The Germanic, Celtic, and Slavic heathens experienced elder in a similar way. The ancient Swedes sacrificed milk for the house spirits at the base of the "house elder"; the Prussians offered the earth spirit beer and bread.

In fairy tales Frau Holle is the queen of the dwarves and elves. It is no wonder, then, that those who fall asleep beneath an elder will soon sense the presence of gnomes, kobolds, and dwarfs. They will be encountered in a good mood or a grumpy one, or even as evil plague demons. Those whose third eye remains tightly closed will probably experience only headaches or body aches or become somewhat dizzy. The Swedes say that whoever sits under a flowering elder at dusk on midsummer's eve will see the elf king and his court go by.

As protector of souls Frau Holle is also a goddess of the dead. Thus it becomes obvious that the little tree sacred to her played a central role in death rituals. The heathen Frisians buried their dead beneath the *Ellhorn* near their house, and their ancestors made crosses for grave sites out of an elder bush that had stood on the land of the deceased. It was considered a very good sign when the wood of such crosses budded once again. Then the dead could sit on it when they took their "vacation" on earth. In Tirol fresh elder branches are stuck in the grave to see if they will sprout, and elder flower tea is drunk at wakes. Until recently, in many places in northern Europe it was customary to bed the dead on elder branches. The coffin maker had to measure out the coffin with an elder reed, and the driver of the hearse was to use an elder switch for the horses. In England grave diggers carried some elder wood with them to protect themselves from questionable ghosts.

To the ancient Germans and Slavs, an old elder that nestled against the side of the house was considered the abode of family ghosts. It not only helped those who crossed over the threshold find their way to the realm of Holle, but it also helped those who returned from there. Thus the tree, called Frau Hylle or Hyllemoer (Mother Holle) by the Danes, was also connected with sexuality and birth. It plays an erotic role in folk songs:

> *Parsley, potherb grows in my garden.*
> *[Name of the girl] is the bride, she shall wait no longer.*
> *Behind an elder bush, she gave her love a kiss.*
> *Red wine, white wine, tomorrow she'll be mine.*[10]

The elder can also speak of separation and false love:

> *The stream runs and roars over there by the elder bush where we sat.*
> *Like many bells ringing, as heart by heart lay, that you have forgotten.*
> —FROM THE FOLK SONG *ADE ZUR GUTEN NACHT*
> ["GOOD-BYE TO GOOD NIGHT"]

In Thuringia during Whitsuntide boys placed elder sticks at the windows of the girls who were known to be somewhat easier. If the girls who were ready to marry wanted to know from which direction their groom would come, they gave the elder bush a good shake on Thomas Day (July 3). If a dog should then bark from any direction, that was the answer to her question. In the *Poetic Edda* it is said of elder tree that "the fruit of the tree of life should be placed in the fire for a woman with puerperal fever and delayed childbirth so that she can push out that which is concealed inside." To build a baby cradle from elder wood was out of the question, because then the elder would take the baby back to the realm beyond. Also one should never raise a child with an elder whip; the child will neither grow nor flourish.

Elder is of a dual nature, like the Goddess of life and death: It is both white (the flowers) and black (the berries), and it is a medicinal plant and a strong poison. The

---

[10] Parsley is considered an aphrodisiac and also an abortifacient. In earlier times streets of commercial love were called "parsley alleys." The English *parsley bed* has an erotic meaning (Beuchert, 1995: 259). In the poem the phrase "red wine, white wine" plays on the taking of the girl's virginity.

house elder was a veritable pharmacy for the common people: From the flowers grandmothers brewed a tea that stimulated sweat and urine, which was helpful for flus, colds, rheumatism, measles, and scarlet fever. Modern phytotherapy has successfully confirmed the medicinal uses of the tea for hay fever and sinus infections as well. The grandmothers made an intestine-cleansing and -stimulating syrup from the black-purple berries. A hot, sweet elderberry soup was always part of the winter nourishment. Recent research has found immune-stimulating and nerve-strengthening activity in the berries. They are even used as adjunct therapy for cancer treatment, because the blue pigment has a positive influence on the oxygenation of the cells. Juice, syrup, and soup made of the berries help cure viral infections, herpes, and neuralgia; dried berries can be stored and then cooked when the flu or other illnesses are going around. The leaves, gathered in the summer, are made into lard-based salves for bruises, contusions, tumors, and chilblains. The cooked leaves are also placed on swollen or infected nipples. The bark is collected in the fall for its dramatic emetic and laxative effects. When the inner rind is scraped upward, it causes vomiting; when scraped downward, it brings on diarrhea. This "superstition" was not limited to Europe; Siberians and Native Americans also used it as a purgative when they wanted to cleanse their bodies. Their faith gave purpose to the physiological effects caused by the glycosides. As always, it is not merely the active ingredients that play a decisive role, but also the appropriate therapeutic word, the power of suggestion, that affects the outcome.

But this pharmacologically "sensible" use of elder was not only for health but also for magical purposes. Because the tree attracts negative energies, or "flying poisons," and "uses them up" or guides them down into the underworld, all kinds of problems and diseases have been "hung" on it. Pus-covered bandages and cloth were draped on the branches. Teeth, hair, and fingernails were buried in its shadows in order to prevent magical misuse. The afterbirth of a calf was buried beneath the elder bush so that neither cow nor calf could be bewitched. The shirts of bewitched children were given back to the elder bush. The bathwater of small children was also poured out there.

To treat a fever, go to the elder bush on the night of the waning moon, wrap a thread around its trunk, and say, "Good day, elder. I bring you my fever, I tie it on, and now in God's name I go." Sometimes the sick would bend down a branch, saying, "I bend you. Fever, leave me now; elder bough, lift yourself up; swine fever, sit on top. I have you for a day; now you have it for a year and a day." For toothaches the afflicted scraped his gums with an elder chip until the affected area bled. Then the chip was placed back on the branch from which it had been taken. As with the fever, the elder guided the toothache downward into the earth. Incidentally, it has also been reported that the woodlands Native Americans use elder magically to get rid of toothaches.

To a tree as powerful and medicinal as this, the farmers have bowed down or respectfully lifted their hats. Arthur Hermes, the farmer-mystic from the Jura mountains in Switzerland, did so until his death in 1986. Nobody would dare to carelessly chop down or burn the wood of an elder. It was believed that the evil powers bound in the bush would attack foolish people and bring them bad luck or even kill them. Only widows and widowers were allowed to gather the wood and burn it, for they had already been touched by death. When cutting it down was unavoidable, the cutters exposed their heads, folded their hands, and prayed, "Lady Elder, give to me of

The horned god in a trance posture, depicted on the Celtic-Germanic Gundestrup cauldron.

The Germanic fertility god, Thor, drives his wagon, hitched to goats, through the air. When he hurls his hammer through the clouds he causes lightning and thunder. The thunderbolt rages lightning-fast to the earth, where it fertilizes the ground.

your wood, so will I give you some of mine when it grows in the woods." In the north in the Frisian Islands, permission to cut down an elder had to be obtained from the tree on the preceding full moon, and an offering was hung in the branches or buried in the roots. The cut branches could not be used in any manner, but had to be returned to the earth. Also elder should not be planted; the Goddess herself finds the right place for it to grow. This is usually not far from the house because elder loves to be near humans. When a house is vacated, it doesn't take long before the elder that grew there dies.

That the tree was an important ritual plant of the Great Goddess is demonstrated by the many different nursery rhyme versions of "Ring around the Rosy." "Ring around the rosy; oh, we are children three; sitting 'neath an elder bush, and calling hush, hush, hush!" The "Ring around the Rosy" songs children sing today are just as much an inheritance of archaic sacred ritual dances as hunting techniques like the bow and arrow are the legacy of Stone Age. Even the Christian missionaries were not able to shake the people's respect for the tree. Although they said that the elder was an evil tree—torturers had beaten Jesus with an elder whip, and that is why, they said, the branches have cracks on their skin—in the end the tree was integrated into Christian mythology. Thus it is said that Mary dried the swaddling clothes of the Christ child on the branches of an elder under which she had found protection from a storm, and that is why lightning never strikes an elder. The traitor Judas hanged himself from the branch of an elder tree. In Allgäu the cross for the "palm" on Palm Sunday must be made only from elder branches. Certainly the sacred wood played a similar role in the spring processions and *Flurumg nge** of the ancient Celts and Germanic peoples.

* These are processions to bless the fields and meadows. (Trans.)

The Buck: The Divine Dispenser

In addition to Frau Holle, the witches were conscious of a further primordial Paleolithic deity when they looked over the hedgerow: namely, the buck, the horned companion of the Goddess, who dispenses pleasure. For the people of archaic cultures the buck, particularly the stag, embodied the divine powers of creation. The relationship is repeatedly demonstrated in the Indo-European languages: The Vedic Indians call God, the dispenser of life and creator of souls, Bhag or Bhagwan.[11] *Bog* is the general Slavic word for God. The *boogeyman* was not only the "black man" who scared children but also the *Waldteufel* (wood devil), the "spring-in-the-field" who jumped on the shepherd maidens or young farm girls when they were collecting berries. The *boggard* was a well-known, unpredictable nature spirit in British folklore. *Boogie-woogie* is the strange, seductive, erotic music of black Americans, which seemed suspect and satanic to the puritanical white Americans. Böögg is still the name of a scary ghost of Alemannic lore, and *Bockert* is the traditional mask worn for Fasching (Shrove Tuesday). In the Himalayas the archaic horned god is still worshipped as Pashupati, "the lord of animals and souls." He is identical to Shiva, the lord of the cave, the possessor of the phallus (lingam) who rides the wild steer. He wears the waxing and waning moon as horns in his long matted

[11] Acharia Rajneesh (1931–1990), the "sex guru," referred to himself as Bhagwan the divine—*nomen es omen*. He assembled a large following among New Age believers but at the same time made many enemies with his teachings, which propagated sexuality as the royal path to enlightenment.

hair. His trident, which actually represents a World Tree (among other things), was reinterpreted as the devil's pitchfork by the Zoroastrian priests (Storl, 2002: 142).

The Chinese remember the archaic horned god in the figure of the primordial emperor, Fu Hsi, who taught the first people how to hunt, fish, and read oracles with yarrow sticks for the I-Ching, and as Shen Nung, who was the first human to teach the people about rituals and ceremonies, herbalism, and agriculture. The Great God revealed himself as a virile steer in Southwest Asia and North Africa. In Egypt he fertilized the sky goddess Nut daily, while as Zeus he fertilized Europe in the form of a steer. The roaring stampede of the heavenly steer embodied thunder, rain, and fertility. The archaic lord of the animals also lives on in Pan, the Arcadian shepherd and hunting god. He has goat's hooves and horns. He lustily chases the nymphs. All nature spirits dance to his flute.

The primordial God mainly appeared to the Neolithic Europeans as a stag with brilliant, radiant antlers. The stag was considered to be the sun in animal form. As the sun he fertilized the earth, the womb of the Goddess, so that vegetation would sprout and grow. His life-bringing light penetrated the deepest corners of the human heart just as it penetrated the dark ravines of the forest. With the advent of Christianity, the sun-stag was transformed into the stag of Hubert or Eustatius. Now it is the light of Christ that radiates from the antlers. Today the stag ekes out an existence on the label of a popular herbal liquor (Jägermeister), which comes in a forest green bottle.

The Celts knew the god with the stag horns as Cernunnos. He is depicted sitting cross-legged like Buddha or the proto-Shiva from pre-Aryan India. He is surrounded by forest animals and rules over all sentient beings. Like Shiva, Cernunnos holds a serpent—the symbol of wisdom and of ever-regenerating life—in his hand. The name Cernunnos comes from the Indo-European root ker, which means "growth" or "to become big and hard." Thus he embodies the principles of growth, copulation, and fertilization. He was also the possessor of the phallus that impregnated the Great Goddess.

The Neolithic farmers of Europe noticed that the yearly growth cycles of the stag's antlers—from the time they were shed in February or March to the scraping off of the velvet from the antlers in August—coincided with the stages of the growth of the grain, as well as the sowing and the harvest (Botheroyd, 1995: 160). Thus they had a tamed stag pull the wagon of the Goddess, and sometimes a tame stag pulled the plow that pushed into the earth and opened it up for the seeds, like a phallus. At harvesttime they danced a stag dance. The stag dance, a tourist favorite, is performed on September 3 at Bromley Abbey in England, during which the young boys carry a huge stag head in front of them. It is a last remnant of the Neolithic harvest festivals. Here and there, the last sheaves harvested are made into stag forms that are still called stag or harvest buck. They are triumphantly driven into the village on the harvest wagon (today they use a tractor). The roots of medicinal herbs, which are sacred to the Goddess, were in archaic Europe naturally dug with an antler, a horn that was possibly worked with gold. Gold represents the sun stag in mineral form (Storl, 1997a: 182).

In Germanic mythology aspects of the archaic god live on in Thor, the favorite god of the farmers. While hurling thunder and lightning, he drives over the land in a wagon drawn by billy goats. The goddess Freya is not resistant to him either: Occasionally she is said to take on the shape of a white goat in rut. The magical animals that are harnessed to the hammer-bearer's wagon are identical to the black thunderclouds. They are rain bringers whose waters make the meadows and fields green and fill the barrels and vats of the farmers. The clouds that swell and rise on hot summer days are still called "storm bucks."

There is a saga that tells how the great thunderer Thor once visited a farm with Loki. As usual, Thor was friendly to the farmer. He slaughtered his goat, skinned it, cooked it in a great kettle, and invited the whole family—husband, wife, and children—to eat it. However, he warned them to carefully collect all bones and to throw them on the goatskin when they were through. The next morning Thor swung his hammer over the skin and there stood the goat, alive again, but lame in his hind foot. The farmer's son had split a thighbone with his knife in order to suck out the marrow. Thor's eyes flashed with rage, and he would have killed the family immediately if their crying hadn't made him take pity on them. As punishment he took two of the children with him, and they served him loyally from then on (Golther, 1985: 276).

Following the example of the much esteemed Thor, the heathen Germanic peoples sacrificed billy goats to the earth goddess. These animals were also visibly resurrected and transformed into corn, wheat, rye, legumes, hemp, or flax—the unhampered and dynamic growth of the agricultural bounty. And when the wind blew through the undulating cornfield it was said that "the goat is racing through the corn!" But this goat, this "vegetation demon," also had to be sacrificed: When the mower is cutting the last row, the Swabians say, it is "cutting the goat's neck." In many places the last sheaves of grain are still called bucks. To thresh is to kill the buck. Often goat is served for dinner during threshing time. The horns of the sacrificed goat are hung on the door to protect the house and barn from black magic and lightning. For a long time people still believed in the protective power of Thor's goats. A few years ago a Swiss farmer told me that he let a billy goat run free around the barn so that if the devil came into the barn, he would take possession of the goat first and leave the other animals alone.

Thor and his goats embodied cosmic sexuality in the imagistic thinking of rural farmers. But Thor's animals could also dispense potency and health to the human root chakra: He who rubs his member with goat tallow will be favored above all other men by the women. The smoke of goat hair was used for the relief of pain in the sexual organ. And the western Slavs believed that a man who was bewitched by a woman could be freed by smearing goat blood on himself.

If we inadvertently think about the billy goat when we hear the word *buck*, it corresponds to the medieval fantasy of the animal that was nourished by a Germanic belief in Thor that later melded with the Pan myth of classical antiquity. The witch hunters believed that at the nocturnal witches' sabbat the devil held court in living form as a lusty, stinking black billy goat. Their spies reported that the sabbat participants danced around in a circle turning to the left, with their faces outward. This is definitely correct, for all archaic round dances turn "with the sun." Music was allegedly made with dead cats, and they drummed on the heads of pigs (Bächthold-Stäubli, 1987: vol. 1, 1427). Enormous amounts of food were eaten and drunk. The witches sat on grassy banks and devoured apples, pears, and the flesh of freshly slaughtered roasted ox. The devil himself served the unsalted roast, the *Bockbier* (buck beer), and the wine. From an ethnological standpoint, this relates to a typical archaic Thanksgiving festival: Among primitive people, the "big man" or the chief divides the meat according to strict ritual rules. The tribal kings of the Celts and the Germanic peoples also divided and shared the meat that had been consecrated to the gods, and in this way ensured the good spirits of their followers. In America the head of the household still ceremoniously carves and serves the turkey on Thanksgiving (the third Thursday in November) (Storl, 1997b: 34).

It is significant that the ox meat was served without salt. During the initiation of the youth in the remote "bush schools" of traditional peoples, the food is almost always salt-free. Many shamans—including the farmer-philosopher Arthur Hermes—do without salt because it causes the soul to bind to matter.

A fertility orgy, which was not very different from other archaic peoples', became connected with the witches' festival. When it is said that the participants copulated with goats, wolves, and other animals, it merely emphasizes the unburdened, orgiastic character of fertility festivals. The horned one himself engaged in coitus with the witches. But they—as it says in the trial records—experienced the embrace as rather uncomfortable, for the large, eternally erect penis was ice-cold, possibly because it was an artificial member that was used in fertility magic.

Demon as a witch's lover. (From Ulrich Molitor, *De laniis et phitonicis mulieribus*, 1489.)

The devil also instructed the participant in all kinds of black arts—weather making, the learning of spells *(maleficii)*, the making of magical potions *(veneficii)*, and other "evil doings." Every witch was given a witches' name and the sign of the devil, which he burned with his goat's hoof on her back, either on her left shoulder blade or in the small of her back. This was almost certainly a tattoo or brand that had to do with an initiatory test of courage, as was customary in earlier times for the Celts.

For a long time after the conversion to Christianity, the followers of the ancient religions probably still gathered in remote areas, in moors with difficult access, or on mountaintops for Walpurgis Night, Midsummer Day, and other magically loaded times (solstice, equinox, quarter days). The authorities had reluctantly endured these rural fertility rituals until the twelfth century, when the fanatical Cathar sects, with an orientation toward Manichaeism, challenged the Church and made it very insecure. The Cathari (from *catharoi*, meaning "the pure") taught a stern asceticism and a dualism between God and Satan. Against these heretics Pope Gregory IX initiated the Inquisition, whose agent was the Dominicans. Many suspicious people were made to confess by torture and were punished by the seizure of their property, imprisonment in dungeons, and burning at the stake (Heiler, 1962: 699). Although the Church brutally tortured the Cathari, they took on elements of their adversaries as well—for instance, the concept of Satan as a powerful opponent to God. A machine was set in motion that brought to light the ancient cults and persecuted them as the products of Satanic oaths.

The World Tree

Another Paleolithic concept that still lived on in the inner life of so-called witches was the image of a powerful tree, a World Tree, or a pillar that holds up the sky. From its branches hang the planets and stars. Its roots reach deep down into the bright regions of Frau Holle, into the spring of life, which the world serpent guards and where the mothers of fate (the Norns) sit spinning. The tree is the ladder to the beyond. The gods, ancestors, and ghosts roam up and down the ladder, and sometimes a shaman flies through the branches, crowing like a raven, or like an eagle reaches all the way to the treetops and looks down upon the entire breadth of the universe.

The participants of the witch cult danced circle dances around the ancient oak, ash, or birch tree, which represented the World Tree. The initiates were probably hung from the trees or bound to them so that their souls might travel up and down into the worlds beyond and encounter deities, ancestors, and helpful magical animals. Native Americans and Siberians still bind initiates to such trees. The Plains Indians pierce the flesh of initiates with hooks and bind them to the World Tree while they

Motif of the World Tree on a Sölkupic shamanic drum.

dance and play eagle pipes and fly into the extrasensory world. As a shamanic god, Odin demonstrated this for the Germanic peoples: For nine days he hung in the tree, starving, thirsty, and sleepless, and drew the wisdom of the runes from Mimir's well (in the primordial memory). In India it was the king's son Siddhartha Gotama who fasted for forty days beneath a mighty pipal tree and discovered enlightenment when his spirit spread out in the crown and root regions of existence. Jesus, known as Christ, also hung on a cross-tree on top of Golgotha, the mountain in the middle of the world. In Christian mythology it was the same place where the tree of the fall of man once stood.

During their initiation, the Siberian shamans experience demons who hunt them, kill them, chop them up, cook them in a great cauldron, and then eat them; this is the representation of the dissolution of the everyday personality. The Goddess in the form of a bird takes the pale discarded bones, puts them carefully back together again, surrounds them in a shell of ice, and incubates them in a nest high up in the world tree. When the young are able to fly, they leave the nest of their mother and fly back to the earth, where they awaken as freshly created shamans. Now they have the wings to fly into the other world, now they can speak with gods and ghosts, accompany the dead part of the way, and greet those who are reincarnating. They can also heal, as they have the power over every disease demon that has eaten a piece of their flesh. Because they know their way around the regions beyond, they can also bring back lost souls who have been kidnapped by demons or sorcerers. They use herbal incense to seduce the souls and sing to them magical songs. All of this is witches' wisdom, witchcraft medicine.

The Flight to the Holy Mountain

Another primordial image that lives on in the soul of the witch is the vision of a holy mountain on whose peak the dispenser of life and happiness is enthroned. The sacred mountain of the gods is found everywhere: It is Mount Olympus of the Hellenists, Mount Sinai of the Hebrews, Bear Butte in South Dakota of the Cheyenne; it is Mount Santis, on whose heights the Neanderthals celebrated the bear cult about seventy thousand years ago; it is Mount Shasta of the California Indians, where the animal spirits and the creator live, and which intergalactic UFOs visit. (California hippies are convinced of this.) In West Tibet it is the sacred world mountain Kailash, on whose snow-white summit Parvati and Shiva are found in a profound embrace of eternal joy *(ananda)*. And in places where there is no natural elevation, the ancient peoples built mounds and pyramids.

Many of the elevated sacred places in central Europe are consecrated to the Virgin Mary or to a saint. On special days, usually at Easter or Whitsunday, people made a pilgrimage to a chapel on the sacred site, sang religious songs, made extensive vespers, and left behind votive offerings. However, other mountains remained under the dominion of the ancient gods and cults. A Munich vesper from the fourteenth century mentioned a *Brochelsberg* as being an abode of nocturnal ghosts and witches. Such "buck mountains," "hay mountains," or "heathen caps," where the last heathen festivals took place, were found throughout Europe. The most famous of these is the Brocken in the Harz Mountains of Germany. The "witches" usually gathered there on Walpurgis Night. They danced the last winter snows away in full "participation mystique." In the sagas they danced so vigorously that they danced through the soles of their shoes. At the same time raging boys went out dressed as werewolves to scare off the enemies of summer.

Flying Ointment

Later, as the persecution increased, fewer and fewer dared ascend to the heights. Now they "flew" mostly in a psychedelic trance. They stayed at home, undressed, and anointed their temples, sexual organs, and other parts of the body where the skin is thin with a flying ointment. They rode on lubricated brooms and pitchforks, or simply sat in the dough tray* before they were elevated through the chimney in a trance. They followed Holda (Frau Holle) or Diana, flying with a whole retinue. Some rode on geese, ducks, goats, pigs, wolves, cats, or other animals (familiars), to which they were connected in their souls. While traveling, or so it was believed, the flying witches rested in the thorny hedgerow and ate hawthorn tips or alder buds. Some farm wives twisted wreaths out of valerian, ground ivy, or centaury and wore them as crowns around their foreheads; this was said to help them see the witches flying.

A witch feeding her familiar. The familiars are shamanic helping spirits.

To make the flying ointment, native plants in the Nightshade family (henbane and thorn apple) were simmered in pig or goose fat. Poisonous plants, such as poison hemlock *(Conium maculatum)*, monkshood *(Aconitum napellus)*, and bearded darnell *(Lolium temulentum)*, were added to this mixture. Harmless herbs, such as poplar buds and mallow, added a synergistic effect. Poisonous herbs like the above can sever the soul (the astral body) from the body; thus it is able to fly into the astral world behind the world of exterior appearances. There the soul not only encounters speaking animals, elementary beings, and nature spirits, but it is also able to take on animal forms. While the body remains in a deathlike posture, the soul can slip into animals and move through the forest as a werewolf, a *Werbär* (were-bear), a *Werkatze* (were-cat), a bird, or a beetle. If not used properly these herbs can lead to fatal poisoning. The shamanic art is, at best, the ability of the soul to find its way back to the body.

Both of these elements—animal transformation and soul travel—are well known to cultural anthropologists. They belong to the repertoire of shamanic techniques of ecstasy of many different peoples. They have been used since the Stone Age, if the cave paintings in the Pyrenees and the cliff drawings from Australia to Tierra del Fuego have been properly understood.

We don't know any more details about the witches' ointment. The ethnobotanist Herman de Vries points out that there are no recipes passed down by women that can be verified (de Vries, 1991: 31). All recipes that are known were written by early scientists, often clerics or doctors. The ointments *(Unguentum populeum)* were not forbidden; they were officially used for the treatment of pain, as a numbing wound dressing, as an executioner's salve, for rheumatism, and for hemorrhoids. The common people were also quite familiar with plants that move the spirit, and used them for love potions and as spices to make beer more inebriating.

The Church sought to establish Satan as the true adversary of God, and thus did not base the witch phenomena on the pharmacological effects of the ointment, because to do this would have created a material explanation that would place the very existence of the adversary in question. The courts themselves made use of such ointments. The inquisitors used them to revive defendants after they had been thoroughly questioned and—due to the effects of scopolamine—used the ointments as "truth serums" to break the resistance of tortured prisoners.

---

* An oblong, shallow bowl used for kneading bread dough. (Trans.)

Holy mountains of the gods are found throughout the world. Depiction of a goddess on an insignia from Crete.

Sex and Fertility Magic

The sex magic the witches were also accused of is ancient women's wisdom. In all cultures women know which herbs to use to make themselves pretty and desirable and which ones to use to attract and seduce a man. They know which plants can ease heavy menstruation, which ones promote fertility, or, if necessary, bring on a missed period. They know plants that make births easier, minimize the loss of blood, stimulate milk production, or quiet a crying child. It is practically common knowledge. But there are also women whose personal experience and spiritual vision have a broader scope than the others. These are the wise women who, as embodiments of the Great Goddess, play an important role in primitive societies.

Such respected and knowledgeable women were thorns in the sides of the celibate priests and misogynist monks. They were rivals in the power struggle over souls. Because of this, these shamanically gifted women, who protected the tribe's fertility and their ability to love, were transformed into dangerous witches who spoiled the fruits of love, who, through knot-tying magic, caused men to be impotent, who feigned false love to innocent young boys, or who killed infants and used their fat to make their witches' ointment. Priests, who damned sexual desire as sinful, turned the love goddess Freya into a lover-demon. Out of the cuckoo, once considered a herald of the beloved Goddess by the Indo-Europeans, they made a satanic bird: *The cuckoo should fetch her!* ("To the devil with her!").

People who are connected to nature love their children. The children are not "had" like one has an automobile or a piece of furniture, nor are they "brought into the world" like superfluous objects. Children are the ancestors embodied. They are the future, they bring joy, and, as the Cheyenne medicine man Tallbull explained, they scare off evil ghosts and problems that assemble like miasma around the foundation of the home. Like other traditional peoples the Cheyenne women intuitively experience the souls coming out of the wilderness and into their wombs in order to be born again. But sometimes they are spirits a woman does not want, perhaps twins that would be a great burden for her, or perhaps the times are so difficult that she could not take care of the infant very well. Then the woman says to the spirits that they should wait awhile or seek out another womb.

In a certain sense it could be said that these Native Americans regulate their fertility in order to live in harmony with nature so that the material basis of life, the game and the vegetation, is maintained. The respected Cheyenne families, the "nobles," bring a child into the world only every seven years. They believe that it takes that long for the father to completely gather his strength again so that a full-fledged *tsistavostan* (true person) can be born. The Cheyenne trace the current population explosion to the fact that more and more individuals are being born who possess only a fraction of the power that a complete person has. Between births, the Cheyenne parents practice abstinence.

Aside from the nobles, the Indians used plants to regulate their fertility. One of the most important plants for the Cheyenne women's ritual is the silver sage or "woman's mugwort" (*Artemisia frigida*). Only women are allowed to touch or use it; it is taboo for men even to speak about it. (The men have "men's mugwort," *he-tan-i-wan-ots [Artemisia gnaphalodes, A. ludoviciana]* for their own rituals and public ceremonies.) The prohibition is so strict that Bill Tallbull did not dare to tell me anything further about the plant. However, the women of other tribes, the Blackfoot and the Arapaho, for example, use it, among other purposes, to stimulate missed menstruation (Kindscher, 1992: 49).

The Cheyenne also know how to use gromwell (*Lithospermum incisum*). They call this plant, which is part of the Borage family, "lame medicine" *(hoh-ahea-no-is-tut)* because they grind the roots, leaves, and seeds into a powder and then rub it on parts of the body that are lame. They also rub a decoction of the plant from the head to toe of a sick person who is going "crazy" from the distress of the illness. And if someone is suffering from insomnia the medicine man chews the gromwell, spits the chewed plant matter in the patient's face, and rubs it on the heart region. Nothing is publicly known about the use of gromwell by the Cheyenne in women's medicine to restrain ovulation in order to induce temporary infertility. The Shoshone women are known to drink a cold infusion of the gromwell roots for a period of more than six months to protect against pregnancy. Other tribes also use the plant in this way.

The great-grandmothers of Europe also harbor such secrets about fertility and birth. The Church brought about mistrust against the daughters of the sinner Eve, which escalated to paranoia during the time of the Inquisition. In theological writings, "woman is the gateway to hell, the way to licentiousness, the sting of the scorpion, a worthless gender." Or else "sin comes from a woman . . . that is why we must all die" (Wolf, 1994: 59). In such an atmosphere feminine wisdom can be nothing other than satanic wisdom.

Weather Magic

Whether or not the fields and gardens will produce a bountiful harvest, whether or not the meadows will become green and the livestock will have enough to eat, is dependent upon the weather. Every culture has "weather-makers" who have a thorough knowledge of ritual techniques to draw down rain, banish lightning and hailstorms, or redirect the weather against their enemies. The practice of throwing burning wood or hot ashes into the air in order to subdue unwanted downpours is nearly universal.

The magic techniques that people use when the rain is absent and the ground withers are similar around the world. The weather shamans spray water, beer, or their own blood on the parched earth while singing magical songs that awaken the rain gods or change their attitude. In ancient Russia the rainmakers climbed up fir trees in the sacred grove. One of the magicians drummed on a kettle in imitation of thunder, another struck flint, sending sparks flying, and a third sprinkled water in all directions with a bundle of sticks (Frazer, 1991: 90). Often the rain is danced in by imitating the rhythm of raindrops with the dance steps. Usually the dancers are naked—they are outside of everyday humans, untouched by civilization, in a natural primordial state. Often the weather-makers are women, for they are "damper" by nature and closer to the water element and the moon. Among the southern Slavs a girl is chosen. She is then cloaked only in grass, herbs, and flowers, and she dances in circles through the whole village with a troupe of other girls. Every housewife must water her with a pitcher of water. If, in India, a drought lasts for a long time, naked women pull a plow at night over the soil—men are not allowed to be present.

Today we find such superstitious practices humorous since we know the objective causes of drought and storms. Satellites mediate the state of the weather, and computers calculate the highs and lows. Today scientific experiments to control the weather are undertaken. All the same, Wilhelm Reich succeeded in causing rain in the 1950s with his "cloudbuster," an apparatus that beamed orgone energy into the

The powerful hallucinogen henbane *(Hyoscyamus niger)* was the most important ritual plant of the ancient Germanic peoples and was connected to the prophetic gods of the Celts, Greeks, and Romans of antiquity. It is one of the most important remedies in witches' medicine. (Woodcut from Otto Brunfels, *Contrafayt Kreüterbuch*, 1532.)

Witches brewing weather. Herbs and all sorts of other magical additives were stirred in the great cauldron. (From Ulrich Molitor, *Tractatus*, 1490–1491.)

Hemp agrimony (*Eupatorium cannabinum* L.), also called water maudlin or water hemp, was used primarily for the liver, for the treatment of wounds, and for the healing of skin eruptions in folk medicine. In homeopathy *Eupatorium* is used in the diseases of the liver, spleen, and gallbladder. In German the plant was named *Kunigundenkraut* after Saint Kundigunde (tenth century), as she had withstood a trial by fire and had to walk through burning fields. (Woodcut from Tabernaemontanus, *Neu vollkommen Kräuter-Buch*, 1731.)

sky. And the United States, which like every superpower undertakes secret projects to control the world, was supposedly able to extend the monsoon season in Southeast Asia an extra week during the Vietnam war. (Incidentally, that would have been a classic example of black magic!)

Even though science makes a big deal out of it, shamans really can influence the weather because they are in contact with the spirits of the elements. Some skeptical ethnologists have had to acknowledge this as well, as did W. H. R. Rivers, who bade the newly converted natives in Malaysia to demonstrate a rain ceremony. At first they refused because the missionaries had forbidden it. Rivers explained to them that an exception would be made this time. The ritual was barely finished when it began to rain.

Naturally the Celts and Germanic peoples also had weather-making shaman women who performed their rituals in an ecstatic state and ritualistic nakedness. They beat puddles with sticks until the clouds formed. They brewed—similar to the witches in Shakespeare's *Macbeth*—weather in a great cauldron in which they put herbs and other magical things. They stirred storm-raising energy with hazel wands. With henbane they woke up the lazy rain out of its sleep.

Heathen rituals such as these were practiced for a long time in rural areas. In the early eleventh century Burchard of Worms reported that a naked girl pulled a henbane plant—once consecrated to Belenos or Balder—out of the ground with the little finger on her right hand and then bound it to her foot. Then the rain-maiden was led to the river and splashed with water while prayers were sung.

Weather magic is also performed with other herbs—for example, hemp agrimony (*Eupatorium cannabinum*), also known as *Wetterkühl* (weather cool) or *Donnerkühl* (thunder/Thor cool). The plant is considered a stag plant because it is bound as sensitively to the weather as the stag is with his antlers. The abortifacient, diuretic medicinal herb was possibly once under the dominion of Cernunnos, the "lord of the souls"—the animal souls and also the cloud souls.

Because those who control the weather also control the harvest, and thus also control the heart and spirit of the people, the weather-disir were considered particularly dangerous. The *Indiculus superstitionum et paganiarum*, the previously mentioned handbook for religious informants, has heavy penalties for such *tempestarii*. The synod of Paris (892) judged: "When men and women who have committed such crimes [causing storms and hail] are discovered, they must be punished with unusual harshness, because they are not afraid to serve the devil completely openly" (Habinger-Tuczay, 1992: 278).

From then on women who were weather-shamans became monstrous storm-raisers, *Wolkenschieberinnen* (cloud pushers), *Schauerbrüterinnen* (shower-breeders), *Wetterkatzen* (weather-cats), *Nebelhexen* (fog-witches), or *Wolkentruden* (cloud spinners), who, it was rumored, had corrupted the crops with hail, tornadoes, and pestilence. The Christian defense against their machinations consisted of weather-blessings by a priest and the weather-ringing of the church bells.

Saint John's Wort *(Hypericum perforatum)*

Saint John's wort is devoted to the sun like no other plant of the flora native to Europe. It usually grows in dry sunny places. The seeds germinate only in sunlight. The effects of the sun are revealed in the intensive flowering, in the sturdy, well-structured stems, and in the many small oil glands that look like perforations in the petals and leaves. The hypericin oil is really transformed sunlight.

Saint John's wort is so saturated with light that it can pass its light effects on to other organisms. Light-skinned ruminants such as sheep, pigs, and cattle can develop photosensitivity; infected, inflamed skin; and stomach cramps when they eat the herb and then go into direct sunlight.

The plant also demonstrates a very definite light effect on people who take it as a tea. Recently *Hypericum* has been used in the United States for the treatment of AIDS (Foster/Duke, 1990: 114); this makes sense, not only because many infected by HIV suffer from depression (which Saint John's wort can alleviate), but also because of the danger of becoming infected with candida yeast. HIV patients die not from the virus but usually from a complete infection of the lungs and blood with yeast. Candida is an opportunist, and when the immune system is compromised the fungus spreads from the intestines to the reproductive organs, to the lungs, and finally to the blood. Yeast, such as candida, cannot stand any sunlight. It needs a dark and damp environment. Because a plant like Saint John's wort is enriched so much by the sun, it is an appropriate remedy for yeast infections.

Saint John's wort also has an inner and spiritual light-bringing effect. Saint John's wort radiates the summer sun into the darkest corners of the soul. The tea—a cup drunk every day over a period of a few weeks—lightens dark moods and chases off melancholy, fear, and depression. Chemists believe that the red pigment hypericin, a phenolic compound, is responsible for the euphoric antidepressant effect.

It is interesting to take the drug (the tea) and to observe the effects in meditation following the homeopathic method of proving. The entopic phenomena of light, the clouds, and lightning that normally appear behind closed lids are unusually bright. Colorful, nearly gaudy light forms ascend, gain in radiance, and freeze suddenly in rigid geometric patterns. Thus, these light phenomena playing on the eye's interior mirror the external appearance of the plant.

The ascending cloudlike entopic light phenomena, probably the result of electric nerve impulses deep in the eye socket, are the raw material from which the images in dreams and visions are woven. Usually we do not notice them as we glide into a dream and lose our consciousness of external reality. But if attention is meditatively placed on this seam between waking and dreaming, then one will become aware of such "light clouds." If grim images resembling dark and threatening storm clouds rise in front of the spiritual eye, these will be absorbed by the power of Saint John's wort's light and will be organized into beautiful, if somewhat rigid, patterns. The plant "creates itself" in our soul; it influences the sunlike energy of forms. Fearful and melancholy thoughts can barely keep spinning under the influence of the *Hypericum* drug.

Of course, this psychoactive effect did not remain hidden from the old herbalist women. The name *hypericum* comes from the Greek *hyper,* meaning "over," and *eikon,* meaning "picture." Thus *Hypericum* lifts the human spirit over threatening internal images, over the diseased imagination. Medieval doctors called the plant *Fuga*

Many species of Saint John's wort were called *Hartheu:* above, the mountain Saint John's wort (*Hypericum montanum* L.); below, the four-petaled Saint John's wort (*Hypericum tetrapterum* Fr.). In his herbal Hieronymus Bock wrote of Saint John's wort that it chased away all poisons and banned all ghosts. "The old women speak thusly / oregano [*Origanum vulgare* L.], / Saint John's wort and bog rosemary [*Andromeda polifolia* L.] / makes the devil violent. Thus it becomes clear what the ancient heathens thought of this herb and what they did with it." (Woodcut from Hieronymus Bock, *Kreütterbuch,* 1577.)

daemonum, which indicates that it forces demons to flee. Paracelsus considered Saint John's wort to be "an *arcanum*, a universal medicine of greatest effectiveness, a *monarchei*, in front of which all must bow." In the language of signatures the small veins in the leaves denote that the herb chases off all *phantasmata* around and beneath humans. By *phantasmata* Paracelsus meant "diseases without body and without substance"—in other words, "imagined voices, insanity and lunacy" (Pörksen, 1988: 75). "So that the heavenly influence works against the phantasmata, the plant must be collected in correspondence with the path of the stars," when Mars, Jupiter, and Venus are in good aspects, but not when the moon is full. The medicinal plants should be gathered at sunrise, with the harvester facing the sun. Paracelsus wrote, "The herb should always be carried, underneath the hat, on the breast, or as a wreath in the hand, and smelled often, placed underneath the pillow, placed around the house or hung on the wall!"

Because of these qualities the rural people called the herb *Teufelsflucht* (devil's flight) and *Jagdteufel* (hunt-the-devil).

Marjoram, Saint John's wort, chicory
make the devil flee.

The grandmothers used charms such as these when they picked the herb under the sign of the lion and put it in the baby's first bath, placed it on the first sheaves of grain, strew it in the feed of bewitched livestock, or placed it crosswise in the window or under the rafters to guard against lightning. In the case of spellbound love, "for one who has lost his senses and become unreasonable because of a love spell," Saint John's wort was soaked in wine.

Old crones also made weather-magic with Saint John's wort. They banished the black clouds and charmed the sun back again. In central Germany it is said, "Saint John's wort and dill makes the storms still." A story from the Saxony-Anhalt region tells of a terrible storm that wouldn't end and that threatened to destroy the harvest in the fields. Suddenly the frightened farmers heard a voice thundering in the dark clouds: "Is there not a single woman who knows about Saint John's wort?" When the farmers' wives placed Saint John's wort in the windows, the storm stopped.

The herb was usually burned, however, as can be interpreted from the traditional saying:

Mugwort and Saint John's wort
burn on and stop the storm!

Is it pure superstition, or is something hidden behind it? Is it possible that one can banish bad weather with Saint John's wort? Ethnologists have repeatedly witnessed how shamans influence the weather, but they have never been able to explain it (Kalweit, 1987: 112). I was the unbelieving witness of a Native American rain dance that brought an end to a long drought in Oregon, despite the fact that the radio had predicted more heat. If we take seriously the holographic model, which says that everything is contained in everything else, then it is entirely possible to influence the weather. One must quiet the internal weather (the atmosphere and the emotions), and the external will adapt itself via resonance.

Women and feminine images have been honored as the Great Goddess since the Stone Age. This statue is known as Venus of Lespugue. (Photograph by Christian Rätsch.)

Above and middle: The billy goat can grow to become an impressive animal. The ancient peoples saw in him a divine being. The goat was reinterpreted from its sacred role in heathen times to the Christian symbol of the devil. (Photographs by Christian Rätsch.)

Below: The archaic custom of bringing the head of a sacrificed animal to the altar and keeping it there as a skull is still practiced today in Crete. (Photograph by Christian Rätsch.)

The young round fly agaric
(*Amanita muscaria* [L. ex Fr.] Pers.)
was called witch's egg or devil's
egg. It is possible that the Orphic
cult of late antiquity saw in it the
world egg out of which the
universe was born. (Photograph by
Christian Rätsch.)

Ergot (*Claviceps purpurea* L.) is a parasitic fungus that affects rye in particular. Black-violet growths ("mother grains," or sclerotia) develop on the ears of grain. In earlier times ergot was used by midwives as a medicine for labor. Albert Hofmann not only developed the psychedelic LSD-25 from ergot alkaloids, but also made methergin (methlergometrin), which works on a long-lasting uterine contraction following labor or a miscarriage. It is still successfully used for postpartum bleeding, lochiostasis, and for delayed regeneration of the uterus following birth. These are the last remains of witchcraft medicine.

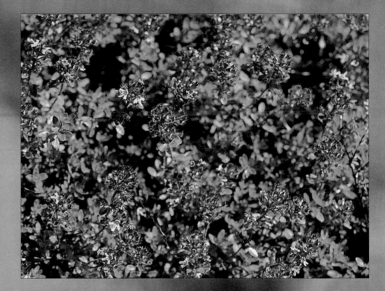

Above: Wild thyme (*Thymus serpyllum* L.) is an ancient medicinal and ritual plant. The aromatic herb has been burnt as magical incense since antiquity. Many Mongolian and Siberian peoples still use wild thyme as shamanic incense. The genus name *Thymus* comes from the Greek *thymon*, "incense brought to the gods as offerings." Before the introduction of frankincense (resin of *Boswellia sacra*) from Arabia, thyme served as the most important incense in Greek rituals. The smoke is supposed to fend off disease-bringing demons. Thyme used to be called "our Lady's bedstraw" and was used in the Middle Ages for many women's problems. (Photograph by Christian Rätsch.)

Below: Marigold (*Tagetes* spp.) has been considered a flower of death since ancient times in Mexico. During the great Masses of the night before November 1, it is placed on family shrines, altars, graves, and open places. During this night the souls of dead ancestors are fed with offerings, and are sometimes made drunk.

Above: Ephedra (*Ephedra alata* Decne.) is found throughout the Near East and was used sixty thousand years ago by the Neanderthals as a flower of the dead; it was placed with the bodies in their graves. Ephedra has been used for at least six thousand years as a medicine for asthma and bronchitis and as a diuretic. The prophets of antiquity named the plant "the food of Saturn." Ephedra was one of the psychoactive ingredients of the Persian haoma drink in pre-Zoroastrian times. In the Himalayas *Ephedra gerardiana* is still known as *somalata* ("soma plant"). Ephedra has a strong, stimulating, awakening, and vasoconstricting effect that lasts for about eight hours. Ephedra is a beloved aphrodisiac for women. (Photograph by Christian Rätsch.)

Below: Hemp (*Cannabis sativa* L.) was sacred to the Germanic love goddess because the female flowers are an outstanding aphrodisiac. (Photograph by Christian Rätsch.)

Above: Saint John's wort (*Hypericum perforatum* L.) used to be called *Fuga daemonium* (ghost's herb) because it was said to protect against ghosts, witches, and black magic. Tabernaemontanus documented the knowledge of the witches in his herbal: "The old women say that this herb is for ghosts when it is carried on the person. That is also why it is called *Fuga daemonium*" (1613). A common name for the antidepressant and mood enhancer is still witches' herb. Naturally Saint John's wort belongs to the ancient heathen medicinal and ritual plants of the Teutons. Saint John's wort oil was the active ingredient in countless preparations from the early modern era (for example, in the magic balm of Pforzheim) used to treat those who were possessed, plagued by nightmares, and disoriented by the consequences of an overdose of a love potion. (Photograph by Christian Rätsch.)

Below: The Saint John's wort native to the Himalayas (*Hypericum choisianum* Wallich ex N. Robson) is now, as before, a sacred plant. Its large yellow flowers are used as offerings for the "witch goddess" Kali. (Photograph by Christian Rätsch.)

Above left: Thorn apple (*Datura stramonium* L.) takes the place of henbane in other parts of the world, such as Central and South America and central and south Asia. When the thorn apple was brought back to Europe, it was immediately recognized as an ingredient of witches' medicine. (Photograph by Christian Rätsch.)

Below left: Autumn crocus (*Colchicum autumnale* L.) is the first to grow leaves in spring. It is considered a plant of Medea, and belongs to the feared poisons of Colchis. (Photograph by Christian Rätsch.)

Above right: Henbane (*Hyoscyamus albus* L.) has been ritually used in Europe since the Bronze Age. It is one of the most important plants in witches' medicine, used as a "traveling herb," an aphrodisiac, and as medicine for asthma and wounds. (Photograph by Christian Rätsch.)

Above: The "witches' broom" on the branch of a birch tree occurs because of a degeneration caused by a mushroom invasion. (Photograph by Christian Rätsch.)

Below: The polypores on the trunk of a birch tree are reminiscent of the steps on the shamanic World Tree.

In any event the moods of humans and animals oscillate with the weather. In the spiritual experience of humans of earlier eras, the internal and external weather was not as radically separated as is now the case in the West. Periods of bad weather, which threaten the harvest and therewith survival, or the fear of lightning and hailstorms can also influence the spiritual climate of a community and lead to an agitated atmosphere, bad mood, and accidents. In the loaded atmosphere before a storm, the sting of the horsefly is particularly harsh, the cows' bellows more agitated as they kick the milk buckets and withhold their milk, and people themselves are nervous and stressed. Therefore it is entirely possible that, when grandmother burns in the house or barn Saint John's wort that has been consecrated to the sun, it helps.

Saint John's wort was not only sacred to the sun, but to Venus as well. As a woman's herb it was mixed with aromatic herbs for giving birth. It was put in emmenagogues to bring on the monthly blood because the flower itself has "blood" in it. Menopausal women also drank it.

Because fair Freya is above all a love goddess, it is not surprising that this solstice herb was used by young women as a love oracle. Usually a girl took a handful of Saint John's wort flower buds that had been gathered on Saint John's Day and put them in a linen sack, squeezed it, thought about her beloved, and said:

If my dear is good, comes red blood.
If he is bad, there is only foam!

If one squeezes the gold-yellow flower buds between the fingers, red "elves' blood" comes out—this is what the above oracle is based on. The heathens called the red juice the blood of the sun god, of gracious Balder, who was sacrificed at the solstice or, rather, who sacrificed himself to Earth. The symbolism was carried over to Saint John, the preacher of repentance, who declared at the baptism of Jesus (the sun of the soul), "He must grow, but I must diminish." In popular Christianity, John the Baptist, who was beheaded after Salomé performed her dance of the seven veils, replaced the heathen sun god.

Many religious legends are entwined with this summer solstice flower. The plant was said to have been created when the blood of Saint John the Baptist fell on the ground. A sweet story from the Upper Palatinate region of Germany tells that Zechariah, the father of Saint John, was saddened that he had had no children, and so he went into the desert. There an angel gave him this little yellow flower, which stayed fresh until Saint John was born.

In order to explain the ancient, indestructible custom of putting Saint John's wort in the windows and doors on Saint John's Day, preachers invented another story. An informant discovered the hiding place of the persecuted holy man Saint John. So that the henchmen could find the place where Saint John was hiding, a spy placed a sprig of Saint John's wort in the window of the house. But a miracle happened! On the next morning the windows in all of the houses in Jerusalem were decorated with the herb.

Another legend tells that the herb is so good and so medicinal that the devil in his wrath attacked it with a needle and punctured it thousands of times. The proof for this misdeed is in the many black spots that look like needle holes on the petals when they are held up to the light. These spots, which are caused by small oil glands, are where *perforatum*, the plant's species name, comes from.

The inquisitors, the Christian witch hunters, were convinced of the elevated status of Saint John's wort. They gave Saint John's wort tea to the brides of Satan because they believed it would negate the oaths the witches had made with the devil. Abundant amounts of Saint John's wort were burned during sessions of "embarrassing questioning" as well, either because the inquisitors were afraid of the devil or because they assumed he would not be able to approach the frightened woman due to the presence of the herb.

Paracelsus classified the red juice and the "needle holes" differently from the priests. He saw in them the signature of Mars, the planetary war god—a sure sign that the plant was suited for slash and puncture wounds. Paracelsus, who had traveled as a surgeon with mercenary armies back and forth across Europe, knew what he was talking about. Compresses of *Hypericum* are antiseptic and heal wounds. The red hypericin oil is also outstanding for all wounds, bruises, and abrasions, and it is good for burns and scalds. But it must be kept in mind that Saint John's wort oil should not be used as a suntan oil, because it can cause photosensitivity. A few drops taken internally are said to help gastritis and ulcers and stimulate the gallbladder.

The red oil belongs in every household pharmacy. It is very effective for neuralgia and nerve inflammation, lumbago, and sciatica when massaged into the painful areas. Saint John's wort oil is easy to make. On a dry, sunny summer day collect the flowers and the buds, put them in a clear glass jar, pour sunflower or olive oil over them to the top of the jar, screw on the top tightly, and leave the jar in the sun for two weeks. Eventually the oil will become a burgundy color. It should be strained and stored in a dark glass jar in a dark place.

The herb is also suitable for tea. Saint John's wort, which belongs to the same botanical order (Theales) as black tea, has a pleasant taste. Because this tea is not a diuretic, a small cup can be drunk before bedtime without a problem. It is particularly recommended during the dark days of winter, when the lack of light depresses the mood. This tea works as a tranquilizer on the limbic system (Weiss, 1991: 35).

Saint John's wort tea works particularly well for children who wet their beds. Bed-wetting does not have to do with a kidney problem; it has mostly spiritual causes. In such cases a psychotropic medicinal plant is recommended.

Midwives: Fertility and Birth

Wolf-Dieter Storl

Our lives begin when the haploid chromosome chain of egg and sperm cells fuses. Our personalities, then, are the result of genetic heritage, but are shaped by natural and social influences. This is more or less how the schoolbooks explain it.

But what did the clairvoyant wise women see in the mirror of their souls when they sat at the hearth or spinning wheel pondering the depths of the mysteries of fertility and birth? What did the old crones know about the coming and going of human beings? Is there any way for us to know? If we listen quietly to ourselves, if we listen to the whispering wind and the sounds of the forest, then the submerged primordial memories will awaken in us as well. At some point, in distant times, in earlier existences, we were also there. We can add to this the traditions of folk medicine, fairy tales and sagas, superstitions and customs, which are like keys to the memory of a society. Language is also a refuge for primordial wisdom. It does not develop haphazardly but mirrors the contours of an ever-transforming eternal being. Language is—in the sense of Rupert Sheldrake—a "morphogenetic field": We sense when it is "right," when it fits with one's being.

Although each tribe has its own particular access to the truths about the path each being takes on its way into existence on the earth and every shaman and every midwife her own particular perspective, we would nevertheless like to say something about what a glance behind the hedgerow or the lowest branches of the shamanic tree might reveal.

The Way into Existence

Hungry for a new body on this beautiful earth, drawn by the hopes of the tribe, by the love of the parents, but also driven by old deeds and seeking balance—guided by Skuld (guilt), one of the three primordial fate-weaving goddesses in northern mythology—the human embryo that had been spread out across the entire universe dives down to earth. It leaves the fixed stars—most primitive peoples consider the Milky Way to be the path of the souls—and wanders through the seven, nine, or twelve realms of the gods and spirits. It climbs down the branches of the World Treeor the sprouts of heaven's ladder. The Babylonian astrologists identified it as the spheres of Saturn, Jupiter, Mars, the Sun, Venus, Mercury, and the Moon. During the descent the human child returning home to earth becomes ever more compact, ever smaller, ever more material.

As the child wends its way through the spheres of the planets, the gods bestow it with both good and disadvantageous qualities. They give it the soul-robe that was destined for that child alone. When the child reaches the damp sphere of the moon, it begins to suckle the milk of life (*soma*) from the breast of the moon goddess—she is also our mother. That is why in many traditions it is said that the children come out of the garden of the moon mother. (It is well known that the moon has a lot to do with fertility, sexuality, and birth; menses follows the rhythm of the syndic moon, if no longer synchronously. The reproductive systems of fish, amphibians, and other primitive animals occur in total harmony with the moon. Many children are washed ashore in this life's harbor in the wake of the full moon. And every gardener knows that growth and germination are strongly tied to the moon.) The natal horoscope of an individual mirrors this descent from the stars and the path over the "seven-colored rainbow bridge" of the seven planets.

When the stories of the ancient Germanic tribes and many other traditional peoples relate how the returning soul matures deep in the interior regions of the earth, in the realm of the earth goddess, and that it gradually ascends through the springs, seas, lakes, and swamps, where it then lives as a little fish or frog, and where eventually a fisherman or a stork pulls it out—these are not contradictions. For in the regions beyond, our logical categories make little sense.[12] The sunny green realm of Frau Holle is found "deep in the earth," but at the same time it is found high above in the sky with Thor the thunderer and the wind and cloud spirits who make the weather. In archaic thinking the goddess who protects the souls under the earth or the ocean is often identical with Lady Sun.[13] As the sun she is a warm, kind mother in whose broad skirts the souls hide like little children. As above, so below—is the sky not reflected in the still sea?

After they have left the realm of the stars, the human seeds drift through the wilderness. They rest on clouds, in trees, on bushes, on flower calyxes, on ponds, and on stones, where they play amusing games with the animals, the elves, and the elemental beings. In the cool earth, in the springs, or in the algae-covered lakes and ponds they rest and suckle themselves full with the precious life energy that only the earth can give.

In traditional cultures it is still known that women can pick up the soul-seed of their children when out in the open countryside. A young woman could accidentally brush up against a stone or rock and a little child might swiftly slip into her. Sometimes the future mother need only see a frog or a rabbit, inadvertently slap a fly, or eat a fish, and the human seed that hangs around these animals will find its way into her and will find her womb a warm, comfortable cave where it makes itself at home. Countless child-seeds are found in springs, ponds, seas, and wells. Thus a woman can become pregnant while bathing or carrying water. In archaic ways of thinking water sites were considered to be the vagina of the Goddess, the entrance to the realm of Frau Holle. According to northern German sagas, Adebar is the stork who gets the children from the swamp, carries them to the house, and drops them down through the chimney.

But plants, in particular the trees, make good homes for the unborn. Vegetation is a reservoir of pure life energy. Sometimes the woman needed only to reach for a beautiful flower and the small spirit, caused by karmic love, was pulled to its future mother—bound to her. Often the little ones were in a fruit tree. The farmers' wives who rested below it or the women who picked an apple or a cherry as they passed by might soon become mothers. In many places in Germany it is said that girls' souls are gotten from plum or cherry trees and boys' souls can be gathered from pear trees.

When women had difficulty conceiving, they went to the wise woman. She knew of herbs to help increase fertility. For example, footbaths made with infusions of mugwort warmed and energized the abdomen. Mistletoe, when used correctly as a tea or tincture with yarrow tea, could prepare the womb for conception. The Celts considered the waxy mistletoe berries to be drops of sperm from the cosmic steer. But when these plants and

Mugwort (*Artemisia vulgaris*) was once also called "red goat." In southern Tirol the plant is still called broom herb, and it is associated with the witch's broom. It is also called bunch herb because it is used to bind the herb bundles in folk customs. (Woodcut from Otto Brunfels, *Contrafayt Kreüterbuch*, 1532.)

---

[12] Like Persephone, the Greek goddess of animals and death, Frau Holle lives simultaneously in the starry sky and in Earth's interior. Our ability to reason, which we have thanks to Aristotle and Descartes, refuses to accept this idea. It collides with every rule of logic. Logic is useful for describing the laws of the physical world, but in the regions in which the visionaries work the laws of earthly logic are suspended or often transmuted. Quantum physicists move on such boundaries as well: Atoms are waves and mass; Schrödinger's cat is dead and alive. The South African Bergdama tribe believes that the dead live in small huts in the sky and that at the same time these huts are the earth mounds in which their bones lie buried. A missionary attempted to show the savages that this was an undeniable contradiction. A gray-haired Bergdama responded, "It is only your head that separates these things. For us, each term includes each other!" (Huxley, 1974: 42). Don't we also bring flowers to our dead at their graves while at the same time believing they are with Saint Peter in heaven?

[13] In the southern countries—for example, those in the Mediterranean region—the sun is hot and penetrating. In those areas the warrior, the masculine aspect of the sun, is pronounced, while the cool, mutable moon is feminine. The Celts, the Teutons, Native North Americans, the Japanese, and many of the Siberian peoples saw the sun as the generous, warm, life-giving mother and the moon on the other side as masculine. (The grumpy man in the moon who carries dried sticks gave all of his water to the earth.)

The linden (*Tilia platyphyllos* Scop.) has been honored as a sacred tree since antiquity. Herodotus reported in his discourse about the Scythians, "the Enareer or the men-women [transvestite shamans] . . . say that they received their prophetic powers from Aphrodite. They use the bark of the linden tree, which they split in three ways, wrap the strips around their finger and then loosen it again while saying their spells" (*The Histories* IV.67). (Woodcut from Hieronymus Bock, *Kreütterbuch*, 1577.)

spells did not help, the wise woman had advice. She knew quiet places—crevasses in cliffs, ponds, caves—that teemed with the souls of children who were waiting for a mother. These places still exist, and even though it is not spoken about these days, they are often still visited. For example, in the Jura Mountains of Switzerland there is place called Vrenelis Lake—I will not betray exactly where it is for it is a sacred place, not something for curious tourists or sensational journalists. In our times, women still bathe secretly there in the stream that roars through the forest ravine. They light candles and offer flowers before sticking their hands in a hole in the limestone cliffs. For the expectant it is the contact with another dimension; they touch the beyond, the realm of the Goddess, who has been camouflaged under the guise of Saint Verena.

The Children Springs at Lolarka Kund

Power spots where children can be obtained are found throughout the world. One of the most famous is Lolarka Kund, a deep spring near Assi Ghat in Varanasi, India. "Once the sun stood still" above the lake—in other words, it touched eternity. A *naga*, a snake king, lives in the waters below. Before the childless couple descends the numerous steps into the damp, cool depths, they knot together the woman's sari and the man's dhoti. They go down to the spring to bathe and leave their old clothing behind. The woman breaks her glass bracelets and sacrifices her favorite fruit, vowing to do without for the rest of her life. Sometimes she sacrifices a round pumpkin, which symbolizes pregnancy. After the bath they climb back up the stairs holding hands and wearing new clothes. In the event that a baby is born, the couple vows to return one year after the birth on the Day of the Sun (Ravivara) and give some of the child's hair to the deity as a demonstration of their gratitude.

Every year nearly ten thousand people go to Lolarka Kund on Ravivara, which falls on the sixth day of the waxing moon of August. The barbers have their hands full; whole mountains of children's hair pile up around the spring. Lolarka Kund—like Vrenelis Lake—is actually a *thirtha*, or ford, over the stream, which separates this world from the other side.

Once there were regular "children-trees." The *Salige Frau* (blessed lady)* lived high in the Alps, in the ancient larches that were often decorated with images of the Virgin Mary. The "blessed lady" appears to perceptive mountain peasants as a beautiful woman with radiant golden hair. For many generations she bestowed children upon the dairymaids, the farm women, and the wives of the coal burners. And when they were too poor to afford a midwife the blessed woman helped them. Entire valleys have been populated by such children-trees.

The ancestral spirits of the Celts and the Teutons reappeared in the village linden, oak, ash tree, or rolling meadows. Such *Holle* trees and *Titti* firs are still found in many places. (*Titti* or *ditti* means "child" or "spirit." Thus children were "fished" out of Lake Titti in the Black Forest.) At the beginning of the twentieth century, wedding parties still found reprieve under such trees; they feasted and drank, decorated the branches with ribbons, and watered the trunk with wine or schnapps. It is said that such trees bleed and scream when an ax is put to them. This saying is not foolish superstition, but is based on an extrasensitive understanding of nature.

Many children in England, France, and Belgium come from the cabbage patch. This is no surprise—cabbage heads are nearly bursting with excesses of life energy. The seeds

---

* The *Salige Frau* is not human, but instead a divinity who lives in the mountains. She sometimes appears to people and occasionally marries mortal men. She is well known throughout the Alps. (Trans.)

germinate and grow quickly. A cut cabbage head grows roots again as soon as it is placed on the moist ground. A poultice of juicy cabbage leaves heals many injuries, not only because of its active ingredients (mustard oil glycoside), but also through the transference of pure life energy.

When Australians, Africans, or Native Americans told nineteenth-century ethnologists that a stone, tree, or flower had made them pregnant, it was considered proof of an animistic prelogical mentality. The sorts of ideas about intercourse and pregnancy that are fabricated and theorized about in university seminars and coffeehouses are astounding! For example, feminists still consider this to be the remnants of a primordial matriarchal society, because for them the idea that a plant made the woman pregnant categorically negates the fatherhood of the male.

However, what the native women told the curious ethnographers was simply what they had intuitively experienced. They had, like Buddha's mother, who saw her son floating by as a white elephant, experienced the spiritual child before conception. Naturally the role that intercourse played was not unknown to them. This just made it possible for the spirit to receive a body.

The child's soul that has taken refuge in the flowers, the trees, the cliffs, or the stones comes near to the mother who is full of curiosity before the fertilization of the egg. The sexual act, in which the lovers melt into one another, makes it possible for the child to bind itself to both parents in the stream of inheritance. The heat of the ecstasy of love, the penetration of all barriers that the ego constructs around the body and soul, allows the child to weave into the fertilized egg, into the DNA double helix. Now cell division can begin.[14]

The Time of Begetting

When the humans were generally still clairvoyant, they paid attention to when and where procreation took place. They oriented themselves to the customs of their forefathers and to the rhythms of the universe. The melting together of man and woman was experienced as sacred ecstasy, as a communion in which the human neared the Divine, not as a random, egotistical, desperate act, as so often is the case today. In ancient European cultures it was considered especially favorable to conceive children in the open countryside—in the meadows, the fields, and, in particular, the woods beneath the hazel tree when the moon was full and the sun was ascending in the yearly cycle. The joyous month of May, when people could take part in the exhilarating greening and flowering of nature, was considered to be a particularly favorable time for impregnation. Only after the conversion to Christianity—as happened in other heathen customs—was a May wedding warned against. For Christians, May is the month of the Virgin Mary and it is dedicated to her chastity; therefore, couples are supposed to refrain from the pleasures of the flesh or else they will produce fools, idiots, or, at the very least, difficult children (Loux, 1980: 66).

Sweet woodruff (*Asperula odorata* L., syn. *Galium odoratum* [L.] Scop.) was once called Sternleberkraut (star liver herb) or Herzfreund (heart friend). It is an old custom to soak the aromatic herb in wine and enjoy it as a May bowl. The distinctive coumarin-scented dried herb was also smoked as a tobacco substitute. Sweet woodruff belongs to the family of plants that fall under the name "Our Lady's bedstraw," and was used in folk gynecology. (Woodcut from Tabernaemontanus, *Neu vollkommen Kraüter-Buch*, 1731.)

---

14 Our top-heavy contemporaries—the modern intellectuals and other people who are unable to release themselves from their ego-based reason—often have difficulty conceiving children. Infertility and impotence, and an exaggerated cult of orgasm and perversion, are symptoms of the loss of the transcendent dimension of sexuality. Our sex is not ecstatic, it is not devoted to the gods, it is not in harmony with nature; it is civilized, cramped, and infertile. Sex takes place "inside the walls," inside the mind, following the instructions from the sex manual—unlike the people who are still bound to nature, the ones beyond the hedgerow. But it is precisely there, in the wilderness beyond the hedge, where the horned god, Frau Holle, and the ancestral spirits dwell, where the reservoir of joy is found, where the source of returning life lies.

Aromatic healing herbs and sometimes whey were added to the "May bath." Men and women bathed together in order to chase off the melancholy of the cold seasons. Somewhat unusual was the "love bath for two." (Woodcut from Hans Schönsperger, *Kalender*, 1490.)

The May festival was a bathing festival. The wise women prepared aromatic herbal baths and brewed strong beer that lent the humans wings. The girls braided flowers into their hair like Freya herself.

The people drank a wine scented with sweet woodruff (*Asperula oderata*), which stimulated desire and eased inhibitions. The May drink is well known; the Benedictine monk Wandelbertus wrote in the year 854, "Pour pearly wine on the sweet woodruff fine." The "May bowls" of today are prepared by very decent, very civilized methods. A few little twigs of sweet woodruff are placed in the wine for a short while, and then a little sugar and lemon are added, and finally some sparkling wine is poured in. People are afraid that too much woodruff results in a terrible hangover. But if these warnings are ignored and numerous handfuls of the wilted forest herb are soaked in the wine, then the reason the plant is called "master of the wood," *Herba matrisylvae* (wood mother herb) and *reine des bois* (forest queen) quickly becomes apparent. It not only excites amorous desires but it also makes the forest, all of wild nature, venture a few steps closer. The wood spirits watch and grin at you.

The quarter days, such as the full-moon festival in May, are free spaces, breaks in the flow of time; they are moments in which the world beyond comes closer to the world of humans. Not only can witches and shamans fly effortlessly during that time, but the otherworldly creatures, elemental beings, fairies, and elves also are able to descend to earth and find reincarnation easier.

During May the youth collected colorful flowers, mugwort, thyme, chamomile, sweet woodruff, ground ivy, bedstraw, and other aromatic herbs—which were sacred to the goddess Freya, or later to Mary—and built beds of them for lovemaking in the blooming meadows or in moss-covered forest groves. In the eighteenth century the young people in France still built "castles of love" (*châteaux d'amour*) out of leaves and flowers that the maidens hid in and the boys raided.

The May festival was also an occasion to "quicken" the young women with birch and hazel branches. Not only is the energy set free from the body in this way, but the branches also transmit the flow energy from the ancestral world to this world.

The children who were conceived in May are born into the world during Candlemas, near the threshold of springtime when the goddess of light reappears. This is also when the bear regenerates and emerges from her cave with her young. The Midsummer and the August festivals were also considered favorable times. On the other hand, the days of November were unfavorable.

Pregnancy

During the early phases of pregnancy, the child is not yet bound fast to the embryo. While the growing fetus goes through the entire evolution of the species once again—from amoeba to jellyfish, fish with gills, amphibian, and so on—in the watery environment within the placenta, the accompanying child-soul can easily leave the belly and sway around the mother. It regularly goes on adventures, dances with butterflies, plays with songbirds and other animals, and delights in flowers and trees. And when it is frightened, it flees back into its warm cave (Rätsch, 1987: 31).[15] During this time strong

---

[15] While in the embryonic state the human soul can very easily leave its body, which is in the process of its development; it is ecstatic in the truest sense of the word (*ec* and *static* mean "out of oneself"). The shamans also find themselves in ecstasy when they are traveling. The ethnopsychologist Gerhard Heller pointed out that in shamans there is a certain degree of regression to prebirth abilities when they are in a trance.

souls (for instance, the future shamans, chieftains, or warriors) play with powerful, exceptional animals—wolves, bears, lions, vultures—that later become their allies or familiars.

This floating around lends the expectant mother her distinct loveliness and her radiant aura. Who has not noticed how much butterflies like to flutter around pregnant women, how birds like to fly close past them, and how ladybugs enjoy landing on them? For these reasons it is nourishing for the pregnant woman to spend as much time as possible in nature. The Hindu *Shastras* prescribe long walks in the garden for pregnant women. This attitude toward nature also explains the custom in which the woman embraces or shakes young fruit trees. The belief, repeatedly confirmed by ethnologists, that children can be strongly influenced by what the mother sees and does during pregnancy is based on this idea (Loux, 1980: 52). Sometimes pregnant women are told not eat strawberries because they could cause strawberry-like birthmarks. A farmer who had stuttered since childhood explained to me that his speech impediment resulted from his mother listening to a radio program in a foreign language while pregnant. In Silesia infants can be born with scaly skin if the mothers eat fish while pregnant. Naturally, eating fish is healthy—in this instance it has less to do with the nutritional and physiological standpoint than with the power of suggestion on the impressionable soul of the fetus.

During the last weeks of pregnancy, with the increasing "souling" of the embryo, the child remains more and more in the belly. Usually humans are not able to remember their prebirth existence. Through hypnotic regression or potent psychedelics—such as ayahuasca and ololiuqui—it is possible to break through this amnesia. Some people have even retained images from their prebirth existence. For example, the English poet Thomas Traherne (1637–1674) sang of the joy he had experienced, "how like an angel I came down," and how everything, the flowers and the trees, shone bright and wonderful (Traherne, 1991: 4).

The ancient Celtic poems also paint a picture of the other side of nature, of the land of the elves where the incarnated souls are found:

> Hair there like primrose and the whole body is the color of snow. White there the teeth, black the brows. All of our guests there are a feast for the eyes, every cheek there has the color of the foxglove.
>
> —FROM "*Lebor na Hidre*," an ancient Irish poem

Birth

When the time of delivery was finally at hand, the village midwife, the "night woman," was called for; often it was the pregnant woman's own grandmother. The midwife was called secretly, given a nod; it was better if no unfriendly ears or malicious spirits found out about the birth. The old woman, whose gaze was fixed not only on the material surface of existence but also on the realms beyond, had already seen the child long before it would be born. Through dreams and signs she could foresee who was coming into the world, which ancestor, which warrior, which healer, or even which deity was on its way to becoming embodied. And because what she said turned out to be correct, the elder seemed like the Norns informing fate.

On her way to the birth the midwife paid attention to signs, the animals that crossed her path, the wind, the clouds, the sun, and the moon. These revealed to her how the birth

The goddess as womb and creator of life (Luristan, Iran, c. 700 B.C.E.). All who give birth take part in her archetype. Her womb was considered by many people to be the sacred door between this side and the world beyond, through which the human could cross only by birth, initiation, death, or the shamanic flight.

was going to proceed. She came in the darkest of nights as well. She had no fear; she was a sorceress who knew the night side of existence and of her own being.

Once inside the house she made sure that the doors and cupboards were open, that aprons and shoelaces were untied, and that the thread or yarn was unknotted so that the infant would not be strangled at the threshold or get stuck. She gave the birthing woman advice with comforting words, and she also knew the magical words used to call the disir, Frau Holle, or the Salige Frau for assistance. The Indian midwives sang Vedic birth mantras. The Germanic peoples carved protective runes:

> I'll teach you lore for helping women in labor,
> runes to release the child;
> write them on your palms and grasp her wrists
> invoking the disir's aid.
>
> —FROM THE LAY OF SIGRDRIFA

The wise woman placed a bundle of mugwort in the pregnant woman's left hand, because the guardian of mothers, Frau Holle or Artemis, is present in this aromatic woman's herb. In addition, she burned soothing herbs and herbs that fended off evil influences in the room and the storage rooms. Mugwort and Saint John's wort were included in this incense.

If the baby lay wrong and a breech birth threatened, the wise woman pushed and massaged the abdomen of the mother until the baby lay right. This method was favored by nearly all primitive peoples.

Although the midwife took care of the important practical aspects, she was also in an ecstatic state: She offered herself as a soul-guide to the baby, which found itself on the threshold of the earthly world. She talked with it, gave it courage, took it by the hand (so to speak), and guided it, while the contractions carried it through the birth canal. In South Africa the midwives often smoked hemp, which eased their way into the transsensory realms.

For many modern women birth is a traumatic experience that requires anesthesia and manipulation by an elaborate medical apparatus—an apparatus that, however unintentionally, causes stress and fear. Often the mothers are not even conscious of the birth of their child. In the so-called primitive societies, on the other hand, birth is an experience of the greatest ecstasy. The woman giving birth does not fight against the pain but rather—under the guidance of a wise woman—gives in to the labor and transcends her mortal ego. She is no longer in the everyday world but is "beyond the hedgerow." In this way the midwife reveals herself as the Goddess. Indeed, the woman giving birth has become divine herself, bound to the most profound instincts, bound to the feminine archetype. Groaning, panting, sweating, leisurely moving her weight from one leg to the other, she dances the birth dance of wild Artemis until the contractions begin.

We hear over and over that for the primitives—*primitive* actually means "close to the origins"—birth is swift, uncomplicated, and nearly painless. The ease with which Native American women brought their children into the world amazed white researchers. "It has often been reported to me that the pregnant squaw simply goes somewhere remote, delivers the baby by herself, washes the child in the stream, and walks again afterwards. They do not stay in bed for a whole month (like civilized women do), but make no more out of pregnancy and birth than a cow does" (Stiles, 1761: 149).

Missionaries and Christian zealots were not so certain that the devil did not have a hand in the easy births of these "godless" savage women. Did God himself in the sacred texts not personally damn Eve, the sinful mother of man, in Eden before he banished her, saying, "I prepare much difficulty for you as soon as you are pregnant. You will bear children with pain" (Genesis, 3:16).

Herbs that the midwife uses if the labor takes too long or other complications arise grow everywhere. Native Americans have passed down many. Katawba women drank decoctions of the bark of the poplar, cherry, and Cornelian cherry bark. The Cheyenne women drank bitterroot tea *(Lewisia rediviva)*, which a respected old woman whose life had not been plagued by bad luck had gathered. To shed the placenta the Navajo and Hopi drank a tea made from broomweed *(Getierezia sarothra)* and the Cherokee drank skullcap *(Scutellaria laterifolia)* (Vogel, 1982: 234). Examples such as these could fill entire books.

European midwives also had a masterful knowledge of the plants—above all mugwort—that encourage birth, relieve cramps of the perineum (with a compress made of cramp bark, *Viburnum opulis*), and minimize blood loss (for instance, ergot, *Claviceps purpurea*, which is administered in precise doses beginning with the third set of contractions). The Inquisition, during which almost all midwives were sacrificed, and the Enlightenment, which made a clinical illness out of birth and thus it had to be entrusted to a doctor, nearly destroyed this native gynecological tradition. Complicated and fatal births became problematic only after the ancient traditions had been eradicated.

The *Hebe-Ahnin* and the Men's Childbed

The father was included in the birth even if he was not immediately present. He also found himself in an unusual state of consciousness and often lay on the ground with no energy—like the Amazonian Indian, who lay for days in his hammock, completely exhausted, while the mother was already up and walking around. This postpartum exhaustion of the man is defined by ethnologists as the *couvade*, or "men's childbirth bed," and is considered "sympathetic magic." Radical feminists talk of the "sign of the beginning of the rights of the father." In reality, however, the man was exhausted because he had sent the woman and the child as much power, as much etheric energy—*orenda*, or whatever one wishes to call it—as they required. During the Middle Ages, the Christian man prayed fervently during labor; today's father numbs himself with alcohol and chain-smoking.

Among the Germanic peoples a ritual took place following the birth in which the midwife was the priestess. As mediator (*midwife* means "mediating woman") between the world beyond and this world, the midwife laid the newborn on the straw-covered earth. Thus she consecrated it to the Earth Mother, to Frau Holle, who is our mother as well. She circled the child three times and inspected it. If it was healthy and viable, she lifted it up—that is where the German word for midwife, *Hebamme* (from Old High German *Hevanna* = *Hebe-Ahnin*),* comes from. As she was the embodiment of the goddess of fate and the ancestors, she prophesied the child's destiny and welcomed it with a blessing. She sprinkled water, the life element, on the baby or bathed the child in it. Then she put the baby on the father's lap. He called the child by its proper name. Usually he had dreamt or "heard" the name—humans bring their names with them; they are not named unintentionally. Often it is the name he had before reincarnation, as in the case of the

---

* *Hebe* = to lift, *Ahnin* = ancestor; *Hebe-Ahnin* means "the lifting ancestor." (Trans.)

great-grandfather or the great-grandmother that is being set on the father's lap as a newborn. The wisdom of the language betrays this: *Enkel*, the German word for grandchild, means "little ancestor."

The ritual of the lifting up and name-giving makes the new arrival part of the living community, which it had left a long time ago, again. Weak, inviable, or crippled children were not lifted up; they were sent back behind the fence and set out (Hasenfratz, 1992: 65). However, after the ritual it was considered murder to neglect the infant.

Midwives continued to practice these "heathen" birthing customs, even while veiling them as Christian, into the Middle Ages. They collected birthing herbs and performed the first ritual handling of the child, bathing the newborn with magically powerful ingredients—an extension of the water baptism—and blessing them. They cut off a lock of the child's hair and threw it to the demons as a sacrifice. This satisfied the monsters, and the demons left the child in peace. The midwives were also valued as bringers of children, for they knew about fertility magic.

All of this pushed the midwives dangerously close to the vicinity of the witches. The clergy and the congregation took a stand against them, among them a Dominican in Breslau in 1494 who accused these women of working with thousands of demons. It was the devil who led the midwives to recite superstitious blessings and other deceptions, according to the Augsburg midwife laws (Bächtold-Stäubli, 1987: vol. 3, 1590). Medicinal law and Church prohibitions determined that a priest must be present at birth to prevent the midwife from practicing superstitious customs. Prayers for bearing down were to replace blessings, and baths and water blessings, which mocked the holy baptism, were to be discontinued.

Bedstraw and Bewitching Herbs

During and after the delivery the mother and child are in particular need of the healing energy of vegetation; thus, they are bedded on scented pillows. The gods and heroes have demonstrated this as well. Ishtar, the Babylonian goddess of love, laid the tiny Tammuz on sheaves of grain. And it is said that in the crèche Mary laid aromatic herbs that had been left over by the oxen and the donkey. Alternatively, the Germanic peoples used the nine sacred plants that were dedicated to Freya to bed down the mother and the infant. When the missionaries of the Gospel converted the heathen lands, these important herbs of Freya quickly became "Our Lady's bedstraw."

Which herbs were used as bedstraw? Traditionally the golden yellow, honey-scented inflorescences of the true yellow bedstraw *(Galium verum)* were used. An English legend holds that this herb once had an inconspicuous white flower but, when the Christ child was laid upon it, it transformed into a radiant sunny gold. It comes as no surprise that the midwives not only placed it in the childbirth bed but also bathed the children in a decoction of the herb when they suffered from cramps and convulsions caused by an "evil eye." In an old recipe book we discovered that a soothing drink was prepared from bedstraw to lessen the pains after birthing.

Common thyme *(Thymus vulgaris)*, the aromatic and calming culinary spice that is still reputed by dowsers to eliminate harmful geomagnetic fields, was always included in the mix. The volatile oil (thymol) in the leaves of this Mint family plant is disinfectant and nervine. The Greeks consecrated it to Aphrodite, the goddess of love. Dioscorides prescribed it along with other herbs to stimulate menstruation, birth, and afterbirth.

In general, thyme is considered protective against evil influences. A saga tells of a girl

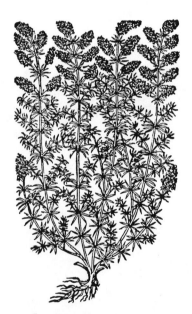

Our Lady's bedstraw (*Galium verum* L.) is related to woodruff. In folk medicine the herb is used for kidney problems of all kinds and as an alterative. (Woodcut from Tabernaemontanus, *Neu vollkommen Kräuter-Buch*, 1731.)

who fell in love with a good-looking foreign traveler. The mother, who did not trust the black-eyed stranger, discovered that her young daughter had arranged to leave with him in the middle of the night. The worried mother fetched thyme and a fern called *Widritat* (from *Wider der Tat*, or "against the deed") and sewed it into the girl's dress. At night, when the stranger came to get the girl, he hesitated and, before dissolving into a cloud of fire and sulfurous fumes, he screeched in a devilish voice:

> *Thyme and fern*
> *Have kept me from my bride!*

No less of an antidemonic action is found in the yellow toadflax or flaxweed *(Linaria vulgaris)*. The yellow-flowered plant in the Figwort family is supposedly loved by toads—symbols of the womb—and avoided by flies. Like flax, yellow toadflax, which grew as a weed in the flax fields, was considered a woman's plant and was sacred to Freya for the Germanic peoples. Among other uses, it was added to a sitz bath as a remedy for discharge.

Oregano *(Origanum vulgare)* also protects the woman and the child after birth. The Greeks consecrated this aromatic herb to Aphrodite as well. The red, lightning-deflecting rose bay *(Epilobium angustifolium)*, called *Froweblüemli* ("ladies' little flower") in Aargau, was also one of the bedstraws, like chamomile, woodruff, sweet clover, ground ivy, and wood betony *(Stachys betonica)*.

Sweetgrass, *Hierochloe odorata*, which smells like woodruff and was known by the Native Americans, was not to be left out. The Native Americans, who burn sweetgrass at all ceremonies, say that it has less to do with protection than with attracting good energy. To the Germanic peoples the aroma embodied gracious Freya.

Bedstraw herbs were used to strengthen the sick and invalids, to comfort the dying, to encourage relaxation, and to stimulate joyous love.

Most of the bedstraw herbs that belong in the medicinal herb bundle are the ones the women gathered on the days between midsummer and the dog days of August. They are herbs with pleasing, antiseptic volatile oils or—as with woodruff, the Mint family, and sweet clover—with coumarins, which release a pleasant and soothing haylike aroma when they are dried.

Many herbs were used by midwives as bewitching or conjuring herbs. Bewitching was understood as evil-tongued gossip and false friendship, behind which jealousy or maliciousness hid; it was also the secret curse on children who seemed to become sick for no reason or did not grow properly. With a nine-herb bath made from flowers that were usually yellow or purple—the colors of jaundice, the skin color that symbolizes envy—the illness was washed away and rinsed off in a stream or river.

After the Birth

The midwife received eggs, flour, flax, and other utilitarian and symbolic offerings. Money was also given to her. It was once the custom to thank the fairy of the farm or village tree for the blessed birth of the child by offering it the umbilical cord or the first bathwater. In certain East African tribes the father plants the baby's umbilical cord with a sapling behind the house. The little tree is lovingly cared for, as it is forever bound to the recent arrival. Christian Rätsch reports that among the Lacadonians in the Chiapas jungle the father plants the dried umbilical cord near the house with some kernels of corn.

"When the corn is ripe, then he takes the ears and hangs it near the place where his wife and child sleep. From then on the ears protect the child from Kisin, the lord of death" (Rätsch, 1987: 36). The midwife wraps the afterbirth in leaves and places it in a hollow tree that only she knows about.

Our heathen forefathers knew similar customs. The northern Germanic peoples buried the "shirt" (placenta) of the newborn and the umbilical cord beneath a tree, or they hung it on branches as an offering to Woden's ravens. For this purpose the trees and shrubs sacred to Freya, such as linden, wild rose, birch, and fruit trees, were used. The fruit trees would then bear a particularly great amount of fruit, and the child would grow and mature like the trees. Sometimes it was the duty of the midwife, or sometimes the father, to bury the afterbirth while silently saying or speaking aloud charms.

This custom has not yet died out in places where home births are still common. The bloodred bathwater is still poured under the rosebush "so that the child will have red cheeks." In many places a birth tree, usually a linden, oak, pear, apple, or nut tree, is planted. The grandfather of Goethe, for instance, planted a pear tree at the birth of little Johann Wolfgang. A vegetative "double" that shares the etheric field with the human during its life is still seen in such trees today. If something happens to the human, the tree will become ill. Likewise, if the tree is harmed—no matter where he is—the human will also suffer.

Wolf-Dieter Storl

The Mother of Death

Just as the wise woman "goes out" to guide the child being born to this side of the harbor, she accompanies the dying in their journey over the threshold as the mother of death, or *Leichenwäscherin* (literally, "corpse washerwoman," the woman who tends to the dead). She usually knows in advance when someone is going to die because the dying process begins long before the afflicted has taken his last sigh. Long before anyone else, she notices when someone has been touched by the withered, cold fingers of death and must dance the dance of death. She is able to perceive death because she has gone over the threshold beyond the hedge and come back again. She has this gift by virtue of birth, through initiation, or by calling.

After the human heart stops beating and the person has taken his last breath, he slips out of his physical skin. He will take the same way back through the cosmic spheres that he descended through before his birth. But at first he is clumsy and insecure; he is like a moist, fragile, thin-skinned butterfly that has slipped out of its cocoon. He has barely become aware of the ancestral spirits, angels, or demons that have come to meet him from the other side. He is still a part of the world on this side. The traditions of all peoples report that the dead person can still see and hear what is happening around him. He requires help establishing orientation. He requires loving attention, just as does the child when it is born. He requires the care of Leichenwäscherin, who takes him in her arms, lovingly caresses his pale skin with her hand, and soothes his fears and confusion with gentle encouragement. "Look, my dear, at how beautiful I am making you! Look what a beautiful new shirt I am putting on you. We will have a lovely party for you, there will be lots to eat and drink!" The Leichenwäscherin even combs the hair and trims the nails of the dead person.

It is understandable that during the time of the Inquisition, the Leichenwäscherin, like the midwife, was in danger of being accused of being a witch or a necromantic, or of making pacts with the dead. She had to be careful to cloak her work in Christian garments. Usually she was deeply faithful anyway; she was Mary Magdalene, who lovingly cared for the corpse of the *Ecce Homo*. In many societies it was she who sang the laments.

After the passing, the family and close friends held a wake. For three days they stayed awake with the dead because the dead remained by its body for three days. During this time the dead person was still very close. He could reveal himself to those to whom he had been connected throughout his lifetime. Even when age, illness, and fatal blows marked him, he appeared in a radiant, beautiful, youthful form to those who were perceptive, for the etheric body remains unmarred, untouched by external influences.

During the three-day death watch, the dead person could still send important messages and give his blessings to those left behind. The light of the candles (the light of death), the smoke of aromatic herbs and resins, and songs and fresh flowers offered the deceased protection from negative influences during this important transitional phase, during this time of metamorphosis. In the Andes the natives played dice games during the wake *(velorio)*; it was the dead who steered the dice and thus made apparent their preferences or indifference.

Flowers for the Dead

Flowers and evergreens play an important role in most festivals of the dead, for the plants are the ambassadors between the worlds—not just between the Earth's darkness and the light of heaven or between the mineral and animal realms, but also between this side and the other. Plants have, as Goethe said, a "sensory" and a "super-sensory" dimension. They have their living bodies in the physical-material world, but as spiritual-sentient entities they also dissolve into the spiritual spheres beyond physical manifestation (Storl, 1997a: 91). Plants are ecstatic (standing outside themselves) in the truest sense of the word. What we call *spirit* or *soul* floats freely around plants in the macrocosmic nature, in the world where the ancestors and gods are also found. To speak with the plant spirits, the gods, and the ancestors, the shaman must also be able to travel outside the body and become ecstatic.

Nowhere is the soul of the plant more tangible in the incarnated world than in the flower. The soul of the plant is best revealed in its color, its scent, its delicacy, and sometimes in the measurable warmth of the flower. Because it is a sentient being, it can touch not only our souls but the souls of the deceased as well. Flowers are the road signs for the dead in the macrocosmic dimension.

The custom of bedding the dead in flowers is ancient and was first practiced more than sixty thousand years ago by the Neanderthals, who buried their dead in a cave in what is currently Iraq. Pollen analysis clearly shows that they laid their dead on beds of bushels of medicinal herbs—yarrow, centaurea, ragwort, grape hyacinth, mallow, ephedra, and others. The ground around the bed was strewn with mugwort. It is possible that mugwort was already considered a plant of Frau Holle and was consecrated to the grandmother of the Earth.

The Mexicans believed that the dead could see the color yellow in particular. For this reason they made a flower carpet out of marigolds *(Tagetes)* that stretched from the house to where the wake was taking place to the table piled high with the dead's favorite food and with cigars, *pulque* (agave wine), fruit, and incense censers with copal (Cipolletti, 1989: 207).

The Festival of the Dead

The custom of having a party along with the wake is nearly universal. Feasting, copious drinking, singing, and dancing mark these celebrations. The dead are invited to celebrate, and when the festivities are over they are thanked for the fun. The celebrants "lift off"; they go, so to speak, a few steps into the spirit world. They are "spirited" or ecstatic.

Since the inception of Christianity, the Christian priests had continual problems trying to subdue this festival. The first action the synod of Litninae forbade was the "blasphemous customs at the graves of the deceased." In the year 1231 the council of Rouen outlawed dancing in the graveyards and in church. In 1405 another council forbade musicians, actors, and jugglers to practice their crafts at the cemeteries (Raiber, 1986: 9). The Church also damned tearing out the hair, scratching the face with the fingernails, and ripping off the clothing as expressions of grief.

In countries not influenced by Christianity, where alcohol is not used to help soothe the mourning, another spirit-moving substance is often used. The Huichol shamans ingest peyote so that they can guide the dead. Iboga plays this role in Africa. But above

The Earth Goddess not only bestows a new life, but she also snatches away the old one. This trait of the cosmic mother of death is particularly apparent in the Aztec statue of their earth goddess, Coatlicue (Snake Mother). Her head is made from two snake heads and she wears a necklace of human hearts, hands, and a skull. Her skirt is woven from snakes.

all, hemp (*Cannabis sativa*) is the sacred herb of death ceremonies. In the *Pen T'sao* of Shen Nung, the most ancient herbal with roots dating to the Chinese Neolithic period, hemp is said to make the body light and enable the human to speak with ghosts. The Scythians, a mounted nomadic people of the West Asian steppes, reportedly placed their dead in a tent with dried hemp burning on glowing stones. The inhalation of the smoke relaxes the soul enough from the physical construct of the body, making it possible to accompany the deceased part of the way into the regions beyond. In India hemp is considered the herb of Harshanas, the god of the death ceremony (*shraddha*). Those who are left smoke ganja at the funeral pyre or eat it spiced with pepper as a delicacy. Those in mourning cut their hair and sacrifice it, as is done for a birth or other important ritual of transformation. With the help of hemp they meditate on the dissolution of the five physical shells of the body (*Pancha Kroshi*). They watch as Shiva, swinging the trident, frees the deceased from his material chains in the wild dance of the flames.[16] They see the demons and the elemental beings who dance with Shiva, and they take delight in the flow of life energy.

In Neolithic China it was the custom for participants of the festival of the dead to wrap themselves in hemp garments. The *Codex Leviticus* of the ancient Hebrews stipulates that the last clothes of the dead be made from hemp fibers. The idea could have come from Egypt, as the bandages of the mummies contain many hemp fibers, and in the mouths of the mummies archaeologists have found hemplike resin mixtures (Behr, 1995: 33). Undoubtedly the hemp seeds that have been found in Germanic graves were thought of as food of the dead. Hemp was, as were all other fibrous plants, sacred to the goddess of fate, the "spinner" Freya or Frau Holle. Hemp seeds are still food for the dead among the Slavs and the Balts of eastern Europe: A hemp soup is cooked and eaten at Christmas or the Epiphany, when the dead visit their families.

Departing gifts are still given to the deceased before he is festively carried to the grave, bound to a tree in the grove of the dead, burned on the funeral pyre, or thrown into the sea from a ship of the dead. Russian women write their men farewell letters. Usually the dead person gets his favorite things. These are also "killed" by being broken or burned so that they can be used on the other side. Even medicinal salve is pressed into the dead's hands so that he can heal himself in the realms beyond. Among the Germanic peoples the *Totenfrau** put good shoes on the dead person's feet for the long walk to the realm of Frau Holle. This ancient custom has been kept alive by the cowboys, who wear their best or often new cowboy boots in their caskets.

It is important for the dead to receive guidance by a relative, a wise woman, or a shaman. The deceased should go farther into the world of the ancestors, the underworld, or heaven. He should not cling to his former life, not return as a bad-luck-bringing *Wiedergänger* (walking dead), not scare the humans as a spook, not bring someone else into the grave. The Celts, the Germanic peoples, and others carried the corpse out through a hole that had been broken in the wall of the house. Afterward the hole was filled so that the ghost wouldn't be able to find its way back in again. Hunters simply left their homes and moved on when someone died. The Germanic peoples and

The Germanic goddess of love, Freya, flew through the worlds with her cat-drawn chariot. Her sacred animals were cats and rabbits; the plants dedicated to her were hemp and flax or linen. Just as the goddess was transformed into a "witch," her sacred hemp was made into a "devil's herb."

---

[16] Shiva, who dances in the fire with his trident, or fork, and his retinue of demons, was the model for the Zoroastrian concept of the devil. The image of Shiva, more than the pictures of horned gods like Pan and Cernunnos, ultimately determined the picture of the devil created by the Pharisees, Christians, and Muslims (Storl, 1989).

* Woman who cared for the dead. (Trans.)

the Slavs bound anyone who died suddenly or violently; they weighed the corpse down with a heavy stone or pierced it with a spear. Shamans and clairvoyant women would have known when anyone came back to the village as a vampire, and they would know different methods—iron nails, juniper smoke, garlic braids, and crucifixes—to make them harmless. They could recognize when a restless dead soul was inside the body of a living one, and whom it wanted to possess. They could also differentiate the walking dead from the friendly dead, who sometimes came, usually during the time of the dead in November (Samhain), in order to warn about the future or to beg for some nourishment—a little light perhaps, or some nuts, apples, or gruel. If their needs were satisfied, they would show their gratitude—the "grateful dead," as they are called in English—and send unexpected blessings from the other world.

The Dead and Vegetation

After the dead person has left his body, he looks for security, for a new shell, which holds his being together as it gradually dissolves into the microcosm. Often a coffin, a hollowed-out tree trunk, a carved fetish, or a boat is used as a transitional "body." The person can rest there before he continues down the path of death.

More than anything else, huge ancient trees were considered dwellings for the dead. Many Native Americans, Melanesians, and Siberians bound the dead to the branches of such trees. The Slavs considered entire groves of trees, where the dead dart from tree to tree like forest spirits, to be sacred. To cut down one of these trees would bring the sinner bad luck or drive him to insanity.

"Guarantee that my soul sets down in the trees which I have planted, so that I may refresh myself under my sycamores," says the Egyptian death prayer carved into a casket lid. The sycamore, a type of fig tree *(Ficus sycomorus)*, is the World Treeof the Egyptians and the residence of Hathor, goddess of the heavens, who dispenses the water of life. The Egyptian Copts still believe that the Virgin Mary has sat in every sycamore tree.

The sagas often mention dead people who transformed themselves into trees. We hear of Dryope, who turned into a poplar, of Daphne, who became a laurel, of the daughter of the king of Cyprus, who, pregnant by her own father, fled his rage and through the graciousness of the gods was transformed into a myrrh tree. We hear of the devoted old couple Philemon and Baucis, who were allowed to continue growing next to each other as an oak and a linden after death. And in the Celtic saga the passionate love of Tristan and Isolde first found fulfillment after death when hazel branches and honeysuckle grew over the graves and embraced each other so tightly that they could not be separated by anybody.

Although it is barely perceptible, the knowledge of the connection of the dead with trees lives on in European culture. The cemeteries are like old parks or even forests. Many of the trees growing in the graveyards have been considered trees of the dead for thousands of years. This is especially true of the poisonous yew, which was sacred to the goddess of death throughout Europe and which protected the dead: "With yew no magic can stay!" The juniper, the elder, the "sorrow-heralding cypress" (Horace), the cedar, and the beech (which is sacred to the reaper Saturn) are classic cemetery trees.

Cemeteries, cremation places, groves of the dead, trees of the dead, and coffins have

The elm (*Ulmus* spp.) has been considered a tree of the dead since antiquity and is classified to the underworld. But in the regions influenced by Germanic culture, the elm is a tree of rebirth, as is clearly recognized in this woodcut in which storks bring the souls of the unborn children. (Woodcut from Hieronymus Bock, *Kreütterbuch*, 1577.)

always been considered the residences of and initiation places for "witches" and shamans. Siberian and Indian shamans were initiated among such trees of the dead. Sadhus (wandering holy men) are initiated at midnight on a cremation site. There they "die"; they take off their clothing, their former lives, their social positions, their caste membership, even their names. From then on they clothe themselves in ashes, in "air," or in the red cloth that echoes the flames of the funeral pyre. Although they are still in their bodies, they are reborn as spiritual beings. They can communicate with other spiritual beings, "fly," see invisible things, and hear inaudible sounds.

The wooden coffin or sarcophagus (from the Greek *sarko-phagos*, which means "flesh eater"), which we have inherited from the Osiris mysteries of ancient Egypt, was actually a tree. Stone Age hollowed-out trunks in which the dead were laid to rest have been discovered. Like the cradle that surrounds the infant, so does the protective motherly wood enclose the human during this phase of its transition from one form of being to another.

In the Indian Vedas, Yama, the first mortal human, is made into the lord of the dead. He lives in a tree and becomes drunk with the gods on the drink *soma*. The dead, robbed of their bodies, seek refuge in the huge ancient tree. There they find entrance to the realm of Yama. The masculine relatives show the dead soul the way: They fix an unglazed, undecorated clay pitcher on the tree trunk and offer the dead water and unsalted rice balls. After two weeks—half a lunation—the clay pot is broken to show the deceased that it is time to move on. Unhappy dead people—those who don't want to go any further—develop into evil spooks *(pisachas)* or vampires *(vetatlas)*. An iron nail must be pounded into the tree trunk to scare them off.

To the external eye the tree in which the dead souls seek refuge is just one of the many mighty fig trees that grow in every location in India. But to the inner eye this tree reveals itself as the World Tree. It is the shamanic tree, the ladder to the heavens, the cosmic spinal column that connects the highest heavens and the depths of the underworld. It is the path on which the witch sits and listens and sometimes laughs her "cosmic laugh."

On every branch of the tree is a universe. Depending on their karma, the dead spend a longer time in one or another universe. Some go to the heaven of Shiva while others go to Vishnu; others go to the terrifying Rakshasas. The Germanic heroes go to Valhalla, where they drink mead with Odin; the gracious go to Freya's Folkvang; the seafarers and the drunks go to Ran, the god of the sea. But most go to the underworld realm of Hel or Frau Holle. Seven or nine such spheres are known by most peoples. The Upanishads mention 333,000,000 divine and demonic realms—they are as numerous as the leaves of the world tree.

The Dead As Dispensers of Fertility

The moon is the first branch of the cosmic tree where a dead spirit rests for a while. This eternally increasing and decreasing planet is brought into connection with the dead and the vegetation gods throughout the world. The syndic moon, the period from full moon to full moon, represents a day and night of the *pitri*, the ancestors, according to the Indian worldview. The dark phase of the new moon is the night when the pitri sleep. The bright half of the full moon is the day in which they are busy working. The pitri's work brings the earth fertility and stimulates the plants to grow.

Gardeners know that seeds germinate and the plants grow faster around the time of the full moon.[17] Because the deceased work from the sphere of the moon on the flourishing of the fields, the herds, and the humans, it is imperative to look after the pitri, to feed them, and to honor them with our thoughts.

The Chinese know about this mystery. The round grave mounds of the ancestors still stand in the middle of the fields and receive the respect they are due—despite the scientific materialism demanded by the Communist Party. In the spring the dwellings of the deceased are meticulously cleaned; in the fall the ancestors are fed elaborate meals. They receive blankets (small pieces of fabric and paper), rice wine, and large bundles of "hell money," which is burned next to the graves. Only then will the Shen spirit bless the fields with a bountiful harvest.

Similar examples are found in Africa. There the fields will become barren and the living will have bouts of bad luck if the Manen are not properly fed and honored.

The Romans sacrificed food, wine, milk, and blood to the dead in February; in May

Yama, the south Asian god of death, is an ancient Indo-European deity. He is identical to Ymir, the first being who was killed, as is told in the Eddas. (From Dahram Vir Singh, *Hinduism*, 1991.)

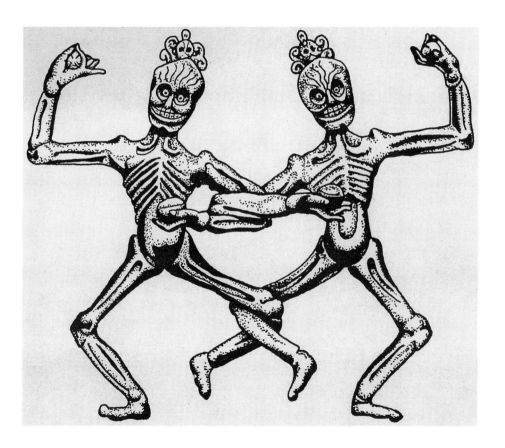

A central theme of Tibetan Buddhism is the confrontation with the transitory. Death is a part of life and is not shut out but is instead understood as a kind of "dance of the molecules," which stand at the beginning of transformation—as can be seen on these grinning skeletons.

---

[17] The pitri are guests of King Soma on the moon. Soma, surrounded by a radiant milk-white aura, is the ruler of all liquids and juices. In the Vedas he is honored as nourisher and guardian of the world, for he moistens the earth with rain, lets the rivers swell, and flows through and enlivens the bodies of the animals and plants with juice. "Penetrating the earth I retain the creations through my power; by becoming a moon full of juice, I feed the plants" (*Bhagavad-Gita*, XV: 13). Soma is also the Lord of the Brahmans, who are allowed to press the sacred soma plant and bring out the intoxicating liquid of the gods as libation. Soma allows the reincorporating souls to stream down to the earth in the water of rainstorms. There they are soaked up by the plants. Inside humans the nutritional plants transform themselves into life energy in semen and sexual secretions. In this manner the souls are able to attain a new body on the Earth.

other spirits of the dead, the Lemurs, are celebrated. The Lemurs, who descend to earth in the rays of the full moon, are also connected to the growth of the plants.

For the northern Europeans these festivals of the dead were held in late fall. Among the Celts the grave mounds, the *sidh-mounds*, opened up in the full moon of November and the Samhain festival of the dead, one of the quarter days, was celebrated. Today it is still considered a typical witches' holiday.

The shamans and the witches can make healing and fertility magic because they understand the connection among the dead, the moon, and the vegetation and also know the rituals that reach into the dimensions beyond. That is also witchcraft medicine.

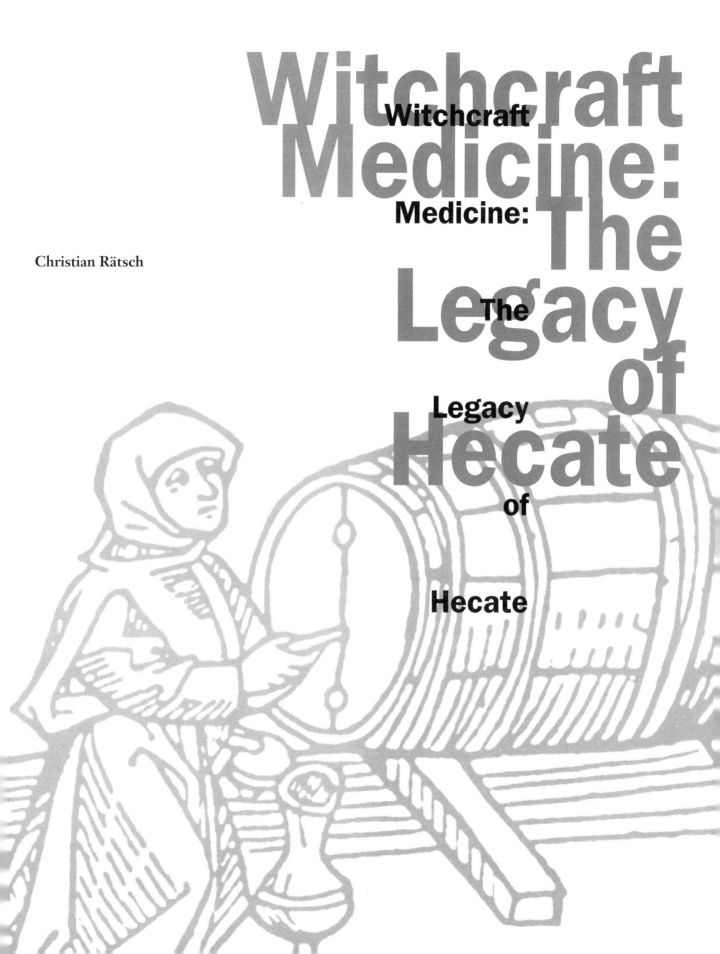

Witchcraft Medicine: The Legacy of Hecate

Christian Rätsch

Plants that demonstrate powerful pharmacological effects must be used with expertise; otherwise, they will cause considerable damage. For this reason such plants are generally feared and in due course demonized. Those who know how to use them correctly are also feared, and all too easily turned into "witches."[1]

Witchcraft medicine is a kind of applied pharmacology of the plants with potent activity. The powers that be have always sought to control the use of strong medicines because, among other reasons, rulers feared they might be poisoned by a skilled hand. In earlier times, however, the powerful activity observed in a substance was considered to have its origins in the supernatural, the magical, or even in the sorcery of witches.[2] In other words, the potency and effectiveness of a substance were considered proof of witchcraft.

Indeed many medical treatments used during antiquity were not based on rational pharmacology, but were a combination of ritual and the use of material substances. Man already believed in archaic times that the plants revealed their power only when harvested with the proper ritual gathering method, and only when the correct accompanying words were spoken.[3] The ancient authors (such as Homer and, in particular, Diocles) wrote of the *rhizotomoki*, the root gatherers of archaic times, that they were the inventors of pharmacological medicine and that they still spoke with the plant spirits (Baumann, 1982: 15; Graf, 1996: 69). These root gatherers observed the gods sacred to the respective plant. They made use of the moon's energy and knew the particular oath formulas for each plant. Witchcraft medicine belongs to the spiritual and cultural legacy of the rhizotomoki. When a scientific theory rationalizing the healing arts emerged with the Hippocratics,[4] ritual and magical medicine was slowly suppressed. It was ridiculed as superstitious and ultimately driven underground. Only certain areas of magical medicine were maintained in the healing cult of Asclepius and were officially accepted into late antiquity (Krug, 1993; cf. Meyer and Mirecki, 1995).

Witchcraft medicine is the healing art of the underground. It is the forbidden and despised medicine, the one oppressed by the Church and/or state, the kind of medicine sanctioned as "alternative,"[5] for it makes decisions over life and death. And it does more than make people healthy—it brings joy and awareness, inebriation and mystical insight.

Witchcraft medicine is wild medicine. It is uncontrollable, it surpasses the ruling order, it is anarchy. It belongs to the wilderness. It scares people. It is one thing above all: heathen.

---

[1] "In the myths and poetry of the Greeks we learn about the great witches such as Circe and Medea. But perhaps they were not originally witches, and were instead goddesses, or even priestesses of gods of a religion that fell a long time ago. Their knowledge of herbs, roots, and mushrooms represented ancient, secretly protected experience and bestowed them with their particular power. In their own culture they were priestesses—the subsequent generations made them into dangerous witches" (Luck, 1990: 46).

[2] "That evil people sometimes use certain substances from which a desired effect ensues, and that various credible, if peculiar, examples were performed by Harsdörf in his great show-place, cannot be doubted. But whether or not such effects are natural or supernatural has not yet been decided. At the very least these substances are as dangerous as they are unreliable; in that they commonly lead to illnesses, robbing of the senses, loss of memory, if not death . . ." was the explanation offered as recently as 1738 in volume 17 of the *Grosses vollständiges Universal-Lexicon aller Wissenschaften und Künste* [Great Complete Universal Dictionary of All Sciences and Arts].

[3] "It must be assumed that without the proper words the ingestion of the medicinal plant did not help" (Graf, 1996: 69). The same holds true for the medicine of the druids: "The magical songs did not work on their own, the two healing methods of magic and plant medicine worked only in unison" (Guyonvarch and Le Roux, 1996: 183). This concept is still widespread among shamans of the Central and South American Indians. They are all in agreement that plants heal only in combination with rituals and magical sayings (see Rätsch, 1997c).

[4] The Hippocratics based their work on the Greek doctor Hippocrates of Kos (c. 460–377 B.C.E.), who developed the teachings of the four humors. They have been preserved by him and his students in numerous essays (*Corpus Hippocraticum*). The Hippocratic teachings influenced the Western medicine practiced by men through the early modern era (Krug, 1993).

[5] Foreign and new healing methods have always been considered competition for the established methods, and those who use the established methods have always feared the new ones. It comes as no surprise that "alternative" medicine continues to be intellectually and scientifically restricted (see also the description of Jütte, 1996).

Witchcraft medicine stems from shamanism and has its roots in Paleolithic times. Witchcraft medicine is mythological, ritualistic, and strongly feminine. Witchcraft medicine is religion—a shamanic healing religion revolving around sacred, in other words, effective, plants.

> Cults, in which the medicinally effective plants and sacred beverages play a role, have always been viewed suspiciously, at first by representatives of the Christian faith, later also by Western medicine. The witches, the last wise women of European culture, fell victim to the Inquisition. In Siberia in the 1930s and 1940s shamans were prosecuted as counterrevolutionaries. Today shamans are also denigrated and ridiculed. So it was in the year 1990 that the Protestant church of the Indonesian island Siberut, which lies east of Sumatra, released a decree forbidding the activities of the medicine men as heathen and blasphemous (Plotkin, 1994: 187).

The most important domains of witchcraft medicine include knowledge about the preparation and use of the *pharmakon* as:

- aphrodisiacs (philters, *Virus amatorius*) and anaphrodisiacs[6]
- birth control and abortifacients (*abortativa*)
- poison/medicine (*pharmakon*)
- inebriants or "traveling herbs" (psychoactive substances)[7]
- life-extending and rejuvenating elixirs

Thus witchcraft medicine was used to increase happiness, for birth control, to heal, to damn, for visionary knowledge, and for life extension. This is why magic was originally called *pharmakeia* (Luck, 1990: 58).

But the ambivalent magic of weather-making, as well as intentional black magic (curses or *devotio, defixions*;[8] ritual maledictions or *dirae*; poisoning; death magic[9]) also belong to witchcraft medicine. Witchcraft medicine also has an affinity for unusual individuals and people with extraordinary abilities (of prophecy, spiritual healing, and so forth).

The initiation for becoming a "witch doctor" took place within the framework of rituals, mysteries, and orgies. Witchcraft medicine stands under the protection of the Great Goddess in her manifestations as Hecate,[10] Artemis, and Diana in particular, but in Aphrodite, Venus, and Freya as well. These goddesses demonstrate distinct shamanic traits, just as the magicians of antiquity (*magoi*)[11] and witches themselves do. And the witches' herbs come from the gardens of the goddesses.

---

[6] Anaphrodisiacs were mostly used for birth control!

[7] All psychoactive substances are communicators. They are used to communicate with oneself, with others, with ghosts, with ancestors, and with the gods.

[8] "Therefore the standard purpose of a curse is to suppress someone under your will and make it impossible for him to act on his own" (Graf, 1996: 110). Defixions are richly represented in archaeological material.

[9] Death magic—causing an enemy or sacrifice to die with a curse—is one of the particularly feared practices of the "witches," Voodoo priests, and black shamans throughout the world (cf. Biedermann, 1974; Christensen and Martí, 1979; David-Neel, 1984; Evans-Pritchard, 1988; Favret-Saada, 1979; Hall and Kingston, 1979; Kapur, 1983; Kluckhorn, 1967; Knab, 1995; Lehmann and Myers, 1989; Lewis, 1989; Mann, 1994; Marwick, 1975; Multhaupt, 1990; Scheffler, 1983; Sepulveda, 1983; Simmons, 1980; Walker, 1989; Wiemann-Michaels, 1994; Winkelman, 1992), and late antiquity as well (Graf, 1996).

[10] The name Hecate almost sounds like *Hexe* (witch).

[11] The pre-Socratic philosopher Heracleitus of Ephesus (c. 500 B.C.E.) classified the magoi with the *nyktipoloi*, the "night wanderers" (Graf, 1996: 72). Heracleitus was an adept of Artemis, for he brought his book *On Nature* to her temple as an offering. Petronius calls them *stridentes*, "those who are floating about" (Wolf, 1994: 39).

The threatening plants with potent pharmacological activity were called magic plants, witches' herbs, or devil's drugs.[12] During antiquity the people who made use of these plants, the "sorceresses" and "witches," were called *pharmakides* or *pharmakeutriai* in Greek (Gawlik, 1994: 150; Graf, 1996: 159). The Greek word *pharmakon* (plural *pharmaka*) simultaneously means "medicine, poison, and magical substance."[13] In the Middle Ages the German word *Kraut* (herb) had the same meaning as "magical substance."[14] In Venice magic or sorcery was even known as *erberia*, which means "herbalism" (Golowin, 1973: 6f).

A typical characteristic of witches' herbs is their ambivalence—to some they cause damage and disease, to others they offer health and protection. Often they ease the problems they have caused, and they are intoxicating or induce trances.[15] They are true *pharmaka*—in the ancient meaning of the multidimensional word. For these herbs the wisdom of Paracelsus—that it is only the dosage that determines whether or not something is medicine or poison—holds true. And with witches' herbs it is extremely important to determine the correct dosage. It is well known that in antiquity the witches' clients were often poisoned or were made "crazy" by the love potions (*amatoria, remedium amoris*)[16] that commonly contained the active pharmaka of nightshade, henbane, or hemlock.[17] But because the users did not heed the maker's instructions out of pure greed, they overdosed. For this reason such substances had already been forbidden by Roman times (Graupner, 1966: 26).

> The person who, even if it is done without bad intention, provides abortions or love potions, because doing so sets a bad example, will be sentenced to the following punishments: People of lower classes shall be sent to forced labor in the mines, members of higher classes are to be exiled on an island after the seizure of a portion of their possessions. If a man or a woman dies because of the treatment, the death penalty will be implemented (*Codex iustinianus*, dig. 48.8; 3.2,3).

The above is the origin of the saying, "The greatest magician is the one who best knows the secrets of the plants" (Golowin, 1973: 7). Herbalists were often called *Kräuterhexen*, or herb witches (Boland, 1983). Today herbalists and women who know about healing, especially ones who live in the countryside, are still described as "witches" and are often viewed with suspicion (Bourne, 1995). Similarly, shamans and other folk doctors are described in ethnographic literature as "witch masters," "witch doctors," or sorcerers; healers and psychics are called "witches" (for example, Donner-Grau, 1997).

In antiquity the term *witch* (*strix, striges*) appears only in later literature. Originally one spoke of magoi (magicians). The term described a certain type of shamanic traveling priest (sometimes known as *Goetians*, from the word *goetia*, which means "magic" or "shamanism"). In later times prestidigitators and carnival conjurors were also called

---

[12] "The evil plants are the poisonous plants which could have sprung solely from diabolical knowledge" (Gawlik, 1994: 245).

[13] In the Roman literature magical substances were called *veneno*, which means "poison." The woman who makes poisons was a *venefica* (cf. Hyginus, *Myths*).

[14] "Magical substances are vehicles of a mystical power which can be addressed using words, spells, or formulas. The substances receive orders and carry them out" (Multhaupt, 1990: 85).

[15] In antiquity the ability to put people into a trance or to be able to heal them was enough to be convicted of being a magoi (Graf, 1996: 74).

[16] These plants were still named in the early modern era as important ingredients of love potions (Kräutermann, 1725: 100).

[17] Cf. Lucian, *Dialogues of the Hetaerae* VIII.

Illegal Aphrodisiacs and Abortifacients

The magical substances *(veneno)* forbidden in ancient Rome by senatorial decree *(senatus consultum)* (according to Pliny, *Natural History* XXV.95; XXVII.2; XXIX.23; cf. Quintlilian, *Declamations* 7.4; 8.5)

Cicuta	Water hemlock, poison hemlock	1. *Cicuta virosa* L. (syn. *Seinum virosum* [L.] E. H. L. Krause) 2. *Conium maculatum*
Salamandram	Fire salamander	*Salamadra maculosa*
Aconitum	Monkshood	1. *Aconitum napellus* L. 2. *Aconitum* spp.
Bubrostim	Buprestem	a species of beetle
Mandragora	Mandrake	*Mandragora officinarum* L.
Lustramenti	Euphorics	diverse substances
Canthariadas	Spanish fly	*Lytta vesicatoria* L.

magicians (from the word *mageia*, which means "sorcery"). Thus in the Greek literature Moses, Aaron, and Jesus of Nazareth were referred to as magicians (Budge, 1996; Graf, 1996: 13). Moses was probably a trickster who was chased out of Egypt and who greatly impressed a dilapidated Jewish tribe with his little theatrical performances (for example, his "Indian" rope trick) and lured them over to monotheism. Moses is also considered the author of one of the most important folk works about witchcraft medicine, *The Sixth and Seventh Book of Moses.*[18] Therein it says:

> How to obtain magical powers: On the eve of the Adelbert festival (June 1) kill a snake, cut its head off, place therein three kernels of hemp [*Cannabis sativa* L.] and bury the whole thing in the ground: When the hemp has grown, twist a rope out of it. If you wrap this around your body, then even the strongest force will be withstood (Bauer, 1984: 151).

The most famous Thessalian witches were called *veneficus Thessalus*. Magic, poison mixing, shamanic practices of the Goetians, and *goetia* (techniques for ecstatic rituals and divination) were classified together under the term *veneficium* in Latin—but in Greek they were classified as pharmakon (Graf, 1996: 45). In other words, magic was originally applied pharmacology.

Gardens of the Gods and Herbs of the Witches

Mount Olympus, the holy mountain of the sages of antiquity, rises precisely on the border between Thessaly, the ancient home of the magicians and witches, and Macedonia. The mountain is 2,917 meters high[19] and can easily be seen from the train that travels to Thessaly:

> It is the eternal seat of the everlasting gods, high above the storms, rain, and snow, surrounded by a brilliant blue and enveloped by a radiant light. There, in the circle

"The Greek word wotani *stood for the meadow herb, grass. This is where the modern scientific plant science, botany, gets its name. Homer's botany was restricted to the groves sacred to his gods, the wondrous herbs of his mythological figures, or to the allegorical plants he was drawn to."*

—HELLMUT BAUMANN,
DIE GRIECHISCHE PFLANZENWELT
[THE GREEK WORLD OF PLANTS],
1982

---

[18] There is also an *Eighth Book of Moses* written on an Anastasi papyrus from the fourth century C.E., which describes a magical ritual (cf. Graf, 1996: 13).

[19] In archaic Greece this mountain was actually identified with Olympus. Later the term *Olympus* was considered metaphoric and was also used for other mountains (Parnassus, Helicon, Ida, etc.) and as a synonym for heaven, Elysium, paradise, the beyond, and so on (Petermann, 1990: 13).

The mildly psychoactive prickly lettuce (*Lactuca virosa* L.) was often mentioned as an ingredient in witches' salves. It was a sacred plant in ancient Egypt. In the early modern era it was used as a substitute for opium. Gerard says that the plant even smells like opium. (Woodcut from Gerard, *The Herbal*, 1633.)

of his gods, Zeus rules with Hera, Hermes, Athena, and Artemis in golden palaces, surrounded by the sounds of Apollonian music played by immortal beings, filled with the blessed joy of the divine. The muses, daughters of Zeus, dance their circle-dance and sing their songs in the wooded cliffs of the mountain (Petermann, 1990: 13).

On Olympus there grew the "garden overflowing with the fruits of mighty Zeus" (Apollonius, *Argonautica* III.160f.). This mountain is also where the *dodecatheon*,[20] or "twelve-god-herb," grows. Pliny placed this strange, not yet identified "plant of the gods" immediately behind the hermetic magical plant *moly*:

> After moly the plant with the highest reputation they call dodecatheon, as a compliment to the grandeur of all the twelve gods. It is said that taken in water it cures all diseases. Its leaves are seven, very like those of the lettuce and sprouting from a yellow root (*Natural History* XXV.28).

It is possible that the plant was a species of *Lactuca* (for example, the psychoactive prickly lettuce *Lactuca virosa* L.). Lettuce was one of the sacred plants of the ancient Egyptians and was often named as an ingredient in the witches' salves.

Marcellus (c. C.E. 400), the Latin author from Gall, wrote in his recipe book *De medicamentis* that the dodecatheon was also called *donax* (XXVII.7). Conceivably he meant the giant reed (*Arundo donax* L.), the sacred plant of Pan, the joyous nature god who was transformed by the Christians into an image of the devil (Borgeaud, 1988). It was recently discovered that the root-ball of the *Arundo donax* contains the highly potent psychedelic compound DMT (cf. Rätsch, 1997b). In earlier times the twelve-god herb had already been identified as primrose (*Primula elatior* [L.] Hill or *Primula veris* L.) and sometimes as butterwort (*Pinguicula vulgaris* L.).[21] In Germanic tradition the primrose is inhabited by nixes, elves, undines, and naiads (Dierbach, 1833: 176f). It is also one of the Germanic plants of the gods, as well as one of the magical herbs of the Celts.

> Primrose was used by the druids for their *drink of enthusiasm*. It must be picked before the new moon and mixed with vervain, blueberries, moss, wheat, clover, and honey. The new young priestesses heated the drink with their breath until it began to smoke (Perger, 1864: 174).

The primrose, known in German as *Schlüsselblume* (key flower) or *Himmelsschlüssel* (heaven's key),[22] is said to be a "key to heaven" or a flower of Saint Peter,[23] and seems to

Primrose (*Primula veris* L.) was known as heaven's key as well as devil's piss. (Woodcut from Gerard, *The Herbal*, 1633.)

---

[20] Also spelled *dodekatheon, dodecatheum.*

[21] Although the primrose *Primula elatior* grows in Greece, apparently the plant was not mentioned in any antique sources. The only primrose (Primulaceae) described by Greek and Roman authors was *cyclaminonn*, the Greek sowbread (*Cyclamen graecum* Link.). Theophrastus, known as the father of botany, wrote that the plant's roots were used for medicine as well as for aphrodisiacs (*On Plants* IX.3, 9). The root powder was moistened with wine and formed into small disks. Dioscorides wrote, "Mixed in the wine it makes you drunk. . . . It is said that the pounded roots are used for making love potions, being fashioned into pastilles for this purpose" (*Materia medica* III.193). Pliny added that "[primroses] should be grown next to all houses, if it is true that there where it grows no magic is effective, which is why it is also called amulet *[amuletum]*" (*Natural History* XXV.9, 66).

[22] According to folk mythology the plant was created by Saint Peter's key chain when it dropped and fell to the earth (Marzell, 1935: 23f).

[23] In South America there are numerous mescaline-containing species of cacti in the genus *Trichocereus* (syn. *Echinopsis*) including San Pedro, "Saint Peter."

have been one of the most important magical plants of the declining Middle Ages. The doctor Johannes Hartlieb, one of the earliest German authors of an herbal[24] (fifteenth century), wrote about the primrose:

> The herb is also called *Teufelspisse* (devil's piss), because the root has holes in it where the devil has pissed through. Those who cook the herb in lye and then dunk their head in will have their stupidity vanquished and their brain strengthened, better than any other measure. The old women perform much magic with it, but neither shall I, nor should I say, anything about it (see Hartlieb, 1980: 33).

A few magical uses of primrose have been preserved in folklore: "Superstitions attribute secret magical powers to this plant, it can reveal places where great treasures lie hidden, and open up the entrance to them" (Gessmann, n.d.: 72f.).

Throughout the world certain plants, usually psychoactive nightshades (henbane, thorn apple, belladonna, angel's trumpet) are given similar attributes. They always have to do with the plants of the gods or goddesses: "If the primrose reveals where treasure lies, then often a feminine figure appears, at the same time she is the key virgin, who symbolizes Freya [the Germanic goddess of love], for a key also lies hidden in the crown of this goddess" (Perger, 1864: 175).

Just as the Germanic goddess of love was a key bearer, Hecate also had possession of the keys to the three realms of the world, most important to heaven or Olympus (Kraus, 1960). Her keys were the magical plants that were sacred to her: the psychoactive plants, especially those of the Nightshade family.

Primrose remains a common medicinal herb in folk medicine. A tea is made from the flowers and leaves and is taken for insomnia, dizziness, neuralgia, migraines, and headaches (Marzell, 1935: 25). A decoction of the roots (a heaping teaspoon per cup) was recommended as an expectorant (Pahlow, 1993: 282). The house doctor of Johann Joachim Becher, the elector of Bavaria, gave effusive praise to the medicinal herb:

> *The primrose it warms, it dries and it soothes,*
> *for quieting pain, for a wound give it soon.*

A witch disguised as a rabbit is led to buried treasure with the help of a demonic being. With bellows the demon blasts into the woman the ability to comprehend the extrasensory. Many plants of the Nightshade family have the reputation, with proper use, to lead one to treasure. In Europe henbane was mainly utilized for such purposes; in Africa thorn apple and other nightshades were used. In Central and South America it is still said that angel's trumpet makes it possible to find treasure. (Woodcut from Sebastian Brant, *Narrenschiff* [Ship of Fools], 1494.)

Zeus transforms a nymph into a tree, or, more precisely, calls to the tree spirits, who appear as nymphs. (English woodcut, 17th century.)

---

[24] He also wrote a book about the divinatory methods of witches and sorcerers, but published it cautiously and defamed those methods as "forbidden art" (Hartlieb, 1989a and 1989b).

The Twelve Suspected Ingredients of the Dodecatheon			
THE OLYMPIANS	**THEIR PLANTS**		**MEDICINE**
Zeus	Oak	*Quercus robur* L.	Bark
Hera	Lily	*Lilium candidum* L.	Root
Poseidon	Cluster pine	*Pinus pinaster* Soland. (syn. *Pinus maritima* Lam.)	Resin
Demeter	Poppy	*Papaver somniferum* L.	Opium
Apollo	Apollinaris	*Artemisia absinthium* L., *A.* spp.	Herbage
Athena	Olive tree	*Olea europaea* L.	Oil
Hephaestus	Myrtle	*Myrtus communis* L.	Leaves
Aphrodite	Mandrake	(*Mandragora officinarum* L.)	Root
Aries	Gramineae	diverse grasses	?
Dionysius	Grapes	*Vitis vinifera* L.	Wine
Hermes	Moly	not identifiable	Root

It expels the gout, for bad animals bite,
primrose is valued as precious and right.

—*PARNASSUS MEDICINALIS ILLUSTRATUS*
[THE ILLUSTRATED MEDICINALS OF PARNASSUS], 1662

According to other sources the dodecatheon was a medicine prepared with twelve plants. It was effective against all illnesses—a panacea (Baumann, 1982: 115). Perhaps this preparation of twelve sacred plants contained herbs that were each, in turn, sacred to one of the twelve Olympic gods (see table above). The flowers should be gathered by the dryads, the nymphs who live in the trees, and given to humans so that they will have an effective remedy against melancholia. It is possible that this divine preparation, which was definitely psychoactive, could transport the partakers to Olympus.

It is entirely conceivable that dodecatheon was an elixir with a wine basis. Perhaps simples (such as oak bark, lily root, henbane leaves, mugwort herbage, myrtle leaves, mandrake root, blades of grass) were steeped in wine. Finally, opium was dissolved into pine resin and olive oil was mixed in, giving the elixir multidimensional activity; it could have been a primordial form of Swedish bitters. Interestingly, over the course of history nearly all of the plants of the Olympic gods have been demonized and classified as witches' herbs. In addition to the different plants identified with moly (thorn apple, belladonna, rue) are others that were later used as additives in the witches' salve (opium, olive oil, mandrake, wine, incense).

Other plants have also been associated with Olympus. Dierbach classified rosemary (*Rosmarinus officinalis* L.) as a "flower of the Olympians" because the aromatic herb was burned as incense *(libanotis)* for the Olympian gods (1833: 163 f.).[25] At the same time Saint John's wort, more precisely Olympian Saint John's wort (*Hypericum olympicum* L.), was also associated with the holy mountain.[26] It has often been identified with *Panakos Cheironion*, the "panacea of the centaur Chiron" (Baumann, 1982: 118), which is an effective antidote for snakebites (Dioscorides, *Materia medica* III.50).

The classical name of *dodecatheon* was later adapted by Linnaeus as a genus name in

---

[25] Rosemary "grows in the ocean regions and in gardens; before incense [frankincense] was known, the people soothed [the gods] with this plant" (*Medicina antiqua* fol. 83v).

[26] In Nepal there is also a Saint John's wort (*Hypericum choisianum* Wallich ex N. Robson), which is consecrated to the great goddess Kali, the Asian correspondent of Hecate.

his system of botanical classification. The genus *Dodecatheon* is in the Primulaceae family and encompasses many species native to North America. In German they are called *Götterblumen* (flowers of the gods), while in English they are known as shooting stars. Native North Americans made a tea out of the leaves of the pretty shooting star *Dodecatheon pulchellum* (Raf.) Merr. (syn. *D. radicatum* Greene), and the *Dodecatheon alpinum* for colds (Tillford, 1997: 136).

The Garden of the Great Goddess

The garden is originally the domain of the woman. There she plants herbs, shrubs, and trees; there she tends to her medicinal plants; there she nurtures her contact with the Earth, the primordial Goddess, the mother of the plants.[27] The Elysian fields are also gardens. In paradise—the enclosed garden,[28] the heavenly garden—grows the tree of knowledge. In Hecate's garden hangs the Golden Fleece; in Freya's garden are the golden apples. The Goddess's fruits bestow divine knowledge, grant a long life, and ensure good health. The tree of knowledge is the original World Tree, the sacred tree of the shamans through which we can travel to the beyond. What the ancient shamans and archaic mystics understood became demonized by the monotheists. The true tree of knowledge was planted by the gods and goddesses in the garden of the first humans so that the people, through the enjoyment of its fruits, could become intelligent and could be initiated into the secrets of life and death. Those who eat from the tree of knowledge in the correct way will be graced with visions of the divine splendor, the blessed paradise, and the Great Goddess herself will be revealed. Shamans enjoy these fruits in order to open the gates to the other world. The tree of knowledge is the original tool of shamanic medicine, as well as the most important medicinal plant in witchcraft medicine. For this reason the most famous witches' herbs are the visionary plants—those that make it possible for healers to walk into the magical world and take up contact with the Great Goddess.[29]

Eve is not only the first woman, but also the first witch. She was originally the creation or the daughter of the Great Goddess and was simultaneously her first priestess. Thus she knew the effects of the sacred tree and offered its knowledge-giving fruit to Adam, the first man and the first mystic. Through the enjoyment of the fruit[30] he was initiated into the mysteries of the Great Goddess and was filled with the understanding of the feminine role in creation.

The Great Goddess has many forms and many names, depending on the times and the influences of culture. During antiquity she was revealed in the Elysian cults as Demeter, in the Zypriotic orgies as Aphrodite, in the Dionysian festivals of Orpheus as

"Sacred Earth Goddess, bearer of all natural beings, you who nurture everything and propagate daily, you alone offer the folk protection, you who rules over heaven and ocean and over all things . . . For good reason you are named the Great Mother of the Gods, because you conquer the divine beings with tender love . . . The plants, which your majesty grows, are given to all people for the sake of their salvation— leave to me your medicine. Let it come to me with all of your healing power. All that I make with it shall it be effective. When I give this medicine to those who receive it from me, let them all become healthy."

—*MEDICINA ANTIQUA*, FOLIO 9V
(ZOTTER, 1980)

The tree of the Hesperides, or the three goddesses with the golden apples, as well as the snake of awareness and the well of remembrance. (Greek vase painting c. 700–400 B.C.E.)

---

[27] In classical Athens there was a place known as *oi kepoi*, or the garden. In the garden was a temple to Urania, the muse or sky goddess, a shrine to Aphrodite, and a sacred statue of Aphrodite of Alcemenes. Next to this was another Aphrodite "who stands close to the temple; her form is as square as that of a herm. The inscription says that Aphrodite Ourania is the oldest of the so-called Moirae" (Pausanias, *Itinerary of Greece* I.2, 19).

[28] "As an enveloping and nurturing area, therefore as 'healing' and 'sacred,' the garden has always been the symbol of culture—therewith thought as well" (Schmölders, 1983: 9). "The earthly garden is the vision of the heavenly paradise" (Zuylen, 1995).

[29] For more information see the extensive literature on the subject: Hansen, 1981; Harner, 1973; Hauschild, 1981; Kiesewetter, 1982; Kuhlen, 1980 and 1984; Lussi, 1996; Metzner, 1994; Perez de Barradas, 1957; Pollio et al., 1988; Schultes and Hofmann, 1995.

[30] In Turkey the psychoactive substance mandrake (*Mandragora officinarum* L.), which was the sacred plant of Aphrodite in antiquity and grew in her *heiros kepos* (sacred garden), is still referred to as "the root of Adam" or "the root of the [first] humans" (cf. Rätsch, 1994).

ISIDIS
Magnæ Deorum Matris
APVLEIANA DESCRIPTIO.

Isis, the great Mother Goddess, as ruler of the world, sorceress, and herbalist. On the left side her various names are listed. She is considered identical to Hecate, among other goddesses. (Illustration from *Metamorphoses* by Apuleius, from the early modern era.)

Hecate[31] (Maass, 1974: 176f.). In the *Metamorphoses* of Apuleius, Isis, the Egyptian goddess and sister/wife of Osiris, reveals herself in all her splendor to Lucius, the hero of the picaresque novel of late antiquity, and during the initiation spoke:

> Behold, Lucius, moved by your prayers I have come, I, the mother of the universe, mistress of all the elements, and the first offspring of the ages; mightiest of deities, queen of the dead, and foremost of heavenly beings; my one person manifests the aspect of all gods and goddesses. With my nod I rule the starry heights of heaven, the health-giving breezes of the sea, and the plaintive silences of the underworld. My divinity is one, worshipped by all the world under different forms, with various rites, and by manifold names. In one place the Phrygians, first-born of men, call me Pessinuntine Mother of the Gods, in another the autochthonous people of Attica call me Cecropian Minerva, in another the sea-washed Cyprians call me Paphian Venus; to the arrow-bearing Cretans I am Dictynna Diana, to the trilingual Sicilians Ortygian Prosperina, to the ancient people of Eleusis Attic Ceres; some call me Juno, some Bellona, others Hecate, and still others Rhamnusia; the people of the two Ethiopias, who are lighted by the first rays of the Sun-God as he rises every day, and the Egyptians, who are strong in ancient lore, worship me with rites that are truly mine and call me by my real name which is Queen Isis (Apuleius, *Metamorphoses* XI.5).

Unfortunately Apuleius, who knew about witchcraft medicine and who was accused of sorcery because of this,[32] has provided us with no information about the fruit of knowledge that his hero had eaten before experiencing the divine revelation. It has been speculated that the mystery cults[33] used psychoactive substances in order to induce psychedelic visions (Wasson et al., 1984; Needham, 1986; Smith, 1970).[34] At the same time it is quite likely that the preparations were made from plants that are sacred to the gods and goddesses (see box on page 89). Very probably they were used in the rites of Deo, the Minoan Great Goddess, who became Demeter in Greece (Kerényi, 1976 and 1991). During intoxicated temple orgies psychoactive mandrake beer was enjoyed in honor of the love goddess (Fühner, 1925; Rätsch, 1994 and 1996b).

---

[31] Hecate was the first goddess on the island of Aigina, which lies on the coast of Attica and on the Isthmus of Corinth. According to legend it is the place where Orpheus established Hecate's mysteries: "Of all the gods the Aiginete honor Hecate the most, and every year they celebrate a festival of Hecate and say that Orpheus, the Thracian, had initiated the festival. Within their surrounding wall is a temple. The religious symbol is a work of Myron made from wood, and includes the face and the entire body on one piece. In my opinion, Alcemenes was the first to make images of Hecate with three on one another, who the Athenians call Epipyrgidia" (Pausanias, *Itinerary of Greece* II.30.I). The sacred mysteries of Isis or Hecate were also written down on papyrus in late antiquity (Graf, 1996: 164).

[32] The author, born in the African province of Madaura (now Mdaourouch, Algeria), successfully defended himself at his "witch trial" between 156 and 161 C.E. His defense *(Apologia)*, which has been preserved, shows him to be a word artist, a *philisophus Platonicus*, and an excellent student of the natural worlds. Thanks to his rhetorical arts his accusers were forced to set him free (Graf, 1996: 61–78). The accusations included the use of a poisonous *lepos marinus* (sea hare, *Aplysia depilans*) and of oath formulas to heal. Apuleius argued, "My opponents must prove that it is necessary to be a sorcerer or *venificus* [black magician] in order to be able to heal" (Graf, 1996: 73).

[33] In "enlightened" Rome most initiatory cults and secret rites were forbidden because they could not be controlled: "Nightly sacrifices by the women should not take place without permission with the exception of those that are performed for the Roman people. And no one should initiate anyone except as it is commonly done for Ceres [Demeter], according to Greek ritual" (Cicero, *On Law* II.21).

[34] Traditional Greek scholars usually vehemently deny the "drug hypotheses" as an explanation of the mystical experience in the initiatory rituals (cf. Burkert, 1990 and 1997). However, their drug paranoia undoubtedly stems from the long-standing campaign to demonize psychoactive substances (see "Witches' Medicine—Forbidden Medicine," page 198).

The Names of the Great Goddess and Her Sacred Plants (selection)

GODDESS	HER SACRED PLANT(S)	
Cybele/Rhea	Pine, stone pine	*Pinus pinea* L.
	Almond tree	*Amygdalus communis* L.
Athena/Minerva	Olive tree	*Olea europaea* L.
	Pellitory	*Tanacetum parthenium* (L.) Schultz Bip (syn. *Matricaria parthenium* L., *Pyrthrum parthenium* Sm.)
	Agrimony	*Agrimonia eupatoria* L.
Aphrodite/Venus	Mandrake	*Mandragora officinarum* L.
	Myrtle	*Myrtus communis* L.
Artemis/Diana	Artemisia	*Artemisia* spp.
	Wormwood	*Artemisia absinthium* L.
	Life everlasting	*Gnaphalium stoechas* L.
Persephone/Proserpina	Plantain, *herba proserpinacia* (herb of Proserpina)[35]	*Plantago* spp.
	Knotgrass	*Polygonum aviculare* L.
	Sweet violet	*Viola odorata* L.
	Mistletoe	*Viscum album* L.
Demeter/Ceres	Poppy	*Papaver somniferum* L.
	Barley, wheat	*Hordeum* spp., *Triticum* spp.
Hera/Juno	Lily	*Lilium candidum* L.
	Weeping willow	*Salix babylonica* L.
	Pomegranate	*Punica granatum* L.
Mâ[36]/Bellona	possibly belladonna	*Atropa belladonna* L.
	Bellonaria[37]	not botanically identified
Hecate/Trivia	Monkshood	*Aconitum* spp.
	Nightshade plants	(Solanaceae)
	"Mandragora"	*Atropa belladonna* L.
	Pontic rhododendron	*Rhododendron ponticum* L.
Nemesis/Rhamnusia	Flowering ash	*Fraxinus ornus* L.
Isis	European vervain	*Verbena officinalis* L., *Verbena procumbens* Forskal
	Water lily	*Nymphaea coerulea* Savigny
	Lotus lily	*Nymphaea lotus* L.
	Sea wormwood	*Artemisia maritima* L. var. *gallica*
	Southernwood	*Artemisia abrotanum* L.

[35] Linnaeus named a genus in the Haloragaceae family *Proserpinaca*.

[36] Mâ is a Cappadocian goddess related to the Great Mother and, like Cybele, is honored with wild orgiastic rituals.

[37] This plant "was used as a necromantic medium, sometimes as an incense, sometimes as a powder" (Gessmann, n.d.: 24).

In the Orphic mysteries and other Dionysian rituals it is possible that psychedelic mushrooms were ingested (Ruck, 1982; Wohlberg, 1990).

The Sacred Herbs of Isis

"Oh Vervain! Let your work be in our favor,
And let your blessings rest on the witch or the elf who gave you to me!"

—Charles Leland, *Aradia—*
Die Lehre der Hexen
[Aradia—The Teachings
of the Witches], 1979

The original Egyptian goddess Isis is called the "the one with magical power," "the magical being," and the "great sorceress." She was the goddess "with the thousand names." She was "great with magical powers," and had the reputation of intelligence, cunning, wisdom, and perseverance. Her soul was identified with Sirius, just as the astral soul of her brother, Osiris, was identified with Orion. There was a plant, which unfortunately has not yet been botanically identified, that was known as the "protection of Isis." In late antiquity the Great Goddess was depicted as a snake (cobra),[38] and thus symbolizes the mystical power of the serpent. Therein she is equal to Hecate and the Asian Kali (cf. Mühlmann, 1984). Isis lives on in the image of the Mother Mary with the baby Jesus.

Isis was all-knowing. Even the secret name of the sun god Ra, the most inner secret of the energy of life, was discovered by her—thanks to her magical powers and cleverness. This is why she was *the* Goddess of the Mysteries (Giebel, 1990). Many prayers to the Great Goddess and magical healers have been preserved. For example:

> Oh Isis, great in the art of magic! Release me, free me from all wickedness, evil, and burdens, from being haunted by a god or goddess, by a dead man or a dead woman, from an enemy who wants to battle me, just as you released and freed your son Horus. For I have gone into the fire and came out of the water, and I will not fall into the snares of these days. I have spoken, [and now] I am young (from the *Ebers Payrus*).

The cult of Isis was not only a mystery cult, but also a mystical healing cult. In the center stood Isis, the divine sorceress, the protective mother and goddess of the medicinal plants and poisons (Budge, 1996: 13). Next to her reigned Osiris as the shamanic god, who was later identified with the Greek physician-god Asclepius. Isis was a true shaman, as has been told in many myths. After Osiris, who had been dismembered, was reborn through his sister, Isis, he copulated with her out of sheer gratitude and joy. Out of this union of the initiated shaman and the Great Goddess came Horus—the all-seeing and all-knowing god with the visionary eyes. In other words, shamanic initiation leads to cosmic wisdom. At first Osiris was a mortal human, and through the divine sorceress was transformed into an immortal god. Because Osiris and Isis were twins, Isis must also have been human. She was initiated through the plants and made divine.

It is said that the plants of Isis sprouted from her sweat as it fell to earth (Budge, 1996: 24). One of her most important plants was vervain (*Verbena officinalis* L.). This plant was also called druids' herb, Juno's tears, or holy herbe; in Dutch it is known as *Iser cruit* (iron herb). The German common name for the plant, *Eisenkraut* (iron herb), comes from the metal iron, the plant's "iron-hard" character in folk etymology, or from Isis herself.[39] Of her sacred plants it is said in the ancient texts:

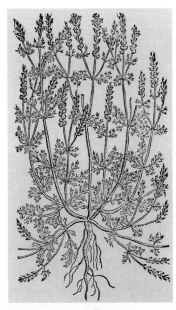

Vervain (*Verbena officinalis* L.) was a sacred plant of the Egyptian goddess Isis and a magical herb of the Celtic druids. (Woodcut from Gerard, *The Herbal*, 1633.)

---

[38] In Berlin in the Egyptian Museum there is a fantastic statue of Isis as the royal cobra that dates from late antiquity.

[39] It is similar to *Eisenhut* (iron hat), the German word for *Aconitum napellus*. It is usually assumed, for instance, according to Marzell (1935: 79), that this name refers to "the helmet or the hat-shaped form of the upper petals." But the earliest example of this name is found in Hieronymus Bock (1539); here the plant is called *Isenhutlein*, which translates as "little iron hat," but more likely means "hat of Isis."

Hiera. The Latin people call it Verbena. It has received this name from the Greeks because the priests use it during purification ceremonies. . . . The entire plant with the leaves and the roots is healing, crumbled in wine for snake bites, as well as laid on wounds and administered as a drink. It is also useful in the case of four-day fevers. For this purpose one drachma, that is three scruples, of leaves with equal amounts of frankincense [turis] is crumbled into a pound of old, hot wine and administered on an empty stomach throughout the four days. [It heals] ulcers and wounds. It soothes [inflammation], when the crushed leaves are used a compress. It cleans contaminated wounds and allows them to heal. Mouth and throat diseases do not proliferate further into the body when the whole plant is cooked in wine and used as a gargle (*Medicina antiqua* 55, fol. 154r).

Pliny used "vervain [sideritis] crushed with stale grease" as an effective aphrodisiac (*Natural History* XXVI.93). The sacred plants, or *heirobotane*, were also famous in other places:

The powder of the plant *peristeron* [dove herb], administered with a drink, cures all effects of poison. It is said that the magicians use it because of its effects, first as the Homeric [moly], then as mithridat and centaurea; administered as a drink, it lifts all bad medicine and guides it through the digestive tract (*Medicina antiqua* 67, fol. 73v).

The *peristereon* or *hierobotane* was called *persefonion*, "plant of Persephone," by the classical prophets. It was known to the people of Tuscany as *demetria*, "[plant] of Demeter," and *bounion*, "plant of Hera/Juno" (Zotter, 1980: 63, 135). It was associated with other goddesses who, according to Apuleius, were identical to Isis. The name *peltodotes*, "bestows love magic," has also been passed down. Pliny, who usually did not make positive references to magic and ritual, described the magical and healing qualities of vervain, the divine plant of Isis:

No plant however is so renowned among the Romans as *hiera botane* [sacred plant]. Some call it *asistereon*, and Latin writers *verbenaca*. . . . With this the table of Jupiter is swept, and homes are cleansed and purified. There are two kinds of it; one has many leaves and is thought to be female, the other, the male, has fewer leaves. . . . It grows everywhere in flat, moist localities. . . . Both types are used by the people of Gaul in fortune-telling and in uttering prophecies, and the Magi (the druids) especially make the maddest statements about the plant: that people who have been rubbed with it obtain their wishes, banish fevers, win friends and cure all diseases without exception. They add that it must be gathered about the rising of the dog star without the action being seen by the moon or by the sun; that beforehand atonement must be made to earth by an offering of honeycomb and honey; that a circle must be drawn with iron round the plant and then it should be pulled up with the left hand and raised aloft; that leaves, stem and root must be dried separately in the shade. They also say that if a dining couch is sprinkled with water in which this plant has been soaked the entertainment becomes merrier. As a remedy for snake bites it is crushed in wine (*Natural History* XXV.105f.)

The Garden of Hecate

According to Hesiod, Hecate was the daughter of the Titan Asteria.[40] Zeus worshipped her above all others, and she was given part of the sky, the earth, and the ocean (underworld), which meant that she could be effective in those places. Among the humans Hecate was the "one of the most honored immortal gods," and was "the teacher of young men from the beginning" (*Theogony* 415, 452).

Hecate lived in a cave, the grotto of Hecate, which was possibly found on Samothrace (Maas, 1974: 176). In Colchis there was a "splendid shrine" to Hecate (Apollonius, *Argonautica* III.842). Hecate was also a goddess of the shamans. She bestowed "illuminating rituals that are, and should be, secret" (Seneca, *Medea* 6). She was called "goddess of the gate," "stealth runner," "the night transformer," "the underworldly one," the "terrible goddess of the leaders," or "raging anger enveloping the flame-eyed dogs," "Tartaros' child," the "goddess of the divine necessity," or even "the excrement eater."

Hecate is the "lady of the underworld," according to Eusebius (c. C.E. 260–339), the Christian and Greek ecclesiastical writer. She is the "mistress of all evil demons,"[41] and also the "black one," or, like Aphrodite, "the demon of love madness." She is the mother of the Italian Circe, and aunt or mother of Medea of Colchis (Georgias), the cosmic "super witch" (Luck, 1962: 61). Hecate brings deep sleep and disturbing dreams, causes epilepsy (the "sacred disease") and insanity (*mania*), and also could bring forth altered states of consciousness: "And propitiate only-begotten Hecate, daughter of Perses, pouring from a goblet the hive-stored labour of bees" (Apollonius, *Argonautica* III.1035ff.).[42]

Hecate is the threefold goddess who often manifests in three separate goddesses: Hecate, Artemis, and Selene (Spretnak, 1984). She has three heads: horse, human, and dog; thus she is also directly connected with Cerberus, who is likewise three-headed: "Cerberus had three dog heads, the tail of a dragon, and on his back the heads of all kinds of snakes" (Apollodorus I.9).

Cerberus is a mythological dog who guards the entrance to Hades, the realm of shadows and the dead. He is the classic image of the "hounds of hell." Cerberus also created the two most important witches' plants in European history. When the half-divine hero Hercules brought Cerberus to the light of day for the first time in the context of his twelve tasks in the underworld, the raging dog angrily sprayed his slave. Where his urine fell to the earth sprouted the first henbane and monkshood[43] (Pliny, *Natural History* XXVII.4–5). After this assignment, Hercules was purified by Eumolpus and then initiated into the Eleusinian mysteries (Apollodorus I.9).

The "herb of Hecate" was a famous magical substance, which was even used by the gods for their own purposes:

The three-headed goddess Hecate with dog, horse, and steer heads. Above left and right, the goddess with six arms. (Woodcut from Vicenso Cartari, *Imagini delli Dei degl'Antichi*, 1647.)

---

[40] Kallimochos left a remarkable note behind. According to it, Hecate was created in Ephesus out of a woman who had been executed, after Artemis hung her own jewelry on the hanged woman (Burkert, 1997: 96). Five centuries after Hesiod, the Roman Cicero discussed whether or not Asteria and Hecate were really gods (Cicero, *The Nature of the Gods* III.46).

[41] "Thales of Miletus (650–560) saw the world full of demons who brought the humans dreams and diseases. According to Xenocrates they live in the region beneath the moon and mediate the interactions between the gods" (Wolf, 1994: 34).

[42] Aegolethron, the pontic rhododendron (*Rhododendron ponticum*, syn. *Azelea ponticum*; Roman field rose), which produces psychoactive honey, also belongs to the sacred plants of Hecate (Dierbach, 1833: 197).

[43] "The name of this plant comes from the name of the hill Aconitos in Pontos, where Hercules brought Cerberus, the hound of hell, up from hell. . . . An extremely interesting plant, important in homeopathy for all conditions that have to do with fear brought on by the hounds of hell" (Gawlik, 1994: 148 f.).

[Pallas Athena] flung at [the human] Arachne juice pressed from one of Hecate's herbs. Touched by those magic drops, Archane's hair fell out; her nose and ears dropped away; her head became tiny; her whole body shrank; and slender, fingerlike limbs grew from her sides as legs. The rest of her was belly, from which she spins a thread to weave as she wove before, for she is a spider now" (Ovid, *The Metamorphoses* VI.139ff).

Henbane: The True Pharmakon of the Witches

Hecate was—astonishingly—intimately connected with the sun god Apollo. Apollo was as alien to the early Greeks as Hecate. He was a wild and ecstatic god of the Hyperboreans and was subsequently displaced through the classical Hellenization of Greece. His original being is made clear in his second name—in the earliest times he was ritually invoked as Hecatos (Kerényi, 1966: 34). He was also a kind of twin of the witch goddess. On the other hand he was the younger twin of the Delik Artemis, who stood by as his midwife even though she had barely been born herself (Apollodorus, *Library* I.4).

Apollo was one of the most important oracle gods. According to Apollodorus (*Library* I.4) he learned divination from Pan.[44] Laurel was sacred to Apollo as well as Hecate. Her most sacred plant, however, was the white henbane (*Hyoscyamus albus* L.).

Henbane was called *apollinaris*, "the [plant] of Apollo," by the Romans.[45] In Latin it is also called *symfoniaca* or *insanin*, meaning "insanity [causing]." The Greeks knew it by the name *Hyoskiamos* (pig bean), or *Pitonionca* (dragon plant). The Celtic Gaels called it *bellinotem*, "herb of the [oracle god] Belenos" (Zotter, 1980: 67). Henbane has psychoactive and strong hallucinogenic activity, and was the most important medium of divination in antiquity. For this purpose the smoke from the herb or seeds was usually inhaled by the Pythians, sibyls, prophets, and Germanic Alrunas. They were able to divine and give oracles through the trancelike or visionary state of consciousness induced by the plant (Rätsch, 1987b).

Henbane was one of the most important plants of antiquity.

For wounds that won't heal and spider bites: crush the plant apollinaris together with old unsalted fat in a bowl of old, odorless wine—[take] one pound of fat—make a kind of salve and rub it on the wound; [the patient will be] healed astonishingly fast (*Medicina antiqua* 23, fol. 41v).

Henbane salve was also used in other ways.

For swelling of the knees or the shin bones or calves, or wherever: putting crushed symfoniaca that has been worked into a salve with sheep manure and some vinegar on it relieves the swelling" (*Medicina antiqua* 5, fol. 25r).

"It is said that Apollo discovered this plant and gave to Asclepius. This is why it bears the name Apollinaris."

—MEDICINA ANTIQUA 23, FOLIO 41V

"Henbane, with its yellow flowers, is one of the favored plants of the women who know about nature, the ones who want to have control over their own wombs."

—RHEA ROTHER, "MODERNE HEXEN, DIE ANF NATURMEDIZIN VERTRANEN" ["MODERN WITCHES RELY ON NATURAL MEDICINE"], 1997

---

[44] In Ovid the god Apollo said of himself, "Because of me what's going to happen, what has happened, and what's happening right now are all known. Because of me words and music make perfect harmony" (*The Metamorphoses* I.515ff.).

[45] Zotter (1980: 91) identified the apollinaris of Pseudo-Apuleius as ashwaganda (*Withania somnifera* [L.] Dunal, syn. *Physalis somnifera* L., *Solanum somniferum* nom. Nud.). Hunger (1935) considered this apollinaris to be the lily of the valley (*Convallaria majalis* L.). Interestingly, it was written in the *Herbarium* of the Pseudo-Apuleius that this apollinaris was called *dicea* or *strigmon manicon* by the Greeks. *Dicea* is usually identified with mandrake (*Mandragora officinarum* L.), *strigmon manicon* with the nightshades (*Solanum* spp.), belladonna (*Atropa belladonna* L.), thorn apple (*Datura stramonium* L.), or nux vomica (*Strychnos nux-vomica* L.).

Since antiquity the idea that women, with bared breasts and magical incense, invoked the gods, demons, or devil has held sway. (Steel-plate engraving by Herbert Horwitz, *Beschwörung* [Invocation], 1901.)

Henbane was also used externally or internally as a pressed juice for hernias, foot or liver pain, and lung problems. The root, when cooked in wine and chewed, relieved toothache. The plant was also one of the gynecological medicines: "Symfoniaca juice, mixed with saffron [*Crocus sativus* L.] and drunk—the wonderful effects you will marvel at" (*Medicina antiqua* 5, fol. 25r).

Henbane was a famous aphrodisiac and for this reason a favorite additive to the love potions of the Thessalian witches. But it is also sacred to Zeus/Jupiter, the god father, as the widespread common name Jupiter bean demonstrates (Schoen, 1963: 36). An invocation to henbane from late antiquity that gives an idea of the former usage has been preserved.

The physician of late antiquity, Alexander of Tralles on Pontes (6th century C.E.) recorded an invocation that he must have somehow heard from the people. It was an invocation of henbane against gout: It was buried when the moon was in the sign of Aquarius or Pisces, before sunset, but without touching any other roots; indeed one must only use two fingers of the left hand, with the thumb and the doctor (ring) finger, digging while speaking, "I beseech you, sacred herb, tomorrow I shall call to you in the house of Phileas, so that you might relieve the flow of the feet and hands [gout, rheumatism] of this man or woman. I swear to you with the great names of Joath, Sabaoth, who is the god, who scorched the earth and made still the ocean despite a great amount of inflowing rivers, who dried the site of Lot and transformed into a salt pillar. Take in you the spirit of the earth, your mother, and her power and dry the river of the feet or hand of this man or this woman!" On the following day the bone of any dead animal is taken, the herb is dug out with it, the root is seized, and the following words were spoken, "I invoke the holy names of Jaoth, Sabaoth, Adonai, Eloi!" Then the roots are strewn on a handful of salt and hung around the sick person, taking care that they don't become wet. The rest of the root is placed for 360 days over the fire (Marzell, 1964: 67ff.).

Black henbane (*Hyoscyamus niger* L.) is also one of the most sacred plants of the Germans and Vikings (Robinson, 1994). In particular they use the plant that is ritually cultivated in henbane gardens, the so-called sacreda acres.[46] Henbane was particularly important in divination, in weather magic, in finding treasure, and as a mead spice for libation and drinking. According to Germanic tradition the magical plant must be dug up by a naked girl "who is possessed by the magical spirit" (Höfler, 1990: 91). This explains the demonization of the plant in the wake of the Catholic conversion of central Europe: the former sacred medicinal plants of the heathens were devalued as satanic witches' herbs (Müller-Ebeling, 1991). In addition, during the Inquisition the use of henbane was considered proof for convicting a person of being a witch (Hug, 1993).

According to sixteenth century legal records from Goslar a witch acknowledged that she bewitched people for money, causing them to buy goods that nobody wanted, regardless of the cost. For this purpose she strew henbane seeds in front of the store as she spoke: "So shall the people like all of my goods, as if Saint John stood on the sacred place" (Marzell, 1964: 47).

---

[46] "The broad distribution of henbane demonstrates that the plant was cultivated for the preparation of an inebriating substance—most certainly the very oldest" (Meyer, 1894, in Höfler, 1990: 91).

Farmer's tobacco (*Nicotiana rustica* L.), once called yellow henbane or English tobacco, contains potent amounts of nicotine. It was well known for its psychoactive effects and was called "drunkenness." The plant was considered by Johannes Weyer to be an active ingredient in witches' salves. Salves made from the leaves of the tobacco plant and olive oil were used for the treatment of tumors and wounds. The plant also served as a pleasurable substance. John Gerard wrote, "It is used of some in stead of Tabaco, but to small purpose or profit, although it do stupifie and dull the senses and cause that kind of giddinesse that Tabaco doth, and likewise spitting; which any other herbe of hot temperature will do, as Rosemary, Time, winter Savorie, sweet Marjerome, and such like: any of the which I like better to be taken in smoke than this kinde of doubtfull henbane." (Woodcut from Gerard, *The Herbal*, 1633.)

During a witch trial in 1648 the accused was charged with giving a farmer whose ox had escaped "nine henbane buttons" so that he could find the animal again (Duerr, 1978: 166). An ancient shamanic practice was present here—namely the finding of lost objects while in a clairvoyant trance induced by a psychoactive substance.[47]

In 1529 a Pomeranian woman in Gotha, Germany, accused of being a witch admitted that she had made a man "crazy" (in other words, lusty), by putting henbane seeds in his shoe. Some of the things that the herb-woman, Konne Bocksdorf, knew about the herb were documented in her trial. On each day of the week she gathered a different herb: "Sunday she wanted to rest. But because it was a blessed day [being the day of the sun god Helios/Sol/Apollo] the poison was banished from henbane, and that is why she quickly picked this herb from the edges of the nearby roads. Those who couldn't sleep because of a toothache placed it under the pillow or burned the seeds on glowing coals and inhaled the smoke" (Ludwig, 1982: 162).

The psychoactive and aphrodisiac traits of henbane were well known at the time of the Inquisition (Fühner, 1919; Heiser, 1987). The burning of henbane as an incense or fumigation probably has a long tradition in Europe (Golowin, 1982b).

In 1586, the celebrated physician Matthiolus said he had observed farm children eating henbane seeds: "They were momentarily mad, foggy, and confused, so that the parents thought they were possessed by evil spirits." In the early modern era henbane seeds were strewn on the hot oven plates in bathhouses "so that the bathers, who sat in the little bathhouse, stumbled into one another" (Höfler, 1990: 91). Henbane, known as *Bilsenkraut* or *pilsner chrut* in German, was the most important beer additive from Germanic times up to the Bavarian beer purity laws in 1516 (Rätsch, 1996b).

Just as witchcraft medicine was forced underground, knowledge about the traditional use of the psychoactive henbane disappeared from public consciousness (Müller-Ebeling, 1991; Schurz, 1969). With the advent of the beer purity laws the medicinal uses of henbane were forgotten. Nevertheless, in this century it was still prescribed in the form of cigarettes for asthmatics, but in medicine it has been replaced by the isolated alkaloid, in particular scopolamine. Nevertheless, henbane remains an official drug and is thus obtainable from pharmacies (DAB [German pharmacopoeia] 8, Ph. Helv. VI). Henbane oil *(Oleum hyoscyami)*, which is particularly good for erotic massage, can also be procured there.

Monkshood As Medicine

Monkshood, "the saliva of Cerberus," was already a feared poison during antiquity. The name *akoniton* came to be used as a general term for numerous poisonous plants (see chart on page 98), but especially for the different monkshoods. Today monkshood (*Aconitum napellus* L.) is considered the "most poison plant of Europe." Hardly any of the ancient medicinal uses of the herb have been passed down. But in India it is still used as a drug; the dried leaves are smoked by yogis and sadhus, in particular the *aghoris*, who are in service to the dark goddess Kali (Svoboda, 1993: 175). Perhaps herein lies a key to the understanding of the role of monkshood in the original cult of Hecate, for this plant is so intimately connected with the witch goddess and her priestesses that it really is considered the classic witches' herb (Bauerreiss, 1994; Hansen, 1981).

---

[47] For this purpose the Nightshade family is usually used (*Datura* spp., *Brugmansia* spp., *Latua pubiflora* (Griseb.) Baillon, *Solanum* spp., *Nicotiana* spp.), as are psilocybin-containing mushrooms (*Psilocybe* spp.). All of these plants were demonized during the witch mania (see appendix).

What was once identified as *akonitum* is also known today as the feared poisonous plant one berry or herb Paris (*Paris quadrifolia* L.). It was especially used as a remedy for gout. Until recent times a ritual for the gathering of the plant was preserved in the Bohemian forest, complete with herbal invocation. In order for the desired healing power to be released, it must be picked by moonshine, after the following charm has been spoken (Marzell, 1964: 77).

Oh one berry, who planted you?
Our Lady with her five fingers true
Through all her might and power
She brought you here to flower,
That I shall have my health.

Only when the divine radiance from the Mother Goddess is combined with the collection ritual does the plant receive its power—a typical characteristic of witchcraft medicine (Storl, 1993a). By the way, one berry is only weakly "poisonous" (Roth et al., 1994: 538); it would be more properly included in the forgotten psychoactive plants of the European flora.

The Shamanic Goddess and Her Shaman, Orpheus

Hecate is also considered to be the wife of Pluto and is often called Proserpina. On the earth she is Diana, and at the same time she is known in the sky as Lucia[48] (Clemens, 1985: 432f.). Thus three goddesses are actually united in her, and she represents a shaman who is bound to the three realms of the world. She describes herself in a classical text of revelation.

I am the virgin of many forms, descended from heaven, with the sight of a steer, three-headed, wild, and with golden weapons. I am Phoebe experienced in the arts; I am Eileithyia [Artemis as birth goddess] who bestows light on humans, she who bears all three links to the threefold nature, like the fiery images of the ether. But with a white team I take possession of the air, while the earth determines the gender of my black children.

Now you should do everything for me, but the image is inside of him. I have the form of Ceres [Demeter], the queen of the divine fruits who wears dresses of all white and golden shoes on her feet. But my girdle encircles larcenous dragons who reach up into the heights with the pure tracks, hanging from their own heads to the tips of their toes, winding around one after the other (Clemens, 1985: 396).

The shamanic goddess was honored above all in Colchis; her garden and initiation hall were also found there.

The garden of Hecate, wherein she grew her poisonous plants and medicinal herbs, was on found Phasis. It was next to the Imperial city of Aetes surrounded by insurmountable walls nine fathoms high, protected by seven bastions and guarded by three iron towers. High on the posts of the tower stood Artemis, radiating a trembling brilliance, with a horrifying gaze that no mortal could withstand, if he did not approach with gifts and purification offerings (Dierbach, 1833: 195).

---

[48] She is also called Lucina, "the guardian of the bridal chamber" (Seneca, *Medea* 1f.)

The demigod Hercules/Herakles abducts the three-headed Cerberus from the underworld. Henbane and monkshood were created from the combination of his spit and the earth. (Woodcut from Gerard, *The Herbal*, 1633.)

"Moon, shine brightly; softly will I sing for you Goddess, and for Hecate in the underworld—the dogs tremble before her when she comes over the graves and the dark blood. I welcome you Hecate, the grim one, stay by me until the end. Make this magical substance as effective as that of Circe, of Medea, and of the blond Perimede."

—THEOCRITUS, *2ND EIDYLLION*, 3RD CENTURY B.C.E.

The Colchian garden of Hecate concealed numerous medicinal plants (see box).

There is a grove in the innermost room of the enclosure,
Where lush green wood ascends with shadowy tips,
Laurel trees and cornelian cherry and slender platanos aloft.
There are also many herbs in this place, arching over the deep roots;
Klymenos, complete with the noble asfoldelos, and adiantos,
Aristereon, most tender of plants, and kypeiros with thyron,
Kyklaminos, like the violet, and erysimon, complete with hormion,
Stoichas, then paionia, surrounded by thickets of polyknemon.
Then polion, mandragoras also, and pale diktamnon,
Krokos with sweet scent, and kardamom, next to kemos,
Smilax, dark poppy, and low chamaemelon,
Panakes and alkeja, with karpason and akoniton . . .
And many others more poisonous rose up from the ground.
—ORPHIC SONGS OF THE ARGONAUTS (910FF.)[49]

A common name for the European white elm (*Ulmus laevis* Paul.) is witch elm. In antiquity the elm was a sacred tree of the gods; it stood together with Hecate and the underworld and was regarded as the residence of dreams. (Woodcut from Gerard, *The Herbal*, 1633.)

---

[49] The *Orphic Songs of the Argonauts*, also known by the title *Orpheus the Argonaut*, were created in late antiquity (c. fifth century C.E.) and were attributed to the legendary singer/shaman Orpheus—yes, the words were placed directly in his mouth. Orpheus speaks as the narrator and participant in the history in the first person singular. The epic mainly follows the *Argonautica* of Apollonius of Rhodius (Storch, 1997: 268).

The Plants in the Garden of Hecate

ANCIENT GREEK NAME	BOTANICAL NAME	KNOWN CLASSICAL MEDICINAL USE
Adiantos	*Adiantum capillus-veneris* L. (maidenhair)	
Aigeiron	*Populus nigra* L. (black poplar)[50]	Gout and epilepsy
Akoniton	1. *Aconitum* spp.: *Aconitum napellus* L. (monkshood) *Acontium* x *cammarum* Emend. Fr. (hybrid) 2. *Paris quadrifolia* L. (one berry)	Gout
Alkeja	1. *Malva rotundifolia* L. (comon mallow) 2. *Malva alcea* L. (European mallow)	
Aristereon	maybe *Aristea cyanea* Ait. (grass-leaved aristea) or *Nivenia corymbosa* (Ker.-Gawl.) Bak. (shrub iris)	
Arkeuthis	*Juniperus* spp. (juniper)	Abortifacient, incense
Asfodelos	*Asphodelus fistulosus* L. (onion weed)	
Chamaemelon	*Chamomilla recutita* (L.) Rauschert (German chamomile) (syn. *Matricaria chamomilla* L.p.p.)	Infections
Daphne	*Laurus nobilis* L. (laurel)	Abortifacient, incense
Erysimon	*Sesamum indicum* L. (sesame) (syn. *Sesamum orientale* L.)	Love potions
Kardamom	*Lepidium sativum* L. (garden cress)	

Wych elm (*Ulmus glabra* Huds.) is called witch hasell in England. Gerard says that the branches and wood of this tree have frequent and widespread use in magic.

---

[50] "Now by the path along the plain there stands near the shrine [of Hecate] a poplar with its crown filled with countless leaves whereon often chattering crows would roost" (Apollonius, *Argonautica* III.927ff.)

ANCIENT GREEK NAME	BOTANICAL NAME	KNOWN CLASSICAL MEDICINAL USE
Karpason	*Unona aethiopica* Dunal (Ethiopian pepper)	Antidote for hemlock poisoning
Kemos	*Teucrium micropodiodes* (L.) (germander) (syn. *Micropus erectus* L.)	Love potions
Kedros	1. *Juniperus exelsa* M. Bieberstein (Greek juniper) 2. *J. communis* L. (juniper)	Wards off demons
Klymenos	*Lathyrus clymenum* L. (pea) (syn. *Cornus mascula* L.)	
Krania	*Cornus mas* L. (cornelian cherry) (syn. *Cornus mascula* L.)	
Krokos	*Crocus sativus* L. (saffron)[51]	Aphrodisiac
Kyklaminos	*Cyclamen hederifolium* Aiton (lit. "pig's bread") (syn. *Cyclamen neapolitanum* Ten., *Cyclamen linearifolium* DC.) (alpine violet)	
Kypeiros	*Cyperus longus* L. (umbrella grass)	
Leukis	*Populus alba* L. (silver poplar)	Wounds
Mandragora	1. *Mandragora officinarum* L. (mandrake) 2. *Mandragora autumnalis* L. (autumn mandrake) 3. *Atropa belladonna* L. (belladonna)	Aphrodisiac, soporific, abortifacient
Mekon keratitis	1. *Glaucium flavum* Crantz (horned poppy or "black poppy") 2. *Papaver somniferum* L. var. *nigra* (black opium poppy)	Decoction to treat dysentery Analgesic
Orminon	*Sesamum indicum* L. (sesame, certain varieties)	
Paionia	*Paeonia officinalis* L. (peony)	Gout, hemorrhoids
Platanos	*Platanus orientalus* L. (Oriental plane tree)	
Polion	1. *Teucrium polium* L. (mountain germander, poleo germander) ssp. *aureum* (Schreb.) Arcang. (syn. *Teurcium aureum* Schreb.) ssp. *polium* 2. possibly also *Mentha pulegium* L. (poleo mint)	Abortifacient, incense
Polyknemon	*Mentha cervina* L. (hart's pennyroyal)	
Rhamnos	*Rhamnus* spp. (buckthorn)	
Smilax	1. *Taxus baccata* L. (yew) 2. *Smilax aspera* L. (Italian sarsaparilla) (syn. *Smilax mauretanica* Poir.)	
Stoichas	*Lavandula stoechas* L. (lavender) spp. *pedunculata* (Mill.) Sampaio ex Roziera (syn. *Lavandula pedunculata* Cav.) spp. *stoechas*	
Thyron	*Solanum nigrum* L. (black nightshade)	

[51] In the *Orphic Hymns* Hecate is invoked as the "Sea Queen in saffron clothing"; presumably she was considered identical to Aphrodite.

The black poplar (*Populus nigra* L.) forms the foundation for the pharmaceutical poplar salve (*Unguentum populi*). The preparation is similar to the recipes for witches' salve. (Woodcut from Gerard, *The Herbal*, 1633.)

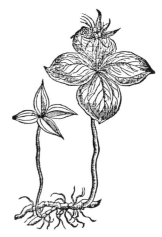

One berry (*Paris quadrifolia* L.) was considered one of the poisonous aconites in the early modern era. However, its legendary poisonous effects have not been confirmed by toxicology. It seems more likely that one berry has psychoactive effects; perhaps it was also an aphrodisiac. In any event, it is called "herbe true love" in England. In Germany one berry was demonized and called *Teufelsauge* (devil's eye). (Woodcut from Gerard, *The Herbal*, 1633.)

In antiquity the seeds of the peony were regarded as an "effective remedy against nightmares," in the Middle Ages as magical protection against bewitchment. (Woodcut from Gerard, *The Herbal*, 1633.)

In the center of this garden[52] stood a sacred tree, a mighty oak, on which the mysterious Golden Fleece hung and "gleamed like the lightning of Zeus" (Apollonius, *Argonautica* IV.184).

> *In the middle, rising to the clouds, an oak stretches over the woodlands*
> *spreading itself out and darkening the forest floor with leafy branches.*
> *See there, hanging from the long branch, shimmering with gold,*
> *Wrapped around it—the fleece; and with his keen eyes*
> *the terrible dragon, the unspeakable monster, guarding it.*
> *And the golden, shimmering flakes imprisoned him*
> *with dreadful sweeping threads striking at him from all sides,*
> *at the horrifying manifestation of Zeus' profound hatred as he watched the fleece.*
> *And the invincible hut he guarded zealously and sleeplessly,*
> *rolling his bluish eyes with inner fury.*
> —ORPHIC SONGS OF THE ARGONAUTS (923FF.)

In a strange way this image is reminiscent of the biblical tree of knowledge, which also stood in the middle of the garden. A serpent wrapped itself around this tree as well. However, this serpent led to the eating from the tree of knowledge while the dragon in Hecate's garden protects the Golden Fleece, which also corresponds to divine knowledge. Just as Eve seduced Adam to taste from the fruit of knowledge, Medea made it possible for Jason to steal the fleece.

The Golden Fleece was the hide of a golden ram that was considered to be the son of the sea god Poseidon and Theophane. Poseidon abducted the pretty maiden Theophane and transformed her into a ewe. Then he took on the shape of a ram, mounted her, and fertilized her. The sheep-shaped Theophane bore the half-god ram who could speak and fly. Hermes, the messenger of the gods, brought this animal to the suffering human woman Nephele. She had found her children Phrixos and Helle racing around the forest, intoxicated by the Dionysian mania. She commanded both of them to climb on the back of the golden ram and fly through the air on his back to Colchis and sacrifice the ram to the god Aries[53] (Apollodorus, *Library* I.9):

> But when they had mounted and the ram had carried them over the sea, Helle fell from the ram; from this the sea was called Hellespont. Phrixus, [*sic*] however, was carried to Colchis, where, as his mother had bidden, he sacrificed the ram, and placed it in its golden fleece in the temple of Mars [Aries] . . . guarded by a dragon (Hyginus, *Myths*).

The "Golden Fleece" is often interpreted as the symbol or epithet of fly agaric (*Amanita muscaria* [L. ex Fr.] Pers) (Allegro, 1970; Ruck, in Wasson, 1986: 171). Was it perhaps a psychoactive mushroom that grew on the tree of knowledge?[54]

---

[52] In later Greek sources the garden of Hecate was usually perverted into the "sacred grove of Aries" (compare Apollodorus, *Library* I.9).

[53] So it was said by Hyginus (second century C.E.), the Roman of late antiquity. He had undoubtedly been influenced by Roman machismo and replaced the Great Goddess Hecate with the warrior god Mars/Aries.

[54] Many mushrooms are mycorrhizal, which means that they grow symbiotically with the roots of certain trees. Thus the fly agaric (*Amanita muscaria*) can only grow with birch (*Betula* spp.) and pines (*Pinus* spp.). The birch is one of the most important Eurasian World Trees and shamanic trees; the fly agaric associated with it is, or was, the most important Eurasian shamanic drug (Brosse, 1990: 41ff.).

This Colchian magical garden, which was more similar to a mountain fortress than a garden, not only contained pharmacologically potent plants but was also a place of initiation into the mysteries of Hecate.[55] There Orpheus, the singer-shaman,[56] burned Rhamnos, or buckthorn (*Rhamnus oleoides* L.), and other plants, such as laurel, as fumigants in order to be initiated into the magical arts of Hecate. The buckthorn was also called *persephonion*, "plant of Persephone or Proserpina," because it was used as a sacrifice for the dead. Branches of it were hung on the door as a sort of protective amulet against poisons (Dioscorides, *Materia medica* I.119). Persephonion was also consecrated to the Eumenides, daughters of Acheron and the night, of the Furies of hell, or of the plague ghosts (Dierbach, 1833: 184).

Virgil described the underworld journey of his hero Aeneas in the sixth book of the *Aeneid*. This journey was only possible under the knowledgeable guidance of a priestess of Hecate or a sibyl, an oracle priestess and prophetess. After Hecate, "the ruler of the depths above and below," had been invoked and an animal sacrifice had been brought, she opened the gates to Orcus, a dark and ghostly place. Then they landed in the "iron chamber" of the Eumenides.

> *In the courtyard a shadowy giant elm*
> *Spreads ancient boughs, her ancient arms where dreams,*
> *False dreams, the old tale goes, beneath each leaf*
> *Cling and are numberless.*[57]
> —Virgil, *The Aeneid* (VI.281–284ff.)

Later they encountered Cerberus, who growled and threatened the intruders. But the sibyls knew how to soothe him; they gave him a magical substance of honey and poppies.[58] After he had swallowed the bait he crawled around, numb from the opium. Without the knowledge of the priestess of Hecate, Aeneas would have been lost. As a true shaman this priestess knows how to deal with dangers of the underworld and other dimensions.[59]

Peony: The Sacred Plant of the Divine Physician

The divine physician Paian (or Paion) was said to have discovered the peony (*Paeonia officinalis* L.), and he used it to heal Pluto (Homer, *The Iliad* V.401). But he must have stolen it from the garden of Hecate in order to do this. This mysterious plant was connected to the cult of Cybele and was considered to be "grown by the moon"—thus its secret name, *selenogonon* (perhaps it was originally the sacred plant of Selene/Hecate). No wonder that the peony—along homeopathic principles—is a cure for somnambulism:

---

[55] Gregorius of Nazianz (fourth century C.E.), in his poem to Nemesios (*Migne* XXXVII: 1571ff.), called the mysteries of Hecate as important as the Eleusinian, Dionysian, and Attic mysteries, as well as equal to the cults of Cybele, Isis, and Mithras.

[56] The songs of Orpheus were so bewildering that when the Moirai fell into their web "the history of the world truly stood still for a moment" (Maas, 1974: 289).

[57] In antiquity the elm was considered to be a transformed Hesperides (Apollonius, *Argonautica* IV.142ff.).

[58] Petronius reported of "oracular responses in time of plague urging the sacrifice of three or more maidens. These ate nothing but verbal dumplings coated in honey, every word and every deed sprinkled with poppy-seed and sesame! Students on this fare can no more acquire good sense than cooks living in kitchens can smell of roses."

[59] "To understand the goddess Hecate—above all in ourselves—means to understand your own inner chaos. It means to undertake journeys in your own underworld, and get to know our dark sister there—she whose existence we are all too quick to deny" (Künkel, 1988: 9).

If a person with stumbling somnambulism ties the peony plant around his neck he will immediately stand up again as a healthy person. If he always keeps the plant at his side then the evil will never touch him again. Bind the root of the peony plant in a linen and wrap it around the body parts that hurt. It has a particularly beneficial effect if you take it with you on a ship journey; it quiets the storm when you use it in its pure form" (*Medicina antiqua* 66, fol. 72v).

The peony has been associated with witchcraft medicine since early times. In his fifteenth-century herbal Hartlieb wrote about the plant:

Isaac the Jew said that when a smoke is made from the seeds of the herb, it is good for people possessed by the devil, the ones who are called *demonaci* in Latin, and for the epileptics as well. The fruits of the herb, drunken and taken with rose honey, is beneficial for the spirits that sleep with the women in the shape of a man, who are called *incubi* in Latin (Hartlieb, 1980: 75).

Another source names fifteen peony seeds in honey as protection from the incubus. Those who wore an amulet made from the plant around their necks were protected from diseases (Meyer, 1884: 61f.).

Invocations and Incense

William Shakespeare (1564–1616), whose name was perhaps a pseudonym of Francis Bacon's, demonstrated in his dramas that he not only had a good knowledge of medicinal plants, witches' herbs, and poisonous plants, but was also familiar with the ancient art of invocation (Tabor, 1970). The magical incantation of the three witches who prophesy the future in *Macbeth* draws on archaic material. Hecate even appears in *Macbeth* after the three witches invoke her.

Hecate was invoked as the most important goddess in many invocations (magical papyri) of late antiquity. She was also known by the names Artemis-Hecate and Isis-Hecate. Usually she was invoked for love magic *(phíltra)*, and was often connected to dogs,[60] even Cerberus. Medea is also invoked in the place of Hecate in the magical papyri (Luck, 1990: 50, 129ff.).

Invocations *(epaoidé, carmen)* are connected with incense. The burning of incense opens the ritual. The incense creates a sacred space and is at the same time food of the gods—a means to entice them. With the invocation a deity or a helping spirit *(daimon, parhedros)*[61] could be made serviceable. With their help one can receive healing, prophecy, or black magic. A magical papyrus indicates this recipe for a cursing ritual *(diabolé)*: "The NN brings you, dear goddess, a horrifying incense offering—colorful goat fat, and blood, and refuse, the corpse juices of a dead virgin, the heart of one who died too soon" (Graf, 1996: 163).

In his second *Idyll* Theocritus named sacrificial grain, laurel leaves, and wheat bran as incenses for the altar of Hecate, to be burned during the invocation. In Virgil *(8th Eclogue)* "masculine incense" was burned for love magic. Myrrh was also named as an incense offering during the rites of Hecate. Storax was the sacred incense of Prothyreia, of the goddess of birth *(Orphic Hymns)*. Storax has the following medicinal effects:

---

[60] Petronius wrote that the witches would "howl like a dog chasing a hare" (*The Satyricon* 63).

[61] "A magician can thus not get on without a parhedros: Only through him will anyone be able to become a proper sorcerer" (Graf, 1996: 100). In this way a sorcerer or magician is equivalent to a shaman.

It has a warming, softening, digestive energy, it is effective for coughs, catarrh, colds, hoarseness, and the loss of the voice, further it is a good remedy for congestion and hardenings in the womb and encourages, when taken internally and in suppositories, and also eases the menstruation. A small amount taken with turpentine resin soothes the body. It is also used to spread on bandages and mixed with the strengthening salves. But it was also burned, crushed, and made to coals, like incense. . . . The storax oil prepared in Syria is warming and powerfully soothing, but it causes headaches, pain (in the limbs) and dead sleep (Dioscorides, *Materia medica* I.79).

Incense of Hecate (Recipe from Late Antiquity)

Take equal parts:

Frankincense (olibanum)	(*Boswellia sacra* Flück.)
Laurel leaves	(*Laurus nobilis* L.)
Myrrh	(*Commiphora* spp.)
Rue seeds	(*Peganum harmala* L.)[62]
Storax	(*Liquidambar officinalis* L.)

Crumble and mix everything together. Then strew the incense on glowing wood embers or on special incense charcoal. The incense is quite aromatic, with the dominant scent of the storax.

---

[62] In a margin note Myrsios mentions the herb *peganon*, whose "odor can chase off snakes." Peganon is the psychoactive rue (*Peganum harmala* L.), which was used in the mysteries, according to Nicander (Burkert, 1997: 215).

The Arts of the Thessalian Witches

During antiquity in Thessaly the servants and priestesses of Hecate were already famous for their witchcraft.[63] Thessaly is a region in northern Greece that borders on Macedonia. It was considered to be the home of witchcraft and magic.[64] In the Thessalian region of Pharsalus an ancient bas-relief (from the first quarter of the fifth century B.C.E.; today it is located in the Louvre) was found on which Demeter and Persephone stand across from one another. They offer each other an identifiable mushroom.[65] Perhaps this image represents the Great Goddess with her priestesses, the "first witch." Could mushrooms, maybe even psychedelic species, have been the secret remedy of the Thessalian witches?

Magical abilities were attributed to the Thessalian witches, and they had magical sayings with which they could "draw down the moon."[66] In other words, these women could make use of the magical power of the moon.[67] The moon had, according to various

"Hecate, also called Daughter of the Night, was particularly famous for her herbal knowledge; she could identify and knew the poisonous, harmful roots as well as she knew the true medicinal herbs. She also taught her daughters about the poisonous and healing plants."

—JOHANN HEINRICH DIERBACH, *FLORA MYTHOLOGICA*, 1833

---

[63] "When someone says that the evil green stuff on the Thessalia soil and the arts of magic might be able to help, then he should try it. That is the ancient way of witchcraft" (Ovid, *The Art of Love* 249ff.).

[64] Many concepts about the Thessalian witches from late antiquity can still be found in Africa. "For the Africans, magicians and witches are people who make use of unhealthy energy for their selfish goals at the costs of other members of the community. When someone has success where others have failed, that person easily falls under suspicion of having used magical means in order to secure his advantage. In its extreme, negative form 'witchcraft' is the general term for all that is evil and threatens to undermine and destroy normal social life. For this reason, those who believe in magic attribute the magicians with a number of negative characteristics. Such anti-societal blasphemers represent the opposite of virtuousness; as a rule sexual degeneracy, incest, and what is in our context particularly important—cannibalism—belong to the stereotypes of the sorcerer" (Lewis, 1987: 373).

[65] It is not a "flower," as it has been falsely identified in the literature (for example, Baumann, 1982: 12).

[66] "Don't you know (she) is a witch; she knows Thessaliaan charms, and can draw down the moon; they do say she flies o' nights" (Lucian, *Dialogues of the Hetaerae* I).

[67] "Every witch who thought highly of herself was at least able to make the moon disappear from the sky; that means she could cause moon darkness" (Luck, 1962: 8).

classical concepts, the ability to perspire magical sweat, which in the hand of a witch revealed truly wondrous powers. There was a magic, called *virus lunare*, through which the moon could be invoked and a liquid secreted from it and dropped on herbs.[68] The moon was considered a container that filled with the divine drink soma, haoma, or ambrosia during the waxing period (Hajicek-Dobberstein, 1995; Wohlberg, 1990).

To the Thessalian witches *(veneficus Thessalus)* were also attributed the ability to transform into animals and an insatiable sexual appetite. They were legendary for their art of brewing love potions *(philter, amatoria)* as well as their knowledge of aphrodisiacs.[69] However, these preparations could "make someone crazy" (Lucian, *Dialogues of the Hetaerae* I). Special love magic could release the Dionysian ecstasy (Graf, 1996: 129). The "old women, the same kind who were said to be found in Thessalia, who understood the magical sayings," also knew the tricks of "how to make a woman, regardless of how ugly she is, desirable" (*Dialogues of the Hetaerae* IV).

The satirist Petronius (first century C.E.) described in his picaresque novel how his hero was made impotent through witchcraft: He was bewitched by a love potion. His search for help from the gods and goddesses, even from the "wondrous Circe," was futile. Finally he went to Oenothea, one of the witches experienced in the Thessalian arts. He was handled quite severely by her:

> Oenothea produced a leather phallus, sprinkled it with oil, ground pepper and crushed nettle-seeds, and proceeded to guide it by degrees up my backside. Then the sadistic old hag sprayed my thighs with the stuff. . . . She mixed nasturtium-juice [*Lepidiu latifolium* L., *L. sativum* L.] with southernwood [*Artemisia abrotanum* L.] and soaked my parts in it. Then she took a bunch of green nettles and with measured strokes began to whip all my body below my navel (*The Satyricon* 137–138).

As far back as the Middle Ages the Thessalian witches have been endowed with cannibalistic tendencies.[70] It was said that they had an enormous appetite for human flesh, used body parts for making love potions and death drinks, and even gnawed on corpses.[71] That is why there were cemetery guards who prevented the witches access to the dead. Eating human flesh or human entrails should—as Plato and after him Pausanias (*Itinerary of Greece* 8.2, 6), reported—lead to one's transformation into a wolf (Burkert, 1997: 98ff.). Petronius described how a man transformed himself on the night of the full moon.

> When I looked back at my companion, he stripped off and laid all his clothes by the side of the road. . . . He pissed round his garments, and suddenly changed into a wolf. . . . He

---

[68] This practice was placed in the mouth of the witch goddess Hecate in Shakespeare's *Macbeth* (act 2, scene 5): "Upon the corner of the moon / There hangs a vaporous drop profound: / I'll catch it ere it come to the ground: / And that distill'd by magic sleights / Shall raise such artificial sprites / As by the strength of their illusion / Shall draw him on to his confusion."

[69] In Serbia numerous recipes for similar love charms, which were attributed to the Thessalian witches, have been preserved into the twenty-first century. Included in the ingredient list is menstrual blood, vaginal secretions, bat blood, stork fat, dragon fat, apples, excrement, and more (Krauss, 1906).

[70] "The Androphagi ('man-eaters') are the most savage of men, and have no notion of either law or justice. They are herdsmen without fixed dwellings; their dress is Scythian, their language peculiar to themselves, and they are the only people in this part of the world to eat human flesh" (Herodotus, *The Histories* IV.106).

[71] The accusation that witches ate humans is found throughout many cultures (Lewis, 1989). Today cannibalism is usually represented as a colonial fantasy. But there are also theories that some humans body parts, particularly the brain, are psychoactive, and that eating them played a large role in the evolution of human beings (Linzenich, 1983).

turned into a wolf, and then he began to howl, and then he disappeared into the woods (*The Satyricon* 62).

The Thessalian witches had further traits of a scatological nature. They allegedly consumed excrement and used all sorts of animal feces and urine for the preparation of their magical and medicinal remedies (their *pharmaka* or *venena*)—an early form of the so-called *Dreckapotheke*, the "filth pharmacy."[72] In the descriptions passed down from antiquity Thessalian witches are even said to "piss long and hard in the face" of a man in order to bewitch him (King, 1988: 17). Today such behavior would be condemned to the realm of bizarre pornography or discussed in the context of urine therapy.

However, the Thessalian witches could also, thanks to their magical arts, produce brews that filled the drinker with Dionysian joy. Ovid described how a drink of this kind was prepared.

> Then [Tisiphone] yanked two snakes from her hair and with a toss of her filthy hand threw them at the pair. They slithered inside the garments and down the sheets of Ino and Anthamas and breathed their morbid breath upon them, but did not wound their bodies: It was their minds that felt the savage blows. Tisiphone [the fury] had also brought a monstrous mixture of deadly poisons: from Cerberus' mouths [henbane, monkshood], venom from the monstrous Echidna [the mother of Cerberus], the wandering blankness of darkened mind, crime, tears [resin, amber], and an insane craving to kill, ground up together, mixed with fresh blood, boiled in a bronze vat, and stirred with a green stick cut from a hemlock tree" (*The Metamorphoses* IV.495ff.).

The saga about the founding of Eritrea through the conquest of Knopos and the Kodriden reports of such a drink.

> Knopos had brought a priestess of Hecate from Thessalia, who in light of the enemies, the former Eritreans, prepared a bull sacrifice. The horns of the animal were gilded, it was decorated with rushes and led to the altar. But he had been given a substance which drove him mad and suddenly the bull broke loose and ran snorting raucously over to the enemies. They caught him and sacrificed him and had a party with his meat. Then all were seized by insanity and were easily taken by the attacking Kodriden (Burkert, 1997: 181, following Polyainos, *Stratigimata* 8.43).

In short, the image of the Thessalian witch was that of a humanized Hecate.[73]

"The plant *Basilica* grows on such places where the snake *Basilicus* is found. . . . those who carry [the plant] with him will have domain over this snake, and no evil eye nor any problems will ever harm them."
—*MEDICINA ANTIQUA*, FOLIO 117R

The three-faced and six-armed Hecate with her serpents. (Copy of a classical Gemme.)

Ancient Chinese symbol of rebirth, with serpents and a sun wheel.

---

[72] "During the initiation of a witch in Northern Italy the candidates drink a brew made up of the excrement of the giant tortoise, hair and ashes . . ." (Graf, 1996: 103).

[73] The witches were her servants too, just as they were to Hecate, the goddess: "there are women about with superhuman powers who flit around by night and bring down the firmament from above" (Petronius, *The Satyricon* 63).

The emblem of the Sumerian physician-god Ningizzida shows two serpents wrapping around a cosmic pillar or the trunk of the World Tree, flanked by two fantastic hybrids. (Illustration from Heuzey, *Catalogue des Antiquités Chaldéenes*, 1902.)

From the Snakes of Hecate to the Staff of Asclepius

Many snakes lived in the garden of Hecate. They were sacred to the goddess. For snakes are as ambivalent as Hecate herself; with their poison they can heal and they can kill. That is why the two snakes are one of the most important attributes of the witch goddess. One symbolizes healing and health; the other sickness and death. Snakes, which were protected in the temple, were also used for divination and prophecy. Perhaps the famous bare-breasted snake goddesses of Crete were forms of Hecate or her priestesses. The oldest oracle of Delphi, the "navel of the world," was Pythos, a female serpent or dragon. Her spirit lives on in Pythia, the prophetic priestess in the temple of Apollo. According to a Delphic myth it was a smoke that rose from the rotting corpse of the python killed by Apollo that Pythia inhaled in order to fall into a prophetic trance (Rätsch, 1987b). Snake handling and snake charming were already part of the witches' arts of late antiquity. "The people of Absoros could not cope with an endless number of snakes. At their entreaties Medea [who flew to Colchis on dragon's wings] gathered them up and put them in her brother's [Abystros] tomb. There they still remain, and should any go outside the tomb, it pays with its life" (Hyginus, *Myths*).

As Hecate was a goddess from Asia,[74] it is very likely that she introduced the tantric symbolism of the snakes into archaic Greece. In tantra the serpent stands for the feminine sexual energy; in this aspect it was called *kundalini*. The kundalini snake is equal in its form to a cobra.[75] At the same time it is a manifestation of the Great Goddess, especially her dark aspect, which is expressed in the figure of Kali. In the Himalayan regions and India, Kali is still considered to be a "witch goddess" (Kapur, 1983). She is still worshipped in secret rituals, invoked by witches, and nourished with blood sacrifices.[76] In general Hecate and Kali have many similarities.[77] Both have six arms, both carry torches as an attribute, and both hold daggers in their hands. Both reveal the dark side of the

Left: The ancient healing god Asclepius/Asklepios with the asclepian staff made of a torch enwrapped by a serpent. (Modeled after a relief on the ancient harbor wall on the Tiber River in Rome.) Right: Adam and Eve in paradise with the tree of knowledge, which has the diabolic serpent wrapped around it. (Medieval woodcut.)

---

[74] It is usually assumed that Asia Minor was the homeland of Hecate (cf. Kraus, 1960).

[75] Certain followers of the Kali cult, for example, the aghoris, fed their kundalini serpent by taking hemp daily. They also sprinkled cobra poisoning (cobratoxin), which contains, among other substances, neurotoxins, enzymes, and cholinesterase, on the hemp herbage to make it more potently inebriating (Rätsch, 1992: 30).

[76] In the Kathmandu Valley (Nepal) belief in witches who are able to cure illness is widespread. The witches (*bokshi*) are mostly women who have devoted themselves to black magic and the dark side of Kali. They send their souls out in order to take over their chosen sacrifice. The possessed man will become sick as the bokshi eats all of his meals and thereby steals his energy. Thus she slowly plagues him to death (Wiemann-Michaels, 1994). When a sickness is recognized as bokshi possession, a shaman or a tantric priest is called to perform an exorcism (cf. Nepali, 1988: 338f.).

[77] In archaic times a vigorous cultural exchange took place between India and Greece. Many Asian concepts infiltrated the early European world. These connections are addressed with great insight by Danielou (1982).

universe, both have destructive but rejuvenating traits—just like their symbolic animals renew their skin. Both have the power to heal and to kill.

In the Asian tantra cult a snake wrapped around stone, an egg,[78] a staff, or a phallus represents the feminine energy that is released during the sexual union between god and goddess, man and woman, leading to an altered state of consciousness (Müller-Ebeling and Rätsch, 1986). In ancient India and ancient China the entwined snakes in combination with disks or wheels are a symbol of rebirth and of the eternally regenerating creation. In Mesopotamia the symbol of the Assyrian medicine god Ningizzida (third century B.C.E.) was a snake staff. In ancient Greece the snake wrapped around a staff or a torch became a symbol of the healing god Asclepius, and eventually a symbol for the medical arts in general. "The snake of Asclepius was considered the primordial form of the god and appears many times as his representative in temple healings. From classical antiquity until late antiquity the snakes generally enjoyed great respect and were often kept as house pets" (Kasas and Struckmann, 1990: 22).

The Dionysian followers of the Orphic mysteries believed that the world was born from a primordial egg that was hatched by a serpent.

Only the monotheists feared and demonized snakes. It was a serpent that seduced Eve, who then seduced Adam to eat the forbidden fruit of the tree of paradise. In tantra humans strive to become like gods and goddesses, to experience the mystery of being, and to receive divine knowledge. This is forbidden to believers of monotheism. Snakes not only were the personification of the devil but also became the primordial image of evil. That is why in many descriptions of witches in the modern era snakes are used as ingredients for magical potions.

The staff of Asclepius was originally the symbol for the tree of knowledge. In the healing cult of Asclepius it became the symbol of ritual medicine. In late antiquity it was considered a symbol of hermetic alchemy and the divine messenger Hermes/Mercury, until ultimately it was reinterpreted as the symbol of scientific academic medicine.

Snakes As Medicine

As is shown in the images on ancient vases, snake venom was taken as medicine or perhaps drunk as an intoxicating additive in wine. In his medicinal teachings Dioscorides wrote: "The flesh of the viper [from *Vipera aspis* Merr. and *Vipera ammodytes* Dum. et Bibr.] cooked and eaten gives one keen eyes; it is also a good remedy for neuralgia and keeps the swelling of the lymph glands down. . . . Some also say that one can reach an old age by eating it. . . . Snakeskin cooked in wine is used as an injection against earaches and as mouth rinse for toothaches. It is also included under the remedies for eyes, mainly from the viper [Asclepius snake, *Coluber aesculapii* Sturm]" (*Materia medica* II.18, 19).

Next to opium, viper flesh (in particular from the aspic viper, *Vipera aspis*) became known as a universal remedy and antidote called *theriak* and *mithridatium* during antiquity, late antiquity, and the Middle Ages. The recipe, which included up to sixty herbs, can be traced back to Andromachus, the doctor of the emperor Nero (C.E. 37–68), King Mithridates of Pontos (132–63 B.C.E.), and Celsus (c. first century B.C.E.). Snake

---

[78] In the Orphic worldview of late antiquity the universe was born from an egg wrapped with a snake. Tantric images are reminiscent of "the world egg of the Orphic mysteries which was split open by the Demiurge to make the universe. . . . For the creation of the world, according to the Orphics, resulted from the sexual act performed between the Great Goddess and the World-snake Ophion. The Great Goddess herself took the form of a snake and coupled with Ophion. . . . The Goddess then laid the world egg which contained infinite potentiality, but which was nothing in itself until it was split open by the Demiurge. The Demiurge was Helios, the Sun, with whom the Orphics identified their god Apollo—which was natural, because the sun does hatch snakes' eggs—and the hatching-out of the world was celebrated each year at the Spring festival of the Sun." Robert Graves, *The White Goddess: A Historical Grammar of Poetic Myth* (New York: Octagon, 1972), p. 248.

flesh is considered an antidote to poison. Theriak can still be purchased in pharmacies, but without either of the main ingredients: viper flesh and opium.

Fossilized shark teeth known as "snake tongues" or "tongue stones" (*Glossopetrae*) have been found since antiquity and were considered the fossilized tongues of poisonous snakes. They have served as protective amulets against poisoning since the earliest times.

Snakes have a reputation as aphrodisiacs. Today in Southeast Asia snake flesh is still considered an aphrodisiac food. In Japan a general tonic and remedy for impotence is made from the venom pressed out of living snakes.

In homeopathy the venom of different snakes (*crotalin*), particularly from the rattlesnake (*Crotalus* spp.), the aspic viper (*Vipera aspis*), and species of the genus *Lachesis*, is used in various preparations. The homeopathic remedy *Crotalus horridus* hom. is used in the third to sixth potency corresponding to the medical picture for a damaged nervous system, and is also used for spiritual functions, blood cleansing, and epilepsy, among other ailments. Snake venom is also used in allopathic medicine, usually in the form of an embrocation or injection, for the treatment of allergies, cramps, epilepsy, circulation problems, high blood pressure, rheumatism, and edema (cf. Madejsky, 1997b).

The Mandrake of Hecate

Just as Hecate and Aphrodite are different forms of the Great Goddess, her mandrakes appear to be two related species with the same qualities. The mandrake of Aphrodite, who also bears the name of Mandragoritis, "the [goddess] of the mandrake," was clearly the true mandrake (*Mandragora officinarum* L.), which grows lushly at her sacred site of Paphos—in the former "sacred garden" (Rätsch, 1993 and 1994). The mandrake of Hecate, on the other hand, was belladonna (*Atropa belladonna* L.). Both mandrakes belong to the Nightshade family (Solanaceae), and both species have been confused with one another since the earliest times. Both are psychoactive, both cause hallucinations, and both are some of the most important aphrodisiacs and ingredients for love potions and witches' salves (Schwamm, 1988).

Belladonna,[79] or "beautiful woman," is identical to the "masculine" mandrake called *morion*, which was known as "others growing near caves." *Morion* literally means "masculine member" and refers to its use as a *Tollkraut* (crazy herb; in Middle High German *toll* meant lust). Belladonna has been used as an aphrodisiac since antiquity. Other psychoactive plants that were used as aphrodisiacs were also called *Tollkraut*, for example, henbane (*Hyoscyamus niger* L.) and scopolia (*Scopolia carniolica* Jacq.). In German *Atropa belladonna* and *Scopolia* are both known as *Walkenbaum* or *Walkenbeere*. These names are said to derive from the word *Walküre* (Valkyrie) (Perger, 1864; Schwamm, 1988: 45).

The botanical genus name for belladonna, *Atropa*, which was coined by Linnaeus, comes from Atropos (the Dreadful/the Pitiless). She was one of the three Moirai, or goddesses of fate (Parcae, Norns), who decided life and death. Atropos is the one who cuts through the threads of life. Hecate was a "daughter of the night" and therefore a sister of the three Moirai (Hesiod, *Theogony* 211–232).

Hildegard of Bingen had already begun demonizing the former heathen ritual plants.

Belladonna has coldness in it, but this coldness also holds evil and barrenness, and in the earth and at the place where it grows, a diabolic influence has some share and

[79] There is also a belladonna lily (*Amaryllis belladonna* L.), which is very poisonous (Gawlik, 1994: 149).

"The true mandragora is the 'tree of knowledge,' and the love that burns when eaten is the origin of the human race."

—HUGO RAHNER, *GRIECHISCHE MYTHEN IN CHRISTLISHE DEUTUNG* [GREEK MYTHS IN CHRISTIAN INTERPRETATION], 1957

participation in its craft. It is dangerous for a person to eat or drink, since it will disorder his spirit, as if he were dead (*Physica* I.52).

Belladonna was further demonized in the early modern era, and was called "devil's berry," "devil's eye," and "devil's cherry." It was considered a dangerous, poisonous, and demonic witches' plant and was associated with witches' salves (see table on page 135). But because belladonna poisoning can easily be fatal, it has never played a big role as a magical plant. Belladonna has probably been used since antiquity in a manner similar to mandrake or scopolia. Belladonna root was possibly used as a substitute for mandrake or as an alternative to it. In any event, rudiments of the belladonna cult have been preserved in related folk customs. In Hungary, for instance, the roots "are dug up on the night of Saint George, naked, after bringing an offering of bread to the nightmarish monster" (Höfler, 1990: 90). In Romania belladonna is called "wolf cherry," "flower of the forest," "lady of the forest," and "queen of the herbs" (Eliade, 1982). Although belladonna is considered the classic witches' plant, only a few bits of information about its magical use in witches' rituals have been passed down. Giovanni Battista della Porta (c. 1535–1615) wrote in his work about "natural magic" that through the use of belladonna one could be transformed into a bird, a fish, or a goose—the sacred sacrificial animal of Odin—for winter solstice and thereby have a lot of fun.

Since antiquity belladonna has been used medicinally as a narcotic for pain. It was often used to "chase off demons"; in other words, it was used for the treatment of depression, psychosis, and spiritual diseases. It was said that "belladonna healing is an effective remedy for the 'traveling'—an 'illness caused by a demonic perspective,' which usually befell the victim suddenly as headaches and pain in the limbs" (Schwamm, 1988: 44). Rudiments of the common psychiatric use have been preserved in North Africa.

In the nineteenth century roots and herbal extracts of belladonna were used for the treatment of jaundice, dropsy, whooping cough, convulsive cough, neurosis, scarlet fever, epilepsy, various skin diseases, eye infections, diseases of the urinary and respiratory tracts, and disorders of the gullet, kidney, and nerves.

A base tincture made from the entire post-flowering fresh plant (*Atropa belladonna* hom. *PFX* and *RhHab1*, *Belladonna* hom. *HAB1)* in different potencies (usually beginning with D4) are often used in homeopathy, corresponding to the medical presentation (Vonarburg, 1996).

The powerful hallucinations brought on by belladonna are usually described as threatening, dark, demonic, diabolic, hellish, and profoundly scary. Many users speak of a "Hieronymus Bosch trip" and are not usually willing to repeat the experiment (Illmaier, 1997).

The Mandrake of Aphrodite

In ancient Athens, Venus was worshiped as Urania "in the garden" (Pausanias, *Itinerary of Greece*). Although we know next to nothing about her cult we can infer from the inscriptions about her cult image, a kind of hermaphrodite, that she was a goddess of fate and the sister of Hecate. Calves were sacrificed to Aphrodite Urania—just as bulls were sacrificed to Hecate. Both goddesses were worshiped by the "sacred prostitutes," the courtesans known as the *hetaerae* (Langlotz, 1954: 28).

During Roman times the Italian Venus who was identified with Aphrodite was considered as goddess of the gardens (Schmölders, 1983: 11). In the Middle Ages the garden of Venus became *Venusberg* (Venus mountain, mons Veneris), "which has been, since the church fathers fanned the flames of fantasy, the place of heightened sensuality and greatest fulfillment of love" (Langlotz, 1954: 34).

The "golden apples of Aphrodite" were the yellow fruits of the mandrake (*Mandragora officinarum* L.) that grew in the center of the sacred garden.[80] It was the *Mandragora femina*: "Many call her apollinaris or malum terre" (*Medicina antiqua* fol. 141r); in other words, the plant was identified with or considered equal to henbane because of Aphrodite's characteristics and effects.

Mandrake has always been an important gynecological medicine, and as witchcraft medicine it was ambivalent and could be used in different ways. It has served the midwives since antiquity to increase sexual desire, to promote fertility and pregnancy, to ease birth, to numb the cesarean section, to kill the fruits of life in abortions, and to expel a stillborn (Gélis, 1989: 61ff.).

The Garden of Medea

"On long tables sat the hellish guests / a witch next to diabolic lovers / they ate aphroditic herbs / sharp spices with chopped salamanders / turtles / snakes / and drank Broyhahn brewed in Hannoverian style."

—JOHANNES PRAETORIUS, *BLOCKSBERG VERRICHTUNG* [THE PERFORMANCE AT BLOCKS MOUNTAIN], 1668

Medea is the original image of the Western witch. She is beautiful, sensuous, and seductive. With secret salves she can make herself old and ugly or bewitch others. She has psychic gifts; she knows the power of the poisons and the effects of the herbs. She is the barbarian from a wild land. Medea is experienced in the secret art; she knows the procession of the stars and works as a priestess of Artemis.[81] She stands under the protection of the Titans and earth goddess Themis, and Artemis, whom she invoked as "sublime." Themis was, like her mother, Gaia, the second oracle goddess of Delphi, before the shrine of Apollo was annexed (Ovid, *The Metamorphoses* I.320f.). Themis, "who protects the oaths," was, as daughter of the Earth Goddess, identical either to Python, who was also born of Gaia, or to a sister of the dragon with a "poisonous

Mandrake As Medicine

"Seed of mandrake taken in drink purges the uterus, a pessary of its juice is an emmenagogue and brings away the dead fetus" (Pliny, *Natural History* XXVI: 156f.).

"It [*Mandragora officinarum* L.] is administered when, in the course of a treatment, an operation must take place, because those made numb with this drink will not feel the pain of the incision. But when you breathe in [the aroma] of the fruits or eat them they will cause sleep and numbness and will rob you of your voice; but the juice, pressed from the rind and the roots and placed in a ceramic container in the sun or over a small fire, [can] be stored for medicinal use, the dried roots can also be stored for many future treatments: for eye infections, for infected wounds, to disperse hardenings and the congestion of harmful fluids, for ergot poisoning, for snake bites, for swollen lymph nodes, for joint pain. A drink made from this plant is taken so as to not feel operations" (*Medicina antiqua* fol. 134r).

---

[80] Mandrake also grew in the garden of the Egyptian goddess of love: "Love, passion, and intoxication are united in the domain of Hathor" (Hugonot, 1992: 19).

[81] She took on the form of a priestess of Artemis for her sorcery (Hyginus, *Myths*).

stomach" (*The Metamorphoses* I.459). Medea selected the goddess Hecate/Trivia, who lived in her "hearth ground," to be her assistant and protector goddess (Euripides, *Medea* 399; Seneca, *Medea* 785). According to Seneca, Prometheus was one of her teachers (*Medea* 820ff.).

Medea can fly through the air on a dragon-drawn wagon[82] or ride through the ether on snakes. She can conjure with incense the wonder of youth and create illusions. She knows the healing arts as well as she knows black magic. Her primordial symbol is the cauldron, in which she brews poisons or makes her sorcery. Seneca, in his drama *Medea*, describes how the sorceress prepared her drink. The main ingredients are snakes and "common worm." The poet also mentions a row of barely identifiable magical plants from the botany of Medea's witches:

> Everything snakelike now evoked, she then
> prepares her fruits of evil, heaping them
> into a pile: all that the wilderness
> near Eryx grows; produce of Caucasus,
> those ridges smothered in endless winter,
> splattered with Prometheus' blood [Ferula communis].[83]
> The fighting Mede, the flighty Parthian,
> the wealthy Arab: she employs toxins
> into which they dip their arrowheads [Aconitum spp.].
> She uses juices Uebian ladies seek
> Amid the dankness of their black forests
> Under an ice-cold sky.
> Her hand harvests whatever earth creates in nesting spring
> Or when brittle frost balds trees' beauty,
> Forcing life inside itself with cold:
> Grasses virulent with dead flowers [Helleborus niger],
> Harmful juices squeezed from twisted roots [Mandragora].
> Mount Athos brought her those particular herbs.
> They came from the massive Pindus. That she cut
> on a high ridge of Pangaeus; when it lost
> its tender, hair-like crown, it left traces
> of blood on the sickle blade. *

"O night, faithful friend of mysteries; and you, golden stars and moon, who follow the fiery star of day; and you, Hecate, goddess with threefold head, you know my designs and come to strengthen my spells and magic arts; and you, earth, who offer your potent herbs to magi; and airs, winds, mountains, streams, and lakes, and all you woodland gods, and all you gods of the night: Be present now."

—PRAYER OF MEDEA TO HECATE, FROM OVID, *THE METAMORPHOSES*

---

[82] According to Apollodorus (*Library*, I.5), Demeter also had a wagon pulled by winged dragons with which she could fly through the air.

[83] *Narthex*, or giant fennel (*Ferula communis* L.), the "umbel of Dionysius," is similar in appearance and aroma to true fennel but grows up to four meters high. The woody, hollow stems were used to make the Dionysian thyro-staffs. On one hand, they were the emblem of the Dionysian cult; on the other, they were subsequent forms of archaic shamanic and magical staffs. According to the sagas the Titan Prometheus brought the gift of fire to the humans with the help of narthex. The jealous Zeus wanted to prevent Prometheus from giving everything that the gods possessed to the humans. But Prometheus stole some embers from Hephaistos' divine smithy, which he carried to Earth in the marrow of a narthex stem. The dried stem is easy to ignite but the mark burns very slowly, so that the stems are actually suitable for transporting fire. The use of fennel stems as symbols and bestowers of fertility continued into the early modern era during the witch trials. In northern Italy the heathen Benandanti, who was persecuted as a "witch," preserved the machinations of the thyro-hurling Maenads (Ginzburg, 1980).

* Translation by Frederick Ahl, *Seneca: Three Tragedies* (Ithaca and London: Cornell University Press, 1986).

Medea is still entirely the shaman, the archaic magician who has a thorough knowledge of botany, medicine, and magic (magical songs).[84] She is not yet the "evil witch" of later eras. She used her knowledge and abilities to protect and heal her friends and allies, and also to harm and destroy her enemies. Those who were afraid of her had reason for their fear; whenever she desired, she could use the "evil eye" (Apollonius, *Argonautica* IV.1670f.). In Euripides' plays she is addressed as a "lioness" (*Medea* 1316), which is possibly an indication that Medea was a skilled shaman who could transform herself into a big cat. During her invocation she bared her breasts,[85] gave her hair a lively toss, and held a snake in each hand (Seneca, *Medea*). Thus she completely resembled the Minoan snake goddess of Crete. Later she became immortal and ruled as queen of the witches and the bride of Achilles over the Elysian fields (Ranke-Graves, 1984: 577).

Medea's beauty—Hesiod called her the "pretty-footed Medea" or the "pretty-eyed"— and her erotic skills and magical arts had already fascinated the ancient poets. But she also inspired fear and disgust. Euripides dedicated an entire tragedy to her. Ovid did as well, and also voluptuously described some of Medea's feats in *The Metamorphoses*; from his play *Medea*, however, only one verse remains (Binroth-Bank, 1994; Heinze, 1997). The poetry of Euripides was used as the model for countless Medea workings in world literature. In the eighteenth and nineteenth centuries many operas were written that took on the Colchian sorceress. The allure of Medea still radiates today. For example, she has become a current topic in women's literature. Not without reason did Ursula Haas produce a *Freispruch für Medea* [Aquittal for Medea] (1991), which Rolf Liebermann set to music as an opera (1995).[86]

Medea, the blond Colchian woman with a "godlike head," came from a country inhabited by "black faced" barbarians (Apollonius, *Argonautica* III.828ff.). Her grandfather was Helios,[87] the great demiurge who cracked open the Orphic world egg (cf. Ranke-Graves, 1985). This genealogy had already been reported by Hesiod. Medea, Circe, and Hecate belong to the clan of Helios/Sol.[88] In other words, witches are the children of the sun! According to Hesiod, Medea bore a son named Medeios from her liaison with Jason the Argonaut, "who was raised in the mountains by Chiron" (*Theogony* 1001). Thus the mother who was well versed in magic had her child trained from birth in the healing arts by the shamanic centaur Chiron, who also raised Hercules.

The Magic Salve of Medea

The "all magic mediator" Medea was a famous healer: "And with oil medicating simples against stark pain [she] gave them for his use" (Pindar, *Fourth Pythian Ode* 221f.). Medea apparently learned the art of making salves from Prometheus: the *Promethion*, the

---

[84] Mühlmann considers her to be a "Scythian shaman" (1984: 74).

[85] "For you I bare my breast according to Maenadian custom, slice into my arms with sacrificial knife," speaks Medea in a prayer to Hecate (Seneca, *Medea* 805ff.).

[86] The Medea saga was used by, among others, Franz Grillparzer (1791–1872) as a trilogy (*Das Goldene Vlieβ*, 1818–1820), Hans Henny Jahnn (1894–1959) as a tragedy (*Medea*, 1931), Dagmar Nick (born 1926) as a story (*Medea, ein Monolog*, 1988), Christa Wolf in a novel (*Medea—Stimmen*, 1996), and Ljudmila Ulitzkaja as a novel (*Medea and Her Children*, 1996). The Medea material was often used for operas (for example, Marc-Antoine Charpentier's *Médée*, Luigi Cherubini's *Medea*, and Giovanni Simone Mayr's *Medea in Corinto*) and has inspired many songs, including Louis-Nicolas Clerambault's "Médée," Antonio Caldara's "Medea: Kantaten für Kontratenor solo," Jiří Antonin Benda's "Medea Melodrama," and Edison Denison's "Choeurs pour Médée." The story of Medea was also written as orchestral music in such pieces as Vincent d'Indy's *Médée suite d'orchestre* and Samuel Barber's *Medea Suite*.

[87] "For all those in the race of Helios were plain to discern, since by the far flashing of their eyes they shot in front of them a gleam as of gold" (Apollonius, *Argonautica* IV.725ff.).

[88] As moon and sun, Hecate and Helios are the parents of the race of witches (Kraus, 1960).

"Prometheus plant," is one of the most important magical substances (*pharmaka*) of Medea. This "plant of Medea" was intriguingly identified by Clark (1968) as mandrake (*Mandragora*). The "substance, which, as people say, is named after Prometheus," had wonderful powers.

> If a man should anoint his body therewithal, having first appeased the Maiden [Persephone], the only begotten [of Demeter], with sacrifice by night, surely that man could not be wounded by the stroke of bronze nor would he flinch from the blazing fire; but for that day he would prove superior both in prowess and in might. It [this plant] shot up first-born when the ravening eagle on the rugged flanks of Caucasus let drip to the earth the blood like ichor* of tortured Prometheus. And its flower appeared a cubit above ground in color like the Corycian crocus, rising on twin stalks; but in the earth the root was like newly-cut flesh. The dark juice of it [the pharmakon], like the sap of a mountain-oak, she had gathered in a Caspian shell to make the charm withal, when she had first bathed in seven ever-flowing streams, and had called seven times on Brimo [Hecate], nurse of youth, night-wandering Brimo, of the underworld, queen among the dead, in the gloom of night, clad in dusky garments. And beneath, the dark earth shook and bellowed when the Titanian root was cut; and the son of Iapetus himself groaned, his soul distraught with pain (Apollonius, *Argonautica* III.843ff.)

Medea gave precise instructions on how to use the magical salve—just like the witches' salves. "She said to Jason the Argonaut, 'And at dawn steep this charm in water, strip, and anoint thy body therewith as with oil; and in it there will be boundless prowess and mighty strength, and thou wilt deem thyself a match not for men but for immortal gods'" (Apollonius, *Argonautica* III.1042ff.).

Thus strengthened, the hero Jason could confront his duties to carry out the initiation into the mysteries of Hecate. Only conquering the dragon who guards the tree of knowledge remained, and here the priestess of the Great Goddess stood effectively at his side. "But she [Medea] with a newly cut spray of juniper [Arkeythoy, *Juniperus phoenica* L.], dipped her substance [*pharmaka*] into a mixture [*kykeon*] and sprinkled it undiluted in the eyes [of the dragon] using the magical formulas, and the enveloping intensive aroma lulled him to sleep" (Apollonius, *Argonautica* IV.156ff.).

The kykeon was the key to the mysteries of the Great Goddess (Wasson et al., 1984). The kykeon was a mixed drink[89] that was prepared from the pharmaka of the goddess—from opium, for example.

The Plants of the Atonement Sacrifice

Medea burned a funeral pyre as an incense in order to practice her magical arts; the magical smoke consisted of juniper wood,[90] kedros (*Juniperus oxycedrus* L.),[91] rhamnos (buckthorn), and poplar—all plants that were already growing in Hecate's garden (Dierbach, 1833: 203).

The Great Goddess, Deo or Demeter, sits bare-breasted beneath a sacred tree and offers her followers or priestesses an opium capsule. (Copy of a Minoan gold insignia ring from Mykonos.)

---

[89] In the *Odyssey* of Homer, Circe also called the magical drink kykeon (*The Odyssey* X.316).

[90] In the magic of late antiquity, as has been passed down in the magical papyri, small temples of juniper were built for magical rituals (Graf, 1996: 101).

[91] This species of juniper is said to have also been sacred to Apollo (Dierbach, 1833: 203); thus it was another witches' plant of the sun god!

* According to Apollonius, *ichor* is liquid that flows in the veins of gods. (Trans.)

Alkanet (*Anchusa tinctoria* L.) is one of the magical plants of Medea. (Woodcut from Gerard, *The Herbal*, 1633.)

In the early modern era the ancient magical plant ephemeron was equated not only with autumn crocus but also with loosestrife (*Lysimachia ephemerum* L., Primulaceae). This plant was cooked in wine and recommended for toothaches. (Woodcut from Gerard, *The Herbal*, 1633.)

For their atonement sacrifices, in order to ritually cleanse themselves, participants used the following additives.

> *The experienced Medea also brought to me many magical plants,*
> *which she picked from the soil of the sacred shrine,*
> *Then I quickly prepared a joyous image beneath the veil,*
> *threw it up to the woods, and finished the sacrifice of the turning point,*
> *Three very dark offspring of the she-dogs worshipped the gods.*
> *With the blood was I mixed chalkanthos herb with strouthejan,*
> *Knekos also, and onions too, along with the red anchusa,*
> *Also the potent psyllejon and chalkimos.*
> *Then with the mixture I filled the stomach of the dog, and laid her on the funeral pyre.*
> —ORPHIC SONGS OF THE ARGONAUTS (958FF.)

All of these plants, the "magical plants of Medea," were important medicines in antiquity.

The Elixir of Youth

Since time began humans have harbored the desire for eternal youth, even for immortality. The people of antiquity also shared these desires. In Sparta the love goddess Aphrodite is called Ambologera, "the one who dispels age" (Kerényi, 1966: 66). The abilities of being able to cure disease, make the old young again, make rain, forge pacts with the dead, and write poetry were attributed to the ancient magoi shamanic figures, for example, Orpheus, Pythagoras, and the brilliant figure of Empedocles (fifth century B.C.E.) (Luck, 1990: 20). Particularly famous in the ancient literature is the drink of youth, or, more precisely, the "rites of Medea."[92]

The Atonement Sacrifice Plants

Anchusa	1. *Anchusa tinctoria* L. (alkanet)
	2. *Anchusa azurea* Mill. (Italian alkanet)
	(syn. *Anchusa italica* retz.)
Chalkanthos	*Chrysanthemum coronarium* L. (crown daisy)
Ephemeron	1. *Colchicum autumnale* L. (autumn crocus)
	2. *Lysimachia ephemerum* L. (silver loosestrife)
	3. *Convallaria majalis* L. (lily of the valley)
	4. *Origanum dictamnus* L. (dittany)
Kedros	*Juniperus oxycedrus* L. (juniper)
	ssp. *macrocarpa* (Sm.) Ball
	(syn. *Juniperus macrocarpa* Sm.)
	ssp. *oxycedrus* (tree juniper)
Knekos	*Carthamus tinctorius* L. (safflower)
Psyllejon	*Plantago afra* L. (plantain)
	(syn. *Plantagospsyllium* L.)
Strouthejon	*Gypsophila struthium* L. (Greek soapwort)

---

[92] People today still dream of a magical remedy that will make them youthful again; at the moment many Americans think they have found it in Botox.

On a classical vase Medea is depicted brewing her elixir of youth. In the cauldron is a goat. The image can be interpreted in two ways: Either the symbolic rejuvenation of the goat is depicted or the goat is a symbol of the Golden Fleece. It was said that the autumn crocus (*Colchicum autumnale* L.) first sprouted out of the ground where a few drops of Medea's magical drink fell. The name *ephemeron* ("one-day flower") indicated that death would occur within one day if this plant was eaten (Carl, 1995: 85). It was called *venena Colcha* (Horace, *Odes* II.13), a phrase that is usually translated by philologists as "witches' poison."

The magical plant of Medea, which was used to make the dragon who guards the Golden Fleece fall asleep, was called *kolchikon* in antiquity. Linnaeus chose this as the genus name for autumn crocus (*Colchicum* spp.) (Baumann, 1982: 111). However, *ephemeron* could not have been identical to the colchicum (Engel, 1978: 18). Of ephemeron Virgil reports that Moeris, the shepherd with magical knowledge, used it to transform himself into a wolf (lycanthropy):

> *This herb here, this poison, gathered earlier,*
> *Moeris himself gave to me; it grows abundantly on Pontis.*
> *With it—often I saw this—Moeris transformed himself into a wolf*
> *and hid in the forest; with it he captures the souls*
> *from the grave, with it he could even transform the crops (Aeneid).*

The transformation from man into wolf was well known in antiquity and was usually traced back to eating human flesh (Burkert, 1997: 98ff.).

This magical plant of Medea was a popular medicine in antiquity.

Ephemeron has the leaves of a lily, but smaller, a stem of the same length, a blue flower, a seed of no value, a single root the thickness of a thumb, a sovereign remedy for the teeth if it is cut up into pieces in vinegar, boiled down, and used as a mouth wash. And the root also by itself arrests decay if forced into the hollow of a decayed tooth (Pliny, *Natural History* XXV.170f.)

The plant was also used externally. "The leaves of the ephemeron are applied in the form of liniments to tumors and swellings that are still able to be dispersed" (*Natural History* XXVI.122).

Autumn crocus is a remarkable plant: It blooms in the fall and produces its leaves and seeds in the spring. Because time is reversed for this plant, *Herbstzeitlose* (fall timelessness), the Germans' common name for it, persists. Through the present time in German folk customs the notion that the autumn crocus is a "docket" (puppet, girl) or a "naked virgin" has been preserved. The common names for the plant have obvious erotic interpretations: *Nacktarsch* (naked ass; Eifel region), *Nackte Hure* (naked whore; Thuringia, Franconia), *Faule Fotze* (lazy cunt; Alsace-Lorraine), *Tittenwecke* (tit-loaf; Gotha), *Hundshoden* (dog's balls), and *Oschsenpinsel* (ox penis). In English it is known as naked ladies. The withered capsule of the autumn crocus contains a brown powder that holds the tiny seeds. These capsules were called *Teufelsküche* (devil's cake) in Ertingen and *Hexenfurz* (witches' fart) in Biberach (Aigremont, 1987: vol. 2, 25f.). Thus in folk traditions the plant is connected with witchcraft medicine. The farm women of Upper Hesse still cook the leaves of the autumn crocus as a vegetable or prepare a salad from them for Walpurgis Night (Marzell, 1943: 1083).

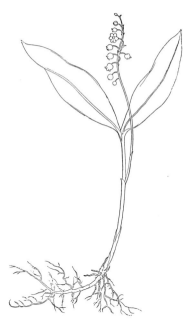

Lily of the valley (*Convallaria majalis* L., Liliaceae) was identified with the Greek ephemeron in the early modern era. A decoction of the roots was used as a mouthwash for toothaches. The pressed juice from the plant was said to strengthen the heart, brain, and liver. According to Fuchs, a decoction of the entire flowering plant was drunk for fainting, dizziness, and epilepsy. (Woodcut from Fuchs, *Neu Kreüterbuch*, 1543.)

Alkanet As Medicine

Alkanet (*Anchusa tinctoria* L., Boraginaceae) grew in the garden of Medea; it has a fleshy root that contains a bloodred pigment. When touched it turns the hands red. The juice from the root was also used as makeup for the cheeks. It was used in antiquity as a vaginal suppository to "draw down the embryo," as well as for the treatment of jaundice, kidney problems, hypochondriasis, and infected wounds. It was one of the most important ingredients for salves: "The salve makers use the roots to thicken the salves" (Dioscorides, *Materia medica* IV.23). According to Dioscorides, alkanet was called "weasel seed" by the prophets, and when "it is placed in wine it is said to cause a good mood" (*Materia medica* IV.126). Pliny also praised the psychoactive effects of alkanet.

> Akin to the plantain follows the buglossos, which is like the tongue of an ox. The most conspicuous quality of this is that thrown into wine it increases the exhilarating effect, and so it is also called euphronsynum, the plant that cheers (*Natural History* XXV.81).

He added: "This plant is called this *[buglossos]* because the raw leaves have a sort of ox-tongue. Some also call it sibillum. It has rough, dark leaves which spread out from the earth. It is used as a cooked food for vegetables and ground as a seasoning" (*Medicina antiqua*, fol. 137r).

The Garden of Circe

"All Circe's magic potions, all Medea's drugs
and all the herbs that sprout in Thessaly,
horse-madness too, that exudation from the mare in season
when Venus breathes her longing into the wild herds
and a thousand other simples, brewed by Nemesis, I'd drink
if only to find favor in her eyes."

—TIBULLUS, *ELEGIES*

Circe, the daughter of the sun god Helios, sister of Hecate, and aunt of Medea, lived on the island of Aiaia, or Lussin (Homer, *The Odyssey* X.135ff.). "Circe with splendid braids, the powerful, commanding goddess," was a master of poisons (pharmaka). According to Theophrastus, Circe lived in Lazio, a region in west-central Italy[93] that produced "the special medicinal herbs" (*On Plants* IX: 15). Today Monte Cicero, the sacred mountain of Circe, still stands on the Italian coast above Sicily.

> Tales everywhere are widely current about Medea of Colchis and other sorceresses, especially Circe of Italy, who has even been enrolled as a divinity. This also explains that Aeschylus, one of the earliest poets, declared that Italy abounds with potent herbs, and may have said the same of Circeii where she lived. Strong confirmatory evidence exists even today in the fact that the Marsi, a tribe descended from Circe's sons, are well-known snake-charmers (Pliny, *Natural History* XXV.11).

The divine sorceress was worshipped in a grove and was clearly a goddess of death and a guide of the souls.

> This [grove] is called Circe's; and here in line grow many willows [*Salix alba* L.] and osiers [tamarisk, *Tamarix* spp.] on whose topmost branches hang corpses bound with cords. For even now it is an abomination with the Colchians to burn dead men with fire; nor is it lawful to place them in the earth and raise a mound above, but to wrap them in untanned oxhides and suspend them from trees far from the city (Apollonius, *Argonautica* III.200ff.).

---

[93] There "Circe certainly is worshipped religiously by our colonists at Circei" (Cicero, *The Nature of the Gods* III.48, translation by Horace C. P. McGregor, New York: Penguin, 1984).

Tamarisks and willows were well-known medicinal plants. The willow, or, more precisely, the white willow (*Salix alba* L.), was used for birth control; thus it was a typical witches' plant. "The willow is a tree known to all; its fruit, leaves, bark, and the juice have astringent power. The finely crumbled leaves, with some pepper and wine, is used for intestinal blockages; taken with water, it prohibits pregnancy" (Dioscorides, *Materia medica* I.135).

Another sacred tree of Circe was the alder (probably the black alder, *Alnus glutinosa* [L.] Gaertn., syn. *Betula alnus* L. var. *glutinosa* L.). "Alders surrounded Circe's Aiaia" and grew on her island (Ranke-Graves, 1984: 101, 139). We can assume that there had been an archaic alder cult that by the Hellenic times had already been suppressed.[94] Alders were considered transformed sisters of Phaeton, the son of Helios and brother of Circe.

The sacred incense of Circe was the good-smelling juniper (*odorata cedrus*—as it is called by Virgil, *The Aeneid* VII.13); therewith it is in the vicinity of archaic shamanism. Juniper is one of the oldest incense materials of the Eurasian shamans (Rätsch, 1996c).

The "glass-shimmering-captivating Circe" (Horace, *Odes* I.17), the "divine Circe," the "daughter and mother of darkness and horror" (Bruno), the "noble sorceress" who was also "compassionless," was originally a healing goddess.

> Ah, if only it pleased the sky, that for us today, like once long ago in happier centuries, this ever magical Circe would appear, who would be able to put an end to things with plants, minerals, poisons, and the magic of nature. I am certain, that despite her pride she was merciful with regards to our misery (Bruno, 1995: 101).

Moly: The Magical Plant of Circe

Moly was the most famous plant of Circe. In antiquity the wondrous moly was considered psychoactive and aphrodisiac.[95] The Homeric moly, like the magical plant of Circe, was interpreted quite early as mandrake, *Mandragora officinarum* L. (Dierbach, 1833: 204; Kreuter, 1982: 29). Dioscorides passed down the name *circeon* for mandrake, as well as *Mandragora Circaea*, the herb with which Circe transformed the men of the Odysseus into "pigs" (this probably means sexually aroused men)[96]: "The mandrake. Some call it *antimelon* ["in place of an apple"], others *dirkaia*, also *kirkaia* [plant of Circe/Kirke], because the root seemed to be effective as a love potion" (Dioscorides, *Materia medica* IV.76).

Pliny writes something similar: "Some give the name circaeon to the mandrake. There are two kinds of it: the white, which is also considered male, and the black, considered female. . . . When the seed is white the plant is called by some arsen, by other morion, and by others hippophlomos" (Pliny, *Natural History* XXV.147).

According to Apollodorus (second century B.C.E.), the most important scholar of his times, it was the κιρκαια ριζα, the plant of Circe, that was an amulet against the black magic of Pasiphae, a daughter of the sungod Helios (Circe was also a daughter of Helios), wife of King Minos, and mother of Ariadne and the Minotaurs (Library frag. II.15).

[94] Alder was unknown to Dioscorides, or, more precisely, it no longer belonged in the first-century medicine chests (cf. Lenz, 1966: 392f.).

[95] Propertius considers the "herb of Circe" to be a powerful aphrodisiac (*Elegy* II.1, 56ff.).

[96] On the island of Circe "beasts, not resembling the beasts of the wild, nor yet like men in body, but with a medley of limbs went in a throng . . . such creatures, compacted of various limbs, did earth herself produce from the primeval slime . . . in such wise these monsters shapeless of form followed Circe" (Apollonius, *Argonautica* IV.670ff.)

The sorceress Circe transforms humans into animals or hybrid beings. (Alfred Kubin, *Circe*.)

A modern comic version of the divine witch Circe with her secret magical drink. (©Verlagsunion Pabel Moewig, Rastatt, 1997.)

Homer only briefly describes moly, the divine magical plant of Hermes. With this moly, which is classified in the original text as a pharmakon, Odysseus protected himself from the sorceress Circe, who had transformed his men into pigs (Schmiedeberg, 1918). The plants of Hermes (Mercury)[97] were harvested in the garden of Circe; thus it was a magical plant that was transformed into a nearly homeopathic medicine by the messenger of the gods.

> [Hermes] bent down glittering for the magic plant
> and pulled it up, black root and milky flower—
> a molü [moly] in the language of the gods—fatigue and pain for mortals to uproot;
> but gods do this, and everything, with ease.
>
> —HOMER, *THE ODYSSEY* (X.342–346)

Generations of alchemists, Hellenists, philologists, pharmacologists, and ethnobotanists have attempted to uncover the botanical identity of the Homeric magical plant. Theophrastus, the "father of botany," already endeavored to establish the identity of the stock plant.

> Panacea, the heal-all herb, grows in greatest abundance and best on the rocky soil near Psophis, moly near Phenos, and on the mountain Cyllene. They say that this plant is like the moly mentioned by Homer; that it has roots like an onion and leaves like the sea holly and that it is used against spells and magic, but it is not, as Homer said, difficult to dig up (Theophrastus, *On Plants* IX.15).

Dioscorides wrote that the sea holly, *Eryngium maritimum* L. (Umbelliferae), which was treasured as an aphrodisiac, was also called *moly* (Rätsch, 1995: 228ff.).

> Eryngion, some call it *erynge*, others *eryneris*, *karyos* [nut], *gorginion* [gorgon herb], *hermion* [sharp arrow, thorn], *Origanon chlunion* [wild boar marjoram], *myrakanthos* [thousand–thorn], *moly*, the Egyptians call it *krobsysos*, the prophets *sisteros*, the Romans *capitulum carduus* [thistle-head], also *carterae*. The Dacians *sikupnoex*, the Spaniards *contucapeta*, the Africans *cherdon*, *oreian chloen* [mountain plant], also *chida*, belongs to the thorn bushes (*Materia medica* III.21).

> Eryngion, known as witches' thistle (*Eryngium campestre* L.; also called snakeroot), "when warmed it cools the infections caused by ergot poisoning [*ignes sacer* = Saint Anthony's fire]" (*Medicina antiqua* 45, fol. 154r).

The mysterious plant called *halikákabon* or *halicacabum* belongs to the group of psychoactive plants known as moly whose botanical identity remains uncertain.

> There is besides another kind [of strychnine], with the name of halicacabos, which is soporific, and kills quicker than even opium, by some called morion and by others moly, yet praised by Diocles and Evenor, by Timaristus indeed in verse with a strange forgetfulness of harmless remedies, actually because it is, they say, a quick remedy for

---

[97] Hermes was a shamanic deity, a soul guide, and the founder of the alchemical arts and erotic magic (Fowden, 1993; Kerényi, 1996). Perhaps Homer was describing a shamanic battle or a witches' war, a widespread ethnographic phenomenon (see Knab, 1995; Multhaupt, 1990; Reichel-Dolmatoff, 1996).

strengthening loose teeth to rinse them in wine and halicacabos. They added a proviso, that the rinsing must not go on for too long, for delirium is caused thereby. . . . The root of halicacabos is taken in drink by those who, to confirm superstitious notions, wish to play the inspired prophet, and to be publicly raving in unpretended madness. The remedy for it, which I am happy to mention, is a copious amount of hot hydromel [honey wine, mead]. Nor will I pass over this: that halicacabos is so antipathetic to the nature of the adder, that if its roots be brought near it, numbs that very power of theirs to kill by stupefaction. Therefore, when pounded it is a help for those who have been bitten" (Pliny, *Natural History* XXI.180–182).

In late antiquity it was assumed that the mandrake was a gift of the Greek-Egyptian god Hermes Trismegistos, the god of alchemy (Fowden, 1993) and that it was well suited for the invocation of ghosts and for the alchemists. Because Hermes/Mercury was sometimes depicted with an opium capsule in the art of antiquity, moly could also be designated as *Papaver somniferum* L.

Bauhinius believed the famous magical plant was rue (*Ruta graveolens* L.). Stannard saw *Peganum harmala* L.in the hermetic moly (1962); he apparently bases this on a section by Dioscorides.

Wild rue. Some designated the wild peganon,[98] including ones in Cappadocia and in Asian Gallatin, as *moly*. It is a shrub out of which a root with many branches develops, it has leaves much bigger and tender as the other peganon [rue] and is of a penetrating scent, a white flower, on the tip of which are small heads, bigger than the cultivated peganon, usually made up of three parts, in which a three-cornered, light yellow seed is found, which is also utilized. In late fall the seeds become ripe and are finely chopped and mixed with honey, wine, chicken gall, saffron *[Crocus sativus]*, and fennel juice *[Foeniculum vulgare]* as a remedy for infirmity. Some also call the same plant *harmala*, the Syrian *besasa*, the Egyptians *epnubu*, the Africans *churma*, but the Cappadocians call it *moly* because it on the whole demonstrates a similarity with *moly*, because it has a black root and white flowers. It grows on hilly and infertile soil (*Materia medica* III.46).

Moly has been speculated to be maritime squill[99] (*Urginea maritima* [L.] Baker; syn. *Scilla maritima* L.) (Rahner, 1957).

The most renowned of plants is, according to Homer, the one that he thinks is called by the gods moly, assigning to Mercury its discovery and the teaching of its power over the most potent sorceries. Reports say that it grows today in Arcadia round Pheneus and on Cyllene; it is said to be like the description of Homer with a round, dark root of the size of an onion and with the leaves like the squill, and not difficult to dig up. Greek authorities have painted its blossom yellow, though Homer wrote that it is white. I have met a herbalist physician who said that the plant was also to be found in Italy, and that one could be brought for me from Campania within a few

---

[98] The word *peganon* or *peganum* is said to be derived from Pegasus. Pegasus was the winged horse of ancient mythology who was born of the sea god Poseidon/Neptune and the snake-haired Medusa.

[99] Lucian (c. 120–180 C.E.) described in his dialogue *Menippos* that during the invocation of the dead *(necromantia)* for oracle purposes the Persian-clothed priests or *magus* (magoi) used squill as a magical plant.

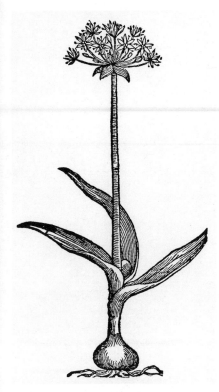

In the early modern era the legendary magical plant moly was interpreted as gold leek (*Allium moly* L.). But John Gerard differentiated among five species of moly; the first corresponds to the moly of Dioscorides and the third to the moly of Homer. (Woodcut from Gerard, *The Herbal*, 1633.)

days, as it had been dug out there in spite of the difficulties of rocky ground, with a root thirty feet long, and even that not entire, but broken off short (Pliny, *Natural History* XXV.26–27).

In early antiquity the word *moly* probably meant something like "magic plant" or "entheogen." It was used as a kind of general term for psychoactive, magically used plants, very similar to the words *haoma* and *soma*.[100] In the Middle Ages moly was also known under the name *immolum* and belonged to the gynecological medicines.

According to the testament of Homer, it is the most famous of all plants. He also attributed its discovery to Mercury [Hermes] and called it a remedy against the evil eye and witchcraft. It has a round and black root the size of an onion. . . . The low growing plant *Immolum album* entirely allays the pain of the womb when laid on top (*Medicina antiqua* 49, fol. 62v).

Plants Interpreted As Moly

Following Dierbach, 1833: 192; Marzell, 1964; Rätsch, 1998; Rahner, 1957; Schmiedeberg, 1918; Schöpf, 1986: 117; Stannard, 1962.

Allium moly L.	Gold leek
Allium magicum L.	Magic leek
Allium nigrum L.	Black onion
Allium sativum L.	Garlic
var. *ophioscordum* Döll	Snake garlic
var. *sativum*	True garlic
Eryngium maritimum L.	Water eryngo
Helleborus niger L.	Black hellebore
Mandragora officinarum L.	Mandrake
Nectaroscordum siculum (Ucria) Lindl.	Sicilian onion
(syn. *Allium dioscoridis* Sibthorp,	
Allium siculum Ucria)	
Nymphaea spp.	Water lily
Papaver somniferum L.	Opium poppy
Peganum harmala L.	Syrian rue
Ruta graveolens L.	Rue
Solanum spp.	Nightshades
Urginea maritima (L.) Baker squill	
(syn. *Scilla maritima* L.)	
Withania somnifera (L.) Dunal	Ashwaganda
(syn. *Physalis somnifera* L.)	

[100] Moly had already been symbolically interpreted during the Middle Ages: "The strange plant of the earth is man himself—with a powerful piece of his being he roots around in the dark of the chthonic realms, and only from the spiraling energy of this black root can the white flower of his bright consciousness spread out against the heavens. This is why there are rhizotomoki of the soul-life who show us how a black root can transform into a white flower, but who also teach us that even in the flower kissed by Helios the primordial energy is still preserved, which rises from the root according to secret laws of the spirits. . . . The human is the reborn rhizotomoki of the soul, an eternal and unwavering illuminate. Always there he must dig his own root out of the dark and hold it up to the light. For only in this way do the roots become medicinal" (Rahner, 1957: 230).

Above: Black henbane (*Hyoscyamus niger* L.) is the most important witches' plant in European history. (Photograph by Christian Rätsch.)

Below: Monkshood (*Aconitum napellus* L.) is considered the most powerful poison in the flora of Europe. It is one of the magical herbs of the witches of antiquity and one of the possible ingredients of the so-called witches' salves. (Photograph by Christian Rätsch.)

Above: The autumn crocus (*Colchicum autumnale* L.) was the most important medicinal herb of Medea. (Photograph by Christian Rätsch.)

Middle: In antiquity the opium poppy (*Papaver somniferum* L.) was considered the sacred plant of the Great Goddess, in particular Demeter and Aphrodite. Its latex yields the psychoactive and pain-relieving raw opium. Opium was mentioned a number of times as an active ingredient in witches' salves. (Photograph by Christian Rätsch.)

Below: The peony of Cyprus (*Paeonia mascula* [L.] Mill), the medicinal plant of the physician-god Paeon, also grew in the magical garden of Hecate. (Photograph by Christian Rätsch.)

Above: The flower of the hallucinogenic belladonna (*Atropa belladonna* L.). Bees collect nectar from it, which they transform into intoxicating or, more properly, psychoactive, honey. (Photograph by Christian Rätsch.)

Below: The flower of the yellow belladonna (*Atropa belladonna* L. var. *lutea).* This relatively rare variety was said to be more potent than common belladonna, and was preferred by witches. (Photograph by Christian Rätsch.)

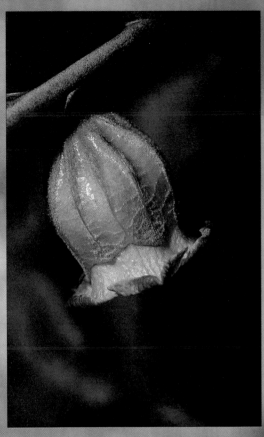

Above: Many of the nightshade plants are called *Tollkraut* (fool's herb) because they have both psychoactive and aphrodisiac properties. This is the bloom of the Asian scopolia (*Scopolia anomala* [Link et Otto] Airy Shaw). (Photograph by Christian Rätsch.)

Below: The bittersweet nightshade (*Solanum dulcamara* L.) is one of the more important European witches' plants. (Photograph by Christian Rätsch.)

Above: Black hellebore, or Christmas rose (*Helleborus niger* L.), is one of the most important medicinal plants of antiquity. It was identified with the magical plant moly and was an ingredient in witches' salves. (Photograph by Christian Rätsch.)

Middle: Herb Christopher (*Actaea spicata* L.) was known as a witches' plant and was one of the medicinal plants of Artemis/Diana. (Photograph by Christian Rätsch.)

Below: Common butterbur (*Petasites hybridus* [L.] Fl. Wett.; syn. *Petasites officinalis* Moench) was feared as a diabolic magical substance of the witches, as can be seen from the common names devil's cap and devil's hand. In the early modern era the plant was considered a "valuable medicine against pestilence"—against diseases that were thought to be caused by witches. (Photograph by Christian Rätsch.)

Above: A northern Peruvian healer *(curandero)* sets up his table, or *mesa*, for a healing ceremony. During colonial times practitioners of this ceremony were persecuted for using witchcraft. This form of ritualistic healing has been preserved in spite of the Inquisition. (Photograph by Christian Rätsch.)

Below: The buds of the poplar *(Populus* spp.), called balm of Gilead in the United States, yield the aromatic tacamathaca resin. In the early modern era this was the main ingredient in the recipe for pharmaceutical poplar salve *(Unguentum populi)*, a preparation similar to witches' salves. (Photograph by Christian Rätsch.)

The threefold "witch goddess" Hecate sits next to her book of magic and invocations, surrounded by her familiars, or animal spirits: ass, owl, lizard, and bat. (Hand-colored print by William Blake, 1795.)

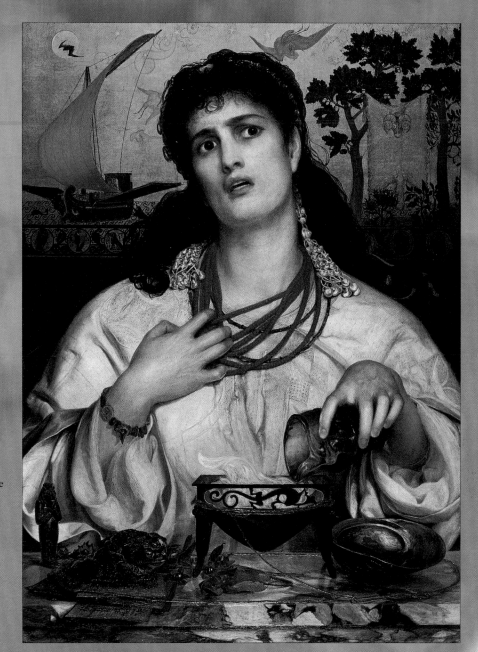

In this pre-Raphaelite painting by the English symbolist Frederick Sandy (1829–1904), the "primordial witch" Medea is depicted executing a magical ritual. For this purpose she makes use of copulating toads, belladonna (*Atropa belladonna* L.), a blood-filled abalone shell, and a censer, and she adds a libation to the compound. Her expression shows that she has already entered another reality. Directly behind her is the garden of Medea. Three of the most important witches' plants can be clearly recognized (from left to right): snakeroot, belladonna, and monkshood. (*Medea*, oil painting, 1866–1868, Birmingham Museum and Art Gallery.)

The Mother of the Witch's Egg

In the early modern era some mushrooms were also included in the plants of Circe.[101] So it was said of the deer truffle (*Elaphomyces granlutatus* L. ex Pers.) by Matthiolus:

> Of the deer truffle the ancients wrote nothing, but indeed it had the power to strengthen unchaste members and Venus-veins, for this purpose one takes a half an ounce of the powder and drinks it with a drachma of long pepper [*Piper longum* L.] mixed in. This drink also increases the milk in women. Burning the mushroom as incense and letting the smoke cover the person from the bottom up quiets the mother in its ascent. The women of Circe also do business with it and use it in love potions (1626: 387).

This mushroom, usually called *Hexenei* (witch's egg) in the vernacular, was used into our era by "evil women" in the preparation of love potions (Aigremont, 1987: vol. 1, 157).

Other mushrooms were also called witch's egg, such as the fly agaric (*Amanita muscaria* [L. ex Fr.] Pers.) and the stinkhorn (*Phallus impudicus* [L.] Pers.).

> It pushes out of the earth like an egg (devil's egg, witch's egg), then the penis rises from this vulva. When it breaks through a horrible odor is released that entices the flies, who then get stuck in the sticky stuff and must lose their life. The penis grows into the shape of a small pillar with a round head (glans) of dirty green color, while the stalk is gray. The final shape resembles precisely an erect penis with the foreskin pulled back. The mushroom has such a shape to thank for its early reputation as an aphrodisiac (Aigremont, 1987: vol. 1, 156).

The witch's egg of the stinkhorn was also called gout mushroom and was used medicinally. "The gout mushroom was cherished as a remedy for gout in the Middle Ages. It was used in sorcery primarily for love potions, sometimes to create love, sometimes to allay the consequences of illegal love" (Gessmann, n.d.: 49).

The Witches' Herbs of Linnaeus

In the sixteenth century the French botanists Dalechamp and Lobel had already designated *Circaea lutetiana* as the magical plant of Circe. From there Carl Linnaeus (1707–1778) took the name and entered it into his botanical nomenclature. Linnaeus described two species:

Circaea lutetiana, enchanter's nightshade (*herbe des sorcières, Circée de Paris, erba-maga comune*), which was distributed throughout Eurasia; and
Circaea alpina L., alpine enchanter's nightshade (*Circée des Alpes, erba-maga delle Alpi*), which was native to the Alps.

In addition, there is a natural hybrid:

Circaea x *intermedia* Ehrh. (*C. alpina* x *C. lutetiana*), intermediary enchanter's nightshade (*Circée intermédiaire, erba-maga ibrida*).

The witches' dance took place in a clearing in the woods. In the foreground is an object that can be interpreted either as fly agaric or a covered table. On the left is a *tumulus*, a door to the other world, and above, right, in the tree grins a Dionysian leaf face. (Woodcut from an English chapbook, 16th to 17th century.)

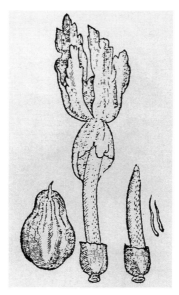

The stinkhorn (*Phallus impudicus* [L.] Pers.) grows out of the "witches' egg" like an erect penis. The foul-smelling mushroom was considered an aphrodisiac and was once an ingredient in forbidden love potions. (Woodcut from Gerard, *The Herbal*, 1633.)

---

[101] During the sixteenth and seventeenth centuries mushrooms were interpreted as weeds of the devil, as the pen-and-ink drawing "the devil sows weeds" by Jacob de Gheyn II (1565–1629) clearly shows.

These plants of the Onagraceae family grow in remote shaded places and flower from June to the end of September. Other common names for *Circaea lutetiana* include great witches' herb, Walpurgis herb, common witches' herb, Parisian witches' herb, and magic herb. In Silesia the herb is hung as protection against witchcraft and cattle rustling (Marzell, 1943: 1006ff.). In English the plant is known as enchanter's nightshade or bindweed nightshade, and the plant has been associated with magical rites (invocations, curses) from very early on. Gerard (1633: 351) had already commented on Lobel's botanical classification and considered it a mistake, because the effects, which are attributed to the ancient *Circaea lutetiana*, have the same qualities as black nightshade (*Solanum nigrum* L.).

The Garden of Artemis

Artemis was an ambivalent goddess; she could bestow sickness as well as health (Asselmann, 1883: 4). She was a foreign sorceress in the Hellenic world. She was also the goddess of the underworld, as Theocritus noted in a prayer: "You, Artemis, you who also moves the gates of Hades and all which is as strong as that." Artemis was often identified with Hecate and compared to the Italian Diana. Ephesus was a religious center of Artemis. Once when the opulent city was beset by a plague the oracle of Apollo informed the people that a cult for Artemis Soteira, the "savior," should be dedicated. In addition, a statue of Artemis with a torch in each hand was to be worshipped. This would cause the wax dolls, through which the plague had been instigated via witchcraft, to melt; thus the illness could be chased away (Graf, 1996: 150).

In Ephesus a many-breasted Artemis was honored. There were also ecstatic mystery cults in Ephesus, whose followers were called *mágos*. The early Christian author Clement of Alexandria polemicized against these heathen rites.

> To whom does Heraclitus of Ephesus prophesize? The devotees of the night—the *magoi*, the bacchants, the maenads, the mystics. He threatens all of them with what comes after death, to all of them he prophesizes fire. For what the people consider pious mysteries are godless initiatory rites (*Protrepticus* 22).

Unfortunately there are hardly any further sources that describe an initiatory mystery cult of Artemis. However, she was highly honored in the Orphic Dionysian rites. During the Orphic rites storax was brought to her as an incense offering.

The garden of Artemis was the wild nature. It was there that the shaman-goddess liked to spend her time. It was where she found her medicinal plants and her magical herbs: "There are three types of Artemisia. All three and their healing effects were discovered by the goddess Diana. She transmitted this medicine chest to the centaur Chiron, who was the first to transform it into medicine. This is why these plants carry the name of Diana, or rather Artemisia" (*Medicina antiqua* 13, fol. 32r).

Mugwort (*Artemisia vulgaris* L.) stands in the primary position. It is a sacred plant of the goddess. In earlier times it was called *Artemisia monoclonos* and was an important medicine.

> When people carry the plant artemisia, they don't feel the difficulty of the path. Kept in the house, it chases away demons, protects from bad medicine, and averts the evil eye. Grinding the artemisia in lard and rubbing it on the feet relieves aches. The

"Hear me, revered goddess, many-named divinity,
You aid in travail, O sight sweet to women in labor;
you save women and you alone love children, O kindly
goddess of swift birth, ever helpful to young women,
O Prothyraia."

—FROM THE ORPHIC HYMN TO PROTHYRAIA (ARTEMIS EILEITHYIA)

A witch roams through the woods. At her feet is fly agaric. The association of fly agaric with witchcraft was developed only in recent times. (*The Witch* by Heinrich Vogeler, pen-and-ink drawing, c. 1900.)

grounded and pulverized artemisia is administered with water and mead as a drink; it takes away the intestinal pain and helps in various conditions of weakness (*Medicina antiqua* 11, fol. 30r).

Tarragon (*Artemisia dracunculus* L.) was called *Artemisia tagantes* and was used not only as a seasoning, but also in many ways as a medicinal plant.

For bladder pain and strangles. For those without a fever, give 2 scruples artemisia juice in a glass of wine to drink; those with one use two glasses of hot water. For hip pain: grind the plant *Artemisia tagantes* and mix it with lard and vinegar; on the third day [the pains] will be healed without complications. For nerve pain: the ground plant *Artemisia tagantes* works good with oil and rubbed on the skin; it heals wonderfully. . . . Light the artemisia and let the smoke go over the child, this will avert all dangers and makes the child happy (*Medicina antiqua* 12, fol. 31r).

Roman artemisia (*Artemisia pontica* L.) was used mainly for nerve pain.

The *Artemisia leptafillos* is ground and worked into a kind of salve with almond oil. Then it is smeared on a clean piece of linen [a bandage is made]; on the fifth day the healing will be complete. When the roots of the artemisia are hung over the threshold of a building no one in the house will be harmed. Make a rub from the juice of *Artemisia leptafillos* and rose oil; it soothes the pain and the trembling and dispels all problems (*Medicina antiqua* 13, fol. 32r).

The Divine Herbs of Midwifery

Artemis is the guardian goddess of birth and abortion and the guardian of midwives. Mugwort, which is sacred to her, is considered a gynecological panacea. But to the flora of Artemis belong many further *Mutterkräuter* (mother herbs)—herbs for the mother and the womb. Therefore it is evident that all of these plants were demonized and associated in the vernacular with the plants of witches and devils. (See the appendix and the box on page 125.)

Poleo mint (*Mentha pulegium* L.) also bloomed in the garden of Artemis. It was used in antiquity as a potent abortifacient and a favorite incense. The witch persecutor Bodin (1591) identified the aromatic herb as the Homeric *nepenthes* ("soothing plant") and demonized it as a witches' herb (Beckmann and Beckmann, 1990: 201).

Savine (*Juniperus sabina* L.) also came under the protection of Artemis. Its common names included "child murder" and "virgin palm." Since antiquity it has been considered one of the most powerful and effective natural abortifacients. However, the use of the branch tips or the top shoots of savine for abortion is not entirely without danger. A decoction of fifty to sixty grams of the tips causes a strong rush of blood in the abdomen, urinary tract infections, and abortions and can also lead to fatal poisoning (Leibrock-Plehn, 1992 and 1993: 81). Nevertheless, most lethal poisoning comes from improper use by the layman. Savine has been one of the most famous abortifacients even into our era, and was demonized by the Church and by the state: "Planting it in public gardens was forbidden in some instances, because the top shoots were regularly discovered to have been harvested" (Leibrock-Plehn, 1993: 81).

Other Artemis herbs of antiquity were used in a very similar ways. The ancient

Because it is poisonous, savine (*Juniperus sabina* L.) is considered a tree of the dead; it was used in folk medicine mainly as an abortifacient. For this reason the plant was connected to witches. Hieronymus Bock wrote in his herbal, "Of it the old witches and whores pay attention to the first sprout / so that the priest or others of stinking Juniper throw palms on the cross / given to the same sprout are said to be good for the hawen and choking / for witchery / evil ghosts / and make with it many adventures / allowing from new offerings / and read masses over it. Finally they lead the young whores / give them seuen-palms powdered / or drink over it / thereby many children will be ruined. Such practices require a sharp Inquisitor and master." The tips of the branches are an important incense of the Mongolian shaman. (Woodcut from Hieronymus Bock, *Kreütterbuch*, 1577.)

Greeks called the true dittany (*Origanum dictanmus* L.)[102] *Artemidion* or *Artemidioncre*, which means "Artemis plant."

> Diktamnos, which some called wild poleo, others call it *embaktron*, *beluakos* [medicine against arrows], *artemidion* [Artemis plant], the Cretes *ephemeron*, *eldia*, *belotokos* [arrow quick birth maker], *dorkidion* [fawn], *elbunuin*, the Romans *ustilago rustica* [coltsfoot]. . . . It has the same effect as the cultivated poleo, only much more potent; for not only drunken, but also in suppositories and in incense it expels the dead fetus. . . . Eating the root is warming and speeds the birth along (Dioscorides, *Materia medica* III.34).

Dittany also was known as *Labrum Veneris*, which means "Venus lips." The name *artemisiod* was a reference to the hunter Artemis, who could wound as well as heal wounds with her poisonous arrows.

> The juice of the ground and pressed dittany plant, administered as a drink, heals extraordinarily effectively [for poisoning]. But the effects of dittany are so great that it kills all snakes by its presence alone—no matter where they are. When its scent is carried further by the wind it kills snakes promptly. As a proof it was added that wild goats or stags, when they are wounded by the [poisoned] shot of a hunter, seek out the plant diptamnum and eat it; thus the animal is able to shake the arrow out and heal the wound while it is eating the plant (*Medicina antiqua* 63, fol. 69v).

The doctor and preacher Otto Brunfels (1498–1534) wrote that dittany was used in a drink or a vaginal suppository for abortion, and the incense also worked as an abortifacient.[103] The entire plant has a volatile oil that contains carvacrol, pinin, cedrol, p-Cymol, and other phenols, as well as bitter properties and tannic acid.

The dittany of Crete is still recommended as a panacea and aphrodisiac: "It is considered a panacea and is often used for colds, stomach and intestinal complaints, for diseases of spleen, for rheumatism, and for delivery. Dittany is a calming tea and a wound medicine" (Iatridis, 1986: 92).

The "Green Fairy": Wormwood and Absinthe

One of the best medicinal plants from the garden of Artemis must certainly be wormwood (*Artemisia absinthium* L.). Ancient literature is full of praise for this herb.

> Grind the plant absintium and administer the pressed juice to drink; after mushroom poisoning such a person will go on to live to be one hundred years old. The plant absintium is cooked in water and placed on linen and a bandage made from it, this clears bruises. For sensitive skin rub it on with honey. Grind equal amounts of the plants absintium, marrubium, and lupinum and cook in honey water or spiced wine and stroke it on the navel to kill worms. Take a stalk of the plant absintium and girdle yourself with it, its healing powers are astonishing (*Medicina antiqua* 102, fol. 1003/100v).

---

[102] The plant, which is native to Crete, is often confused with *Dictamnus albus* L. (burning bush), which was also called witches' horn or devil's plant.

[103] "In the Middle Ages dittany was used to make the famous Benedictine liqueur, and even in recent times mugwort wine was seasoned with the strong aromatic herb" (Baumann, 1982: 121).

The "Mother Herbs" in Witchcraft Medicine

Following Aigremont, 1987; Beckmann and Beckmann, 1990; Leibrock-Plehn, 1992 and 1993; expanded by Rätsch.

Folk Name	Stock Plant	Known Use(s)
Bärlapp (bear cloth)	1. *Huperzia selago* (L.) Bernh. ex Schrank et Mart. (fir club moss) 2. *Lycopodium* spp. (club moss)	Menstrual and abortion medicine
Bärmutz (bear cap)	*Atropa belladonna* L. (belladonna, deadly nightshade)	Abortifacient
Frauenblümchen (woman's little flower)	*Bellis perennis* L. (daisy)	Abortifacient
Frauenkraut (woman's herb)	1. *Melissa officinalis* L. (lemon balm) 2. *Hypericum perforatum* (Saint John's wort)	Menstrual problems
Frauenwurz (woman's spice)	*Tanacetum balsmita* (syn. *Chrysanthemum majus* [Desf.] Aschers., *C. balsamita* [L.] Baill. non L., *Pyrethrum balsamita* [L.] Willd., *Balsamita major* [Desf.]) (costmary)	unknown
Jungfernkraut (maiden herb)	1. *Lycopodium clavatum* L. (wolf's claw, common club moss) 2. *Papaver rhoeas* L. (corn poppy) 3. *Papaver somniferum* L. (opium poppy) 4. *Achillea millefolium* (yarrow) 5. *Artemisia absinthium* L. (wormwood)	Abortifacient Abortifacient Abortifacient Abortifacient Abortifacient
Jungfernpalme (maiden palm)	*Juniperus sabina* L. (savine)	Abortifacient
Jungfernstrauch (maiden shrub)	*Ribes nigrum* L. (black currant)	unknown
Jungferntrost (maiden comfort)	*Herniaria glabra* L. (rupture wort)	Hernia
Jungfernweck (maiden loaf)	*Peucedanum officinale* L. (hog's fennel)	Birth
Mutterblume (mother flower)	1. *Chamomilla recutita* (L.) Rausch. (syn. *Matricaria chamomilla* L.) (German chamomile) 2. *Pulsatilla vulgaris* Mill. (syn. *Anemone pulstilla* L.) (pasqueflower) 3. *Pulsatilla pratensis* (L.) Mill. (meadow pasqueflower) (syn. *Anemone pratensis* L.)	To stimulate menstruation, abortifacient Birth
Mutterkorn (mother grain)	*Claviceps purpurea* (Fr.) Tul. (ergot)	Abortifacient

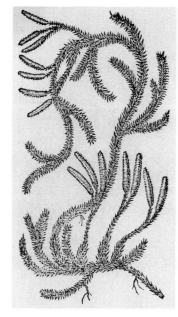

Common club moss (*Lycopodium clavatum* L.) is one of the most important magic plants in European history, as can easily be seen in its common names: druid foot, druid grass, witches' herb, witches' moss, witches' dance, devil's band, devil's flower, wolf's claw. In the Middle Ages club moss was used in gynecology. Into the twentieth century the spores of the club moss were offered in pharmacies as "witches' grain," used mainly as a wound powder. Today club moss still has a multifaceted use in homeopathy (Lycopodium hom.), particularly in diseases of the genitourinary tract. In Peru many different species of club moss become psychoactive when used in connection with the San Pedro cactus (*Trichocereus pachanoi* A. Berger). (Woodcut from Gerard, *The Herbal*, 1633.)

FOLK NAME	STOCK PLANT	KNOWN USE(S)
Mutterkraut (mother herb)	1. *Marrubium vulgare* L. (horehound)	Abortifacient
	2. *Artemisia vulgare* L. (mugwort)	Universal gynecological medicine
	3. *Tanacetum parthenium* (L.) Schultz Bip. (syn. *Chrysanthemum parthenium* L., *Leucanthemum parthenium* [L.] Gren et Godr., *Matricaria parthenium* L., *M. parthenioides* [Desf.] hort., *M. capensis* hort. non L., *M. eximia* hort., *Pyrethrum parthenium* [L.] Sm.) (feverfew)	Uterine disorders
	4. *Alchemilla xanthochlora* Rothm. (syn. *A. vulgaris* auct. non L., *A. pratensis* auct. non Opiz) (lady's mantle)	To enlarge the breasts
	5. *Melittis melissophyllum* L. (bastard balm)	
	6. *Anacylcus pyrethrum* (L.) Link (syn. *Anthemis pyrethrum* L.) (pellitory)	Menstruation, abortifacient
	7. *Veronica chamaedrys* L. (speedwell, germander)	
	8. *Salvia officinalis* L. (sage)	Aphrodisiac
	9. *Ledum palustre* L. (marsh tea)	Abortifacient
	10. *Thalictrum flavum* L. (meadow rue)	
	11. *Sedum* spp.: *S. telephium* L., *S. reflexum* L., *S. album* L. (stonecrop)	Strengthens the reproductive organs
	12. *Matricaria* spp. (chamomile)	
Mutterkrautwurz (mother herb spice)	*Ophioglossum vulgatum* L. (adder's tongue)	
Mutterkümmel (mother caraway)	*Cuminum cyminum* L. (syn. *Cuminum odorum* Salisb.) (cumin)	For women's problems
Mutternägel (mother nails)	*Syzygium aromaticum* (L.) Merr. et Perry (syn. *Eugenia caryophyllata* Thunb., *Caryophyllus aromaticus* L., *Jambosa caryophyllus* [Spr.] Ndz., *Myrtus caryophyllus* Spr.) (nettle)	For women's problems
Mutterwurz (mother spice)	1. *Astrania major* L. (masterwort)	
	2. *Meum athamanticum* Jacq. (spikenel)	Birth
	3. *Arnica montana* L. (arnica)	Birth
Wild mutterkraut (wild mother herb)	*Leonurus cardiaca* L. (syn. *Leonurus villosis* Desf. ex Spr.) (motherwort)	Birth

Wormwood is still used in a similar manner today: Extracts of the fresh flowering herb are administered as foundation tincture (Absinthium Ø) in modern phytotherapy and in complementary medicine as a tonic for states of exhaustion that accompany depression and present through digestive problems (one to three drops are taken one to three times a day, before or after meals).

But wormwood not only delivers an outstanding medicine; it is also a psychoactive substance. Absinthe was the name of a legendary drug favored by artists and bohemians at the end of the nineteenth century (Conrad, 1988). It consisted of schnapps that has been distilled from herbs, foremost from the thujone-containing wormwood. Schnapps made from absinthe has a much stronger and more unusual effect than other kinds. Among other properties absinthe is a strong abortifacient, due to the thujone content. Because it was both an intoxicating drug and an abortion medicine, it was made illegal at the end of the nineteenth century because of a supposed "escalation of abuse" (Vogt, 1981).

But in this case, as always throughout the history of the legal bans, the illegal substance continued to be distilled underground. Today absinthe is forbidden throughout the world, but it is still distilled behind closed doors in Switzerland (Lussi, 1997). The absinthe drinkers, who call their product the "green fairy," care little about the prohibitions on its use. In Switzerland absinthe was forbidden mainly because it was used, or rather abused, for abortions. Those who are caught distilling it must pay a fine of a hundred thousand Swiss francs (Rätsch, 1996a).

Secret recipes for absinthe are carefully protected. In addition, other herbs are distilled in the mixture. Absinthe is clear, green, or yellowish in color. A Swiss person once explained that absinthe is the "most psychedelic alcohol there is."

Because experiences with the thujone-impregnated schnapps are very rare, I would like to offer a short description of what I experienced. The taste reminded me very much of anisette or Pernod. It was diluted (about 1:1) with water. The mixture was milky and cloudy. The absinthe truly had an intoxicating effect on me, but totally different from "normal" schnapps. Absinthe is quite a powerful stimulant; it woke me up and kept me awake for a long time. At times I was flooded with aphrodisiac feelings, and at other times I flowed out of myself. As the effects increased I had the feeling of floating. It was like the kiss of the green fairy. As delightful as the intoxication the night before, so too was my head painful the next morning. I have never had such a brutal hangover.

In Switzerland on October 7, 1910, absinthe was outlawed. This contemporary caricature shows a Bible-thumping priest who has "killed" the "green fairy" with his religion (a knife in the form of the Christian cross)—the Church triumphs over heathendom. But the green fairy, a last manifestation of the witch goddess Artemis or Diana, lies hidden in home distilleries and still inspires absinthe drinkers.

Herb Christopher and the Solstice

Once when Artemis and her nymphs were bathing naked the Greek hunter Actaeon spied on them. The goddess noticed the secret admirer and became angry. As punishment she transformed him into a bellowing stag, and then fed an herb to her hounds, who went crazy and ripped the stag to shreds (Hyginus, *Myths* 181). This remarkable herb of Artemis retains the name of its sacrificial victim: Actaeon.

The plant was later named herb Christopher after its patron, Saint Christopher, because of its supposed effectiveness against the plague. "The ancient figure of Christopher was a human with a dog head *(cynocephalus)*, who mediates between life and death" (Beckmann and Beckmann, 1990: 119). Thus Christopher belongs in the company of Hecate and is one of the guardians of the travelers. It is interesting to note that the folk name *Heydnisch Wundkraut* (heathen woundwort)[104] was used for a long

---

[104] Usually goldenrod (*Solidago virgaurea* L., Compositae) is called heathen woundwort.

European heliotrope (*Heliotropium europaeum* L., Boraginaceae) was also called herb Christopher or cancerwort. Praetorius reported that the magical plant grows only on the Brocken, or Blocksberg (Harz Mountains), and is gathered there by witches. Nevertheless, the plant is actually found in southwest Switzerland. (Woodcut from Gerard, *The Herbal*, 1633.)

Herb Christopher (*Actaea spicata* L.) is one of the most important plants of witchcraft medicine. (Woodcut from Gerard, *The Herbal*, 1633.)

time. Today herb Christopher and baneberry are common names for *Actaea spicata* L. (syn. *Actaea nigra* [L.] Ph.).

Herb Christopher (*Actaea spicata* L.) was a famous magical and poisonous herb, hence the names "conjuring herb," "bewitching herb," or "witches' herb." Its shiny black berries are poisonous; they are used as *Mutterbeeren* [mother berries, Eifel region] for women's problems (Aigremont, 1987: vol. 2, 68f.)

In the early modern era baneberry was called *Aconitum bacciferum* and classified with the aconites because of its poisonous berries. Although it has the same qualities as monkshood, it was not used medicinally (Gerard, 1633: 980). In Norway the plant is called troll berry (Beckmann and Beckmann, 1990: 119); in Swabia it is simply known as *Hexechrut* (witches' herb).

The cunning with which the devil uses natural things to win new brides is attested to by the shiny black, enticing berries we often see when we walk through the woods. Because birds eat them without harm it seems as though they would not harm a human, and so the children pick these fruits. Their poison causes fever and when the little one starts mumbling confused words the people think that the child is bewitched, perhaps even by the person who showed him the herb. The juice of the odorless root, also called black root, is emetic and is used against the plague, to push the evil out of the body. This drug is also taken against asthma and consumption (Ludwig, 1982: 149).

Herb Christopher was also identified with heliotrope or cancerwort (*Heliotropium europaeum* L.; European heliotrope). According to the ancient sagas, this plant comes from a nymph who was in love with Helios, the tribal father of the race of witches who was abused by the sun god.

As for Clytie . . . the author of light no longer came to her and made love to her no more. She wasted away after that, driven mad by her passions. For unable to endure the company of her sister nymphs, she sat out in the open on the bare ground night and day, her head uncovered and her hair uncombed, and went without food and water for nine whole days, sipping only a little dew and her own tears, and remaining on the ground, not moving, only watching the god, following him with her gaze as he crossed the sky. They say her limbs grew into the ground. The part of her that was pale and wan changed into bloodless leaves while her face, the part that was tinged with red, became a flower most like the violet. Though she is held fast by her roots she always turns to face the sun, and though she has been transformed she loves him as much as ever (Ovid, *The Metamorphoses* IV.256–271).

Of the heliotrope, also known as *emeatites* (Titan's blood),[105] is said that "it grows everywhere, on cultivated and bare places, and on meadows. The flowers of this divine plant follow the path of the sun, and when it sets the flowers close; when the sun rises

---

[105] Perhaps this name is an indication of the identity of the legendary Prometheus plant, which was also created by the blood of the Titan Prometheus.

again the flowers open again. It is effective in many medicinal remedies" (*Medicina antiqua* 50, fol. 52r). The finely pulverized plant in good aged wine "removes all poison" (*Medicina antiqua* 50, fol. 62v). Of heliotrope it is also said that "where this plant grows, no magic will approach and no witches. . . . If one carries it with them, then no demons and no witches will harm them" (*Medicina antiqua* 50, fol. 152r). Because heliotrope is very rare in central Europe it is believed to have grown on the most famous of German dancing places for witches, the Blocksberg, or Brocken, in the Harz Mountains: "The heliotrope only grows there and nowhere else. All witches ride there on long-haired lusty bucks"[106] (Praetorius, 1668 [1979]).

Heliotrope was also said to have been an ingredient in witches' salves (Beckmann and Beckmann, 1990: 160): "In magic it is called a witches' herb, one which must be gathered on Sunday if it is to have any sort of magical effect. It was used as protection against bewitchment" (Gessmann, n.d.: 87). During the nineteenth century it was sold in pharmacies to women and prostitutes because the aroma was known to make men amorous (Aigremont, 1987: vol. 1, 15).

The Mother of the Witches

Artemis/Diana was reinterpreted during the Middle Ages as a witch goddess par excellence. The Church's perspective was made clear by Regino of Prum in his *Canon episcopi* from the ninth and tenth centuries. He named "certain immoral women, who had been perverted by the devil, who are seduced by illusions and fantasies, who believe and admit that they ride through the night on animals with Diana, the goddess of the heathens, and that countless women ride out, and that they put great distances behind them in the deadly still of the night, following the orders of their mistress" (Naegele, 1997: 14).

Flying Ointments and Lovers' Salves As Medicine

The famous witches' salves, the substance with which the alleged witches "traveled out"[107] during the night, is not an invention of the Inquisition; it had already been mentioned many times in ancient texts (Luck, 1962).

> It is certain that the use of witch's salves is very ancient and that their application reaches back into prehistoric times (Fühner, 1925).

In archaic Greece the *baetulos*, or fetish stones, were worshipped with salves—or, more precisely, with rubbing the salves on.[108] To the Greeks the salves (*unguentos*) were ambrosia, the primordial food of the gods (Hajicek-Dobberstein, 1995: 109). In late

Goldenrod (*Solidago virgaurea* L.), just like herb Christopher, was once called heathen woundwort. It is an ancient wound medicine. (Woodcut from Fuchs, 1545.)

"Witches on a trip lay numb and stiff at home."

—WILL-ERICH PEUCKERT, *HEXENSALBEN* [WITCHES' OINTMENTS], 1960

---

[106] The buck is used as a symbol of intoxication and sex—on Attic vases, for example.

[107] The "trip" is one of the arts of the Greek *goetians*, or witches (Burkert, 1962): "An ancient shamanic motif is namely the 'trip' in an imaginary wagon. The 'trip' begins with a song. The goetians also took such a trip. This has been preserved as a motif over the centuries and was found everywhere the ancient Orphic traditions were still perceptible or some relic of the Orphic was yet tangible. The most defined . . . is found when Permenides is encountered. He took a trip beyond the thresholds, where the paths of day and night intersect, into the realm of the 'goddess,' the lady. . . . This trip or journey of the shaman, or more precisely of the Mycenian *goetia*, is so identified with the song that the [Greek] expression for 'trip' is also a common word for 'song'" (Böhme, 1970: 303). The goetians had the ability to transform themselves into wolves (Burkert, 1997). "It appears that these people practice magic, for there is a story current among the Scythians and the Greeks that in Scythia once a year every Neurian turns into a wolf for a few days, and then turns back into a man again. I do not believe this tale; but all the same they tell it, and even swear the truth of it" (Herodotus, *The Histories* IV.105).

[108] Today in Nepal the sacred stones and the unshaped ones are placed in shrines for worship (*puja*) and smeared with pigment offering (*tika*) and clarified butter (*ghee*).

Hellenic times the salves that were used in magical rituals (*prâxis*) were called *mystérion*, the "secret thing" (Graf, 1996: 90). This places magic and witchcraft in the realm of the mystery cults.

> The magician understood himself as a mystic, as someone who created a ritual experience, who had close associations with the members of the known mystery cults of the Imperial times. In ritual . . . the magician also sings, for he too has been initiated into the mystery cults. . . . Magic and mystery cults are secretive; they seek direct contact with the Divine, but access is only attainable after a complex initiation ritual (Graf, 1996: 91).

Did the "secret" salves serve the initiation into the mysteries through their psychoactive qualities? Regardless, according to the so-called Mithraic liturgies the initiates had salve rubbed on their eyes during the ordination so that they would see visions (Graf, 1996: 05).

The first mention of a "flying ointment" stems from the "father of poetry" himself, Homer:

> *These shining doors the goddess [Hera] closed behind her,*
> *and with ambrosia cleansed all stain away*
> *from her delectable skin. Then with fine oil*
> *she smoothed herself, and this, her scented oil,*
> *unstoppered in the bronze-floored house of Zeus,*
> *cast fragrance over earth and heaven.*
>
> HOMER, *THE ILIAD* (XIV.169–174)

Hera[109] anointed herself with the "food of the gods," with ambrosia, in order to travel from Olympus over Thrace's snowy mountains, to soar "over the highest peak, and never touch the earth," to fly to Zeus on Mount Ida. Zeus was profoundly stunned at how fast she was able to make the trip—entirely without horse and wagon! (*The Iliad* XIV.289f.) The answer is very simple: Hera flew by way of ambrosia. Thus Hera can be considered the discoverer of the "flying ointment."[110]

What Was Ambrosia?

The name *ambrosia* was not only used to describe the "food of the gods," but was also used as a general term for different plants both mythic and real. According to Pliny the plants were also called artemisia, "the plants of Artemis" (*Natural History* XXVII.28, 55). Dioscorides described the plants and their medicinal effect more precisely.

> Ambrosia—some call it Botry, other Botrys Artemisia, the Romans Caprum silvaticum, also Apium rusticum, the Egyptians merseo—is a small, many-branched shrub three spans tall. At its base it produces small leaves like the rue *[Ruta graveolens]*. The thin branches are full of small seeds (similar to small grapes) that

"When the moon shines Artemis is present, and the animals and plants dance."

—KARL KERÉNYI, *DIE MYTHOLOGIE DER GRIECHEN* [THE MYTHOLOGY OF THE GREEKS], 1966

---

[109] "It is generally assumed that Hera's name is the Greek word for 'lady,' but it could also be the elided form of *He Era*, 'the earth.' She was the pre-Hellenic 'great goddess'" (Ranke-Graves, 1984: 42).

[110] Ovid also described the ability of Hera/Juno to fly through the "air of the beautiful sky" (*The Metamorphoses* IV.475ff.).

never flower, with a winelike smell. The root is delicate, two spans long. In Cappadocia it is woven into garlands. It has the power to stop pressing juices and to push them back; it has an astringent effect when used as a compress (*Materia medica* III.119).

The ambrosia plants of Dioscorides are considered to be grape artemisia (*Botrys artemisia* L.), goosefoot (*Chenopodium botrys* L.), or sea ambrosia (*Ambrosia maritima* L.). It is very doubtful that any of these plants could cause the magical effects of the ambrosia flying salve. The divine ambrosia was also compared to soma or haoma—in other words, to psychedelic or entheogenic sacred drugs—and was often interpreted as fly agaric (*Amanita muscaria*) or magic mushroom (*Psilocybe* spp.) (Hajicek-Dobberstein, 1995; Graves, 1960 and 1992; Wohlberg, 1990). Psychoactive mushrooms could actually induce visionary "trips" in other realities—in the world of myth!

To assume that fly agaric was included in the witches' salves is to fall prey to an illusion of the twentieth century.[111] The only example of a possible use of mushrooms for the preparation of witches' salve is found in a statement by Peter Fosselt, who was executed on May 20, 1689, in Gleichenberg:

> He had, when the desire came to him, smeared himself with witches' salve, and went around in hybrid form either to Stradner or he flew over the mountaintops . . . The devil had given him and his wife a black container with a blue-green salve (Wolf, 1994: 450).

In other words, the "sorcerer" had produced a salve while gathering mushrooms with which he transformed himself into a goshawk and could fly through the air. Perhaps one can read into this that the preparation contained mushrooms, possibly fly agaric or another psychoactive species (*Psilocybe* spp.). Sometimes fly agaric is associated with the old Scottish witches who achieved literary fame through Shakespeare's *Macbeth*.

> It is not known if the witches of the New Forest region added hallucination-causing stuff to the bear lard for their salves, but it has been reported that they ate fly agaric in small amounts (Hall and Kingston, 1979: 231).

A famous witches' salve is mentioned in the best-known heroic story of late antiquity, the *Metamorphoses, or the Golden Ass* of Apuleius (second century C.E.). Therein the hero is Lucius, a member of the magical practitioners and sorcerers of Thessaly, "the native land of those spells of the magic art which are unanimously praised throughout the entire world" (*Metamorphoses* II). According to the story the Thessalian witches knew how to animate mandrake manikins and send them out to cause damage according to their wishes. And the witches could even change their form according to their desire and travel out.

> First Pamphile took off all her clothes. Then she opened a box and removed several small jars from it. She took the cover off one of these and scooped out some ointment, which she massaged for some time between her palms and then smeared

---

[111] For example: "The magic . . . [flying] mushroom is used throughout the world for magical purposes, and the witches were no exception. They brewed tea and drank it then just before the witch gatherings, or also, in order to become prophetic" (York, 1997: 137).

all over her body from the tips of her toenails to the top of her hair. After a long secret conversation with her lamp she began to shake her limbs in a quivering tremor. While her body undulated smoothly, soft down sprouted through her skin, and strong wing-feathers grew out; her nose hardened and curved, and her toenails bent into hooks. Pamphile had become an owl (Apuleius, *Metamorphoses:* III.6–18).

Unfortunately, no Thessalian recipes are still in existence. Medieval sources remain silent on this theme. Only toward the end of the late Middle Ages was there speculation about witches' salves, both those used for the witches' flight and those for the purpose of animal transformation (Haage, 1984; Leubuscher, 1850; Völker, 1977). With the Renaissance an interest in antiquity emerged, as well as interest in all other possible narcotic salves whose recipes apparently had antique roots in folk medicine and in surgery (Piomelli and Pollio, 1994). Many of these recipes appeared to be based on ancient traditions. In ancient times medicinal salves, pomades, and oils were much more commonly used than in the subsequent eras (Budge, 1996: 29ff.; Clarkson, 1992: 293–310).

Poplar Salve As Medicine

From the beginning those who speculated about the recipes of witches' salves—usually physicians of the early modern era (Vries, 1991)—attributed the effects to the plants of the nightshade family, the true "traveling herbs" (Duerr, 1978; Evans, 1978; Fühner, 1925; Harner, 1973).

For many inquisitors—Pedro Ciruelo, for example—it was obvious that the alleged witches did not really fly to the sabbat but created hallucinogenic experiences with the salves (Dinzelbacher, 1995: 209).[112] Today the other realities into which one enters with the help of psychoactive substances (hallucinogenics) are still called "Lucifer's garden of light" (Kraemer, 1977).

There has probably only been one time in the history of the witch trials that a commissioner found an actual salve that elicited its attributed effects. In the year 1545, when the Duke of Lothringen lay very sick in bed, a married couple were arrested and accused of casting a spell on the duke. Both of them admitted to witchcraft at the trial. During a subsequent house search a jug with a salve was found. The papist physician Andrés de Laguna (1499–1560) investigated the ingredients (Rothman, 1972). He recognized in the salve *un cierto unguento verde como el del Populeon* ("a certain green salve like that of the poplar"; Vries, 1991). Laguna guessed that this salve contained *Cicuta* (water hemlock), *Solanum* (nightshade, probably belladonna), *Hyoscyamus*, and *Mandragora*, and tested it on the wife of the hangman. She fell into a kind of coma or deep sleep for three days, and was annoyed when she was wakened from this sleep full of sweet dreams and erotic adventures. Apparently this was not an isolated effect; in *Tractatus de magis* (1591) Goedelmann wrote about a girl from Magdeburg:

After she had anointed herself, she fell in such a deep sleep that she could not be woken, neither during the night nor on the following days. When she finally came

---

[112] "In the sixteenth century scholars such as Cardano or Della Porta formulated a different opinion: animal transformation, flight, manifestations of the devil, were the effects of malnutrition or the use of hallucinogenic substances that were found in decoctions of plant material or in salves. But these explanations have not yet clarified their fascinating effects. No kind of deprivation, no substance, no technique of ecstasy can, taken alone, induce the reoccurrence of such complex experiences. Contrary to all biological determination it is vital to stress that the key to this codified repetition can only be a cultural one. Of course, the deliberate ingestion of psychotropic or hallucinogenic substances does not entirely explain the ecstasy of the adherents of the night goddess, the werewolf, and so on, for their visions are not merely established in an exclusively mythical dimension. Can the existence of the framework of such rituals be established?" (Ginzburg, 1990: 296f.)

back to herself she could not be talked out of the fact that she had not really been at a dance on the Blocksberg (Peuckert, 1960: 170).

Particularly informative are the comparisons of the witches' salve and poplar salve, which was often used medicinally (Vries, 1991). A poplar-bud salve had already been described by Dioscorides.

> The leaves of the black poplar with vinegar helps for the pain of gout. The resin of the same is mixed into the salve. The fruit drunk with vinegar helps those who suffer from epilepsy. It is said that the tears that flowed from Eridanus hardened and became what is called amber, which is called Chrysophoron by some. When rubbed it smells good and has a golden color; when it is finely ground and drunk it works against dysentery (*Materia medica* I.110).

The doctor Valentino Kräutermann wrote in his vernacular introductory book *Der Curieuse und vernünfftige Zauber-Artzt* [The Curious and Practical Magic Doctor, 1725] that one should eat lemon balm (*Melissa officinalis* L.) after the evening meal in order to have happy dreams. "The same does borage [*Borago officinalis* L.] and oak fern [*Polypodium vulgare* L.] and white poplar buds, that is why the poplar salve is good for happy dreams as well" (Kräutermann, 1725: 96f.).[113]

For poplar salve the European poplar (*Populus nigra* L.) was mainly used, but American species were also used. In North America the resinous poplar buds from the balm of Gilead poplar (*Populus gileadensis* Rouleau), from black cottonwood (*Populus trichocarpa* Torr. ex A. Gray ex Hook.), and from quaking aspen (*Populus tremuloides* Michx.) are are all called balm of Gilead; the resin is called tacamahaca when it is separated. The buds are picked during the spring from beneath the branches and are extracted in alcohol. This solution is still used in wound salves (Tillford, 1997: 114f.; Vries, 1991). Balm of Gilead is favored as an apotropaic incense for modern wicca rituals.

Since the fifteenth century medicinal poplar salve has been included in almost all herbals and pharmacopoeia. In the *Gart of Gesundhit* (Garden of Health) from 1485 poplar buds are mentioned along with the following ingredients in equal parts: opium poppy leaves (*Papaver somniferum* L.), houseleek (*Sempervivum tectorum* L.), lettuce leaves (*Lactuca sativa* L., *L. virosa* L.), orchid (*Orchis* spp.), nightshades, henbane leaves (*Hyoscyamus niger* L.), and mandrake leaves (*Mandragora officinarum* L.). Everything is crumbled up and boiled in lard. How it was administered is also interesting: the salve was rubbed on the temples and the navel area. In later recipes belladonna (*Atropa belladonna* L.) and hemp (*Cannabis sativa* L.) were mentioned as additives (Vries, 1991). In other words, all psychoactive and aphrodisiac witches' herbs, with the exception of monkshood, were combined in the poplar salve. In the early modern era this sort of poplar salve was widespread and very beloved, and was used as a general pain medicine as aspirin is today. It was probably found in most households. This, however, had the drawback that at any time it could be identified by the Inquisition as a witches' salve and would be considered proof of witchcraft.[114]

Orchids (*Orchis* spp.), known as *Knabenkräuter* (boy's herb) in German, have been used since antiquity in the production of love potions. The testicle-shaped root-balls are used for this purpose. A flour made from the root-balls is still sold as an aphrodisiac at the Egyptian bazaar in Istanbul. (Woodcut from Gerard, *The Herbal*, 1633.)

---

[113] "That wonderful things appear in dreams. Take the blood of the wiedehopfen bird, smear the veins with it, the temples and the forehead, and lie down to sleep and you will see wondrous things while you sleep. The nightshades also have this same effect [*Atropa belladonna*, *Solanum* spp.] or mandrake herb [*Mandragora officinarum*] eaten at night, or the herb *apollinaris* [= henbane, *Hyoscyamus niger*] makes it possible to see beautiful, lovely things at night while you sleep. (Kräutermann 1725: 97). In a witch trial from 1758 the following ingredients of the salve were recorded: "Mandrake root, henbane seeds, nightshade berries, stomach seed juice [= opium]" (Grünther 1992: 24). In other words, a witch had admitted to having used the recipe from Kräutermann.

[114] For this awareness I thank pharmacist Patricia Ochsner (personal communication).

In the year 1854 Ludwig Bechstein reported about the astonishing medicinal effect of the *Hexenschmiere* (witches' grease):

> When a sick person is smeared with it he will become healthy, and when a healthy person is smeared with it he will become sick and die (Bechstein, 1986: 224).

The association of witches with medicinal salves reached into the twenty-first century. In the nineteenth century the pharmaceutical preparation *Unguentum nervinum*, nerve salve, was still called "devil's salve" in the vernacular. *Oleum philosophorum* was "devil's oil," and a camphor-soaked bandage was the "devil's bandage" (Arends, 1935: 226). A nerve salve was prepared from the pressed oil of laurel berries and other plants (Mercatante, 1980: 58). *Unguentum flavum* was called gland salve (Arends, 1935: 63). The German word for gland, *Druse*,[115] derives from druid, but it is also reminiscent of *Drude* or *Trude* (nightmare), which originally meant the *Druck* (pressure) of nightmares and was also a term for scary demons (Reinhardt, 1993).

The pharmaceutical poplar salve *(Unguentum populi)* was also called by the somewhat ironic common name apostle salve (Arends, 1935: 15). Poplar salve still exists in pharmacies, but it is now made without the psychoactive—the actually effective—ingredients. The salve is suited for infections of the sinus passages, hemorrhoids, wounds, burns, and more.

In the 1938 edition of *Hagers Handbuch der pharmzeutischen Praxis* [Hager's Handbook of Pharmaceutical Practice] there is a "true" witches salve recipe, a blended poplar pomade:[116] "Pomatum Populi compositum: 100 T. each of powdered, dried belladonna, henbane, poppy, and nightshade leaves are mixed, soaked thoroughly with 400 T. alcohol (95%), after 24 hours in water bath 3 hours long with 4000 T. rendered pork lard, then add 800 T. dried poplar buds (not over one year old), leave a further 10 hours in water bath, sqeeze out vigorously, let sit and then strain" (vol. 2: 513).

Yew: The Healing Tree of the Witches

Hoffmann (1660–1742), the chemist from Hall, Germany, expanded the ingredients in the witches' salves and the visionary "sleeping salves" to include the nightshade plants and opium in addition to the poison of the feared yew (*Taxus baccata* L., Taxaceae).[117] Yews can live to be five thousand years old and are some of the oldest trees in the world (Chetan and Breuton, 1994; Hartzell, 1991). The yew is a shamanic tree, a World Tree, a tree of life, for it is simultaneously a poison, a medicine, and an intoxicating substance—in other words, another true pharmakon. The words *toxic* and *toxicology* derive from the Latin name for yew *(Taxus)*.

> Sextius says that the Greek name for this tree [the yew] is *milax*, and that in Arcadia its poison is so active that people who go to sleep or picnic beneath a yew-tree die. Some people also say that this is why poisons were called "taxic," which we now pronounce as "toxic," meaning "used for poisoning arrows." I find it stated that a yew becomes harmless if a copper nail is driven into the actual tree (Pliny, *Natural History* XVI.51).

---

[115] The ancient dream interpreters were called *Drusus* and were regarded as part of the class of *magi*, or magicians (Graf, 1996: 53).

[116] This entry is not included in the current edition.

[117] Although the yew is regarded almost everywhere as highly poisonous, it is nevertheless used in ethnomedicine. In India a few pieces of bark are cooked with some salt and ghee to make a drink called *jya*, which bestows spiritual strength and vitality (Shah and Joshi, 1971: 4199). The Hindus also use the powdered bark for their *tilaka* (forehead mark).

"In Brittany it was believed that only one yew tree, which was considered the tree of the dead, could grow in a cemetery because its roots descend into the mouths of all of the dead who were buried there."

—JACQUES BROSSE, *MYTHOLOGIE DER BÄUME* [MYTHOLOGY OF THE TREES], 1990

Ingredients of the "Witches' Salves"

Included among these plants are countless species that were greatly honored in heathen contexts, and most of the herbs also have psychoactive effects. Today the majority of the plants listed here are considered to be poisonous or dangerous; two of them (hemp and opium poppy) are even illegal.

PLANT PRODUCTS AND THEIR ASSUMED PLANT SPECIES

Aconitum	1. *Aconitum napellus* L. (monkshood)
	2. *Paris quadrifolia* L. (one berry)
	3. *Actaea spicata* L. (baneberry, herb Christopher)
Acorum vulgare	see Fieldwort
Ambrosia	"food of the gods"
Apium	*Apium graveolens* L. (celery)
Betelnut	*Areca catechu* (betel palm)
Bewitching herb	*Conyza* spp. (plowman's spikenard)
Blue wolfwort	*Aconitum napellus* L. (monkshood)
Botrychium lunaria	*Botrychium lunaria* (L.) Sw. (moonwort)
Celery	*Apium graveolens* L. (celery)
Celery juice	1. *Apium graveolens* L. (celery)
	2. *Aethusa cynapium* L. (fool's parsley)
Dog parsley	*Aethusa cynapium* (fool's parsley)
Eleoselinum	*Apium graveolens* L. (celery)
Calamus	*Acorus calamus* L. (sweet flag)
Circuta[118]	1. *Cicuta virosa* L. (water hemlock)
	(syn. *Selium virosum* [L.] E. H. L. Krause)
	2. *Conium maculatum* L. (poison hemlock)
	(syn. *Cicuta maculatum* Gaertner)
Darnel	*Lolium temulentum* L. (darnel)
Devil's bite	*Scabiosa succisa* L.
Devil's dung	*Ferula asafoetida* (asafetida, devil's dung, food of the gods)
Dragon's blood	*Resina draconis* (red resin) from
	1. *Dracaena draco* (L.) L. (dragon's blood)
	2. *Dracaena cinnabari* Balf. F. (Zanzibar drop)
	3. *Daemonorops draco* Bl. (dragon's blood palm)
	(syn. *Calamus draco* Willd.)
Faba invers[119]	assumed to be *Atropa belladonna* L. (belladonna)
Fieldwort	1. *Acorus calamus* L. (sweet flag, calamus)
	2. *Iris pseudacorus* L. (yellow flag)
Fingerwort	*Potentilla* spp. (cinquefoil)
Five-fingerwort	*Potentilla erecta* (L.) Raeusch (bloodroot)
Flying mushroom	*Amanita muscaria* (L. ex Fr.) Pers. (fly agaric)
Hemp	1. *Cannabis sativa* L. (hemp)
	2. *Cannabis indica* Lam. (Indian hemp)
Horehound	1. *Ballota nigra* L. (black horehound)
	2. *Marrubium* spp. (horehound)
Hyoscyamus	1. *Hyoscyamus niger* L. (black henbane)
	2. *Hyoscyamus* spp. (henbane)
Incense	Frankincense, the resin of *Boswellia* spp.

The unusual moonwort (*Botrychium lunaria* [L.] Sw., Botchrychiaceae/Ophioglossaceae) is one of the classic witches' plants. It is said to be an ingredient in witches' salves. In the Middle Ages moonwort was used as a remedy for abscesses and wounds. A common name for the plant, which grows on mountain meadows, is Walpurgis herb. It is said to assist in finding hidden treasure. (Woodcut from Gerard, *The Herbal*, 1633.)

In antiquity the white lily was a sacred plant of Hera/Juno. In the Middle Ages it was sacred to Mary and was considered a symbol of chastity. But the aromatic plant was also used as an aphrodisiac. (Woodcut from Gerard, *The Herbal*, 1633.)

---

[118] It has sometimes been written that water hemlock is in and of itself psychoactive. As both *Conium maculatum* and *Ciruta virosa* are two of the most thoroughly researched medicinal and poisonous plants, we can assume that the supposed pharmacological psychoactivity has not remained hidden for the past three thousand years. Both hemlocks contain highly toxic alkaloids, furanocumarine, and the bioactive polyacetylene (Teuscher, 1992).

[119] According to Wyer the *faba inversa* is the plant "which the Italians call belladonna" (cf. Peuckert, 1960: 172).

In antiquity the white poplar (*Populus alba* L.) was sacred to Hercules. Dioscorides mentioned that a salve made from the leaves and honey would alleviate infirmity. The salicine found in the bark was considered medicinal up through the modern era. (Woodcut from Gerard, *The Herbal*, 1633.)

PLANT PRODUCTS AND THEIR ASSUMED PLANT SPECIES (CONTINUED)

Lactuca	1. *Lactuca virosa* L. (wild letuce)
	2. *Lactuca serriola* (prickly lettuce) (syn. *Lactuca scariola*)
	3. *Lactuca sativa* L. (garden lettuce)
Lily	1. *Iris* spp. (iris)
	2. *Lilium candidum* L. (white lily, madonna lily)
Madwort	1. *Scopolia carniolica* Jacq. (scopolia)
	2. *Atropa belladonna* L. (belladonna)
	3. *Hyoscyamus* spp. (henbane)
Mandragora	*Mandragora* spp. (mandrake)
Maniacum solanum	not identified[120]
Nightshade	*Solanum* spp. (nightshade)
Napellus	*Aconitum napellus* L. (monkshood)
Nasturium	*Nasturtium* spp. (nasturtium)
Nymphae	1. *Nymphaea alba* L. (white water lily)
	2. *Nuphar lutea* (L.) Sm. (spatterdock)
Olibanum, incense	resin from *Boswellia sacra* Flückiger, *Boswellia* spp. (frankincense)
Opium thebaicum	opium from *Papaver somniferum* L. (opium poppy)
Ottermennige	*Agrimonia eupatoria* L. (agrimony)
Papaver ruber	*Papaver rhoeas* L. (corn poppy) (syn. *Papaver strigosum* [Boenn.] Schur.)
Papaver niger	*Papaver somniferum* L. (opium poppy)
Poplar branches and buds	*Populus* spp. (poplar)
Pastinaca[121]	*Pastinaca sativa* L. (parsnip)
Pentaphyllum	*Potentilla* spp. (cinqufoil)
Pepper	*Piper nigrum* L. (black pepper)
Populi	*Populus niger* (black poplar)
Portulaca	*Portulaca* spp. (purslane)
Saffron	*Crocus sativus* L. (saffron crocus)
Searose	1. *Nymphaea alba* L. (white water lily, water nymph)
	2. *Nuphar lutea* (L.) Sm. (yellow pond lily)
Smyrna paste	opium
Solano, Solanum	1. *Solanum* spp. (nightshade)
	2. *Datura stramonium* L.(thorn apple)
Solstice	1. *Artemisia vulgaris* L. (mugwort)
	2. *Hyoscyamus niger* L. (black henbane)
	3. *Heliotropium europaeum* L. (European heliotrope)
Sneezewort	1. *Veratrum album* L. (white hellebore)
	2. *Helleborus* spp. (hellebore, Christmas rose)
Soot[122]	1. grain parasite (*Ustomycetes*)
	2. *Claviceps purpurea* (Fries) Tulasne (ergot)

[120] This plant was also used in the preparation of love potions (Gessmann, no year: 62).

[121] *Pastinaca* was the name for a poisonous freshwater stingray that has been associated with the poison mixing of the magicians (Graf, 1996: 68).

[122] In his book *The Oyntment That Witches Use* the English politician, philosopher, and writer Francis Bacon (1561–1626) discussed the recipe of the Italian Cardano, but underestimated the nature of the "rust," for he replaced it with wheat flour. But the rust almost certainly was the wheat parasite, or even the ergot of rye (*Claviceps purpurea* [Fr.] Tul.). Bacon also conjectured that the New World plants tobacco (*Nicotiana tabacum* L., *Nicotiana rustica* L.) and thorn apple (*Datura stramonium* L.) were serviceable ingredients.

Stramonii	*Datura stramonium* L. (thorn apple)
Stomach seeds	*Papaver somniferum* L. (opium poppy)
Tobacco	1. *Nicotiana tabacum* L. (tobacco)
	2. *Nicotiana rustica* L. (wild tobacco)
Thebaicum	opium
Tormentill	*Potentilla erecta* (L.) Raeusch. (cinquefoil)
	(syn. *Potentilla tormentilla* Stokes, *Potentilla sylvestris* Neck.)
Verbene	*Verbena officinalis* L. (European vervain)
Water-Merck	1. *Apium graveolens* L. (celery)
	2. *Sium* spp. (water parsnip)
Wolfwort, Wolf-root	1. *Aconitum* spp.
	2. *Aconitum napellus* L. (monkshood)
	3. *Lycopodium clavatum* (common club moss, wolf's claw)
	4. *Euphorbia* spp. (spurge)
Wolf's milk	1. *Euphorbia* spp. (spurge)
	2. *Chelidonium majus* L. (celandine)
Yew	*Taxus baccata* L. (yew)

ANIMAL PRODUCTS

Badger lard, bat blood, bird blood, cat brain, child blood, child fat, fox lard, hoopoe blood, infant blood, menstrual blood, milk, owl blood, screech owl blood, Spanish fly (*Lytta vesicatoria*), toad poison (*Bufo bufo*), wolf blood, wolf fat, wolf lard, vulture fat

OTHER

Bitumen, Communion wafers, oil, rust, salt, soot, wine

Ancient yews often grow in cemeteries. But they were not planted by the cemetery groundskeepers; the Celtic druids planted them long ago. This ancient yew is grown over with ivy, the vine of Dionysus. (Copper engraving, Dibden, England, 1837.)

According to Lucan (C.E. 39–65), the yew was one of the trees sacred to the gods of the underworld and thus was connected with Persephone, Proserpina, and Hecate (Lenz, 1966: 390). The yew also grew in Hecate's garden. People carved out of yew wood "images of the gods in the most ancient times in the Mediterranean region" (Golowin, 1973: 25). The yew was sacred to Diana Nemorensis, the Diana of the forest. The Celts considered the yew to be the "oldest of the trees," and it was a sacred plant of the druids— they planted it on sacred sites (Chetan and Brueton, 1994). The Gaels made an arrow poison from the yew. The Irish druids used yew wood staves to carve the ogham script that was so important for their prophetic arts (Guyonvarc'h and Le Roux, 1996: 184). Some authors consider the Germanic World Tree Yggdrasil to be not the ash tree, as is commonly believed, but the yew, which is called "evergreen ash" in skaldic poetry (Chetan and Brueton, 1994: 110). Regardless, for the Germanic peoples the yew was a sacred tree and was connected to the runes *eihwaz* and *yr*. The peace symbol of the hippies was derived from the latter rune.

It has been repeatedly reported that yew has psychoactive properties.

> Only by way of his residence under the shadow of yew trees was Professor Kukowka able to discover the "psychedelic." In other words this plant transformed his consciousness in an extraordinary way. Who will doubt that the same process did not occur thousands of times in the sacred woods of the primordial age among the Celts, Romans, Greeks, and Semites? In these places the initiates of the early culture dreamed their way into the realm of the ghosts and gods (Golowin, 1973: 26).

The yew has a gained a role in folk medicine as an abortifacient. Fifty to a hundred grams of yew needles are decocted in water and drunk for this purpose (Roth et al., 1994: 695). However, this amount is also dangerous for the expectant mother—the abortive dose is nearly identical to the fatal one! The yew, like all sacred plants, is to be enjoyed with respect and caution. Keep in mind that one must spit out the black seeds; they are just as poisonous as other parts of the plant.

The yew species native to the Pacific Northwest, *Taxus brevifolia* Nutt, has become famous in recent years because the substance taxol has been isolated from it, and this substance has been successful in the treatment of cancer.

Modern Witches' Salves

In the burgeoning literature about "new witches," which is usually pseudofeminist and directed at the esoteric market, recipes of the alleged witches' salves from the early modern era have been thoughtlessly reprinted. At the same time, despite the fact that none of the "modern witches" themselves have any experience with the plants, they warn about the poisonous additives. In this literature, which is as superficial and empty as the elaborately fashionable themes of tantra and shamanism, it is considered trendy to brew "modern flying ointments, guaranteed to be not poisonous." The recipes are nothing more than ineffective rubbish. One recipe circulating among the authors consists of mugwort (*Artemisia vulgaris* L.), parsley (*Petrosilinum crispum* [Mill.] Nym.), catnip (*Nepeta cataria* L.), orchid (*Orchis* spp.), jasmine oil *(oleum jasmini)*, and valerian root (*Valeriana officinalis* L.) (for example, in York, 1997: 135).

Nevertheless, in Mexico there are still salves sold on the "witches' markets" called *pomada de toloache* that contain toloache, the Mexican datura (*Datura innoxia* Mill., syn. *Datura meteloides* DC.):

> It is very rare that a toloache salve from pork lard and datura leaves is still made in Mexico. There are still "witches" who sell their datura pomade, because it is supposed to make the men superfluous. This is an exact counterpart to the witches' salves of the Middle Ages, which were made from henbane and thorn apple (Schenk, 1954: 79).

Nevertheless, thorn apple and henbane still belong, or, better said, belong once again, to the "traveling herbs." A medicated Band-Aid with the active alkaloid from these plants, scopolamine, is placed behind the ears as a remedy for motion sickness (Grünther, 1992).

Pharmakon Wine

Ecstatic dance cults already existed in the Stone Age; at least that is what the cliff paintings in South Africa suggest. Communal dancing with the goal of the collective transformation of consciousness until ecstasy is reached appears to be a kind of "cultural archetype" that clothes itself in a new cultural costume, depending on location and epoch. The dances take place at night in nature; the ritual participants ingest various pharmaka in order to become intoxicated, dance to pounding rhythms, and pour themselves into the mystical realms of a god. During these dances the rhythm of the music and the rhythmical movement of the body has a harmonizing effect on humans. It is as if they are shaken rhythmically through and through until the inner conflict, division of the spirit, and tension and cramping of the body are put into harmony again. This leads to spiritual freedom and creativity, physical happiness and enjoyment, erotic desire and ecstasy—in brief, to health and healing.

These ecstatic dance cults do not belong to any organized religion, nor do they follow any absolute dogma of hierarchic institutions. They usually are not bound to a specific place; in other words, they are nomadic. Dance cults are found throughout the world. Well known are the Native American powwows, the African trance dances, and the Asian Shiva festivals. The modern rave and technoculture also belongs here, in particular the parties in Goa with their psychedelic trance music.

Besides the little-known and rarely documented dance cults of Hecate and Artemis, the ancient dance cults of Dionysius were another manifestation of the genre. The Dionysians, named after the wine god Dionysius, commanded an incredible audience during antiquity. People met at night in the forest—for example, in the conifer forests on Parnassus, above Delphi—to celebrate at these intoxicating festivals. There they danced to wild music, made themselves drunk on drug-impregnated wine,[123] fell on one another in erotic excitement, and, finally, gripped by the god, exploded in collective ecstasy. Women were especially attracted to the cult. They are remembered in history as being bare-breasted maenads or Bacchae. The men of Dionysus were dressed in animal skins and they pranced around with splendid erections invigorated by the aphrodisiac wine. They were immortalized in the typical form of the Dionysian followers—as satyrs, fawns, seleni, centaurs, and Pan.

However, by antiquity the state was already eyeing the dance cult of Dionysus with suspicion. It was an anarchic, uncontrollable thorn in the side of the complex state system. The cult was demonized in public opinion. Its women were accused of killing living animals or men and of having extramarital sex. In puritanical Rome the Dionysian cult was entirely forbidden in the year 186 B.C.E. (Giebel, 1990: 77). But its powers of attraction were too strong and the experiences it offered too seductive. The prohibition did not lead to the cult's disappearance but instead pushed the cult, which was antagonistic, to the underground.[124] The Dionysian and Thracian followers of Sabazius,[125] just like those of the dance cults of Hecate/Artemis/Diana,[126] remained until the beginning of the early modern era. During the Middle Ages they were demonized and forbidden by the Church. Dionysus became Satan, the Great Goddess was turned into the witch goddess, the maenads were transformed into witches, the satyrs became the disciples of the devil. The heathen and erotic dance cult received a new name: sabbat, or, more precisely, witches' sabbat (Lussi, 1996: 136).

---

[123] The wine had different psychoactive plants or substances added to it (Ruck, 1982). There are a number of indications that the wine was "improved" with psilocybin-containing mushrooms. Orpheus, patron of the ecstatic cults, was often depicted wearing a Phrygian cap, which today is often considered a symbol for the potent psychedelic mushroom with the conical cap known as liberty cap *(Psilocybe semilanceata)*. In the cathedral vault of the Historic Museum of Pfalz in Speyer there is a Thracian or Phrygian amphora from the fifth century B.C.E. It is made of bronze, the interior is gilded, and it is cast in the form of a mushroom cap (cf. Grewenig, 1996: 55).

[124] "A priestess from the Campania allowed men entrance to her mystery rituals, which had previously been exclusively for women. She performed five nighttime initiations per month. The men, according to Livius, fell into ecstatic physical movements and discharged prophecies. The women stormed to the Tiber river with their hair flying, dipped flaming torches into it and pulled them out burning again, for they had been previously dipped in sulfur and undissolved lime. Among them reigned the foundation of absolute freedom of the individual from the moral laws of society, 'nothing was forbidden' was their primary rule" (Giebel, 1990: 77). But the initiates were accused of cultivating "unharnessed promiscuity" and committing ritual murder.

[125] "The importance of the cauldron is demonstrated [by the fact] that among the followers of Sabazius, the Phrygian Dionysus, the cauldron-bearer was a position of honor" (Golowin, 1973: 107).

[126] The mystics of Dionysus carried white poplar garlands "because this tree grows in Hades" (Burkert, 1990: 85). Thus they are decorated with a sacred plant of Hecate.

The word sabbat . . . has absolutely no connection to the biblical sabbat or to the number seven, but rather it is, as Summers thought, most likely derived from Sabazios, a Phyrgia god who is often compared to Zeus or Dionysos and is considered the patron deity of orgies and obscene practices (Castiglioni, 1982: 34).

In the late Middle Ages, and particularly in the early modern era, the heathen dance cults became such a thorn in the side of the Church and the rulers that the groups were totally defamed with the help of broadsheets, papist bulls, and the *Hexenhammer* (hammer of the witches, or *Malleus Maleficarum*). The written testaments—similar to what might be found in the *National Enquirer*—manipulated popular opinion.

During the Inquisition people who were under suspicion of having taken part in "diabolic orgies" were tortured and murdered. The state, for its part, sanctioned the consumption of heathen intoxicants. In particular, the "beer purity laws" of 1516, written by the Bavarian duke Wilhelm IV, represented an attack on the heathen nature religions and witchcraft medicine (Rätsch, 1996b: 170 f.). With this ordinance, which is often misunderstood today as nutritional laws, the use of the dangerous witches' plant henbane was forbidden.

Some early authors mention that witches' wine was used as a sexual stimulant: "On the witches' sabbat beer, apple wine, pear wine and water in which witches' wort [henbane] had been soaking, brought the people to dance . . . but in a smooth, pleasant way, demonstrating no trace of epileptic or violent movement." Father Sebastian Michaelis declared that the witches favored drinking a wine that had been stolen from the wine cellar in order to stimulate sexual desire. . . . The witches' wine was often described as dull and with little taste (Wolf, 1994: 451).

The Sabbat on the Allmend

"In the canton of Lucerne the forbidden dance of the night took place on the Allmend. The Allmend is an area that belongs to the villagers communally and that is used by them according to a specific law. Animals are grazed there, and hemp and flax is cultivated in unfenced gardens. Different forms of love magic demanded a visit to the flowering hemp fields. This often caused states of aphrodisiac intoxication. The forbidden dance on the Allmend, and the ingestion of the consciousness-altering plants that grew there, encouraged illicit intimate relations between the youth. Nightly dancing outside the village, aphrodisiac plants, and erotic sentiment went against the dominant moral codes. The happenings outside of the village were demonized and forbidden as being witches' sabbats" (Lussi, 1996: 115f.).

Witches' wine has moved the soul throughout history and continues to do so today. Because wine was known to be an aphrodisiac, it was assumed to be the foundation of the love potion made by the Celtic "herb witch" Isolde, whose history can be read in the countless early and late workings of the story of Tristan and Isolde. Wine was identified as a love potion and therewith automatically belonged to the alleged repertoire of witchcraft medicine. In the opera *L'Elisir d'Amore* [The Love Potion], by the Italian composer Gabriel Donizetti, the magical drink is nothing more than red wine. Although wine was associated with the outlawed machinations of witches, it has never been—except during Prohibition in the United States—truly forbidden. To the contrary, the Church lifted the sacred use of wine from the Dionysian orgies and used it as the wine for their Mass. However, they forgot—or maybe they left them out on purpose?—to add the psychoactive ingredients of the Dionysian drink to the Mass wine. Wine is also the preferred food in cloisters, and it is one of the most beloved intoxicating drugs of the upper classes. But just as wine can have ambivalent effects, like a true pharmakon, it was always viewed with ambivalence by society and politicians.

Even champagne was considered a "satanic wine" as late as the seventeenth century! That was perhaps the inspiration for one of the most spiritually moving novels of the early German Romantic era. In 1815 E. T. A. Hoffmann—a well-known alcoholic and laudanum drinker—wrote a classic of the Gothic novel genre with the multifaceted title *The Devil's Elixirs*. This book refers to a historical wine from the writings of Saint Anthony[127] that is supposed to be like Syracuse wine in appearance, smell, and taste. Those who taste this wine, "the wonderful drink with spiritual strength," will have their minds strengthened and will be bestowed with the "joy of the spirit." The aroma of the wine is said not to be "numbing, but more pleasant and benevolent"—in other words, not narcotic but stimulating and uplifting.

Hoffmann described the effects of the wine of Saint Anthony as if it were a psychedelic like LSD: "I gripped the box, the bottle, soon I had taken a powerful swallow!—Embers streamed through my veins and filled me with an incredible feeling of happiness—I drank once again and the desire for a new, beautiful life rose up in me!"

The cloister brother who could not or would not resist tasting the drink, which was kept in the reliquary, broke out of the cloister afterward, out of the stern structure of hierarchical power, and stumbled like a modern anarchist into the chaotic sensations of the world. Were it not for his conscience, had he not been caught sleeping in his own cell, and were he not bound by horrible feelings of guilt he would have had a beautiful life, free from all societal demands—Dionysian through and through. E. T. A. Hoffmann convincingly demonstrated in his novel how a Christian upbringing leads to spiritual uncertainty and schizophrenia.

Surprisingly, the witches' wine, the former "blood of Dionysus," can still be enjoyed these days. In Baden the late-season Burgundy red wine Hex von Dasenstein can still be found.[128] Countless modern types of German beer are named after witches and devils: Halloween Pumpkin Ale, Hexenbrau, Satan, Lucifer, and so forth. But because they all are brewed according to the purity laws, they are all legal drugs.

Wine As Medicine

Since antiquity wine has been known as an intoxicant, an aphrodisiac, a medicine, and a poison—in short, it has been known as a pharmakon. But in medicine wine serves primarily as a carrier for other ingredients.

Ananamide has been discovered in red wine. This substance is made into a neurotransmitter. Ananamide binds to the same receptors as THC, the active ingredient in hemp, and transports the person to a pleasant feeling of contentment. Ananamides are also found in chocolate and cocoa (Grotenhermen and Huppertz, 1997: 58ff.).

A witch taps the wine with the help of a nail while a demonic helper spirit protects her. During the early modern era wine was demonized because of its intoxicating, medicinal, and destructive properties. (Woodcut from Hans Vindler, *Buch der Tugend*, Augsburg, 1486.)

---

[127] In Austria there is actually a Saint Anthony's wine that is stored in consecrated vats, but it was stolen during a march of the troops of Wilhelms von Châtillon. This wine was used for the treatment of Saint Anthony's fire. Unfortunately, it has never reappeared (Behling, 1957: 145).

[128] Brandy was still called "druid's brandy" and "witch's schnapps" in the vernacular into the last century (Arends, 1935: 63). Today there are still herbal liquors marketed under the name "witch's drink."

Ingredients of the "Witches' Brew"

The three witches in Shakespeare's *Macbeth*, who fell under the protection of Hecate, prepared a "charmed cauldron" whose ingredients are precisely listed (act 4, scene 1). In the kettle, which is surrounded by elf spirits, the first witch placed the first ingredient, a toad.[129] The second witch added more ingredients:

> *Fillet of a fenny snake*
> *In the cauldron boil and bake:*
> *Eye of newt, and toe of frog,*
> *Wool of bat, and tongue of dog,*
> *Adder's fork, and blind-worm's sting,*
> *Lizard's leg, and howlet's wing.**

The third witch had still more to offer:

> *Scale of dragon, tooth of wolf,*
> *Witches' mummy, maw and gulf*
> *Of the ravined salt-sea shark,*
> *Root of the hemlock, digged i'th' dark;*
> *Liver of blaspheming Jew,*
> *Gall of goat, and slips of yew,*
> *Slivered in the moon's eclipse;*
> *Nose of Turk, and Tartar's lips,*
> *Finger of birth-strangled babe,*
> *Ditch-delivered by a drab,*
> *Make the gruel thick and slab.*

For the finale, Pavian's blood is added. Unfortunately, Shakespeare does not reveal how the witches' gruel is used.

In this recipe two plants are named directly: henbane *(Hyoscyamus niger)*[130] and poison hemlock *(Conium maculatum, Cicuta virosa)*. The other ingredients seem to be parts of animals, but these designations were probably secret or ritual names of plants. The *rat's blood* is called "slips of yew," and *wolf's teeth* is a folk name for ergot (Golowin, 1973: 42). The author, who dabbled in herbalism and alchemy, probably did not write down a general recipe for the witches' potion, but preserved for eternity a preparation of ingredients whose names were kept secret (cf. Tabor, 1970). These plants belong to the pharmacologically active ingredients of the witches' drink.

---

[129] Toads were in use in the Middle Ages for love magic (Meyer, 1884: 263).

[130] Shakespeare also reveals his knowledge of henbane and its medicinal effects in *Hamlet* (cf. Tabor, 1970).

* In the German translation of *Macbeth* henbane is used in place of howlet's wing. (Trans.)

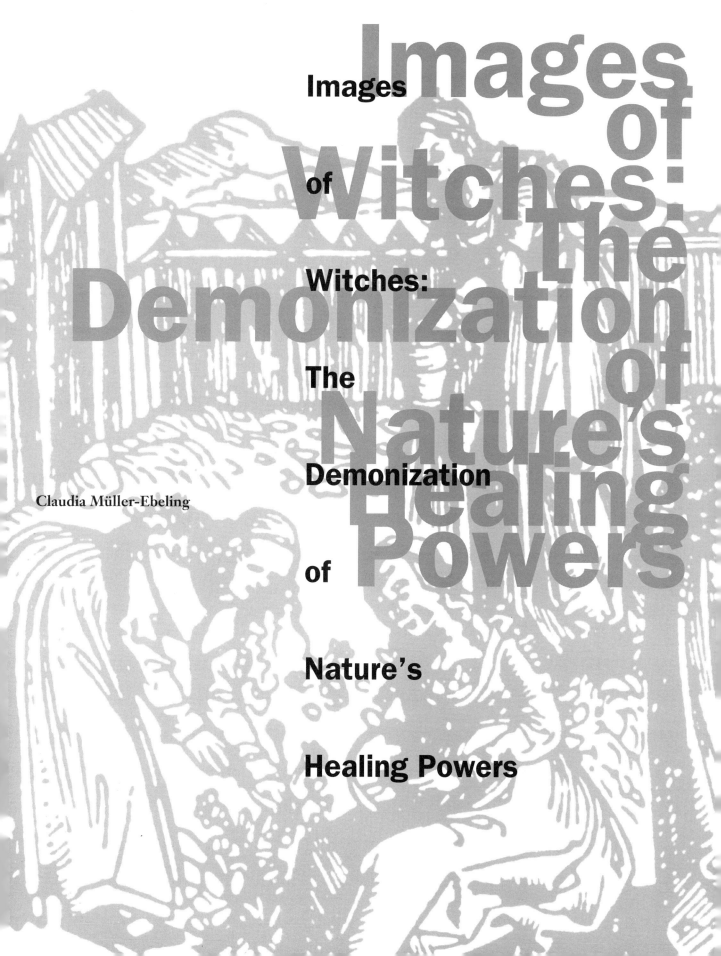

Images of Witches: The Demonization of Nature's Healing Powers

Claudia Müller-Ebeling

The Image of the Witch

Books about witches overflow with illustrations and pictorial manifestations of the witch's legendary existence. Yet even with close scrutiny it remains difficult to find any reference to witchcraft medicine in such pictures; identifiable plants are depicted all too rarely and rarer still is any evidence of the witch-women as herbalists or healers. Before the greatly obscured connection between women healers and the herbs and plants they used can be traced through culture and art history, it is essential first to visualize the image with which the witch has been branded and to seek out different aspects of the activities of the witch.

This reconnaissance mission will first lead us to the woman who is the healer of humanity, the one employed and validated by the Church; naturally, she is not the witch. Then we shall travel into the depths of a demonized nature, where the path leads to sensuousness and finally to the woman who mixes poisons and is a healer. But she left no written records to explain the practices of this tradition, and reports on witches by the Inquisition, which sought to exterminate them, while of interest, are obviously biased. How then are we to proceed with our mission?

Renaissance painters may provide the best documentation of the witch and the powers attributed to her by her contemporaries. The works of Bosch, Dürer, Grien, and other artists of the time hold significant clues for reconstructing the actual religion of the witches and its practices involved with healing, weather control, and divination. Though we cannot know if an individual painter's inspiration was prompted by Church propaganda or a secret sympathy for the tradition, the consistent use of various elements and motifs in these works provides a valuable portrait of the spiritual tradition these women inherited from Europe's pagan past. Furthermore, there is another special role played by pictorial works that I will examine below that makes these works particularly relevant to our mission.

A witch whose demonic helping spirit lurks in her blowing hair approaches a wounded man with gestures of invocation and healing. (Detail of a woodcut illustration from Cicero, *Officia*, Augsburg, 1531.)

Presumably none of us has ever seen a witch and yet most of us have a relatively concrete picture of what a witch looks like. Where does this originate—this tangible idea we have of a figure that exists only in an imaginary reality? Why does every child know what a witch looks like?

Ideas are always pictorial—*bildlich*. The picture is created—*"das Bild bildet"*—and finally it makes culture—*Bildung*. These words are related by virtue of their connection with the pictorial image. For the purpose of our search, understanding the expression of spiritual energy inherent in the pre-Christian syllable *bil* proves informative.[1] This prefix is found not only in terms within the same general realm of meaning, such as *Bildung* (culture), *bilden* (to form), *Bild* (image, picture), *Bildnis* (portrait), and so forth, but also in *Bilsenkraut* (henbane), whose psychoactive effects indicate that it is a sacred plant. There is also something magical and intriguing emanating from pictures of witches, and the idea of the witch continues to stimulate the pictorial fantasy of painters and illustrators even in our own times.

Our cultural consciousness has been filled with various images of witches based on pictures left for us by painters and illustrators. (And as a rule these artists were men.) Our imaginations have been shaped by paintings and engravings by artists such as Hans Baldung Grien, Hans Weiditz, Francisco José de Goya, and Ludwig Richter that have influenced our fairy-tale idea of the witch. We usually think of a witch as being an old, stooped hag with a crooked nose and warts, and we imagine her testing the flesh on

---

[1] Herman de Vries discusses the etymology of the syllable *bil* at length (de Vries, 1993: 77).

Hansel's body with long, withered fingers or preparing magical potions. But she has also appeared in many pictures as a lusty and naked young maid, in her bloom of life, who seems to be engaging in a nocturnal orgy with other naked women. Although the picture of the crooked-nosed old witch of fairy tales and children's books is dominant in our collective imaginations, these two very contradictory pictures of the witch exist side by side in the culture in which the witch arose. [2]

Let us place ourselves in the sphere of dualities for better orientation—for only because of the fact that there is day do we know what night is. Such a juxtaposition is entirely appropriate to our context; after all, the witch is first and foremost "nocturnal," just as are certain animals and plants (predominantly those of the Nightshade family). "The night is the friend of the spirits—secret and still," understood the physician and philosopher Philippus Aureolus Theophrastus Bombast von Hohenheim (1493–1541), who is best known by his nickname, Paracelsus. Besides, the witch is a Christian invention, and if her virtuous, chaste, dutiful sister did not exist, then she—the heathen unbeliever, the sinner, and the evil one—would have never seen the light of day (or, we might say, the dark of night). The witch embodies the suppressed nature of Mary, and Mary contains all that the witch is not allowed to be—or, more precisely, all that has been suppressed in our cultural picture of the witch.

Mary: The Chaste Cultural Heroine

On the side of the day and the virtuous is Mary, the mother of God. She, Our Lady of the Sorrows who endures so much suffering, is considered the conqueror of demons and thus can be addressed as the "healer of humanity" in a figurative sense, as von Laufenberg's fifteenth-century poem demonstrates. Mary is not depicted in a direct relationship with healing and medicinal herbs,[3] but as the mediator between the humans, the saints, and God she accepts the healing medicine that humans offer her in order to integrate it into the divine order.

In this sense Mary stands in direct opposition to the witches, who speak directly to the plant spirits—who speak to nature in the "shape" of these plant spirits. Mary is the mediator of knowledge but she herself does not possess it.

Who was Mary? If we are to believe the biblical sources and the scholarly brotherhood as they have presented it, Mary was brought by her parents, Joachim and Anna, to the temple to work as a servant until her marriage to the aged carpenter Joseph. She was visited by a winged messenger who told her that the Holy Spirit—a divine lover—would come upon her and she would conceive the child of God. Thirty years later Mary was witness to the brutal murder by torture of her son. But she was rewarded in an unusual way for her life's work. She went to heaven, where her son was also lodging, became his "bride" (for in the Bible Jesus is known as the Bridegroom of Heaven), and was crowned the Queen of Heaven.

So much for the particulars. The most important questions for our study are these: What sort of picture did the artist paint of Mary, the witch's virtuous sister? And what can the settings of these paintings tell us of the worldview the Church sought to oppose to the natural world of the witch?

In paintings, drawings, and woodcuts by northern European artists Mary is usually

"This, the world of medicine see, with the weeds removed from sight. This is a rose, of thorns free, with a lily's chastity bright."

—HEINRICH VON LAUFENBERG

---

[2] Under the entry for the word *Hexe* (witch) in the 1877 edition of *Grimm's Wörterbuch* [Grimm's Dictionary], one definition is an insult for an "ugly old woman, because people think of witches as wrinkled and blear-eyed." The word is also defined as a "kind of term of endearment for a young and supple maiden."

[3] Mary, however, is indeed invoked as a magical healer in the world of folk customs. Examples have been cited by Eva Labouvie in van Dülmen, 1987: 59, 61.

dressed in expensive clothes and appears regal—even amid the dreary scenery of the manger. As the embodiment of the Mother she holds the baby Jesus in her lap. This image of the mother with child was modeled upon the Egyptian goddess Isis with her baby, Horus. In ancient Egypt and the traditions of late antiquity, Isis was the authority on medicinal herbs. Isis cults existed in the southern Germanic regions up to the beginning of the Christian conversion.[4]

As a rule, in paintings Mary has been represented in an environment created by humans. As the intercessor for the fallible humans, who turn to her and to heaven, Mary is often surrounded by lofty and elaborate architecture. Thus in the early fifteenth century the worldly and Churchly dignitaries—as well as the common people, whose primary source of theological instruction came from the art displayed in the churches—encountered their heavenly mediator kneeling on decorative tiles in lavish halls with ornate columns and surrounded by bull's-eye windows, as in the painting of the Annunciation by Jan van Eyck. In the distance are cities, symbolizing the sacred city of Jerusalem, and trade ships sailing on rivers. Even when the monks and abbots who beseeched her heavenly grace encountered Mary's image in "the fields of paradise,"[5] she was not out in nature but inside walled temples.

When one does see Mary in nature—for instance, during her escape with Joseph and the child of God to Egypt—it is an exotic fantasy of nature, where the trees almost genuflect to the divine descendant and in the distant sky threatening clouds announce the drama of the Bethlehem child-murder that was left behind. In devotional paintings, scenes of the baby Jesus playing unself-consciously on Mary's lap are also often presented in lavishly adorned environments. If a natural area is depicted, it is a carefully laid-out garden surrounded by a hedge, a wall, or a well-tended rose screen, depending on the fashion of the times. (In Germany, "Mary in the Rosebush" is an independent genre of Mary images extant since the thirteenth century, with its apex occurring in the fifteenth century.) In the well-known examples of this genre by Stefan Lochner (c. 1448) and Martin Schongauer (1473), one sees a domesticated nature in which the leaves of the roses, the strawberry plants, and the lilies are woven together into a tapestry. Therein the "beloved Virgin" finds herself well protected and sheltered, as if in a jewelry box. Her long golden hair, which symbolizes the sun and its radiance (an attribute of the light-gods of the Old Norse Eddas*), flows loosely on her shoulders, while her buttoned-up dress ensures that no glance of her body will detract from her motherliness. The shawl around her head, like that which Muslim women wear, is in the traditional color of Mary: blue or red. The blue of the sky and the red of the Eucharist blood are also contained in this color symbolism, chiefly as the blood of Mary's sacrificed son, Jesus, which the faithful "ingest" during Mass in the form of red wine.

Like the colors, the environment and the few animals and plants that have surrounded Mary in art since early Christian times have symbolic meanings. The enclosed garden is a dominant symbol for the chastity of the Virgin Mary, who is—as can be seen by her loose hair—not a married woman but more like an innocent girl, pure and

In the middle of flowering plants stands a woman with a high-necked vestment, accompanied by two cherubs. It must be Mary, for lilies of the valley, carnations, and especially the lily on the right side are symbols of the Mother of God. (From Lonicerus, *Kreüterbuch*, 1679.)

---

[4] The religion of Isis crossed the Mediterranean into Greece from Egypt and was thence carried throughout the Roman Empire by its legions. It found fertile soil in the more southern regions of Germany, where it persisted until Christianity began to prevail, following the conversion of the Frankish king Clovis in the late fifth century. See Giebel, 1990: 149–194.

[5] The stories of the Middle Ages collected by Joseph Klapper contain the visions of an abbot who found himself transported "to a beautiful meadow in which a temple stood. . . . And he entered the temple and waited, and saw the most Holy Virgin come and cut flowers from the trees that stood in front of the door, and braided six splendid garlands from them" (quoted in Hartlaub, 1947: 30f.).

* The Eddas are a collection of prose and poetry from medieval Iceland that detail the mythic material of pre-Christian Scandinavia. (Trans.)

chaste. This plane of symbolism is also the one addressed in the pictorial theme of "Mary in the Corn Dress": Hinrik Funhof of Hamburg (died c. 1484) depicted the Mother of God standing with folded hands and flowing hair; fertile life sprouts from her corn dress, which stands for the cultivated fields of the Middle Ages. This painting represents Mary as the field of God and an immaculate temple servant.

In the Song of Solomon the enclosed garden symbolized the closed womb of Mary, the virginal Queen of Heaven. The iconography in this scene of the well-cultivated garden surrounded by rosebushes or battlements is related to the Garden of Eden. In the oil painting Paradiesgartlein [Garden of Paradise] from circa 1410 executed by a master from the Upper Rhine, Mary is shown in an enclosed garden surrounded by lilies, lilies of the valley, strawberries, irises, primroses, fruit, and the deciduous trees of feminine saints, as if she were part of a courtly society.[6] (This painting can be viewed in the Frankfurt Städel museum.) All of these plants—especially the lily and the rose—refer to the chastity and faith of the Holy Virgin. They are the symbolic plants of Mary not because of their medicinal powers (or if so, only very tangentially), but because of their beauty, their pure white innocence, their Eucharist red color or their heavenly blue color.

The herb garden is depicted as a *Hortus conclusus*, an enclosed garden. (From Wahlafried Strabo, *Hortulus*, 15th century.)

These pictures of Mary indicate a path to the hidden cultural messages in the pictorial images of witches. The lily is white and immaculate. "Spring delight is the purity, and immortality always sprouts luxuriantly from her white blossoms," mused Methodius of Olympus on the lily. The Song of Solomon compares these sensuous and aromatic flowers with the Church and its true believers: "Be happy, sweet smelling lily! Lady, fill the faithful with your scent!" The song continues with the comparison that, like the "Virgin under the Jews and heathens who persecuted her," the lily remains "blinding white and brilliant through faith." Because the lily grows among thorns in Palestine, the land where Jesus was born, and because the flowers of the rose rise up on a thorny stem, both of these flowers became the symbols of the strength of Mary's faith amid an unchaste, unbelieving, and later apostate environment.[7]

In the year 430 the poet Sedulius attempted, by way of verse, to atone for the comparison between the rose and Mary, who had "atoned" for the actions of her sister, Eve, through the Immaculate Conception.

> *How innocently the rose blooms amidst the sharp thorns,*
> *with no wounding prickers it crowns the mother shrub with honor,*
> *And so too from out of the sacred clan of Eve came Mary full of grace;*
> *The Virgin atones, the new one, while the earlier Virgin fades away.*

The Christian mind-set that made an immaculate act out of conception and transformed a mother into the heavenly bride of her divine son influenced the cultural example of womanhood that ordinary women were meant to follow. But this was not apparent during the conversion of the former Roman Empire to Christianity. The early years of Christianity were marked by great suspicion and loathing of the female sex by

---

[6] Similar to the incorporation of pagan sites and beliefs into Christian practice, the pagan belief in tree spirits survives in the association of deciduous trees with female saints (who replace the former dryads in this Christian context).

[7] The common names of many plants mirror their symbolic classification. Often the same plant was associated with the divine as well as with the demonic. For instance, common German names for orchids (*Orchis* spp.) include *Unserer lieben Frau Hände* (our beloved Lady's hands), *Muttergotteshand* (Virgin Mary's hand), *Marienhand* (Mary's hand), *Teufelsoarsch* and *Teiwelwarsch* (devil's ass), *Bockwürze* (buck wort), and, in English, satyrion. The divergent symbolism is even contained in one expanded name, *Gottes Hand und Teufels Hinterbacken* (God's hand and devil's rear).

the fathers of the Church, who took their cues from Saint Paul in this regard. The effloresence of the cult of the Virgin Mary accompanied a widespread cultural reevaluation of the place of woman that gained ground in the eleventh century and grew stronger over the following centuries. Initially this led to more tolerance for women in general, not merely witches. But then, with the shock waves caused by the Black Plague, the Renaissance, and the Reformation, the Virgin mother and witches became paired in a dual relation, the celestial brilliance of the one matched by the infernal powers of the other.

As the cult of the Virgin Mary began gaining ground in the late eleventh century, emphasizing what the Church regarded as most virtuous in women, only a woman capable of imitating the Virgin Mary's example would be deemed worthy of sharing in her sacred exaltation. But what woman is capable of this? What bride does not fall into lust's "sink of iniquity" by fulfilling her marital duties? And what woman, after laying eyes on her love's masculine fruit and granting admittance to the fire of nuptial desire, could come away unburned?

The acrobatic efforts required to heed the example set by the Virgin Mary necessitated that some things be left behind—the qualities that were shunned were those that distinguish humans as part of nature, as sensuous beings. This dichotomy presumed evil in human nature and in the world (including the plant world) on the part of the early Christians. Such a presumption can be recognized in God's words as rendered in the first book of the Old Testament, when God chastises Adam for listening to Eve and eating from the tree in the middle of the Garden of Eden: "Cursed is the ground because of you; through painful toil you will eat of it all the days of your life. It will produce thorns and thistles for you, and you will eat the plants of the field" (Genesis 3: 17–18).

If we keep in mind how art has positioned the image of the witch in opposition to the Virgin Mary, the witch's transformation in the Christian imagination will become more clear. Nature is moody and unreliable. What it bestows upon humans in the form of insurmountable obstacles or natural catastrophes does not always coincide with humans' personal desires or requirements. Because we have, in our cultural circle, already bestowed the role of the benefactor—the all-knowing, the holy, and the good—upon God, his son Jesus Christ, the Virgin Mary, and the saints who act as mediators between the human and the divine spheres, the negative role was left to others, namely the devil and his human assistants: the warlocks and, above all, the witches.

If Mary is the rose or the lily among thorns, then the witch embodies the thorns.

The Symbolic Plants of Mary

LILY (*Lilium candidum* L.)

"In mythology and symbolism these lovely flowers with a delightful aroma have a double meaning. When the baby Hercules suckled on the divine breast of Hera he immediately demonstrated superhuman strength. He suckled so powerfully that part of the mother-milk flowed into the universe and thus the Milky Way was created. A drop fell on the earth. There where it dampened the soil the first lily bloomed. When Aphrodite saw the pure white flower she became jealous and out of spite made an enormous, obscene stamen, the 'donkey penis,' grow out of the middle of the white blossom. Therewith the plant guardian of chaste marriage became a symbol of the amorous adulteress. During the Catholic Middle Ages it once again became a symbol of chastity, and even of the Immaculate Conception—thus the name Madonna lily." (Rätsch, 1995: 216f.).

STRAWBERRY (*Fragaria vesca* L.)

Strawberries have been found in the northern European pile-dwelling settlements of the Neolithic period. They were possibly the remains of berry offerings for the wood spirits. In antiquity one finds reference to the strawberries that the "lady with the stinking husband" (Faun or Pan) sought out in the protected grove. For example, as Horace reported, "She goes around scot free in protected groves searching for hidden strawberry bushes and thyme from the path, the lady of the stinking husband" (*Odes* I: 17). To the Germanic peoples the red, sweet-smelling, good-tasting, and seductive fruit was sacred to their love goddess, Freya.

Christianity did not take up this sensuous symbolism but concentrated instead on the strawberry's lack of thorns, seed, or skin, from which the Christians strangely derived a symbolic connection with righteousness, modesty, and humility. The red flesh of the fruit became the symbol of the incarnation of Christ. The small white flowers of the strawberry plant became the symbol of Mary's innocence.

Folk medicine attributes to the plant an apotropaic, or demon-repelling, activity. In the art of the Middle Ages and the early modern era strawberries are found exclusively in the context of Mary and the Passion play of Christ.

ROSE (*Rosa* spp.)

To the family of the rose belong the hedge rose and the pleasant-smelling cultivated multiflora rose. Symbolic meanings associated with the rose are as multifaceted as its different species. The Germanic peoples consecrated the hedge rose to Frigga, the stern wife of their father god Odin/Wotan, who watches over moral laws. The red rose hips held thunderstorms and magic at bay.

In antiquity *Rosa centifolia* stood in close proximity to the love god Eros and was also an important ally (and thus an attribute) of Aphrodite, as its aroma excites erotic desire. Not only were the Romans and the Greeks under the spell of the rose's beauty and scent; poets of all cultures and times have been enthralled with this flower.

According to Gallwitz, "The early Christians detested the rose cult of the Romans . . . until they brought the rose's thorns into connection with Christ's crown of thorns" (1992: 204). For instance, the early Christians associated the five petals of the flower with the five wounds of Jesus Christ, and the flower, which sits on a thorny stem, with the chastity of Mary's Immaculate Conception.

The common people of the Middle Ages, and indeed even into the early twentieth century in rural areas, used the rose for love oracles. Other than rose hip tea, the rose, which has hardly any medicinal activity, was not used in a healing context.

LILY OF THE VALLEY (*Convallaria majalis* L.)

During heathen times the aromatic lilies of the valley were considered sacred to Ostara, the Anglo-Saxon and Germanic goddess of spring.

In the Christian context the small woods flower symbolized the Immaculate Conception, the Annunciation, the birth of Christ, and, ultimately, the Ascension, as well as modesty and humility. Painters depicted the plant, with its small white bell-shaped flowers, in images of Mary.

In the sixteenth and seventeenth centuries the lily of the valley was so well known as a medicine for strengthening the heart and brain that it became a heraldic symbol for physicians.

The Celtic druids ritually gathered this yellow-blossomed spring flower and treasured it as a medicine—one that also showed the way to buried treasure.

Because of its similarity to a key ring it is called "Saint Peter's key" in the Christian context. During the Middle Ages, Saint Hildegard of Bingen called the primrose *Schlüsselblume* (key flower) and wrote that it was used as a remedy for lameness and strokes. It also had the reputation of repelling demons.

In Christian art the primrose is an attribute of the Virgin Mary, especially in pictures of her Ascension but also in images of the Annunciation. The lily of the valley, however, often symbolized the Incarnation of Christ.

The Witch: The Sensuous Natural Woman

When one studies the drawings and the paintings of the witch that have been conveyed to the world through the European imagination since the end of the fifteenth century, one will recognize a world opposite that of the Virgin Mary. According to Christian understanding Eve, damned by God to carry thorns and thistles and to give birth in pain, was redeemed by Mary.[8] It is the offenses of this "earlier virgin," who was seduced by the serpent and ate from the tree of knowledge, that Mary atones for. [9] On the Cologne cathedral there is a statue from circa 1520 of Mary standing on a crescent moon,[10] inside of which is an image of the serpent wrapped around Eve and the apple; the "sinner" Eve stands in the middle of an unruly nature that eludes humans' toilsome attempts at cultivation. In contrast, Mary lives in the spiritual and cultivated domain of the world.

Mary has been depicted predominantly in an architectural, or man-made, environment. Pictures of Mary are solemn and static with a timeless, ideal quality. There is no place for emotions, much less passions, in these works of art. Through these images the Virgin Mary has been promulgated as the guardian of culture. From her sister, however, from the lady of the woods who is at home in the thorny brush, emanates a continual lurking danger that threatens all cultural achievements, including the moral and spiritual. In the pictures of witches we have a world where everything is in motion—a world that makes space for the forces of nature and the surge of emotions, a world in which the woods and the thorny wilderness impart a passionate, dramatic environment for the women, who are in ecstatic exultation.

From the late 1400s, when images of witches first began to appear in manuscripts and frescos, until the nineteenth century, when a more evenhanded attitude toward the witch began to prevail, witches were settled in an unwelcoming wilderness. In his thorough 1863 study of the sorceress (*La Sorcière*), which he worked on for more than thirty years, the broadly educated French naturalist, historian, and author Jules Michelet offered an answer to the question, Where are the witches? "In the most impossible places, in the

The herb considered the magical plant of Circe is still called enchanter's nightshade (*Circaea lutetiana* L.). (Woodcut from Gerard, *The Herbal*, 1633.)

---

[8] Many examples of this pair of opposites in medieval art were recognized by Ernst Guldan for his study *Eva und Maria: Eine Antithese als Bildmotiv* (Graz and Cologne: Hermann Böhlaus Nachfolger, 1966).

[9] In a 1504 engraving of the fall of man by Albrecht Dürer, Eve is surrounded by cats—the witch's traditional companions—and rabbits, both of which were attributed to the Germanic love goddess Freya.

[10] In this example the image of Isis again flows into the symbolism of Mary, as the Greek authors interpreted Isis as the moon goddess. As Mary does in this statue, Isis was commonly represented as standing on the crescent moon. There are other similarities to be found in the common artistic representations of Mary and Isis; the most preeminent is the resemblance of the Christian pietà to the many sculptures of Isis holding the dead Osiris across her lap. It is widely considered that the Black Madonnas found throughout Europe represent a transitional stage of the transformation of Isis into the Virgin Mary. Isis was also worshipped everywhere as the guardian of the dead; thus she was demonized and turned into a witch, to whom the night is sacred.

thorny woods, on the moors, there where hawthorn and thistle block the path. During the night in many an ancient megalithic grave."[11]

The illustrator Hans Weiditz, who worked in Strasbourg at the beginning of the sixteenth century, drew the witch in the "thorny woods." Weiditz created a woodcut for Francesco Petrarch's *Book of Philosophical Comfort*; written in 1468 and published in German in Strasbourg in 1532, the book is about how man walks on the path of virtue and through good and bad strokes of fate can grow morally. The woodcut by Weiditz is referred to as the "weather-witch" *(Wetterhexe)* or the "herb-lady" *(Kräuterfrau).*[12] In the middle of the thorny woods, surrounded by thistles, nettles, and brushwood, an old stooped woman with unkempt long hair stands on a stone pedestal. Like Atlas, on her shoulders she carries the world, in which the path of the moon and the stars has been inscribed. With her distaff she appears to influence not only the luxuriant growth of nature but also the raging thunderstorms and hailstorms that rain down on the fenced fields.

The eloquent art historian Wilhelm Fraenger poetically characterized this witch as nature's personification. "The woods woman is barely differentiated from her surroundings. Her furrowed face is the grooved bark. Her bent figure is a crooked stalk. Her crippled feet are like the roots, and her blowing hair is like the night wind." She is "so absolutely immersed in and akin to the nature that surrounds her" that she has an effect "as if she were the mythical symbolic embodiment of vegetation and atmosphere." And it appears "as if the stormy, stifling heat of a summer night, the knotted, dense woods, and the strange plants were embodied in the symbol of this old field spinstress" (Fraenger, 1985: 88, 89).

Hans Weiditz put much effort into the depiction of the plant world, and in 1529 he produced true-to-nature watercolors as drafts for the woodcuts of the herbal by the preacher and botanist Otto Brunfels, whose finely engraved system of plant roots is reminiscent of the blowing hair of the herb witch.[13] In the drawings of Weiditz, the witch, the nature woman, is not depicted as radiant and sensuously seductive. Instead her frightening physiognomy and her stooped posture are associated with plants that block the path for humans and cause them pain if they touch the herbs; this association endured through the centuries; thus, it is predominantly the thorny, prickly plants with burning nettle hairs that are known as "witches' herbs" in Grimm's Dictionary.

Albrecht Altdorfer (c. 1480–1538), one of the most important representatives of the Donau school, placed his witches in a dramatic wooded landscape such as the one in the drawing at right from the beginning of the sixteenth century.[14] Only one of the women depicted in this early drawing by Altdorfer wears the clothing of the time; the others are sparsely covered in scarves. With exalted expressions they seem to be influencing the boiling thunderclouds, which are being led to the sky by four witches riding on goats.

Hans Baldung Grien (1484–1545), who more than any other artist made the witch

Hans Weiditz depicts the weather-witch in an unwelcoming woods. She appears to be determining the path of the stars and conjuring stormy weather. (*Die Wetterhexe*, Woodcut in Petrarca, *Von der Artzney beyder Glück des guten und widerwertigen*, 1532.)

In the middle of the forest the witches surrender to the inebriating side of nature with ecstatic gestures and bared bodies during the witches' sabbat. (Albrecht Altdorfer, *Hexensabbat*, white-highlighted pen-and-ink drawing, Paris, Louvre, Cabinet des Dessins, 1506.)

---

[11] From the original French edition (Michelet, 1952: vol. 1, 9).

[12] Hans Weiditz's birth and death dates and the influence of his work are to a large degree unknown. He is referred to as a student of Albrecht Dürer. According to Woldemar von Seidlitz, the woodcuts in the book by Petrarch were attributed to a "Petrarch master." In 1904 Heinrich Röttinger identified the initials of this master as those of the Strasbourg resident Hans Weiditz. Fraenger (1985: 85ff.) refers to this identification as well, but the attribution is a very controversial topic in art history. In regard to the authorship of any illustration from that era, keep in mind that in the sixteenth century an artist would present watercolor sketches to an illustrator, who then made them into outline drawings. In turn these outlines served the woodcutter as a model, and finally the print was integrated into the typography.

[13] In 1930 W. Rytz discovered these watercolor sketches in the herbarium of the Bern Botanical Insititute, and they proved to be the original draft for the woodcuts in Otto Brunfels's *Contrafayt Kreüterbuch*. Rytz published these fifteen pieces in 1936.

[14] The 1506 date is contested, as it was written by a later hand.

Witches are the embodiment of nature. With their steaming bodies and long flowing hair, which Baldung has depicted like electrical streams of energy, the women arouse the forces of nature and liberate themselves from earth's gravity during the witches' sabbat. They were not bound to human form and were able to transform themselves into animals, usually cats, which the reading cat in the lower half of the picture suggests. (*Hexensabbat*, copy from Hans Baldung Grien, pen and ink, Strasbourg, Musée de l'Oeuvre Notre Dame, c. 1515.)

the protagonist of various drawings and even painted an oil on the theme, also depicted a dramatic and unleashed nature where the clouds race across the sky, lichen-hung trees are whipped by the wind, and steam rises like explosions from cauldrons or pots. Like Hans Weiditz, Hans Baldung, a painter from the Upper Rhine region who since his youthful entrance into the painting studio Grien had been called "the younger," was also a student of Albrecht Dürer and was acquainted with the Strasbourg botanist and preacher Otto Brunfels.[15]

In Baldung's earliest chiaroscuro from 1510 (see color plates)—one of the first examples of this subject matter and the technique of connecting dramatic light and dark shades with the picture's content—three naked witches crouch on the floor around a lidded pot decorated with perplexing symbols. A fourth rides backward through the air, sitting on a goat. She uses a pitchfork to transport a jug that has bones jutting out of it. In the clouds above left are two more witches who are being carried away by the storm, and another witch participates behind the central group of women. Bones and skulls lie on the ground along with a tassel and a hat, which is known to have been the headgear of the pilgrim monks.[16] A cat with its back to us and a hidden billy goat accompany the event.

The scenery in this chiaroscuro is determined predominantly by its nocturnal nature and atmospheric suggestions, as well as by the mimicry and dramatic expressions of the two young witches. The old witch, who while conjuring throws a plate into the air on which an animal-like cadaver is faintly recognizable, contributes to the dramatic atmosphere. Perhaps the animal lost its life in the cauldron. An inexplicable steam seethes from the cauldron despite the fact that a lid covers it and there is no fire beneath. The steam clouds that give dynamism to the picture emanate from the witches, who seem to be melded together as if by centrifugal force, their arms raised and legs stretched out.

In later drawings by Hans Baldung the plump bodies of the women, whose unified energies cause the atmosphere to surge, dominate the picture. In a copy of a drawing by Baldung dated 1515 and owned by the Strasbourg Musée de L'Oeuvre Notre Dame, the women themselves clearly create the dramatic thunderclouds with their body steam and unruly hair. Using magical formulas Baldung's witches handle rose garlands, as a perverted symbol of their normal role in Mary iconography, with pitchforks reminiscent of Neptune's (or Shiva's) trident. Usually an old witch assists a younger one in anointing her body, or the elder helps the youth escape gravity. Cats howl or peek out from the edges, and remains such as arm bones and skulls let the viewer guess what the disgusting ingredients of the potion, which is usually located in the center of the activities, might be.

Images such as these are the polar opposite of the serene and stately settings painters chose for depictions of the Virgin Mary. The wild and chaotic images of the witches created by painters in the fifteenth and sixteenth centuries would later assist in inspiring the fear that drove the witch hunts, a central feature of European life following the Reformation.

Because woman is closer to nature than man due to her physical cycles and her ability to create life, the reasons why Eve—the seducer of Adam—and her daughters became characterized over history as conflicting, ambivalent, disease-bringing, and opaque become obvious. The development of this negative projection is mirrored in the way the meaning of the words *hag* and *Hexe* (witch) have changed over time—both words can be

---

[15] Lottlisa Behling mentions this acquaintance in her 1957 investigation of the *Pflanzen in der Mittlealterlichen Tafelmalerei* [Plants in Medieval Altar Painting].

[16] Such a hat appears as the headgear of Saint Jerome in the left wing of the high altar of Freiburg, also painted by Hans Baldung Grien.

The devil is held responsible for the existence of all plants that the educated believe belong in the hedgerow. These include not only the so-called weeds, but also the plants that have the ability to alter consciousness. In the foreground of this painting, called *The Devil Sows Weeds*, the devil has even planted mushrooms in the fields. (By Jacob de Gehyn II [1565–1629], *Der Teufel sät Unkraut*, 1603.)

traced back to *hae*, which means "hedgerow" or "grove." At one time *hag* and *Hexe* simply meant "lady of the hedge" or "lady of the grove."[17] But the wilderness will always grow over cultivated gardens—the witch will always threaten the realm of Mary. Thus, from a monotheistic or Christian perspective, the activities of the lady of the hedge could be understood only as destructive. This cultural underpinning informed the editor of Jacob Grimm's 1877 edition of the German dictionary when he decided that the definition of a witch was "she who destroys the crops, fields, and soil."

A biblical passage from Matthew underscores the opposition between the good and cultivated plant world and the wild and untamed one:

> But while every one was asleep his enemy came, sowed darnel [weeds] among the wheat, and made off. . . . The sower of the good seed is the Son of Man. The field is the world; the good seed stands for the children of the Kingdom, the darnel for the children of the evil one. The enemy who sowed the darnel is the devil. The harvest is the end of time. . . . As the darnel, then, is gathered up and burnt, so at the end of time the Son of Man will send out his angels (Matthew 13: 25–40).

Thus the witch became identified as the "weed between the wheat," so to speak.

The witches and the devil stand in alliance in the untamed world. The majority of art devoted to the image of the witch depicts her as the devil's henchman more frequently than her masculine colleague, the warlock, is depicted as such. According to concepts borne in the early Renaissance, women were more often visited by the devil than men because women—as Hermann Wilcken, who was elected rector of Heidelberg University in 1569, believed—were more easygoing, forward, and vindictive than men. Women's

Plant Classification in the Visual Arts

MARY (Cultivated plant)	WITCH (Wild plant)
lily	thistle
rose	henbane
strawberry	nettle
lily of the valley	mandrake
primrose	belladonna

[17] Wolfgang Behringer suggested the first time the term *Hexe* appeared in connection with black magic was in 1293 (in van Dülmen, 1987: 134). Since the fifteenth century *Hexe* has been synonymous with the unusual and the destructive. Ralph Metzner (1994: 152), proceeding from the Germanic word *Hagezussa* (hag or sorceress) and the medieval *zunrita* ("she who rides on the fence"), thought about the idea that shamans and soothsayers go through the hedge, which signifies a threshold and border, and that they travel out of the mundane reality into the world beyond. This is made possible by altered states induced by plants.

The plumeless thistle (*Carduus acanthoides* L.) is one of the few identifiable plants found on images of witches from the early modern era. A decoction of the roots was drunk as a remedy for poison. (Woodcut from Fuchs, *New Kreüterbuch*, 1543.)

talkativeness also contributed, for it helped quickly disseminate the devil's information; for this reason the devil was more likely to teach women his black arts than men. And women were associated more with the idea of seduction, which men, in their fear of impotence and physical inadequacies, have always confronted in a rather apprehensive manner. As far back as the fifteenth century the authors of the disastrous *Hexenhammer* [*Malleus Malificarum*, or Hammer of the Witches]* had written that the heresies of witches must be addressed, yet those of warlocks, whose numbers were said to have diminished, were not as important.

While the time of the Renaissance and Reformation brought about great cultural advances, it was also a time in which traditionally more tolerant attitudes toward witchcraft changed drastically. Following the devastation of the Black Plague in the fourteenth century, Catholics and Protestants alike became convinced of the existence of malign conspiracies seeking to destroy the Christian realms through magic and poison, both areas in which the witch was alleged to be proficient. The insecurity caused by the rapid changes in European culture found a ready target in the demonized figure of the witch, and thousands of women were persecuted even into the eighteenth century.

During the witch trials women were repeatedly accused of assaults on the physical and spiritual health of others in the community, on the cultivated plants, and on neighbors' domestic animals. But the first offense the Church accused people of was hanging on to their heathen practices and leaving the path of the true believers in order to bring destruction to society. The 1484 papist bull *Summis desiderantes affectibus* [Desiring with the greatest anxiety] by Pope Innocent VIII, whose name is nothing if not ironic, fanned the flames of fear and hate against warlocks and witches. This papist bull accused "many persons of both sexes" of activities that directly threatened the rest of the citizenry as they struggled to maintain their farms and homes by cultivating nature in order to survive. In it he said:

> [These people] unmindful of their own salvation and deviating from the Catholic Faith, have abused themselves with devils, incubi and succubae, and by their incantations, spells, conjurations, and other accursed superstitions and horrid charms, enormities and offenses, destroy the offspring of women and the young of cattle, blast and eradicate the fruits of the earth, the grapes of the vine and the fruits of the trees; and also men and women, beasts of burden, herd beasts, as well as animals of other kinds; also vineyards, orchards, meadows, pastures, corn, wheat, and other cereals of the earth. Furthermore, these wretches . . . torment with pain and disease, both internal and external; they hinder men from generating and women from conceiving; whence neither husbands with their wives nor wives with their husbands can perform the conjugal act. [18]

In the end the witch was more likely to be seen as offering her services as a black

[18] Quoted in the original German edition from Biedermann, 1974: 18. Quoted here from Robbins, Rossell, *The Encyclopedia of Witchcraft and Demonology*, New York: Crown Publishers, 1959, pages 264, 265.

* The *Hexenhammer* is the German title of the *Malleus Maleficarum* [Hammer of the Witches], a tract written in Latin by two Dominican scholars, first printed in Cologne in 1486. It is without a doubt the most influential and sinister work on demonology ever written, and is the source material and inspiration for all other treatises on witchcraft. The *Malleus Maleficarum* sought to codify folklore as black magic and relate it to the Church dogma on heresy. In particular the tract cast women in a negative light, stating (falsely), for instance, that *femina* derives from *fe* = "faith" and *minus* = "less." The *Malleus Maleficarum* provided the primary source material for the Inquisition. Interestingly, the tract was also accepted as an authority by the Protestants, who otherwise opposed the Inquisition. It was reprinted numerous times in German, French, English, and Italian and was used as a textbook for witch-hunters into the seventeenth century. It remains in print to this day, albeit as a curiosity. (Trans.)

magician and weather-demon, as a representative of "unholy" nature who brings disease, than her masculine counterpart. Perhaps the woman witch was more strongly anthematized because of the fears she inspired of being able, like Eve, to coerce and cajole others into doing her bidding. Though not actual embodiments of the devil themselves—he was depicted as in attendence with witches at their Sabbaths—like Eve, witches emerge from the left or sinister side, traditionally viewed as the devil's realm. Accordingly, her trance journeys, her plant knowledge, and her ability to control the weather were no longer viewed as socially beneficial, as they had been in pagan times, but as devices of the devil to seduce godfearing men from the Christian way.

In 1985 Herman de Vries made this four-part work *monumenta lamiae*. It consists of four plants with the reputation of having once been ingredients in witches' salves. They are (from left to right): monkshood *(Aconitum)*, rye with ergot *(Claviceps)*, belladonna *(Atropa)*, and valerian *(Valeriana)*. (Herman de Vries, *Vierteiliges Monument aus getrockneten Pflanzen;* photo by N. Koliusis.)

The Symbolic Plants of the Witch

MANDRAKE (*Mandragora* spp.)
During Christian times the root of this herb was called *Hexenkraut* (witches' wort), *Unhold Wurzel* (monster root), or Satan's apple. In German it is called *Alraune*. It was so treasured as a panacea that it was called *Artz-wurzel* (doctor root), [19] and quack doctors even carved fakes out of other roots and sold them for high prices. Into the sixteenth century a wise woman or a witch was called an *Alraundelberin* (mandrake bearer). Golowin (1973: 33) discusses these women and refers to various examples from the fifteenth century and onward in which women were persecuted because they used mandrake for magical purposes. Those who kept mandrake in their homes received information about the hidden connections of the present and the future. A mandrake was even found wrapped in fabric in a very small box under the nuns' chairs in the choir at the north German cloisters at Wienhausen. The art historian Horst Appuhn explained that such forbidden possessions could be safely sacrificed in such a sacred place. [20]

---

[19] This is the term used by Williram von Ebersberg in his exegesis to the Song of Solomon in 1060 (see also Müller-Ebeling, 1987: 144).

[20] See Horst Appuhn, *Der Fuund vom Nonnenchor*, Wienhausen: Kloster Wienhausen, 1973: 52: "Protection against evil and fear of punishment were thus united with sacrifices and the hope for the blessing of the highest one." The cloister itself was established in 1221 and moved to Wienhausen in 1231. The nun's choir at the cloisters was built in 1305.

HENBANE (*Hyoscyamus* spp.)

Hildegard of Bingen mentions henbane oil as an ingredient in a bath that was purported to be a remedy for leprosy. In art henbane has played only a subordinate role. For example, the plant was identified on a panel by Albrecht Altdorfer (Behling, 1957: 126f.) that depicts John the Baptist and Saint John the Evangelist. The painter placed the henbane near the lamb, the symbol of the death of Jesus, and John the Baptist prophetically points to the animal. Henbane was described by Albertus Magnus to be a plant that invokes demons, so we can interpret that the demons are driven out through Christ. Henbane only rarely appears in pictures of witches, although it is referred to repeatedly in literature as an ingredient in the witches' brews and salves.

THISTLE (various species)

Because rainwater gathers in the leaf bases on the stems of thistles, these thorny meadow plants, of which there are three genera and numerous species, was known as the *Labrum Veneris*, or "the bath of Venus," during antiquity. (*Labrum Veneris* can also mean "the lips of Venus.")

Because of its prickly appearance, thistle is a symbol of negative characteristics and their attendant circumstances. Thus thistle was considered a sign of laziness, decay, or corruption, although its prickliness was also thought to guard against demons and witches. If the plant is hung in the barn, the thistle protects against black magic.

In art thistle is found now and again in pictures of witches, and it is also found (along with the goldfinch) on images of the flight to Egypt, in which the thistle symbolizes the salvation of souls.

NETTLE (various species)

Konrad of Megenberg wrote that nettles awaken lust. Thus Albrecht Altdorfer logically placed the plant in a picture of Susanna at the bath in which two lascivious men lie in wait and watch Susanna, though she was able to resist their indecent intentions. Nettle played an important role in pictures of witches because the plant represented the wilderness and weeds. The botanical name for blind nettle, *Lamium album*, is derived from the Latin word for witch, and the herb appears on the Isenheim panel by Matthias Grünewald as one of the components that were being worked into a remedy for Saint Anthony's fire.

MONKSHOOD (*Aconitum napellus* L.)

The common name of this plant probably derives from the similarity of the flower to a monk's hood or a knight's helmet, as it is also called. In German its common names include *Sturmhut* (storm cap) and *Eisenhut* (iron cap). But the name of the Egyptian goddess Isis can also be found in Hieronymus Bock's 1539 rendition of a picture called the *Isenhütlin* (Little Iron Hat). Heavenly and divine associations also become animated in the southern Austrian names *Himmelmutterschlapfen* (heavenly mother slipper) and *Venuswägelchen* (little chariot of Venus) that Marzell (1935: 80) found in nearby regions. Venus also came to mind for the French when they gazed on this poisonous blue-flowered plant, and thus they call it *char de Venus* (chariot of Venus) (Gawlik, 1994: 14).

The depiction of the Virgin Mary with the baby Jesus derives from the model of

Isis with the baby Horus. In ancient Egypt and the tradition of late antiquity, Isis knew about medicinal plants. Isis cults in southern Germany were active until the conversion to Christianity. Over the course of the Christian conversion the love goddess was demonized and transformed into a witch, and monkshood was mentioned repeatedly in her flying salves. The association of the medicinal and poisonous plant monkshood with goddesses that belong to different religious realms is a long cultural tradition.

The Demonization of Nature and Sensuality

In the pictures of witches that we describe here, the elemental violence of nature is depicted. This usually includes a wilderness that has been left alone, without any cultivating or domesticating interference. Storms rage in this wilderness. Life triumphs over transitoriness, and in a countermovement transitoriness triumphs over life: The young witches' plump bodies, in their prime, are placed in sharp contrast to the skulls and bones on the ground, while animals and, it appears, children are sacrificed in the cauldron. Among the witches themselves the old and the young do not fight. They are not as uninterested in one another as they are in other images in which naked women are grouped together, such as the three Graces, or as representatives of the different stages of life. Quite the reverse is true: The witches are bound together in a communal cult activity in an ecstatic way.[21] Old women with wrinkled skin and drooping breasts anoint the bodies of their younger colleagues, who are in the flower of their life. "Nature" is represented by the forest landscape with trees (often dead trees), and moss and lichen offer a nourishing ground. Unbridled nature is also shown in the untamed, trancelike ecstasy of the women, who, with their obscene farts, coquettish exhibitionism, and blasphemous consecration of sacred objects, reveal that there is more to their actions than a lack of modesty or good behavior.

With their ecstatic comportment and naked bodies the witches represent the unruly and intoxicating power of nature itself.[22] However, despite all the fertile lusciousness suggested in witch images, the women do not represent motherly, decent, and charitable femininity but rather the threatening, raging, destructive part of feminine nature that is repulsed not even by infanticide.

When we compare such images of witches in the wilderness with depictions of the environment surrounding the Virgin Mary, we see that in the latter the divine clearly shows itself as a spiritualized form of nature. The wooded landscape of the witch's scene

"The first Christians slandered nature as a whole and in detail, in the past and in the future. They cursed nature in and of itself. They damned it so completely, that even in a flower they only saw evil incarnate—a demon embodied. . . . Not only were we [the humans] demonized—for goodness' sake—but all of nature was demonized. If the devil is already found in a flower, then he must really be present in the dark forest."

—JULES MICHELET, *LA SORCIÈRE* [THE SORCERER], 1952

---

[21] During her research into the depictions of witches made between 1885 and 1920, Ulrike Stelzl (1983: 119) made the startling observation that there are neither gender nor generational conflicts—a democratic atmosphere reigns among the people in these pictures. In general neither animals nor nature is oppressed. Stelzl came to the conclusion that the artists had portrayed witches as "figures of opposition" to the norms of their time rather than as "enemies" of their time.

[22] If the subject of a picture by Baldung had not been chosen by him but was instead painted in an academic context, then this emphasis on the intoxicating and erotic content might be seen as a reflex of the conflict between academic medicine and authoritative theology. As we know from Paracelsus's conscious disassociation from the doctor Galen (129–c. 199 C.E.) (who also played a role in the philosophy of the fifteenth century), "The physicians observed . . . that in the suppression of the sexual drive there was a serious danger that could become fatal under certain circumstances. The retention of certain juices that by their nature are supposed to be excreted was thought to make them convert to serious poisons in the body. For this reason the advice was to secrete them through coitus and onanism. A medium for restoring the exhausted life-spirit in the brain was seen in intoxication. Therefore the [medical] advice was to get completely drunk once a month." In his extremely thorough study *Über den Einfluß der autoritativen Theologie auf die Medizin des Mittelalters*, Paul Diepgen (1958: 19) discussed this opposition between medicine, which is interested in physical health, and theology, which concerns spiritual health. With the Lateran council in 1215, Pope Innocent III made a prohibition against such therapeutic measures. In the Christian context Baldung's emphasis on intoxicated behavior represented sin, and sin caused disease—for which the witches were ultimately held responsible.

stands in contrast to the architectural landscape or the enclosed garden in which Mary sits with the baby Jesus and the saints. The naked body stands in contrast to the concealed one, as do the ecstasy and the solemn peace, the unleashing of desires and their subjugation, the wilderness and the world of cultivated plants. The divine sphere is thus understood as a perfect example of the spirit. If humans understand themselves as spiritual beings and the creation of God "in his own image," as it says in the Bible, then the task is to distance oneself as far as possible from nature and to make one's separation from nature as distinct as possible.

This path has been argued since the beginning of Christian culture. The more humans, through the strength of their will and their capacity to reason, shield themselves from their inner nature and the nature they encounter in plants and animals, the more those humans can, according to Christian doctrine, participate in the sphere of the spiritual and become closer to God—a masculine god, of course. The spiritual and moral duty of humans to fence themselves off from nature inevitably leads to a polarization of values: Nature is bad, spirit is good. Such a value judgment leads to the spirit becoming "divine" and nature, in contrast, becoming "diabolic." In this context it is revealing that the medieval paintings of the heavenly spheres depict an abstract gold background (or deep blue arches), and paradise is built up like a kind of heavenly Jerusalem, while lush nature is allowed a presence only in hell. In the cultural sphere of the West (and this is the only one we are speaking about here) animals and plants were discovered very late as suitable subjects for art, and it was not until even later that they were depicted as the sole feature of a composition.

The human's desire to distance himself from nature leads not only to a liberation of the forces of nature, which the heathens saw embodied in gods and elemental spirits and whose forces the human allegedly felt surrendered to (as authors still emphasize today), but also to distancing, to an alienation from nature—and ultimately to its destruction, which, as we know, has had devastating consequences.

Places where the untamed forces of nature manifest became, in the Christian perspective, workshops of the devil. These were predominantly the white-water rapids, mountain ponds, high ridges, deep mountain ravines, and steep cliffs. In these picturesque places nature spirits once revealed themselves to humans. The high mountains were where the Rübezahl—the mountain spirit, weather god, and herb spirit—lived, and such wild places were called "Rübezahl's gardens" or "Rübezahl's pulpit." These places were later renamed "devil's ground" or "devil's pulpit."

People's enduring belief that nature beings live in cliffs where the weather has left its traces or in ancient knotty trees that the powers of imagination have turned into bizarre images and faces recently became clear to me. On a trip to the Massa Marittima in Tuscany I came to a small village called Magliona. There stands an olive tree (*Olea europaea* L.) that is called *olivo della Strega*—the "olive tree of the witches." If one believes the families who live there, who can date the olive trees in their own garden four hundred years back, then the olivo della Strega, which is found near an old church, is nearly six hundred years old. Out of its totally hollow, knotty, enormous trunk grows a new trunk that still bears green leaves and olives. When you walk around the tree, which is fenced in as if it were a shrine to nature, the hooked-nose profile of an old woman can be seen in the twisted, overgrown bark. However, this imagistic association with the witch is not why the tree got its name. When asked why this tree is called the olive tree of the witches, an old native olive farmer explained that tree nymphs still live in such ancient trees, and over time they have become witches. Thus not only did the farmer know the philosophy of his ancestors, but also he knew something about the wondrous transformation from nymph into witch.

Sinister Companions of the Witch

Identifiable plants that are associated with witches are seldom found in portrayals of witches. Ultimately this comes as no surprise—after all, one is not horrified by a plant like henbane, with its pretty blossoms. Despite all interpretive efforts this poisonous plant radiates nothing that could be construed as negative. But when it comes to the prickly thistle, thornbush, or nettle it's a different story. When we see these plants we are all too quickly reminded of direct painful encounters. Thistles, thornbush, and nettles are occasionally found in pictures of witches, such as the one by Hans Weiditz.

The frightening elements of the plant world are better expressed in written form. In the end, the illustrative scenes of witches were meant to convince the observer of the evil endeavors of these notorious women. Thus, certain animals are customarily represented; due to their appearance or habits, the animals that are depicted have a sinister aura and can elicit revulsion and fear. Examples from the "revolting menagerie" include spiders, toads, owls, and snakes.[23] The witch craze itself contributed to the fear-inducing image that was attached to the animals: For example, their black color had disastrous effects on the cultural fate of ravens, cats, bats, rats, and various insects, which over time were turned into diabolic animals and disease demons.[24] Because of this tradition of demonization, most of these animals must seriously fight for their survival, because humans barely grant them the right to exist.

Over the course of Western history humans have increasingly claimed the living space of the wild animals for settlements, farmland, and pastureland for their domesticated "working" animals. Humans thus wound up in conflicts with animals such as the bear and the wolf, which were demonized as beasts. This mind-set has prepared the soil for the animals' extinction. A call for the elimination of "pests" has been systematically fed in pictures and words, and the resulting notions can still be observed today. For example, in *Brehms Tierleben* [Brehm's Life of Animals] from 1878 the wolf is called "a destructive predator." The 1895 edition, published by Brockhaus, reported that the wolf was known for its blood lust and cowardice, and that the "best way to exterminate it is by clearing the forests and shooting it." This goal has been fulfilled, and the announcement of the wolf's extinction was recorded in the 1974 edition of the book.[25]

Back to the time of the witch trials. As humans congregated into settlements, they set themselves up behind high city walls and forts and in protected rooms. The more they moved out of the country and into the city, the more they distanced themselves from nature, alienating themselves from nature's way of being and appearances. The local deities and nature spirits—the nymphs of the springs, the sylphs, and the fairies of the air—became alien. And beings that become alien because their way of life is no longer

The salamander, symbol of alchemy, is one of the typical ingredients of the magic potions brewing in the witches' cauldron. The poison in the salamander's skin contains psychoactive compounds. In Slovenia a psychedelic schnapps is still distilled from live salamanders. (Woodcut, 16th century.)

---

[23] Feelings of revulsion against these creatures lasted for centuries and were resistant to all enlightened knowledge. Insects, amphibians, and small mammals that live underground not only have a position high up on the scale of revulsion, but members of this group reappear again and again as ingredients of witches' potions. In this context the creatures' possible healing attributes were turned into their frightening opposite. The results of a contemporary survey conducted by the Marplan Institute revealed that 40.1 percent of those surveyed are afraid of rats, 32.3 percent are afraid of spiders, and 24.7 fear snakes (Kokrotsch and Rippchen, 1997: 80).

[24] Such creatures were also considered the cause of disease even when they were attributed with healing activity. For example, the Greeks used cockroach flour with rose oil for ear infections, and the pharmaceutical manufacturer Merck included powdered cockroach as a medicine in 1907 (Kokrotsch and Rippchen, 1997: 62).

[25] Cf. Müller-Ebeling, 1991: 163–181.

known mutate into frightening ghosts. In the imagination of the city dwellers, behind the gates of their growing settlements monsters lurked in the woods, the swamps, and the mountains, where they laid in wait for their victims.

Inside settlements, on the other hand, the forces of nature lose their immediate threat. For this reason humans have become increasingly fearful of the images of their own spiritual life, of the inner life of the human. People fear their own personal thoughts and desires, suffering increasingly from centuries of rhetorical bombardment by clergy promulgating dramatic images of teeth-bearing and clawing demons of desire.

According to heathen ideas, the presence of the gods is revealed in nature. Subsequently, animals stand close to the Divine; animal-human hybrids represent the numinous. But in Christian thought animals do not have souls, which is why the incarnation of the devil must be tamed by the culture of humans. Beloved depiction of such taming is embodied in the archangel Michael or in Saint George fighting the dragon.

Saint Augustus taught that *aves sunt daemones* ("birds are demons"). Birds are no longer symbols of the soul, as they were in ancient tradition; these animals threaten humanity's peaceful soul. Hence predators such as the owl and raven, who are traditional companions of the witches, are frequently portrayed as threatening.

The owl. The owl is sinister. Its flight is silent and its feather dress allows it to blend in with the forest, where it often sits perfectly still on a trunk and observes the area with its phosphorescent eyes and its head, which can turn almost 180 degrees.

In antiquity the owl was a symbolic bird of Minerva, the goddess of knowledge and wisdom. The Romans, who worshipped her as the patroness of the arts and crafts, identified her with the Greek goddess Athena, whose "headquarters" were in Athens. But the owl's story was different during Christian times. According to old sources and pictures from the Netherlands, including those of Bosch, the owl is a diabolical animal that embodies lies, blindness, ignorance, insanity, and drunkenness. The owl appears in many depictions of the temptation of Saint Anthony in conjunction with sexual seduction and as a symbol of heresy.[26]

The raven. People who live in connection with nature, such as Native Americans on the West Coast of North America, honor the raven as a totem animal—a sacred messenger between the shamans and the gods. Among the Greeks the raven was the bird of Apollo. In Germanic mythology ravens, called *Hugn* and *Munin* (thought and memory), were companions of Odin/Wotan. To all northern peoples the raven was a transmitter of culture, and some even believed that a raven made the human race.

In the Christian context the raven was denigrated as the embodiment of the devil because of its black color. Its screeching, which rings through the fog on cold autumn days, has a haunting effect. These shrieking birds feed on carrion. When the gallows were still part of daily existence, people encountered ravens there and at cemeteries; for this reason they were feared as unclean birds of bad luck. The raven, like most animals that surround the witches, are under the rule of the planet Saturn, and became the traditional companions of the witch. This idea influenced the collective consciousness so much that ravens stereotypically sit on the shoulders of witches. In a variety of cultures fly agaric, the psychoactive *Amanita muscaria* mushroom, is called raven's bread.

[26] The moral symbolism of these animals in Bosch paintings was identified by the art historian D. Bax in his comparison *Hieronymus Bosch and Lucas Cranach: Two Last Judgement Triptychs, Description and Exposition*, (Amsterdam, Oxford, New York: North Holland Publishing Company, 1983).

The toad. In the next section we will learn about a group of medicines that were known as "toad herbs." In the first century C.E. Pliny had already reported on the poison from the gland secretions of the toad, and bestowed this amphibian with negative associations that easily awaken unpleasant feelings. The toad lives in the swampy morass, where humans feel insecure. In folk beliefs the toad, and its close relative the frog, plays a significant role.[27] In Christian iconography the toad is encountered as a symbolic animal of the devil, and it also represents transience and burdens. This negative complex is dramatically seen on the sculptures of Lord of the World and Lady World found on Gothic cathedrals. The sculptures offer the observer a seductive view, but when one looks behind the beautiful appearances one will see that toads and worms are gnawing on Lady World's spine.

The dragon. With the dragon, various fear-inducing aspects are melded together to form a new hybrid: one that slithers like a snake, has the wings and claws of predatory birds, and shows the teeth-baring jaws of predatory animals. Such threatening primordial beings put heroes to the test, haunted saints, and forced themselves on innocent virgins. Dragons naturally appeared as the embodiment of terror and sin in many variations of images of the witches' kitchen or the witches' sabbat.

The billy-goat, ram, and ibex. With their horned aggressiveness these animals embody masculine sensuality and potency, and they became in the Christian imagination the perfect example of the devil and the deadly sin of lust. In the countless and often drastic scenes of the horror of the Last Judgment, during which Satan pulls the damned from all social classes into his hellhole, the devil and his assistants are depicted with goat legs. Satan, who as an incubus with lecherous intentions visits women who are easily seduced, reveals his true nature on various woodcuts, on which he has horns that poke through his gallant hat or goat's hips that jut out of his pants. During the witches' sabbat the devil, in the shape of a black goat, plays a central role, and the witches demonstrate their respect by kissing him on his rear end. The Greeks, on the other hand, worshipped the goat-legged one as Pan, the flute-playing god of fertile nature.

The bat. The bat is a nocturnal animal that moves silently and orients itself in total darkness by ultrasound tones that are beyond the range of human senses. Thus, for seers and mystics the bat was a symbol of the receptivity of natural forces that usually remain hidden to humans. Although there are only a few bloodsucking bat species,[28] this harmless animal was connected to the idea of the vampire. In art the wings of this flying mammal—an animal that lives in caves—are used to symbolize a diabolic nature. In depictions of the witches' sabbat and the witches' kitchen, as well as in written accounts, bat's blood has been repeatedly named as an ingredient of magical potions.

Blood and all other forms of animal excretions have always been associated with the underworld, the chthonic energies, and the witches' brews, and have been included in medicine chests known as "filth-pharmacy" since ancient Egyptian times. (Woodcuts from Lonicerus, *Kreüterbuch*, 1679.)

---

[27] Frogs were generally considered more lucky. One belief held that frogs carried the souls of dead children and thus it was unlucky to kill one; another that a precious stone could be found in a frog's head.

[28] While no bats native to Europe are members of the bloodsucking species, the bloodsucking vampire bat can be found in the Americas. The range of the Phyllostomidae Desmodus, or common vampire bat, extends from the northernmost areas of Mexico into the southwestern border of the United States to as far south as Argentina.

The cat was a sacred animal to the Germanic love goddess, Freya. In the early modern era the goddess was demonized and turned into a witch, and the cat became a witch's animal. Witches are said to transform themselves into cats in order to practice their sorcery. (Print illustration from Schmach, 1679.)

"The thorny branches became entangled in a brewing turmoil. The plants that stand their heavy, jagged leaves on end, and that raise up their flower heads and grape-like umbels in the night, and the herbs that cover the ground in fertile lushness, reminds us of the terrible science of the herb-witch who sowed such plants, who brewed and dried them, and who knows how to extract magical drinks, elixirs, and medicine from them."

—WILHELM FRAENGER,
HIERONYMUS BOSCH, 1975

The cat. Cats have minds of their own. They are dependent only when they feel like being so, and they do not submit to the needs of humans. This has given cats the reputation of being "false." As a rule, cats are loners. At night they hunt animals that humans find cute, such as birds and rabbits. With their whiskers, and their eyes that flash at night when a light hits them, cats have several keen senses at their disposal. In Germanic mythology the chariot of the love goddess, Freya, was pulled by cats—perhaps because they were the symbol of fertility.

The bad-luck-bringing black cat remains the proverbial symbol of superstition. The fate of witches was tightly bound to that of cats, for often cats too were burned alive in order to destroy evil. Witches allegedly transformed themselves into cats. As late as 1850 the physician Leubscher wrote in his paper on the history of psychology that witches transform themselves into cats in order to creep up on children "to satisfy their vampiric desires." The German word *Ketzer* (heretic) is said to derive from *Katze* (cat). And the term *Kathars* (Cathari, a sect with dualistic theology from the Middle Ages, the members of which were accused of being heretics), is said to come from *Kater* (tomcat). Satan, the lord of the cats, is depicted not only as a buck but also as a tomcat whose rear end the witches kiss on Walpurgis Night.

"Poison Mixers" and Healers

In 1930, when Wilhelm Fraenger, an art historian with an interest in folklore, contemplated the "terrible science of the herb-witch" in his description of the picture by the Petrarca master Hans Weiditz (see the illustration on page 151), he demonstrated how enduring the patterns of association established in the fifteenth and sixteenth centuries have proved to be. The activities he described are similar to those of the world of hell, and the science of the witch is "terrible" because of the bones, skulls, animal cadavers, and even small children that were seen strewn about in the witches' environment or boiling in their cauldron. The imagination blended together such grisly set pieces and fashioned them into the props of a poison mixer, child murderess, and cannibal who was more likely to instigate bad weather than good or to mix black-magic potions than medicine.

Surprisingly, whether the witch-women used their magical and healing knowledge to heal *or* to do damage was not so important to the Church. In 1975 Barbara Ehrenreich and Deidre English quoted an English witch hunter who must have really been fearful of these women:

> For we must always keep in mind, that under witches we not only understand those who kill and torture, but all soothsayers, sorcerers, story-tellers, all magicians who are generally called wise men and wise women . . . and we also include all good witches, the ones who do not harm, but who do good deeds, the ones who don't corrupt and destroy, but who save and protect. . . . It would be a thousand times better for this country if all witches, but in particular the charitable ones, were killed.[29]

The Kartäus monk Johannes Hagen (c. 1415–1475) had a comparably healthier attitude toward witches. Hagen worked in Erfurt and gave himself the nickname Indaginis. Although he rejected—like almost all physicians of his time—the magical invocation of nature for the influencing of good and bad luck, he was, like the other doctors, at the same time convinced of the reality of demonic activities. But in the case of

[29] Unfortunately, this quote from the feminist-oriented authors is not dated. It comes from the edition by Opitz, 1995: 26.

one woman he took a different position. The "witch of Blomberg" was a woman accused of desecrating the host in 1460. She admitted her deed under torture but pleaded her innocence at the execution place, whereupon a heavy hailstorm came down. This storm, which was interpreted as a heavenly indication of the woman's guilt, was the reason they burned her. A decade later this incident still occupied the learned Kartäus monk. Hagen suggested that the bad weather had not necessarily been related to the witch and he accused the responsible clergy of possibly having the death of an innocent women on their shoulders.

In addition to the ruthless attitude of the English witch hunter quoted earlier, we shall consider an insightful, measured individual in order to paint a picture of the Church's attitude toward the healing arts, which they believed to be aligned with the so-called witches. In more than five hundred preserved texts, Johannes Indaginis represents the views of the reform theology of his order on the topic of the healing arts. The following is from the edition edited by Klapper, who relays Indaginis's writing in 1960.

> Forbidden are all "blessings" for the healing of diseases, for those against the attack of wolves, against the gnawing worms, for healing wounds, for removing bullets, to stop blood from flowing. Herbs and stones are only to be used according to their natural powers. It is deadly sin and murder when women and old ladies kill the unborn in the mother's womb with herbs, potions, or other methods.

Theologian Klapper sees Hagen in "the middle of a cultural process in which the bourgeois world was being released from concepts that still have their roots in pre-Christian concepts of folk wisdom."

Around 1462 the monk Hagen turned with vigor against these traditional "alien teachings" when he judged (here I am following Klapper's style) "magical things, magical treatments, conjurations, poisonous drinks, soothsaying, blessings, diabolic deceptions, witchery, divination, fortune-telling, seeing future events, day-choosing, sky gazing, solutions, pacts with the devil in the black arts, fortune telling with fire [and] earth, and other prognostications."[30] These are all activities of the witches who had been accused of diabolic activity. Their enumeration demonstrates how fluid the borders between magic and medicine were in the fifteenth century and how effectively medicinal knowledge had been pushed into the realm of superstitions as merely a diverse accumulation of false and alien teachings. In a spiritual sense this battle should primarily be viewed in front of the backdrop of the Church's exclusive claim on healing.

In contrast to our pragmatic times, in the fifteenth century medicinal and botanical knowledge was planted in the mystical spheres. According to the Church the *unio mystica*, the only connection to God permitted to the Christian, was—to use the allegorical terms of that era—via the mystical bride (personified by Mary) of God's divine son. Mary is the one who conveys the knowledge of humans about a plant's healing properties to the divine spheres and thereby integrates them in the divine order. She represents Ecclesias, the wisdom of the Church, and as such watches over the spiritual health of man. This ideology was recommended to all who willingly subordinated or were forced to subordinate to the dictates of the Church.

The witch, however, turned to the plant spirit itself. She was consulted by people who wanted to receive healing for certain afflictions, because the witch herself turned to

Three wise women in bourgeois dress approach a bedridden patient with pots of ointment. (Anonymous woodcut from *Compendium maleficarum*, Milan, 1626.)

---

[30] Klapper, 1960: 99–109 (about the witch of Blomberg); 76, 77 (about superstitions).

In dramatic shades of light and dark the elderly healer with her censer gives the impression of an old witch in the *Invocation for the Sick Person*. (S. Grocholski, *Krankenbeschwörung*, steel plate, end of the 19th century.)

the wisdom of nature. The witch stands in the center of nature and incorporates the animals and plant ingredients into her brew, which she has found in nature. Accessing the hidden healing powers of nature directly, and not through the intermediary of the Church, was defamed as inadmissible magic and witchcraft. The woman who was vilified as a witch, and who usually lived apart from the Church people in nature, had physical recovery in mind and caused this healing with the help of plants. For this she must atone.

The sixteenth-century encounter of Paracelsus with the accusation that he was a black magician demonstrates how reprehensible it was considered to turn directly to nature with conjuring formulas and to therewith violate divine laws.

> If I had otherwise invoked a spirit, a person, an herb, a root, a stone, or anything like this with its holy name, then one could say with truth and righteousness that I had taken the name of God in vain and therewith angered God, but not before. Let the theologians and sophists say about this what they want, the truth shall not be any different, even if they go against me severely and call me a sorcerer, a magician, an abuser and breaker of divine law, I shall not pay heed.[31]

Paracelsus got off the hook one more time. But Giordano Bruno, who was burned at the stake as a heretic on February 17, 1600, on the Campo de'Fiori in Rome, did not. When one reads his statements about magic and magicians in the context of the phobia of all thoughts that did not originate in the moral-theological breeding ground, one must wonder how he was able to live to fifty-two years old in such a climate of mutual denunciation (to which he ultimately fell victim). In his tract *On Magic*, written between 1586 and 1591, Bruno planted the term *magician* in a historical process of development between the wise and the miracle workers. He called such a person *malefic* "when he tends toward evil. When he tends toward good, he should be considered amongst the

[31] Paracelsus in vol. IX of *Philosophia occulta*, 1989 edition, *(Mikrokosmos und Makrocosmos: Occulte Schriften)* p. 308.

practitioners of medicine." And when he causes death, he should be called "poison magician."

The Christian dignitaries, however, could not care less about such differentiation. According to Bruno they brought the term *magician* to discredit: "For this reason his name does not sound as good to the wise or grammarians, because certain cowl wearers make demands of the term magician. Such a Capuchin monk was the author of the 'Hexenhammer.'"[32] What an appropriate evaluation of heresy!

From today's perspective it seems very strange that someone such as Paracelsus, who turned to the people with the intention to heal and who searched for medicines in nature, was accused of sorcery and witchcraft—and that *medicine* and *magic* were named in the same breath. The logic behind this is as simple as a stereotype: It is not the plants themselves that are sacred but the spiritual principle that created them. To call plants "by their sacred names" meant to criminally confuse them with God. God rules over life and death, and those who claim to rule over therapies, medicines, or recipes to fight disease or to lengthen life are ultimately in league with the devil. Those who are struck by disease are being punished by God for their sins, and if they heal, they owe their life to God's will and their atonement of their sins. This concept can already be discerned in the fourth century A.D. in the writings of the Church theoretician Athanasius, who praises Saint Anthony thusly: "The sick he convinces to be patient and to understand, and that the healing did not come from him at all, but from God alone, who causes it, when and on whom he so desires."[33]

Paracelsus takes what we would consider a more enlightened position. When he spoke about medicine in his *Astronomia magna* (chapter 10, p. 239), he wrote that having the courage to use this healing art resonates with God, for God himself is the physician and whether the person gets healthy or stays sick is in his hands.[34] Eventually, in the nineteenth century, Jules Michelet attacked this attitude of the Christian Church when he wrote that during the time of the witch trials life was considered to be merely a test given to humans. Therefore people were encouraged not to harbor any desire to prolong their lives. Within Christian circles medicine was viewed as simply a properly resigned attitude to await death and even hope for death. But who, then, could be a healer? Michelet says, ironically and provocatively, "It was a broad field for Satan. As he was physician and healer of the living and furthermore even their comforter."[35]

That he thoroughly hit the nerve of the early modern era with these surprising words was confirmed by Martin Luther. The turbulence of the early sixteenth century can be traced back to the effects of his Reformation: "We are all subordinate to the devil with body and soul as guests in this world, whose Lord and God he is himself." Thus those who attempt to exercise a certain amount of control over their bodies can, in a magical sense, come only from "bad parents"; in other words, they have made a pact with the devil, who has given them unusual abilities.

Medicine, as it was practiced in the folkways of the countryside, was connected with divination, namely the prophetic awareness of the origins of disease and their therapy. A healer was often a seeress who determined life or death with her recommendations for the sick person. As long as the healers used their knowledge for soothing or healing the sick, people happily consulted them and looked past the ecclesiastical restrictions of

---

[32] Bruno (from the 1995 edition, p. 115ff.) actually means two authors, namely the Dominican monk Jakob Sprenger and Heinrich Institoris.

[33] Athanasius, 1987: 82.

[34] Paracelsus, after Behling, 1957: 127f.

[35] Michelet, 1952, vol. 1: 13.

In *The Dream of the Doctor* Albrecht Dürer shows unequivocally that it is the bat-winged devil who uses a bellows to instill ideas about the healing powers of nature in the physician. The Venus/Nature who extols her gifts looks like a naked witch. (*Traum des Doktors*, copperplate, Nürnberg, Germanisches Nationalmuseum, 1498–99.)

A winged devil shakes the repulsive disease over a syphilis victim. The sores rain on the sickbed from a cornucopia that has been perverted into Pandora's box. (Woodcut, Zentralbibliothek, Luzern, 1512.)

On a woodcut from the 1578 edition of Lonicerus, women are shown playing a variety of roles in the pharmaceutical process, from gathering the medicinal plants to their application in the sickroom. (Lonicerus, *Herbar/Kreüterbuch*)

On the frontispiece of the 1679 edition of Lonicerus the woman gathering herbs and the female pharmacy assistant are missing. Only the physician stands at the sickbed.

visiting such wise women. But if the disease got worse or the afflicted person died, people were all too quick to blame it on sorcery.

Many authors, and in particular female writers, who have dealt with the themes of the witch craze or the witch trials have pointed out the central role of the woman in the folk medicine of the fifteenth and sixteenth centuries. Based on their own experiences of giving birth, women have always worked as midwives and passed down their knowledge of nature from generation to generation. The woman's knowledge of physical processes and medicinal herbs has always gone hand in hand with magical formulas that chase off disease demons and encourage the healing process on the plane of thought.[36] From a feminist perspective the competition between the healing abilities of the women, which were based on traditional experiential knowledge that had been handed down over generations, and the physicians, who had been trained at the university and who based their knowledge on written documents, represents a significant factor in the witch trials.[37] But others came to the conclusion that this competition should not be given too much weight, as the doctors worked more often with the nobility and in the cities and for this reason barely saw the women healers, who were consulted by the country people, as competitors. Besides, upon closer examination one sees that healers and midwives were not well represented in the horrifyingly high number of women murdered from the fifteenth through the eighteenth centuries.[38]

The competition theory is not so easily laid to rest, however, as can be demonstrated by comparing images from different editions of the *Kreüterbuch* of Adam Lonicerus (1528–1586) (see illustrations above). In a woodcut from the 1578 edition the artist depicts the entire pharmaceutical process, from finding the plants to their processing and

---

[36] The degree to which the imagination plays a role in the progress of disease and health can be seen from a modern perspective when one realizes the serious role the diagnosis serves. When the doctor explains that a nonlethal virus caused a sickness, there is no need to worry anymore, and one's focus turns to therapy and health. On the other hand, a diagnosis such as AIDS or cancer can have the same effect as voodoo, because the afflicted is confronted with a hopeless, often fatal diagnosis.

[37] Cf. especially the essays in Opitz, 1995.

[38] Some researchers take a different position—for example, the pharmacist Larissa Leibrock-Plehn (1992), who researched the abortion medicines used by the so-called witches in their healing practices, and the historian Ingrid Ahrendt-Schulte (1994), who compared the fantasy constructions to the actual realities of the lives of the tortured women.

utilization. In the background are woods in which a well with a heathen figure is found and where an herbalist is gathering plants. To the right of this a gardener cultivates certain plants. In the foreground a person (whose gender is not clearly identifiable) brings the collected material to a group of men, whose gestures and garments distinguish them as educated. The plants are then prepared by a female assistant and ground in a mortar by a pharmacist. The vessels in the left foreground indicate that the herbs are being prepared for distillation. The use of the preparations, in the middle left of the print, brings an end to the process. Three people are gathered around a sickbed: a woman who grinds plant material, a doctor who checks the dosage (which he administers to the patient), and a female assistant.

A mirror image of this example graced the title page of the edition of 1679. It depicts the same processes at all stages; however, all female participation has been removed. There is no herbalist, no pharmacist assistant, no female attendant at the sickbed. Only one background figure is female, and she seems to be more for decorative purposes: She carries a kind of fruit basket on her head and moves from the group of scholars in the direction of the garden.

Such a transforming of the women into men was also noticed by Gerlinde Volland in her study of mandrake depictions in two herbals from the sixteenth century. One is clearly based on the other in composition. In the illustration below from the German edition of the *Gart der Gesuntheit* [Garden of Health], which appeared in Antwerp in 1533 and 1547, one sees a woman gathering plants, including a male and female mandrake in anthropo-morphic forms, in an unfenced garden. In a subservient posture she carries the plants in her apron to a male scholar. Volland questions, with justification in my opinion, the younger date of the woodcut at right from the London *Grete Herball* (1526), which is much more simplified in its composition. The awkward style of the picture and the reduction of the compositional details, as well as the fact that a man in the dress of a scholar is in a strange subservient posture and is depicted as the plant gatherer, seems to me to be a later, simplified replica of the more complex example.[39]

This simplified composition of the medicinal garden, which is obviously derived from the more complex picture below, includes only the scholar, who in this image has been turned into a plant gatherer. (*Grete Herball*, London: Peter Treveris, 1526.)

In the *Garden of Health* are found medicinal plants such as these two anthropomorphic mandrakes. The woman gathers herbs in her apron as a scholar gives her advice. (*Gart der Gesuntheit*, Antwerp, 1533 and 1547.)

[39] Gerlinde Volland, "Mandragora-Ikonographie einer anthropomorphen Zauberpflanze," in *Jahrbuch für Ethnomedicin und Bewußtseinsforschung*, Berlin: VWB, 1997. The insights of Diepgen (1958: 11, 17) are also historically revealing. He considers that over the course of the relentless struggle for primacy between medicine and theology in the Middle Ages, "the value of a *servus medicus* became the same as that of a midwife." In addition, due to competition with women healers, the physicians of the early Middle Ages were duty bound to produce the medicine themselves.

With the help of burning incense, the Germanic seeress, an *alruna*, prophesies for Arimin the outcome of the decisive battle with Germanicus. (Steel-plate engraving from a drawing by F. Leeke, end of the 19th century.)

If folk medicine was based on magical practices that had a strong divinatory component and the magic was in the service of explaining the past and predicting coming events—connecting one's physical state with one's sins (or atonement for one's sins) and foretelling wellness or death—then it is proper that such medicinal plants, which not only acted on the body but were also related to the spirit and the soul of humans (thus they were psychoactive), also held lofty status in the minds of the people who utilized folk medicine. The strength of the connection between women healers and the medicinal plants that act upon the spirit is demonstrated by the name the healing women were called by. The narcotic and consciousness-altering magical root of the mandrake, the plant that creates hallucinatory access to the secrets of the universe, was etymologically associated with the witch as a kind of godparent. *Alruna* was the name the northern European people gave to their seeress, who had vision into the hidden realms. The German word for mandrake, *Alraune*, contains the word *rune*, the German system of writing based on beech staves that the father god Odin discovered in a prophetic way when he hung from a beech tree in order to gain knowledge of cosmic connections. This mythical process can still be seen in the German word for the letter *Buchstabe* (beech stave) The verb *raunen* (to whisper) contains this unconscious access to the inner connection of the universe as well.

The Demonization of Medicinal and Poisonous Plants

As much as the medicinal plants were honored by the people who used them, so were they demonized by the Church; in fact, the demonization of certain natural medicines can still be observed today. Of course the psychoactive substances are demonized above all others, but with these plants—as Paracelsus already knew—the dosage determines whether a plant has medicinal or poisonous effects. For example, consider *Echinacea purpurea* (L.) Moench (syn. *Rudbeckia purpurea* L.), the immune-enhancing root of the purple coneflower, for which the pharmaceutical industry has the North American Indians, who have always made use of its preventive activity, to thank. On May 24, 1996, the headline of the *Hamburger Abendblatt* read, "Fatal Shock: Experts Warn About the Use of Echinacea Products." That the plant can bring on shortness of breath and edema was determined from the results of repeated injections of the concentrated plant, which had been administered to people who were allergic to plants in the Sunflower family. For this reason the media used dramatic words to warn against taking ordinary preparations of the entire plant, including its common forms of capsules, tablets, tea, and tinctures. But the reality is that echinacea was only available to the consumer in oral preparations or as a salve for external use, and the fact that only doctors were allowed to administer injections from ampules was not relevant to the eager journalist.[40] When dealing with nature and natural medicine the following formula still holds true: Shake out every last shred of danger while seeking a sensational story, never pause to ask what these dangerous stories might mean, do away with any sense of reason, never incorporate knowledge that might present the danger in a relative context but immediately offer information on the right way to deal with the danger.

---

[40] No risks or side effects worthy of mention are included in *Echinaceae: Handbuch für Ärzte, Apotheker und andere Naturwissenschaftler* (edited by Rudolf Bauer, M.D., and Hildebert Wagner, Ph.D., from the Institut für Pharmazeutische Biologie at the University of Munich, Stuttgart: Wissenschaftlichen Verlagsgesellschaft, 1990).

Medicinal Plants of the Witches[41]

MANDRAKE AS MEDICINE

Tacitus, the Roman historian from pre-Christian times, handed down the word *Alruna* for a Germanic seeress. In the sixteenth century the term *Alraundelberin* was used for a wise woman as well as a witch.

During antiquity the root of the mandrake (*Mandragora* spp.) was used as an anesthetic, antiseptic, tonic, and narcotic. Mandrake wine was also administered in the Middle Ages and the early modern era to treat insomnia. However, such a medication could prove to be the undoing of the person who administered it. For instance, case files from Basel dating as early as 1407 report that in this Swiss city in the Oberrhein a woman who had used mandrake root was prosecuted. In 1416 a "pharmacy wife" who had administered mandrake root powder was exiled from the same city.[42] In his 1578 edition of the *Kreüterbuch*, the Frankfurt physician Lonicerus (1528–1586) based his entry on mandrake on traditional knowledge of its use, especially when he emphasized the sedative and numbing activity of the rind of the mandrake root when used externally and internally. In women's medicine the plant was used to expel a stillborn baby.

HENBANE AS MEDICINE

The plant called *Hyoscyamus* that was used in witches' salves grows from the Mediterranean to Asia Minor. In antiquity it was used as an ingredient in incenses prepared for divination and medicinally as a narcotic. Henbane seeds were also burned in the bathhouses during the Middle Ages, which led to increasingly vigorous opposition by the Church against the sensuous excessiveness between the two sexes,

An old witch sells society ladies a mandrake manikin. (*Alraun*, painting by Otto Boyer, title illustration for the magazine *Daheim*, year 63, n. 20, 12/2/1927.)

---

[41] I have limited myself in the description of therapeutic uses, in particular to the German doctor Lornizer—Lonicerus in Latinized form—whose herbal appeared in 1578 and was reprinted in 1679. Lonicerus processed the traditional wisdom of Dioscorides. Even though it was written and published at the same time as the witch trials, this herbal is surprisingly free of any demonization of the feared poisonous plants that were associated with witches, such as henbane and belladonna.

[42] From Golowin, 1973: 32f.

In a German farmhouse a healer falls into a trance in order to find the origins for the toothache of the patient in the right foreground. (Detail of a steel-plate engraving, c. 1870.)

who visited these places of pleasure together. Lonicerus added to the "energy and effects" of "Bilsamkraut" (henbane) that it had damaging, poisonous qualities and made one crazy and sleepy. The seeds also work against pain in the eyes, ears, teeth, and joints—activity that has to do with the sedative, or somniferous and quieting, characteristics. In addition, when the crushed seeds of henbane are mixed with wine and made into a compress, the herb soothes chest pain.

THISTLES AS MEDICINE

The habitat of the prickly thistle (*Carduus* spp.; see illustration on page 154) symbolically corresponds to the realm of the witch, who usually lived on the edge of the village near the uncultivated wilderness. Lonicerus included various species of thistles, which as a rule are of medicinal value only in the post-bloom stage. In women's medicine the dried herbage of the teasel (*Dipsacus silvestris* L., syn. *Dipsacus fullonum* L.p.p.) helps prevent discharge and heavy menstruation. Since the *Materia medica* of Dioscorides (around 20 C.E.), teasel crops up in similar manuscripts as a remedy for eye complaints, dyspepsia, and muscle tension, and for stimulating the milk flow in pregnant women. In folk medicine a decoction of thistle was used for worms, melancholy, and "inner pricking," as is indicated by the doctrine of signatures.

TOAD HERBS

According to medieval understanding the *Krott* (toad) or the *Krottenalp* (toad elf) was responsible when a woman miscarried. The toad became the symbol of a sick womb. In order to heal such a problem or to protect themselves from miscarriages women either left pictures of toads as offerings in church or gathered the so-called toad herbs. Included in these are dandelion (*Taraxacum officinale* Web., syn. *Leontodon taraxacum* L.), also called toad bush; chamomile (*Chamomilla recutita* [L.] Rausch, syn. *Matricaria chamomilla* L.); and navel herb (*Umbilicus* spp.).[43]

NETTLES AS MEDICINE

In antiquity stinging nettle, which was widely distributed, was used as a drastic aphrodisiac. A common name in German for *Urtica dioica* L. is *Teufelskraut* (devil's herb; see appendix). Nettles appear in the witch trials as one of the final painful martyr materials, for the witches were dressed in nettle shirts when they were led to the funeral pyre. This also signified that they were in league with the devil. In 1578 Lonicerus included a mixture of ground nettle seeds and honey wine as a cough remedy. Of the numerous therapeutic uses of the nettle species named in that text, only a few are mentioned here. When externally applied, nettle seeds encourage the healing of wounds. Ground nettle leaves laid on the stomach are said to have soothing effects on the womb and to hasten birth. Nettle roots soaked in wine are said to dispel lumbar stones, while the seeds are more effective for bladder stones.

[43] In 1992 Esther Gallwitz presented a virtual treasure chest of plant symbolism that is also relevant in the context of witches. She based her work on the pictures by the old masters in the Frankfurt Städel museum. The herbs' medicinal and magical significance have been derived over the course of history from, among other characteristics, their similarity with certain organs and body parts (following the doctrine of signatures, or sympathetic magic). Accordingly, they were organized into groups based on their activity and according to ancient folk traditions. In addition, some knowledge from the Germanic, classical, or Arabic medicine was included in the classifications. Thus, for example, the toad herbs were those attributed with having a healing effect on the womb, the member herbs were those that affect the reproductive organs, the aphrodisiacs were the ones that enhanced love.

The Healing of the Microcosm and the Macrocosm

For people who live in harmony with nature, the healing arts draw not only on their own bodies, but also on the body of the universe, on the macrocosm, into which humans are integrated. Every living being is governed by the weather, the seasons, and the cycles of nature that provide sustenance while also bringing decay and transitoriness. If the crops do not grow, if the harvest fails due to bad weather, or if a family is struck by illness and death, primitive peoples interpret this event as either a naturally occurring event or as a disturbance in the natural balance of all earthly and heavenly energies. Shamans have the ability to exert an influence on events by going into a trance and entering the reality of the world beyond, where they can receive knowledge about the causes of the imbalance.

Art historians who study images of witches have repeatedly remarked on the trancelike, somnambulistic condition of the women depicted by Albrecht Altdorfer and Hans Baldung (see illustrations on pages 151 and 152).[44] The trance is a shamanic technique found in all cultures; it transcends the mundane world, with its obligations and limitations, in order to break through the boundaries of consciousness and open to associations, inspirations, and intuition.[45] In this state shamans are able to recognize the origins of a disease and practical, therapeutic measures that can be taken against it. According to the shamanic vision of the world, humans are not separate from nature but are a natural component of it. This is demonstrated in the invocation of Manuel Córdova-Rios, who was trained as a shaman by the Amahuaca Indians of the Peruvian Amazon basin:

> *O most powerful spirit*
> *of the bush with the fragrant leaves*
> *we are here again to seek wisdom.*
> *Give us tranquility and guidance*
> *to understand the mysteries of the forest,*
> *the knowledge of our ancestors.* *

Human culture reflects in a complex way on the basic principles of nature, which is understood as a cyclical process of becoming and decaying and as manifesting the poles of masculine and feminine. In his treatise *On the Mysteries of Egypt* (4.2), Iamblichus (250–325 C.E.) explained the magical influence on natural processes in the following way.

Through subtle streams of energy the shaman is "rooted" in his plant and animal environment. This drawing shows the animal transformation of a Siberian shaman. The form on his shoulders (which resembles the veins of insect wings) indicates his flight to the worlds beyond. The elk horns on his head connect him to the sacred king of the woods. (Detail of a drawing on Samoyed shamanic clothing.)

---

[44] See Hartlaub (1961: 15) for example.

[45] In her collection of reports of the experiences of shamans, magicians, and visionaries, the American anthropologist Joan Halifax accurately described the *payé*, the shamans of the Desana people who live in Colombia: "The *payé* is a mediator and moderator between the spirit elements that govern the field of life and the social network that is vulnerable to supernatural forces." Quoted for this edition from Joan Halifax, *Shamanic Voices: A Survey of Visionary Narratives*, New York: E. P. Dutton, 1979, 138.

* Joan Halifax, *Shamanic Voices: A Survey of Visionary Narratives*, New York: E. P. Dutton, 1979, 143. (Trans.)

Every kind of theurgy[46] has a mirror aspect. On the one hand it is practiced by humans and maintains our natural place in the universe; on the other hand the practice is supported by divine symbols because they are connected to the higher powers; it is able to ascend to the heights. It moves harmoniously in unison with their commands and can actually take on the appearance of the gods themselves. In accord with this difference the magician can naturally invoke the powers of the superior beings, for he who calls to them is a human being, but he can also give commands to them, for he has taken on the appearance of a God with secret formulas.

Christians who visited the Samis (Laplanders) in the 17th century for the purpose of converting them were not able to recognize the Sami's shamanic healing trances as being anything other than a pact with the devil. (Pen-and-ink drawing by Dibei Fe, following Manker, 1963.)

Weather magic should be understood as an effort to reestablish a lost balance. Since prehistoric times, and to this day in tribal cultures, rainmaking plays an important role in the work of male and female shamans.[47] Those who put herbs in a censer and burn them imitate atmospheric processes on a small scale. The leaves, resin, and resin-containing bark—for example, from henbane, laurel, and frankincense—become ash, which is later put on the soil as nutrition, ensuring further generations of plants. The smoke rises and thickens into foggy clouds. It condenses and sinks like fog on the fields and as barely noticeable sediment on the plants. In this way man imitates the desired weather processes of the macrocosm on a microcosmic level.

This is exactly what the women who are still connected to such natural processes and their heathen traditions do. Such sympathetic magic can be imagined, in the foreground of the witch trials, through this confessional inquiry transcribed in the nineteenth book of the collection *Deutsches Bußbuch* [Church Decrees] by the Bishop of Worms (died 1025).

Did you act as certain women are wont to? When they need rain and have none, they gather several girls and select a young virgin from among these to act as a kind of leader. They remove her clothes and lead the naked one to a place outside the settlement where they find hyoscyamus, which is called *Bilse* in German. They have her pull out this plant with the little finger of her right hand and tie the uprooted plant to the little toe of the right foot using any type of cord. Then the girls, each of whom holds a rod in her hands, lead said virgin, as naked as she is, back from the river to the settlement by her hands while she places her feet down and moves them like a crab.[48]

Because this magical "conversation with nature" was interpreted as a prohibited intervention in God's plan, the witches had to atone for this heinous act with their lives.[49] By turning the magical invocation of rain, which brings fertility to the earth, into its destructive opposite—as it was stereotypically portrayed in all contemporary pictorial and written sources as hailstorms and thunderstorms—the ecclesiastical authorities severed access to heathen tradition and manipulated public opinion as they desired.

---

[46] *Theurgy* is the art of communicating with the gods through magical practices.

[47] See, for example, Werner Petermann, *Regenkulte und Regenmacher bei bantu-sprachigen Ethnien Ost- und Südafrikas*, Reihe Ethnomedizin und Bewußtseinsforschung, Berlin: Express Edition, 1985.

[48] From the appendix by Rätsch in Metzner. Rätsch considers this to be the oldest literary example of the use of henbane as a Germanic magical plant, and points out that such rituals were also performed for another plant, namely the mandrake, which also has a close relationship with the witches. Quotes for this edition from Ralph Metzner, *The Mead of Inspiration*, Boston: Shambhala, 1994, p. 239. (Trans.)

[49] Because agriculture was dependent on the weather "for growth and decay" and the people of Europe have been dependent on the productivity of the fields and the animals since the early modern era, this circumstance, which Leibrock-Plehn (1992: 175) commented on, is not surprising.

Medieval painters and illustrators did not show the primordial midwife bringing blessed rain to nourish the growth of the fields and to fertilize the earth, but they did show her influencing devastating thunderstorms. The women in these paintings are not shown in a joyous frenzy; rather, their naked limbs are orgiastically contorted and betray the ominous influence witches were believed to have on the natural world. This vision essentially reproduces the Church's negative conception of nature, especially its more nocturnal and aggressive manifestations, which are believed to have a demonic source. This idea was even demonstrated by the scientifically oriented doctor and philosopher Paracelsus. In an event in Basel that is still much discussed in literature, Paracelsus openly burned the writings of the Greek-Roman physician Galen and some of his medical predecessors in order to exclusively allow his path to be lit by "the light of nature." Nevertheless, Paracelsus was entirely rooted in the Christian faith. He considered rain and clouds to be "excretions" of the "hellish ghosts":

> And if they come out of their dwellings and into the heaven so they allow their secretions and its action which are in their nature, to move outwards; but that is nothing other than wind, hail, thundershowers, sun, and many more lavish and more destructive than the other rays of firmament.

Paracelsus considered the witches to be part of such diabolical atmospheric machinations when he wrote: "Thus the work of witches is nothing more than a secretion from the hellish ghosts who are violent due to their diabolic nature and as such create thunderstorms" (Paracelsus, 1989: 138f.).

Christianity can be seen as a smear campaign against ancient nature religions and the natural interconnection between people even when those targeted by the Church are obviously not operating out of these traditions, as is the case with Paracelsus.[50] With the Christians' monotheistic claim that there is only one (masculine) God and the entire Creation in all of its manifestations emanates from him alone, not only did all worship of nature fall under suspicion, but the entire magical worldview was distrusted as well. "For know in truth that all forces of nature are small compared against the power of the devil— but even greater is the power of the good angel," wrote Hartlieb in 1456 (1989b: 40). In different sections of his book on the forbidden arts Hartlieb encouraged his reader to recognize "how the four elements were poisoned with the cunning and deceit of the devil" (1989b: 69). Since the early Christian era the Church fathers have never tired of talking their followers out of worshipping water, cliffs, mountains, trees, plants, and animals, with the instructions that only he who created these natural phenomena deserves honor—not the creation itself. Thus Athanasius (1987: 100), who lived as a bishop in Alexandria from 295 to 373 and also endured exile in Rome numerous times, criticized the heathens:

> What could you, with regard to the irrational animals, attribute to them besides stupidity and wildness? When you, as I have heard, want to ensure that you only understood this as a myth, and when you allegorically . . . call the air Hera, the sun Apollo, the moon Artemis, and the sea Poseidon, you nevertheless do not honor God himself, but worship the creations without regard to God, who created everything. If you have developed such ideas because the creation is beautiful, you are only

---

[50] As Paracelsus used the medicinal herbs himself, he was attacked often enough for being a "black magician" and a "breaker of the holy laws," against which he vigorously defended himself (cf. Paracelsus, 1989: 308). See also page 164.

allowed to go so far as wonderment, and not make the creation divine. For honor is designated for the God of creation, not the created.

These words are found in *Vita Antonii* [The Life of Anthony], written around 356, which is a description of the life and work of Saint Anthony, the godfather of all hermits. Athanasius held up Saint Anthony as an example the Christians were supposed to imitate. This saint, whose varied temptations by demons and sensuality were passed down in many images, will occupy us in the following section, for witches have romped around in his environment since the impressive paintings of Bosch. In *Vita Antonii* Athanasius thundered against all forms of divination, healing, and magical arts, drawing attention to the new religion: "Where the sign of the cross appears magic loses its power, and witchcraft is ineffective." Only saints like Anthony are permitted to work such wonders, for he is humbly conscious of the almighty God.

This division of a (permissible) wondrous power in the sacred name of God and the good and the wondrous power that causes destruction and evil has been firmly anchored in the Christian mind-set over the centuries. A division such as this, and the judgment of nature as fundamentally negative while the spirit of God that stands behind it is sanctified, became the basic theme of theologians, priests, thinkers, and researchers, regardless of whether they were Catholic, Protestant, or of Enlightened mind-set.[51] In the 1630s Otto Brunfels declared in his introduction to his herbal that God was his witness, that he always had the worship of almighty God in mind, and that his multifaceted work would praise the "wondrously strange little plants."[52]

In front of this backdrop every attempt of a person to see her- or himself not primarily as a creation of God but as a part of nature, the influence of which can be guided in a certain direction with magical practices, seemed reprehensible. Even when the magical intention was positive the intention to reach into the divine plan was considered in and of itself a break with God. When examining written sources on the nature of witches, even the nineteenth-century dictionary entry I consulted on the subject,[53] a thoughtful balancing act is in evidence.[54] This has to do with an interest in magical practices on the part of scholars, preachers, and painters, many of whom were obviously fascinated by magic[55] and acquired a

---

[51] This concept of a spiritual force that stands behind the creation of nature does not necessarily have to lead to a distancing or alienation from and demonization of nature. This is illustrated, for example, in a statement by the Sioux Indian Petaga Yuha Mani: "We live off nature." (From Joan Halifax, *Shamanic Voices: A Survey of Visionary Narratives*, New York: E. P. Dutton, 1979, 175.)

[52] According to Behling, 1957: 157.

[53] In the third edition of the *Realencyclopädie für protestantische Theologie und Kirche*, published by A. Hauk (Leipzig, 1899), the entry for *witch* contains references to witchcraft as a practice that "uses the help of unnatural energies, in particular subordinate ghosts." The authors saw such a practice that can be "punishable because of its preconceived intentions" as a break with God, although they were incensed that the Catholics, the early fighters of the Reformation, and Luther himself had fallen under the spell of the beliefs of witches. Their expositions stated that "only the most faithful connection with the pure, innocent, and full truth of the evangelism" was able to free them from the bondage of superstition.

[54] See, for example, the obvious contradiction in the following statements by Hermann Wilckens: "They make weather, inopportune rain, thunder, hail, snow, ripeness, frost, beetles, and other insects, so that grain, wine, acorns, and other fruits in the field and in the woods are destroyed." At the same time Wilckens determined that old women were not capable of such deeds because "weather-making is God's and not human's work. Humans are not as clever and as powerful as they think, especially crazy, old powerless women, and it is doubtful that they could achieve such a thing. On the contrary, if these old ladies could make weather, then one should not kill them, but honor them for their ability to make weather whenever and however we like" (Wolf, 1980: 476).

[55] For example, a broad knowledge of the heretical texts and folk magic practices must be attributed to Hieronymus Bosch because of the grotesque hybrid creations he placed in his magical world. However, it seems as if he never really distanced himself from the Christian way of "righteous belief," for no sources indicate that he was ever accused of being a heretic or had any conflict with the Church. The same holds true for Hans Baldung Grien, as well as for Frans Francken the younger. See Härting, 1983: 177.

thoroughly profound knowledge of it through the literature that had been handed down. But they used their knowledge in order to tirelessly warn others about the dangers of its practices in detailed descriptions. This can be observed, for example, with the physician Hartlieb. Although he thoroughly disseminated all of his vast knowledge about the magical practices of his time, he was still repeatedly assigned by the margrave Johann von Brandenburg to hunt out these practices among his underlings and prevent it.[56]

Rübezahl: Herbalist and Weather God

Besides interceding in matters of human health, another way in which folk medicine and shamanism were seen as interfering with the natural order of things was the practice of weather magic. In court witches were accused of destroying the harvest with hailstorms and stopping the milk flow of the neighbor's cow. The connection of shamanic and folk-medicine ways with weather making offered the Christians someone besides God to blame for interventions in the natural course of life. When the weather is in harmony with the needs of humans and when it is beneficial to the harvest, then there is no need for an explanation—for God, in his eternal goodness, reveals therein his fondness for the creatures he has created. But when man is at the mercy of the forces of nature he encounters powers that the nature spirits were once held responsible for—a concept that has survived into present times in rural areas, although it has been long since layered over with Christian interpretations.

Much less demonic and more like an Old Testament father god or Zeus, the masculine weather-spirit Rübezahl gazes from the heights of the mountaintops, from "the Silesian Parnass." His trident is also known from Neptune and Shiva—and also from the witches. The ravens and the root manikins belong to Rübezahl's domain. (Illustration by Ludwig Richter, 1848.)

Examples of the deeds of mountain and wood spirits, of water nymphs and field spirits, in which the polytheistic spiritualization of nature has survived, are found in many sagas. The stories about Rübezahl, the weather god and spirit of the Silesian mountains, preserve some of these ancient concepts. His name contains not only the words *Rüben* and *zählen* (root counting), but also the Old German word *Zagel* (tail) and the modern German word *Rübe*, which means "root," "turnip," or "fleshy taproot." From these terms the power of Rübezahl, lord of the medicinal roots the mountain inhabitants can benefit from in the event of illness, can be elucidated. But the name also offers clues for understanding Rübezahl as an earth spirit with a tail—in other words, a field demon.

It was reported that even as late as 1814 the inhabitants of the Silesian mountains made pilgrimages to the summit of the mountain, near the source of the Elbe River. There they sacrificed black roosters and hens and said prayers and invocations to Rübezahl in order to pacify the mountain spirit and divert the path of the threatening floodwaters as they roared down from the mountain. The people brought springwater and herbs and roots back home with them, and used these to wash their cows and stalls.

With regard to Rübezahl, Johannes Praetorius (1630–1680), whose reports about the witches at Blocksberg have been passed down, wrote:

> There was a root-man who always brought herbs and roots into the pharmacies. The same man knew the way to the spirit of his root garden; it was called the devil's ground. Therein he had his garden and his special herbs and roots. Not just any man received them from him, the spirit would only give them to those with good intentions. If someone attempts to get them from the spirit through violence or conjurations, he must be perfect in his work, or he will have his neck broken, or otherwise great bad luck will befall him. (*Historien von Rieben-Zahl*, 1738).

---

[56] See Hartlieb, 1989a, 16 and 1989b, 13.

A conjuring spell from 1630 was quoted by Klapper (1936) as an invocation to Rübezahl: "You great man, you doctor, come before us! He who honors you awaits your presence." Around 1566 the Heidelberg theologian David Pareus reported on an encounter with a weather spirit who surprised him with a tornado while he was walking to a white-water source: "The people attributed [it] to an evil spirit . . . which lurks in the lower valleys and often disturbs the water. The inhabitants call it *Riebenzahl*."[57] Moritz von Schwind (1804–1871) depicted Rübezahl as a wood spirit with a red beard, in the same sort of environment that witches are found—a forest with knotted trees and flaming red fly agaric mushrooms (in the collection of the Bavarian Staatsgemäldesammlungen, Schack Gallery, Munich).

> In connection with the thunderstorms the so-called witches' brooms or thunderbrooms are growths which are similarly nestlike and as a rule are caused by parasitic mushrooms on white fir, birch, and cherry trees. People of earlier times liked to attach them to the house gables for protection against lightning and fire. From the symbolic character of such botanical malformations—which is what the witches' brooms are—the folk superstition sought to derive a connection to lighting. The "broom" is firstly a symbol of separation, of air and of heaven's purifying lighting. Thunderclouds often appear broomlike and "sweep" the sky—the sea people call the west wind "heaven's broom" (Engel, 1978: 60).

Seeress and Goddess of Fate

During the time of the great witch hysteria, the churches—both Catholic and Protestant—negated all possibilities for humans to exert a positive, fertile influence on natural occurrences. Thus in the fifteenth and sixteenth centuries the clergy demonized the practices of conjuring natural forces and divining from the signs of nature, practices that were still alive in broad segments of the rural population.

In heathen times the Germanic peoples were more likely to know prophetic women than men. They practiced weather oracles, oracles of the bridal night, and water divination. But Church leaders interpreted such methods as human attempts to become all-knowing, like God. In the second half of the sixteenth century soothsayers were "shit out by the devil into the world because the humans are brazen and want to know more than they should," according to the Heidelberg rector Wilcken. He also warned, "We are created by God, and it has been preordained by him what we can know" (Wolf, 1980: 473).

In one small detail the painters of witch images have left us a clue as to why the people of the fifteenth and sixteenth centuries perceived the activities of witches as being an offense against the divine order. With surprising regularity a distaff can be found in pictures of witches. It first appears in the hands of a haggard witch in Dürer's 1505 allegory (see illustration at left), which we shall study in greater detail below. We also notice it in the context of the herb woman of Hans Weiditz (see illustration on page 151). And in the washed pen-and-ink drawing on page 177 by Jacob de Gheyn II (1608) a witch in the left foreground holds a distaff clamped between her legs. An almost magical force seems to emanate from this distaff, for hailstorms and thunderclouds are brewing in the direction in which it points.

In his allegorical copperplate engraving 1505–07 Albrecht Dürer represents Aphrodite Epitragidia, "she who rides on a buck," as an old witch with love gods. In her arm she holds a distaff.

---

[57] Klapper (1936: 26, 27) explained that the Rübezahl's weather making and his ability to reveal himself in numerous forms must have been particularly reprehensible to theologians. Therefore they wrote him off as a devil or Satan, and erected a chapel on the highest peak of the snowcapped mountain. The chapel was dedicated to Mary in 1681, wherewith the spook was banned (29).

Is the distaff a tool of the devil, with which the witch draws her energy for black magic? And could these images be saying that in the hands of witches harmless objects can easily be turned into dangerous weapons? Could this tool, which was found at that time in all homes for spinning yarn, indicate that any normal farm wife or city woman could be a witch? A distaff in a single-page woodcut by Hans Baldung Grien, dated 1513 (see illustration on page 178), suggests divination and the three goddesses of fate. Grien has placed three women in front of a leafless lichen-hung tree whose barren branches spread out across the scenery. The youngest, with long wavy hair, sits on a tree stump, holds the distaff, and looks at us with a mischievous grin. Behind her the eldest, with her full loose hair contrasting with her emaciated body and the haggard lines on her face, bends forward to the bushel of hemp behind the child. With a large pair of scissors she cuts the threads, which the motherly plump woman, who wears the typical old German bonnet of a married woman, is spinning. She sits on an embankment across from the young woman, who like the elder also cuts the strings of life; at her feet a small naked boy picks a flower. The group, in a shady valley in front of a sunny, hilly landscape, could also be a depiction of the different stages of life—childhood, youth, maturity, and old age. Their nakedness, the enigmatic expression of the youth, their long loose hair, and the dead tree are all reminiscent of witches.

Indeed the ability of witches to influence health, life, and death—and therewith the threads of life—is connected thematically to the Greek Moirai (the Roman Parcae). In classical mythology they were associated with grim spirits of the dead as well as with divinatory spirits of birth, and had—as daughters of the almighty sky god Zeus and Themis, the all-knowing earth goddess—responsibility for overseeing the orderly process of the universe. The Moirai's influence on the human world—for which Homer repeatedly used the metaphor of spinning a thread—disappeared from human awareness. Hesiod describes them in the most ancient sources as "daughters of the night."

An Orphic hymn reveals how the classical man characterized these goddesses of fate, who spin the threads of life and, at the given time, cut them:

Boundless Fates, dear children of dark night,
hear my prayer, O many-named dwellers on the lake
of heaven where the frozen water by night's warmth

Jacob de Gheyn II disseminated extremely grisly witch scenarios. This drawing, called *Witches' Sabbat*, includes the witches' cauldron, which escapes through the chimney, and visibly farting witches. Also depicted are skulls and bones and corpses, which are taken to the cellar to be stored for future procedures. Witches from higher levels of society who carry, among other things, the decapitated head of a child also appear. In addition, in the left foreground is a witch with a distaff. (*Hexensabbat*, washed pen-and-ink drawing, Berlin, Museen preußischer Kulturbesitz, Kupferstichkabinett, 1608.)

Hans Baldung Grien depicts the three Parcae, or the three goddesses of fate, as witches who sever the threads of life from the distaff. (*Die drei Parzen*, Einblattholzschnitt, 1513.)

is broken inside a sleek cave's shady hollow:
from there you fly to the boundless earth, home of the mortals,
and thence, cloaked in purple, you march toward men
whose aims are as noble as their hopes are vain,
in the vale of doom, where glory drives her chariot on
all over the earth, beyond the goal of justice, of anxious hope,
of primeval law, and of the immeasurable principle of order.
In life Fate alone watches; the other immortals
who dwell on the peaks of snowy Olympos do not,
except for Zeus' perfect eye. But Fate and Zeus' mind
know all things for all time.
I pray to you to come, gently and kindly,
Atropos, Lachesis, and Clotho, scions of noble stock.
Airy, invisible, inexorable, and ever indestructible,
you give all and take all, being to men the same as necessity.
Fates, hear my prayers and receive my libations,
Gently coming to the initiates to free them from pain.

In Baldung's picture Atropos is represented by the old woman, Clotho is the motherly spinner, and Lachesis measures and distributes fate—in this instance with a suggestive sneer.

The Norns were the Germanic equivalent of the goddesses of fate. They lived beneath the World Tree, the ash tree Yggdrasil, and were called Urdh (fate that has already become, or the past), Verdandi (fate that is becoming, or the future), and Skuld (present).[58] Like the witches, the Norns combined plant knowledge with the powers of divination. If one compares the Germanic "evergreen ash" (yew) with the leafless tree in Baldung's woodcut, one sees a great discrepancy between the two. Though its trunk was perpetually rotting and its roots eternally gnawed by the dragon Nidhogg, Yggdrasil, unlike the tree behind the three women in the woodcut, always remained vibrantly green with life. The reason for this was that the Norns constantly looked after its welfare, patching the rooted portions of the trunk with healing clay and sprinkling water they had drawn from the well of fate over it. This difference between the tree images was not necessarily based on the personal perspective of the artist, who nevertheless demonized heathendom as a dead religion. More likely the difference is based on the fact that the reigning religion (which significantly determined the political reality in Germany in the early modern era) influenced the humanistic art of the German Renaissance and colored it with such an interpretive position. At the start of the sixteenth century—during the time of societal and religious unrest and on the eve of the religious wars, when terrible epidemics such as the plague and syphilis threatened the life of individuals and the hygienic conditions under which the threads of life of many women and children were severed—the inescapable fate awaiting every human being must have seemed particularly

---

[58] In his inspiring investigation of Germanic mythology Ralph Metzner, the psychotherapist and deep ecologist, came to a different temporal classification of the three "all-knowing maidens" and placed such a linear definition as a whole into question. Metzner makes an etymological connection between the three Norns and the increased demonization of divination and magic: "Most scholars agree that the word *urd* is related to the Old Germanic *wurt* (destiny) and the Anglo Saxon *wyrd*, which means 'destiny' but also 'power,' or 'magic,' or 'prophetic knowledge.' In English the concept *wyrd* only remains in *weird*, which has come to mean 'strange.' In Shakespeare's time, *weird* still retained its associations with magic and divination: the witches in *Macbeth*, who repeatedly warn the King of misfortunes about to befall him, are called 'the weird sisters'" From Ralph Metzner, *The Mead of Inspiration*, Boston: Shambhala, 1994, p. 217.

threatening.

In Greek sources it is said that "in life only the Moirai alone —and none of the other eternal gods"—see and know everything about humans. Some classical authors present even Zeus as subject to the will of the Morai. Such an idea is unimaginably sinful for Christians, for to them God is supreme. A dialogue between Sofia and Saulin written in 1584 by Giordano Bruno (1995: 247) gives us a means for thinking about this abomination. Giordano quotes, in the figure of Saulin, the Roman poet Seneca:

> Fate leads us, we shun destiny, / The fine threads of the winding spindle / Does not permit the release of worrisome thought. / What we do and endure from above is it / Pre-determined, and from there comes everything. / The unforgiving sister of fate / Never pulls the fallen threads back up again, / According to a certain order the Parcae work, / While from us ever history swings against us which we do not know."

To Christians, on the contrary, God alone determines human life and the order of the universe. Those decisions are not made by elemental goddesses. According to the Christian perspective, when the Parcae (or the witches) are able to influence the weather with their distaffs, as we have seen in pictorial examples, then the devil that God has sent to put humans to the test must be part of the game.

But why should the distaff be an indication that the witch, as sorceress and soothsayer, threatens the divine order? Let's once again consult Hans Baldung Grien. In his pen-and-ink drawing *Hercules and Omphale*, in the collection of the Paris School of Fine Arts, the powerful Hercules takes the distaff from the Lydian queen Omphale while she wears his lion fur and carries his cudgel. This illustration, based on an ancient Greek myth, is a vicious allusion to the Christian belief that such a woman turns the natural— in other words, the divine—order on its head. The text that Baldung wrote in the beam on the left edge of the picture—"What does Cupid not conquer when the grim hand of the lion killer is sentenced to spinning work, which makes heroes into weaklings"— documented the general consensus of the time about such a reversal, an attitude that persisted at least into the eighteenth century. The poet August Kotzebue was quoted with a similar verse in *Grimm's Dictionary* under the entry *distaff*, where he defined it as a typical work tool of women. Noble men must "like Hippocrates / strive toward higher things / and should not, like Hercules / play with distaffs."

In the same way, in Albrecht Dürer's 1505–1507 copper engraving of the allegory "Witch with Cupids" (see the illustration on page 176), the old woman, with the haggard body and drooping breasts, rides backward on a buck through the air, contrary to the nature of God. The goat veers to the right but the hair of the witch, who sits backward holding on to the horns, does not blow in the same direction as her strange mount (which is not moving on the earth), but rather as if the wind, which also drives on a hailstorm, was coming from the left, the western direction. The cupids also twist in strange ways as they laboriously attempt to pull themselves up from the ground. The presence of these diminutive gods of love makes sense in either the context of a lover who shoots a beloved with arrows or as companions to the love goddesses Aphrodite and Venus. All traces of the lover are missing from Dürer's print; however, Venus is present, although she has mutated into an ugly old woman.

An examination of art history research could easily substantiate that the famous

---

[59] Sigrid Schade evaluated the literature that had been the classical models for Dürer in her contribution in van Dülmen 1987: 177ff., as well as in others.

German artist Dürer was actually inspired by classical paintings.[59] During antiquity art depicted flying rams that carried Phrixos and Helle over the sea,[60] as well as Aphrodite Epitragidia ("she who rides on a goat"). But why did Dürer portray his Venus with such an angry expression? The classical sources offer a point of reference for such a transformation—Aphrodite as Urania, an underworld goddess who belonged to the world of the dead and was worshipped as the eldest Moirai. In the second century after Christ, Pausanias, who came from Asia Minor, reported in his travels through Greece of an abstract square shrine of Aphrodite at the Acropolis: "The inscription said that Aphrodite Ourania was the eldest of the so-called Moirai" (Pausanias, *Itinerary of Greece* I: 104). The love goddess belongs entirely in the environment of the goddesses of fate.

From the Goddess to the Witch

While the northern lands of fifteenth-century Europe fought hard for a reformation of the religious and moral foundations of spiritual life, sunny Italy opened itself up with all of its senses to the rediscovery of classical sculptures of the gods as well as to texts that were bought from the cloisters by the art enthusiast Cosimo de'Medici. An educated Italian intelligentsia conveyed a new concept of nature's beauty to painters and visualized the congenial side of the human character more than the sinful. This stark difference between northern and southern Europe is mirrored in the art of the time. While the Italian Renaissance investigated new realms such as human anatomy and perspective, in the Netherlands and in Germanic lands pictures of the infernal hell, of witches' kitchens, and of dances of the dead were created. It is barely comprehensible that the panel paintings of Hieronymus Bosch were created at the same time as the master works of Leonardo, Raphael, and Michelangelo!

This difference between these cultures is also recognizable in the few Italian pictures of witches. For example, in a drawing attributed to Filippino Lippi from the 1480s, two lovely youthful women with bared breasts stir a steaming brew in a decorative vessel that rests upon animal paws and is ornamented with pig heads and harpies. Without the title (probably added later) and the classical-looking cauldron, the two women with flowing hair and clothes could be identified as priestesses from antiquity. If one studied each of the surprisingly few demonized heathen women to be found in southern European art of this time, then one could agree with Jules Michelet: "This innocent woman conceals a secret inside that she has never revealed to the Church. She keeps the memory of the poor old gods in her heart, with which she has empathy and who have been degraded into ghosts" (Michelet, 1952: 46).

Frau Venus

The heathen world was devoted to happiness in this life. From the myths that have been handed down it is clear that the gods and goddesses the pagans worshipped behaved as if they shared those sentiments, if anything with even less restraint. Equally wholesome were the Greek and Roman sculptures the Renaissance man brought into the light of day from their centuries-long sleep behind the thorny hedge of roses.

Upon closer examination of the images of witches it becomes apparent that the entire complex of the Aphrodite cult rediscovered in the Renaissance was transferred to the

This drawing by Filippino Lippi, who was the fruit of a forbidden relationship between a nun and the monk and painter Filippo Lippi, was executed entirely within the Renaissance tradition of the emerging interest in antiquity, as can be seen in the way the witches are depicted around a brewing cauldron, like classical priestesses. The three-footed vessel is decorated with the three dogs' heads of Hecate, as well as three harpies, or sphinxes. This is reminiscent of the magical powers of the classical witch-goddess and the powers that bubble out of the cauldron of mystical knowledge. (Drawing, Florence, Uffizi, c. 1480.)

---

[60] This was written down in the "Sagas of Antiquity" by Hyginus before 207 C.E. However, Dürer could have hardly known them, as the (subsequently lost) manuscript first appeared in the Bavarian region in 1535—in other words, after Dürer's allegory. But the passage is also found in Apollonius, who, along with Virgil and others, found respect in the Renaissance.

witch over the course of religious unrest and the radical transformation of society that took place in the fifteenth and sixteenth centuries. This transference was especially prevalent in the lands shaken by the Reformation, where Protestant theologians utilized the discoveries of their more tolerant colleagues in the south to refine their condemnation of the witch. Thus we encounter the love goddess as a young witch with a beautiful body who follows the example of Aphrodite Kallipygos, she "with the pretty posterior." A similarly seductive view of her back is shown in a copper engraving from 1612.[61] The love goddess, who knows about love potions—which were named *aphrodisiacs* after her—became a witch who made men impotent. In Sparta she was honored as Ambologera, she "who banishes age"—an ability that fell under the domain of healers and was also conceived as black magic in the early-modern-era concept of witches. Aphrodite Genetyllis, in her function as the guardian of births, also belongs in this context. In 1544 Leonhard Culman, a Nuremberg preacher of humanist tendencies, wrote a moralizing drama that brought the classic world of the gods into this Renaissance city. In the drama he accorded the devil these words:

> *There where the lust is coveted*
> *my kingdom is also increased*
> *where boys of Venus go to meet*
> *her box is taken up*
> *but the box is only lust and joy*
> *and from it comes the greatest woe.*[62]

In 1668 Johannes Praetorius was witness to how vivid the worship of "Frau Venus, who was the most noble and decried nymph of all the spirit-beings" still prevailed among the Saxons in Magdeburg. He described how they carried an image of Venus through the streets on a wagon—and he did not forget to include the fact that she was naked.

> Her head is crowned with myrtle, on her breast she carried a burning torch, in her right hand the globe of the earth, and in her left three golden apples. After her came the three

Allegories, from left to right: Fortuna on Dürer's woodcut (1500), with her distaff and long hair reminiscent of those of a witch.

This Venus, who is gazing into a mirror and has a horned animal at her feet, could also be an allegory of Luxuria. (Woodcut from Paracelsus, 1537.)

This anonymous print from the 16th century depicts the personification of lust with the ram as an accompanying animal.

A personification of the witch with instruments of torture.

The naked woman with the hourglass and the skull could be an allegory of time. But the title that has been handed down is *Hexe, den Schädel Manuels durch die Lüfte tragend* (Witch, Who Carries the Skull of Emmanuel through the Air). (Niklaus Manuel Deutsch, pen and ink, Kunstmuseum, Bern, c. 1513.)

---

[61] By Maleuvre, in Pierre de Lancre, *Tableau de Inconstance*, an illustration in van Dülmen, 1987: 110.

[62] From Schade, 1983: 98 f.

graces. . . . It had once been in the mountains, caves, and cliffs, where often great arches and caves were found, where she had her home, congregation, and armies. Friday[63] is in particular the best suited among the days for a ghost to appear in a small body. . . . Her movement is like the most beautiful and brightest star[64] (Praetorius, 1979: 139).

Despite these words of praise the author did not forget to include a moral warning: Those who fall prey to Venus's seductions must recognize that she is only a ghost.

Particularly revealing about Praetorius's exposition of these heathen customs is that Aphrodite was obviously still at home in the wild places of nature—indeed she had never left. These are the very same places whose hellish characters appear in the nocturnal scenes of pictures from the Netherlands on the themes of the witches' kitchen and of the temptations of Saint Anthony. Praetorius's description of the naked Venus with long hair, the globe, and other attributes evokes an image of the feminine personification of sensuality, of sumptuousness, or of the unpredictable nature of Fortuna, the goddess of fate. Later generations had a difficult time identifying the individual allegories when they were not clearly labeled, for it was not rare that both Fortuna and Venus, as well as Lust, were models for the witch.

Characterizations such as nakedness and long, unbound hair and attributes such as thistles, skulls, and goats could indicate that these were representations of witches; but those attributes could also have to do with Venus, Sin, Luxuria, or Fate. The 1513 drawing by Niklaus Manuel Deutsch (1484–1530) titled *Hexe, den Schädel Manuels durch die Lüfte tragend* [Witch, Who Carries the Skull of Emmanuel through the Air] shows a nude on a globe with a feather-decorated death's head and an hourglass that flies through the air.

Despite the unbearable "lust and joy" that came from a goddess such as Venus and flowed abundantly from Pandora's box, the Renaissance man had to grapple with a difficult demand, for the gods and goddesses in the rediscovered texts of antiquity maintained a strangely ambiguous attitude that defied the contemporary dichotomies that viewed everything as either good or evil—these gods and goddesses were good *and* evil. For example, Aphrodite/Venus was a love goddess as well as a death goddess, as Karl Kerényi demonstrated in his *Mythologie der Griechen* [Mythology of the Greeks].[65] To the Christians, who looked to the classical sources with renewed interest at the beginning of the modern era with the intention of blending this knowledge with Christian concepts, according divine characteristics to the gods and goddesses of antiquity was simply too much to ask. Christianity knows only one God. In Venus's nicknames Melaina and Melainis, "the Black One," are references to her dark aspect; these became crystallized in the image of the witch.[66] We have noted the prevalent theme of the witch riding on a goat. The impetus for that image likely comes from Sappho, the Greek poet from the sixth century B.C.E., who also sings of Aphrodite as a flying goddess.[67]

[63] Friday the thirteenth of August is still considered to be a sacred day of the witch goddess Hecate, or, more precisely, of her successor Diana. This day, which comes only every few years, still continues to cause fear and panic (Reinhardt, 1993).

[64] This description was also used in the nineteenth century by Flaubert in order to present his Saint Anthony, with Venus as his temptation. (Gustave Flaubert, *Die Versuchung des heiligen Antonius*, Frankfurt: Insel, 1979.)

[65] In earlier times her dark aspect found expression in the Black Madonnas located throughout Europe. The Black Madonna provides a visible link between the pagan cults of Isis and Aphrodite and the Virgin Mary cult that caught fire in the later Middle Ages. The aspects of these goddesses that were at odds with contemporary theology were then cast upon the witch, who as we have seen became a figure of fear and derision in proportion with Mary's success.

[66] Sappho enjoyed great popularity in Europe following her rediscovery by Renaissance scholars and poets in the fifteenth century.

[67] See Kerényi, 1966: 66. According to Kerényi, Aphrodite was also known as Androphonos, "the Murderous," and as Anosia, "the Disastrous."

"Aphrodite and materia, Venus and nature are sysnonumous and interchangeable terms. . . . The goddess is omnipresent and animates nature with her desires and instincts."

—PETER GERLITZ, *MENSCH UND NATUR IN DER WELT-RELIGIONEN* [MAN AND NATURE IN THE WORLD'S RELIGIONS], 1998

In pictures from earlier centuries, caves and decaying ruins are depicted as evidence of heathen times. A frightening impression of those times is shown in the scenes of hell, the witches' kitchen, and the witches' sabbat. These scary images also appear in scenes of the temptation of Saint Anthony, where the heathen areas are depicted as a hotbed of bats, monstrously deformed people, and aged witches who mix dreadful ingredients into ruinous mixtures. (Jacob de Gheyn II, Frankfurter Goethemuseum, Freies Deutsches Hochstift, 1600.)

Deathless Aphrodite of the spangled mind,
child of Zeus, who twists lures, I beg you
do not break with hard pains,
O lady, my heart . . .
yoking your chariot. And fine birds brought you,
quick sparrows over the black earth
whipping their wings down the sky
through midair—*

Diana

When we imagine the witches' nocturnal ride through the air to the dance site, the image of the Roman hunt goddess Diana comes to mind. In 907 C.E. in the *Canon Episcopi* we can read: "It should also not be overlooked that certain criminal women perverted by Satan, seduced by illusions and phantasms of demons, believe and openly profess that, in the dead of night, they ride upon certain beasts with the pagan goddess Diana, with a countless horde of women, and in the silence of the night fly over vast tracts of the country, and obey her commands as their mistress, while they are summoned to her service on other nights."[68] The hunters waited for her command and took care that certain killing and sacrificial rites were maintained; if they were not upheld, she could become very unpleasant.

In Christian art Diana commands "the wild army," as Urs Graf represented her in his painting *Das wilde Heer*. She was depicted on intaglios, in bronzes, and in stone sculptures of the Roman imperial times as the Lady of the Animals, usually in the company of dogs, lions, and especially stags. In this way she offered a fitting model for the witch, who is shown in the company of ravens, cats, and owls. A comparison of the paintings of Diana's hunt with images of the witches' sabbat reveals both subjects to be similar in their portrayals of the orgiastic activities of naked women in the middle of a usually wooded natural setting.

Since the Renaissance, Diana, whom the Italian Sabines saw as a goddess of fertility, guardian of wild animals, and protector of birth for humans and animals, has nourished artists' fantasies of wild feasts in the countryside with naked women. This goddess also enriched the repertoire of the witches' sabbat. (Domenico Zampiere [Domenichino, 1581–1641], Rome, Galleria Borghese.)

---

[68] Quoted in German from Sallmann, 1991: 29. In this edition quoted from Robbins: 76.
* Translation by Anne Carson from *If Not, Winter: Fragments of Sappho*, New York: Knopf, 2002, p. 3. (Trans.)

The goddess Natura (who is the same as Venus or Aphrodite) sits with her cornucopia, surrounded by plants, on the banks of a river in which Neptune is swimming with his trident. A Roman supplicant is turned toward her. On the back side of this book illustration the first line, "Oh Holy Goddess Earth, she who brings the natural things forth . . .," was replaced with "Oh Holy God . . ." in the Middle Ages. (Illustration from *Medicina antiqua*, Libri IIII medicine, *Codex vindobonensis* 93: fol. 9.4., early 13th century.)

Goddess Nature

Eventually the personification of nature, an image that is surprisingly rare in Western art, was pushed into an ever-increasing demonized realm beyond. The beginnings of this process are depicted in an example from the illustrations in *Medicina antiqua (Codex vindobonensis:* 93) from the early thirteenth century (see illustration above). The codex, which was assembled in southern Italy, contains an illustration showing an invocation of the divine Mother Earth. She stands in classical clothing on the banks of a river in which the river god Neptune can be seen sitting with his trident on a snake. Mother Earth holds

Above: The Barong dance on the island of Bali presents both sides of the world. The left side symbolizes the negative aspect, the dragon on the right the positive side of the universe. The dance reveals to the audience that neither side has more power and neither side can win. (Photograph by Claudia Müller-Ebeling.)

Below left and right: This olive tree (*Olea europea* L.) is approximately six hundred years old and is still called *Olivo della Strega*, "olive of the witch" in Magliano (Tuscany, Massa Marittima). The hooked-nosed profile of a witch can be seen in the bark. (Photographs by Claudia Müller-Ebeling.)

Above: The yellow pheasant's eye (*Adonis vernalis* L.), also known as false hellebore, sweet vernal, and spring Adonis, one of the sacred plants of antiquity, was eventually demonized and called a devil's eye or devil's flower. *Adonis* provides an important homeopathic medicine. (Photograph by Christian Rätsch.)

Below: Wolf's milk, or cypress spurge (*Euphorbia cyparissias* L.), was one of the feared plants of the witches. Today it is known only as a poisonous plant. (Photograph by Christian Rätsch.)

Above: The common thorn apple (*Datura stramonium* L.) has been known in Europe since the 16th century. Because of its psychoactive activity and toxicity at higher dosages it was considered a witches' herb and was included as an ingredient in the legendary flying ointments. Although thorn apple is one of the most powerful hallucinogens known, it is not subject to narcotics laws. Nevertheless, thorn apple has been stigmatized as a devil's herb, and in more recent times as a poisonous plant. Botanical gardens and plant books still warn about this dangerous plant. (Photograph by Christian Rätsch, in the Botanical Gardens, Hamburg.)

Below: The "golden apples of Aphrodite" are the ripe fruits of the mandrake (*Mandragora officinarum* L.). (Photograph by Christian Rätsch.)

Above: In Chile *Lobelia tupa* L. is still called *tabaco del diablo,* or devil's tobacco. The plant has mild psychoactive effects when smoked, which led to it being banned by authorities and generally demonized. (Photograph by Christian Rätsch.)

Below: Two smokable plants that have been vigorously demonized: tobacco *(Nicotiana tabacum)* and henbane *(Hyoscyamus niger)*. Yet tobacco was one of the most important shamanic plants of the New World, and henbane was the most important sacred plant of the Germanic peoples. (Photograph by Christian Rätsch.)

Above: The three Moirai, or goddesses of fate, from late antiquity, depicted on a floor in the house of Dionysus on Cyprus. (Photograph by Christian Rätsch.)

Below: These three women on a classical mosaic in Pompeii also appear as the goddesses of fate. They are called the "three tragic masks" in literature. The objects on the table can be recognized (from left to right) as a grass or henbane panicle, a censer, and a flat box with a lid. The three women, with tragic expressions, are drinking; the substance, presumably, is intoxicating. (Photograph by Alinari, National Museum, Naples.)

Left: During antiquity the ithyphallic satyr was one of the intoxicated followers of Dionysus, the god of ecstasy. Because of the satyrs' buck attributes, their bundled energy, and their intoxicated excesses, they became the icongraphic model for the Christian image of the devil. (Photograph by Claudia Müller-Ebeling.)

Above right: Two postcards illustrate scenes from the film *Alraune and the Golem*. On the left a woman, using a conjuring gesture, approaches a patient whose nerves are at the breaking point. On the right are a Rumpelstilskin-like mandrake manikin and the spirit that commands it.

Below right: Around 1870 Robert Bateman (1842–1922) depicted the unusual magical practice of pulling the capricious mandrake root from out of the ground beneath the gallows. Like the three Norns, the women use threads and gazes of invocation to help them in their operation. (Wellcome Institute Library, London.)

Above: Hans Baldung Grien disseminates the world of the witches in great detail: The witches' cauldron, billy goats, a cat, phallic sausages, skulls, bones, and profaned objects from the clergy, such as the pilgrim's hat in the right foreground, are depicted here. With this painting the artist was duty-bound to the existing ideas of the time and based the motif on predecessors such as Albrecht Dürer. He had considerable influence on the concept of the witches' sabbat with this chiaroscuro woodcut *Preparation for the Witches' Sabbat* (1510), which was widely spread and often copied in numerous variations. (Fine Arts Museum of San Francisco.)

Below: Fred Weidmann, a painter who lives in Munich, collected the most important European psychoactive plants on this airbrush painting: fly agaric, mandrake, angel's trumpet, monkshood, hemp, belladonna, and poison hemlock.

a cornucopia in her arms and is surrounded by stylized palms and fantasy plants. In front of her is a Roman supplicant. The fifty-one-line invocation on the back side of the paper was destroyed in the Middle Ages by the hand of a monk and "corrected" so that the masculine god is in the place of the feminine goddess Gaia; thus the invocation no longer says, "Sacred Goddess Earth, bringer of the natural things . . ." but, "To the Sacred God . . ." (Biedermann, 1972: 79).

The Witch As the Temptation of Saint Anthony

The transformation of the goddess of fate into the disease-bringing witch has already been discussed. This same connection between disease and fate can be seen in the Germanic goddess Holda, who has been preserved as Frau Holle in fairy tales (c.f. Rüttner-Cova, 1988). Like her sisters Venus and Isis, Holda, who is also titled Queen of Heaven and who ruled over household matters (one of her symbols is the spindle), was demonized and cast out as a witch. As a rule I think it can be safely said that most of the heathen goddesses eventually "end up" identified as the vilified and disparaged witch.[69] Beneath these demonized appearances it was actually the goddesses' true divine nature that led Saint Anthony into temptation.

What does Saint Anthony have to do with witches? First, a brief look into his life.

Anthony's existence has been historically substantiated. He lived in Lower Egypt during the third and fourth centuries C.E., at the temporal threshold between heathendom and Christianity. He was the son of well-to-do farmers of Egyptian origin. When he was barely twenty years old Anthony gave away his inheritance and went to live an ascetic and solitary life in the neglected ruins of ancient Egypt. He spent his whole long life on the run, dying in 356 in the biblical era at the age of 105. He moved ever deeper into the desert, fleeing the streams of disciples willing to be ascetics who stormed his settlements with questions. They wanted to learn from him how one could survive without satisfying the basic physical needs of eating, drinking, sleeping, and sex.

These early Christians were convinced that only such a life would really be pleasing to their god. They had many vigorous arguments with the Egyptian, Greek, and Roman heathens, and tried to convince them that neither nature nor their gods were sacred, but that only the Christian God and the spiritual principle were valid. With such an attitude, which allows no other gods and truths to exist, one seldom makes friends. The Roman emperor who ruled Egypt during that time violently persecuted the Christian sect.

Perhaps this is the reason why Antonius Eremita fled from worldly life with his disciples, even though Athanasius, the author of his life story, depicted Anthony's flight more as a steadfast stand against the seductions of power and wealth. However, in the decayed temple sites where Anthony settled, he encountered the divine ancestors of his Egyptian past. He saw them as monsters with pointed beaks, sharp claws, and fangs who attacked him. Anthony, as the legend tells, did not allow these confrontations with his demonlike ancestors to deter him from his own still-youthful belief. But it was precisely the ancient Egyptian gods—excuse me, Anthony's demons—who made him famous and holy. Athanasius took care of this when he wrote the life story of the exemplary hermit from Egypt just after Anthony's death in 356, so that all Christian monks could follow his

Saint Anthony is tempted by a Venus-like witch and by Pan, who has been turned into a bat-winged demon with panpipes, in this 1515 illustration by Albrecht Dürer.

---

[69] However, artists of the fin de siècle consciously took up the depiction of witches from pre-Christian and archaic examples, as Stelzl discovered (1983: 11), and rehabilitated them by blending witches with the iconography of the Parcae.

example. With stereotypical declarations of war against heathen ways of thinking, Athanasius hammered out sentences such as the following:

> The demons, who the heathens consider as gods, are not gods; yes, that they [the Christians] step on them and torture them, because they are the seducer and destroyer of man—in Jesus Christ, our Lord, who is splendid in eternity. Amen (Athanasius, 1987: 118).

But what has this got to do with the temptations of Saint Anthony, and what does the witch have to do with him?

According to modern psychological theory one stays "right on the heels" of those very things one most suppresses. Personal desires take on seductive forms, and what one is secretly afraid of manifests in frightening images. Anthony, alone in the unvarying desert without enough to eat, always on the edge of thirst, and without the distraction of any sensuous desire, was entirely subject to his inner world. All of the seductive women he has spliced into his concept of desire visit him in his desert settlement. In his withdrawal from desire the fantasies of boundless power, endless wealth, and notions of his own greatness pressed to the forefront of Anthony's delirious brain. Eventually all of the falcons, cows, and crocodile-headed gods of the ancient Egyptian pantheon that he could see in the bleached frescoes around his settlement became animated.

We don't know what really happened. But Anthony's friend, the bishop Athanasius of Alexandria, in his hagiography of the legendary hermit convincingly secured the belief that Anthony was victorious over all of these challenges and continued on with his unshakable convictions. Athanasius interpreted the visions of the canonized Anthony as being temptations of the devil, who tested him in the form of seductive women and hideous demons in order to deter him from the path of righteousness—in other words, from the path of Christian belief.

This legend of the saint exerted a substantial influence on Western spiritual and cultural history. Whenever and wherever Christians are confronted with opinions and concepts of reality that their church has not blessed, they people their surroundings with devils, demons, and witches. As only one single god and one single world were canonized or permitted, the devil became the perfect sorcerer and transformation artist and manifested in an endless number of forms. He demanded his Christian opponents recognize his true diabolical nature behind the facade of beautiful women, eloquent monks, followers of different faiths, and even in cat's fur and raven's feathers. Thus the artists, particularly in times of unrest, captured in their pictures the various tempters and temptresses as Jews, Muslims, Cathari, Waldenses, or reformed Lutherans. True to the legend of Anthony they place the usually frightened and cowering saint on the borders of the paintings and confront him with the demonic activities of hybrid creatures in whose bodies all that man is afraid of is unified. They present Anthony with toothless women and, more often, richly dressed or seductively undressed women. These temptresses were the diabolic embodiment of the seven deadly sins, particularly of lust and pride. In them the heathen goddesses Freya, Aphrodite, Diana, Artemis, and Hecate rise again.

Hieronymus Bosch (c. 1450–1516) was the first to recognize that all of the inner images that Christianity suppressed were still preserved in the form of the witch. He integrated the witches' sabbat in his peculiar depictions of the temptation of Saint Anthony, which were created in the period between 1475 and 1500 (they are difficult to date). The great impact of his creation of monstrous hybrids—in which not only actually existing animal and plant species were paired with his newly invented creatures, but pots, jugs, musical instruments, and other lifeless objects were also transformed into body parts—can be seen in his many imitators, the most enthusiastic of them being Pieter Brueghel the elder.

In Bosch's puzzling pictorial worlds that have led authors to interpret the most varied of meanings from the paintings without finding the key to the answer, the artist depicts, as Frater José de Siguenza put it, "humans as they truly are inside." Although I do not want to go extensively into the heretical contents of his pictures at this point, a brief description of one of them may help to clarify the question of how such blasphemous altar paintings by the Brabant artist from 's Hertogenbosch might actually fulfill Frater Siguenza's contention of the painter's ability to capture both the angelic and the demonic components that combine in every human being.

At this point I would like to describe Bosch's famous Lisbon triptych, *The Temptation of Saint Anthony*, thought to have been created after 1490.[70] As in all depictions of the temptation, at first it is difficult to make out the hermit among the turbulence. The saint is found kneeling on a small wall in a half-destroyed ancient tower, with his gaze on the observer. He and the strange entourage surrounding him are depicted on a bridgelike plateau. A bearded man with a cylindrical hat, red clothing, and a severed foot who has spread a cloth out in front of him leans on the opposing wall—he has apparently fallen sacrifice to the so-called Saint Anthony's fire.[71] Except for his head, turned out of the painting toward the viewer, Anthony is facing a crucifix in the middle of the dark tower. Next to the panel is the martyred physical shell of the resurrected, self-manifested being—the man on the cross. To the left, near Saint Anthony, is a woman in contemporary clothing whose body turns into that of a pointy snake: the caricature of a false believer, a hypocrite. She passes an old nun a jug of red wine—the Eucharist blood of the crucified. A procession of three strange women is next to the kneeling woman. One of these three "priestesses" turns to Saint Anthony with a piercing gaze and passes him a mug. She wears helmetlike head protection, out of which snakes slither, and a long-sleeved dress. To her side stands an unusually pale woman wearing an oriental-styled, thorn-decorated hat, on which is fixed a veil that partially covers her face. A bizarre object of worship is held in the air over a round table. The table is approached by a crawling cripple, a knight with a mandolin, and a hedgehog head on which sits an owl. The end of the procession is made up of a black man with red cardinal-like robes who is holding the bizarre object: a plate, on which sits a frog holding an egg in the air.[72]

---

[70] The date suggested here follows that of Charles de Tolnay, *Hieronymus Bosch*, Eltville, Germany: Rheingauer Verlagsgesellschaft, 1984: 357.

[71] Saint Anthony's fire, or *Ignes sacre* (the sacred fire), was the name of an illness that appeared in epidemics during the Middle Ages. It is caused by ergot-poisoned rye flour—the primary food for gruel and bread. The afflicted, whom the disciples of Anthony took care of in great numbers, had horrible visions that were similar to those of Saint Anthony; thus he became their patron. In extreme cases of this affliction necrosis would occur, causing limbs to atrophy and fall off. Cf. Veit Harold Bauer, *Das Antonius-Feuer in Kunst und Medizin*, historische Schriftenreihe, Basel: Sandoz, 1973.

[72] To the medieval mentality this symbol-rich depiction could almost be read like a text. There were traditional meanings attributed to each of the elements Bosch has used here. Animal symbolism was especially prominent in medieval iconography. The association of Christ with the lamb has endured into modern times. Frogs were generally viewed with the same suspicion as the toad, and their aquatic environment was viewed by the medieval compilers of bestiaries as synonymous with the pleasures of the flesh. The egg, which was a well-known alchemical symbol to signify the transformation of base matter into a higher, more spiritual form, was also a symbol of sexual creation and a natural corollary to the frog holding it. The owl was associated both with spiritual wisdom and with the forbidden wisdom of the witches. The hedgehog, in addition to being a common medieval symbol for both theft and prosperity, would be equated with the hedge, widely viewed as the domain of the medieval witch.

Wilhem Fraenger interpreted this whole symbol-laden and puzzling scene as a "black mass." He characterized the three women as "snake, moon, and swamp women," whom he places in the mythological vicinity of the Egyptian frog-goddess of Antinoë, Heket, the primordial mother of being, who can be traced back to the four primordial gods of Egypt.[73]

Whether or not one agrees with this interpretation of the painting, in the context of this book the inclusion of the witchlike temptresses in *The Temptation of Saint Anthony*, and the heathen practices that can be deduced from them, is of importance. Temptresses had already been depicted in earlier examples of this genre; as a rule they symbolized Luxuria, whose "diabolic" nature can be deciphered by her bat wings and clawed feet. But Bosch was the first to connect the temptress with ritual practices of heathen origin, which were contested by the Church for being heretical. "Bosch delivers a thoroughly un-simple, wrested from all conventions confessional picture, whose polemic excessiveness dipped the virtuous stuff into a witches' cauldron."[74] On the eve of the Reformation the representatives of the Christian church vehemently declared themselves for the destruction of heathen customs.[75]

After Bosch, witchlike temptresses are found in countless examples of Dutch art of the fifteenth and sixteenth centuries—the period when this theme reached its apex. Integrated into the world of the ascetic recluse, women seduce Anthony in their witches' kitchen, in rock archways, or during the witches' sabbat in isolated forests. In pictures by Joachim Patinir, Cornelis Massys, and Jan van de Venne, witchlike old women with bared breasts and distorted expressions appear as modestly clad matchmakers or as naked temptresses, as well as in other guises. Here, too, they offer the saint the apple of Eve that caused the fall of man as believed by the Christian world, or else they offer him heathen idols, sacks of gold, or plates of delicious food. All heathen concepts of the sensuous joy of life embodied by their goddesses were regarded not only as threatening Saint Anthony but also as corrupting all of Christianity; they all combine in the image of the witch.

Only in the nineteenth century did the once divine nature that had been vilified and made diabolical reenter consciousness. The writer Gustave Flaubert, who fashioned a character for a novel out of Anthony, gave the ascetic memories of his encounters with gods and goddesses such as Isis, whom he originally experienced as nothing more than horrible demons. He then recognized these figures for what they represent—Egyptian gods—although in an alien animal form: "When I lived in the temple of Heliopolis, I often looked at the pictures on the wall—scepter-carrying vultures, lyre-playing crocodiles, snake bodies with men's heads, cow-headed women who worship ithyphalic gods."[76]

Mathis Gothart-Nithart, known as Matthias Grünewald (c. 1455–1528), created a panel with three sides that is dedicated to Saint Anthony. The piece was commissioned by the Antoniterhospital [St. Anthony Hospital] in Isenheim around 1512. *The Temptation of Saint Anthony* is the most impressive of the plates. On it are not only a demon horribly attacking the saint, but also, to the left and below, a victim of Saint Anthony's fire with a bloated stomach. The fantastic scene gives the impression of originating in a nightmare. On the left-facing side Grünewald placed the meeting of the two hermits, Anthony and

---

Medicinal Plants for Saint Anthony's Fire[77]

Blind nettle (*Lamium album*)

Bulbous buttercup (little rose of Saint Anthony *Ranunculus bulbosus*)

Clover (*Trifolium repens*)

Couch grass (*Agropyrum repens*)

Cross-leaved gentian (*Gentiana cruciata*)

Cypress grass (*Cyperus fuscus*)

Long plantain (*Plantago lanceolata*)

Plantain (*Plantago major*)

Red poppy (*Papaver rhoeas*)

Spelt (*Triticum speltha*)

Swallow's wort (*Vincetoxicum officinale*)

Veronica (*Veronica chamaedrys*)

Vervain (*Verbena officinalis*)

Water figwort (herb of Saint Anthony, *Scrophularia aquatica*)

---

77 Following Kühn, 1948: 332.

---

73 Fraenger, 1975: 346. Illustrations 117 to 131 in this book *(Hieronymus Bosch)* show the panel that has been described here. It can be seen in the Lisbon Museu Nacional de Arte Antigua.

74 Fraenger, 1975: 342.

75 Without naming specific sources, Michelet (1952, vol. 1: 127ff.) cites as examples various heathen customs of the Middle Ages that were dedicated to the cults of Diana, the moon, and Hecate.

76 Gustave Flaubert, *Die Versuchung des heiligen Antonius*, Frankfurt: Insel, 1979: 112f.

Paul, who find themselves in a conversation in a wooded environment. Wolfgang Kühn made a botanical identification of a total of fourteen medicinal plants that are to befound on the hermit's plate (see page 188), and eight were listed in herbals of the time as remedies for Saint Anthony's fire. The other six were used in the treatment of "burns, infected wounds, and old sores." Kühn assumes that the fourteen plants that were represented were also the ingredients of the Saint Vinage vinegar or the Saint Anthony balsam (Kühn, 1948: 330f.), for which the Isenheim order was famous. Some of the plants—for example, vervain *(Verbena officinalis)*, blind nettle *(Lamium album)*, corn poppy *(Papaver rhoeas)*, and one of its relatives, the opium poppy *(Papaver somniferum)*— have been identified. All of these plants are closely associated with witches—the blind nettle even has witches *(lamia)* to thank for its Latin name.

Saturn: Master of the Witches

The person of antiquity addressed the planetary god Saturn with the invocation shown here. He did this in order to move the powerful divine authority so that Saturn might influence events in a beneficial way. From this invocation-prayer we can determine that in the heathen past negative aspects were not equated with the evil and demonic or pushed beyond the boundaries of the reality of life, but were considered to be facts that determined life.

The qualities that were associated with Saturn in classical times—cold, isolation, age, petrifaction—can also be gleaned from this invocation. These traits have been derived from astrological observance since Babylonian times, which noticed that Saturn makes the longest path around the Sun of any planet. It is one of the closest planets to Earth. In the third century C.E. Saturn was equated by the Romans with the Greek Kronos, and before them the ancient Italic peoples also considered him to be a god of the fields. Kronos, the god of time, who eats his own children, bestowed Saturn with additional death-bringing qualities. Christian art has borrowed from him in corresponding images of the reaper of death or the sickle of the grim reaper. As is clear in the invocation, Saturn also unites in himself two opposing aspects. He was the god of the golden age who initiated intoxicated celebrations.

In medieval treatments of the so-called "planetary children," in which certain occupations and temperaments were placed under the domain of different planetary influences, one finds nearly all the protagonists of our book collected under the domain of the ruler Saturn. People such as hermits—in particular, Saint Anthony—along with outsiders such as witches, those stigmatized by society (such as cripples, criminals, and women in the stocks), as well as artists and field workers can be recognized in depictions of this planet's children. Artists, geniuses, and Saint Anthony were associated with Saturn because of his temperament, which tended toward the melancholy; in Spanish *saturnino* means not only "being under the influence of Saturn," but also "melancholy." In 1531 in his *Occulta philosophia* Agrippa von Nettesheim added: "All who are under the influence of Saturn and can handle his *furor melancholicus* and those in whom the imagination is stronger than reason could become wonderful artists and craftsmen, for example painters or architects."[78] Artists such as Francisco de Goya, Hans Baldung Grien, and Albrecht Dürer also use Saturn as an embodiment of age, of melancholy, or of the imagination.

---

[78] From Folke Nordström, *Goya, Saturn and Melacholy: Studies in the Art of Goya*, Stockholm: Almquist and Wiksell, 1962, p. 198.

"Oh master, whose name is sublime and whose power is great, supreme master; Oh master Saturn, you—cold, infertile, dark, injurious; you, whose life is serious and whose word is true; you, wise and solitary, imprenetrable; you, who keeps your promises; you, who is weak and tired; you, who more than all others is laden with worry; you, who knows neither pleasure nor joy; wise elder, well-versed in all arts; you, deceptive, wise, and rational; you, who brings prosperity as well as decline; you, who makes humans happy and sad! I implore you, oh mighty father, in your great favor and benevolent spirit, do for me this and that . . ."

—Jean Seznec, *La Survivance des dieux antiques* [The Survival of the Ancient Gods], 1940

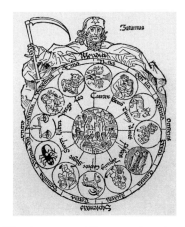

The planetary god Saturn as the ruler of the zodiac, which determines the fate of the earth. (Woodcut, c. 1499.)

The wagon of the sickle-carrying Saturn, "patron of the witches," is drawn by dragons. The child begs for his life. (Crispin de Passe, etching, Bibliothèque Nationale, Paris, late 16th century)

Let us recall the witch allegory of Dürer once again (see illustration page 176). This provides us with another reference to pre-Christian pagan times that explains why Aphrodite was transformed into an old woman by medieval Christians. Namely, Dürer, influenced by the humanist, astrological explanation of Saturn, interpreted the planetary position of the god in the allegory. It is in the god's honor that Saturnalia is celebrated in Rome around the time of the winter solstice. This festival makes it possible to annul strictly defined societal order and hierarchies in permissible ways. During this period in December slaves could dance on the heads of their masters, women had a say, and subordinates could mock their rulers without punishment. It was a truly upside-down world, and this tradition continued into the modern era in boisterous carnivals in the northern regions of Europe. However, religious sects fought this celebration with lectures on morality; later, educated secular theorists—like Sebastian Brandt in *Narrenschiff* [Ship of Fools]—contested it.

Allegories of the "world turned upside down" found a wide range of opportunity in the art of the fifteenth century; one might think of pictures by Pieter Brueghel the elder, for example. The witch allegory by Dürer has been interpreted as the "allegory of the upside-down world," a title that offers a key to interpreting this unusual engraving.[79] The witch appears as a "planetary child" of Saturn—as a person who, like hermits, artists, and the crippled, stands mainly under the influence of this planetary god of time and age. In this context the goddess Venus would be an embodiment of the astrological sign of Capricorn, which is ruled by Saturn. To depict the witch as a planetary child of Saturn and to show Venus as an old witch is explained less by way of the symbols of antiquity and more from a humanist standpoint, which often interprets antiquity from a Christian perspective.

In light of this classification it seems logical that Saturn, with his astrological symbol of the goat, became "patron saint" of witches. At the end of the sixteenth century Crispin de Passe depicted Saturn (based on Martin de Vos) as a hunched, if muscular, old man. He swings a sickle and his wagon is pulled by dragons—animals that are associated with him.

Because the believed influence of the stars and planets on the meteorological and political events in the years preceding, during, and directly following Dürer's life were

[79] Among others, see Sigrid Schade in van Dülmen, 1987: 177 f.

Plants of Saturn[80]

Belladonna	*Atropa belladonna* L.
Black hellebore	*Helleborus niger* L.
Black nightshade	*Solanum nigrum* L.
Celandine	*Chelidonium majus* L.
Celery	*Apium graveolens* L.
Cinquefoil	*Potentilla erecta* (L.) Raeusch.
Coffee	*Coffea arabica* L.
Cypress	*Cupressus sempervirens* L.
Elm	*Ulmus glabra* Huds. (Ill. 11)
Enchanter's nightshade	*Circaea lutetiana* L.
Hemp	*Cannabis sativa* L.
Henbane	*Hyoscyamus niger* L.
Juniper	*Juniperus sabina* L.
Male fern	*Dryopteris filix-mas* (L.) Schott
Mandrake	*Mandragora officinarum* L.
Monkshood	*Aconitum napellus* L.
One berry	*Paris quadrifolia*
Opium poppy	*Papaver somniferum* L.
Plantain, common	*Plantago major* L.
Poison hemlock	*Conium maculatum* L.
Rock brake fern	*Polypodium vulgare* L.
Sage	*Salvia officinalis* L.
Sassafras	*Sassafras albidum* (Nutt.) Nees
Satan's bolete	*Boletus satanas* Lenz
Shave grass (Saturn's food)	*Equisetum arvense* L.
Shepherd's purse	*Capsella bursa-pastoris* (L.) Medik.
Solomon's seal	*Polygonatum multiflorum* (L.) All.
Spruce	*Picea abies* (L.) Karsten
Tobacco	*Nicotiana tabacum* L.
Violet	*Viola tricolor* L.
Wintergreen	*Gaultheria procumbens* L.
Wolfsbane	*Aconitum* spp.
Yew	*Taxus baccata* L.

[80] According to Gessmann, no date: 118, and Jeanne Rose, *Herbs and Things*, New York: Grosset and Dunlap, 1981: 274.

The planetary god Saturn (Kronos) as the embodiment of time, about to eat a child—following Hesiod's description. Behind him to the left is Aquarius, the zodiac sign ruled by him. To the right is a buck, the symbol of fertility and the orgiastic Saturnalia festival, which is celebrated in Rome during the sign of Capricorn (also governed by Saturn).

seen as wholly negative by his contemporaries, a Dürer image such as this one depicting a witch riding in a rage is totally explicable. The prevailing belief in these kinds of influences and their unwholesome nature are corroborated by contemporaries of Dürer. In 1470 the noted Kartäus monk and reform theologian Werner Rolevink from Cologne (1425–1502) published in a chronicle that in the year 1472 Halley's comet would cast a shadow over the world, after which would follow "wars and plagues in different countries." Johannes de Undagine, called Rosenbach (c. 1467–1537), was a clergyman and astrologist who worked in the Frankfurt region. He was in contact with Matthias Grünewald as well as with Otto Brunfels, the clergyman and botanist. In 1522 Rosenbach's portrait was drawn by Dürer's student Hans Baldung for a woodcut.

Rosenbach wrote during the same year of unrest, which was influenced by the Reformation, to Dr. Zobel, the Mainz vicar from Giebelstädt. "I divined from the stars a new condition of the Church, more wars, the movement of many peoples, one regime against the other, pestilence, and many deaths. We see this already partially fulfilled, partially it is still to come."[81]

All in all the time between the second half of the fifteenth century and the first half of the sixteenth—the apex of depictions of witches—was religiously and politically, to put it mildly, a thoroughly unpleasant period. This could be read in the stars, despite the fact that the divine power of the stars had been subject to serious challenge since antiquity. To protect himself against possible accusations of worshipping false powers by the Church, the astrologer would also have emphasized that the stars are the "interpreters of the divine will" and can sometimes indicate what decisions Christ has made regarding the world of humans.

According to certain attributes some plants are also placed under the influence of Saturn.[82] When woody plants show the rings of the years, they remind us of Saturn/Kronos, of the god of time. Gray and dark leaves, bark, and a woody consistency symbolize the god's old age. Unpleasant and pungent odors, such as that of valerian root, make us think of age and decay.

Also in Saturn's environment belong the poisonous plants, especially those with mind-altering activity. Many of the plants classified under Saturn correspond to the presumed ingredients of witches' salves. With the help of these plants one could experience Saint Anthony's state of altered consciousness, which approached a condition of withdrawal so severe it achieved near total sensory deprivation, causing his inner images to manifest in the form of temptations. Like other outsiders in society, Anthony was under the influence of the planetary god Saturn.

The Painters of Witches

One question remains, and remains possibly unanswerable: What could have moved artists to paint witches, and what was their personal position on this phenomenon? Did they share a secret sympathy for the subjects of their painting or did they feel their work was advancing the good cause? We will end with a look at some of the individual painters whose subject matter included the witch and see what, if any, clues to their personal position in this regard might be unearthed from their works.

Throughout the course of this text we have described a number of pictures of witches and compared them with the ever-present panels of the Virgin Mary, which were commissioned by many ecclesiastical orders and later by the nobility or bourgeoisie. But it requires a longer, more assiduous search for evidence of Mary's nocturnal sister. Unlike the depictions of the Virgin Mary, which can be found in every collection of early Renaissance art in the world, the pictures of witches are rarer and often in collections that are not readily accessible to the general public.

The image of the witch first entered the Christian imagination in the middle of the fifteenth century; initially only a few artists dared capture the witch fully on paper, and even more rare was a witch image committed to canvas. Equally rare at that time was the witch's presence in the genre of free art, art that springs from an artist's personal interest. These artists raised this subject to an independent category of pictures not embedded in an illustrative or mythological context. They primarily used drawing as their medium,

---

[81] Quote from W. K. Zülch, *Der historische Grünewald*, Munich: Bruckmann, 1938: 404f.

[82] Cf. W. B. Crow, *The Occult Properties of Herbs and Plants*, New York: Samuel Weiser, 1980.

only rarely making prints, and in just one instance—by Hans Baldung Grien—was the witch depicted in a "salon-quality" oil painting. Drawings are not made on commission from outside sources; in drawings artists have the possibility of putting to paper their own ideas of motifs and themes that are of personal interest. Therefore such pictures can be used to gain a glimpse behind the curtain at what personally moves an artist and how he interprets these subjects of interest.

Depictions of witches are found in three artistic contexts but rarely in the domain of the self-chosen subject. More often—predominantly in the sixteenth century—these depictions are in the context of commissions from well-to-do circles or are in the realm of the applied arts, including illustrated books.

The drawings of Baldung belong in the first category of artworks done for the artist's personal interest. The second category of commissioned pieces is represented by such works as the cabinet picture *Hexenküchen* (Witches' Kitchen) by Frans Francken the younger, who satisfied the desires of his client by making different variations in this romantic "shocking" genre. Also in this category are countless other Flemish and Dutch painters, who embellished the themes of "Vorbereitung der Hexen zum Flug" (The Witches Prepare for Flying) and the "Hexensabbat" (Witches' Sabbat). These commissioned works reveal information about the tastes of the time and about the secret desires of the bourgeoisie for forbidden things. There are also many pictures of the temptations of Saint Anthony that should be included in this category, beginning with those of Hieronymus Bosch, who around 1470 was the first to make detailed renderings of heretical nonbeings enriched with images of witches (although it has seldom been established for whose commission Bosch's panels were created). One encounters witches in the third category concerning the realm of the applied arts, where artists place their talents in the service of publishers who surround their moral and theological texts with powerful images. Included in this category are, for example, illustrations for a 1575 pamphlet by Ulrich Molitor called *Von Hexen und Unholden* [Of Witches and Monsters] and the *Compendium Maleficarum* by Francesco Maria Guazzo (1626), in which the authors created a demagogic atmosphere against the witches.

What connects these three levels of artistic examination of the witch theme is the Christian spiritual worldview. What differentiates them is the degree to which the image of the witch corresponds to the moral and theological position of the time. So, for example, artists who of their own free will draw a witch are permitted to do so because it provides an opportunity for them to depict a naked, sensuous woman under the pretext that it is really a picture of a witch. An example of this is Hans Baldung's thematic development starting with a witches' sabbat (see last color plate, this section) and culminating in his monumental depiction of the naked bodies of the weather-witches (above). The examples in this first category show a strong dependence on the art of antiquity, which can be seen in artists such as Dürer (less so in Baldung), who had more extensive contact with educated humanists of the time).

Many mythological picture themes of the Renaissance can be traced back to the advice of humanist advisers who sought to create a synthesis of their newly found knowledge of antiquity with their Christian position. This confrontation of Christian worldview with classical examples of witch motifs is mainly found in drawings in which the artists realized their personal idea of witches (of course these works were not created in a vacuum uninfluenced by the zeitgeist).

In the two other picture categories, all the classical concepts became totally

The two weather-witches present themselves to the viewer with self-assurance. Baldung's picture oscillates between a connection to the classical archetype of Venus Kallipygos, Venus "with the pretty posterior," and the Christian allegory of lust and sin, which is illustrated by the presence of the billy goat. (Hans Baldung Grien, *Zwei Wetterhexen*, oil painting, Frankfurt, Städel, 1523.)

unrecognizable through the demonizing filter of the times. These illustrations offer the most powerful theological exegesis of witches; therefore, they are the best suited for the reconstruction of the historical and political dimensions of the witch persecution.

In the many depictions of the witches' sabbat and the witches' kitchen created in the Dutch provinces, a more unspecific image of witches was developed. These images fed on an interest in the forbidden and depicted repulsive or seductive worlds. This interest in the aesthetic of the forbidden has more to do with the development of images of witches (the ones created under commission) than any fanatical moral and theological position.

Hans Baldung Grien (1484–1545)

From which position can we explain Baldung's pictures of witches? How did the painter from the Upper Rhine view witches and the characteristics the Church attributed to them? Only assumptions can be made in this regard.[83]

Baldung devoted himself predominantly to religious themes. However, sacred themes increasingly took a background position to secular creations and classical themes in his work, and not just because he was becoming popular with clients of the private sector. Baldung worked mostly in the Upper Rhine area. As an educated citizen with a position on the town council, he spent many years as a member of the guild in Strasbourg. In light of the entire body of his work, Hans Baldung Grien seems to have been a painter with a humanist education who could follow his own personal goals independent of court or denominational duties.[84] His drawings, engravings, and oil paintings are less revealing of any specific Christian or even heathen creed and provide more evidence of standard painterly concerns.

In general, painting in the Renaissance had emancipated itself from a denominational corset—as can be recognized in examples by most of the artists of that era. Through the writings of the humanists, the classical knowledge of man and his natural anatomy moved to center stage—even though this took place against the background of Christianity. Thus images of the naked female body became an increasingly important subject matter in Baldung's later works. He explored traditional subject matter such as the depiction of stages of life in a more radical way. He also dealt with the transitory nature of life, which can be found in his variations on the theme in *Tod und Mädchen* [Death and the Maiden] and in Christian allegories of lust and its subsequent fallout. These generally included representations of woman depicted as Eve, as Venus, as goddess, or even as witch. Linda Hults, for whom the various stages of life speak an ambiguous language, concluded from

---

[83] Gert van der Osten (1983: 16) attributes the painter with an enlightened position in his monograph *Hans Baldung Grien: Gemälde und Dokumente* (Berlin, 1983: 16) when he states that Baldung was making fun of witches and the witch craze in his Städel painting *Die Wetterhexen*. That the artist was able to distance himself from the phenomenon has been supported by a number of authors, including van der Osten (1983: 33) and the art historian Sigrid Schade (in van Dülmen, 1987). They claim that during the first two thirds of the sixteenth century witch trials were extremely rare in Strasbourg, Baldung's place of work. Certainly it is important to compare biographical dates with the actual consequences of the witch trials in a certain place: for example, the fact that the notorious Hexenhammer, written by the Dominican inquisitors Jakob Sprenger and Heinrich Kramer, who was known as Institoris, was published in 1487 in Strasbourg and that in 1508 in this same city the cathedral priest Johann Geiler von Kaisersberg (1445–1510) selected a series of sermons based entirely on the orthodox position on superstition and witchcraft (which he supported with texts that had been previously published). In light of this it seems very risky to me to assume that the people of Strasbourg had resisted the persecution of witches as a result of a liberal atmosphere or because of Baldung's critical attitude toward the Church's position on witches.

[84] This is revealed in the diptych *Sündenfall*, which was created around 1525 and presently hangs in the Budapest Museum of Fine Arts. Deviating from the traditional theme, it is Adam who looks the (female) serpent—a creature usually associated with Eve—in the eye. Without such an independent artistic position, which interpreted Protestantism as "external dry conformity" and had apparently attained independence from the old church (as van der Osten emphasized [1983: 33]), Baldung's drawing of the resting naked couple (currently in the collection of the Stuttgart Kupferstchkabinett), would be unthinkable. The attempt to categorize Baldung's art in either a Christian or a mythological context is most often futile.

this development that Baldung was influenced by other spiritual streams toward the end of his life rather than merely the Christian one.[85]

Baldung's depictions of naked women are open to multiple interpretations. They all depict the same type of female with long curly blond hair, similar facial expressions, and comparable body types. This same basic type can be found in the classical heathen Venus, which hangs in the Museum in Otterlo, as well as in the representation of Judith holding the decapitated head of Holofernes from the Old Testament (Nuremberg) and in his depiction of the Christian Eve (Budapest).

In this context it is good to keep in mind that we usually have not only the artists themselves to thank for the titles of the paintings, drawings, or engravings, but also the iconographic interpretation of art historians. For example, the painting that hangs in the Frankfurter Städel museum under the title *Wetterhexen* [Weather-witches] was purchased by the museum in 1879, at which time the title was changed to *Himmlische und irdische Liebe* [Heavenly and Earthly Love]. The current title has been used only since 1938. With such an unusual subject as the weather-witches the search for sketches of similar figures that appear in subsequent paintings could prove to be revealing. But in this case such a search leads only to further confusion. Without a doubt a drawing preserved in the Berlin Kupferstichkabinett can be traced to the same person who stood as a model for the standing witch. Her haughty expression, the posture of her head, and her hairstyle are noticeably similar to the coquettish over-the-shoulder-looking witch in *Zwei Wetterhexen*. However, the question of whether or not this drawing, known by the name of *Venus als Siegerin, den Apfel des Paris haltend* [Venus As Victor, Holding the Apple of Paris], actually has anything to do with the fall of Eve, or represents a sketch Baldung drew in preparation for that painting,[86] or was created on its own after the painting remains unanswered.[87]

This female nude with the apple could be the model for Eve as well as for Venus, who was chosen by Paris with an apple to be the most beautiful goddess (Hans Baldung Grien, Berlin, Museen preusischer Kulturbesitz, Kupferstichkabinett.)

Frans Francken the Younger (1581–1642)

We have mentioned how a number of artists had already worked clandestinely in their private studios, with a relative amount of freedom, on the world of witches. In some cases these works even saw the light of day in engravings, where they later paved the way for other artists at the beginning of the seventeenth century to translate these sketches from graphics into paintings. An example of this is the work of Frans Francken the younger. From 1606 to about 1617 he worked on countless small-format pictures on the theme of the so-called *Hexenküchen* (witches' kitchen), in which nearly two hundred years of witch demagogy had gathered in the heads of his contemporaries. This category includes the old witch who anoints her younger colleague for the *Himmelsflug* (sky flight),[88] and female

---

[85] Linda Hults's essay about Baldung's relationship to the Reformation in the exhibition catalog *Hans Baldung Grien, Prints and Drawings*, Washington, D.C.: National Gallery of Art, 1981.

[86] A study of the painting was assumed by G. von Tèrey in his catalog of the drawings of Hans Baldung Grien, published in 1894–96. Tèrey identified the drawing as Eve, based on the apple the model holds in her hand.

[87] Carl Koch regards the drawing as an independent composition that was created after the painting, in *Die Zeichnungen Hans Baldung Griens*, Berlin: Deutscher Verein für Kunstwissenschaft, 1941: Cat. no. 126.

[88] According to conventional belief the witch is able to leave behind the gravitational pull of the earth with the help of the witches' salve. Her destination is an earthly one, namely witches' gathering places such as in Blocksberg. For her flight the witch used her broom as a vehicle. In short, it is quite fitting to speak of "witches' flight" or "flight through the air" in this context. On the other hand, these experiences of physical independence from earthly gravity can also be interpreted as *Himmelfahrt* (journey to the sky or heaven—the Ascension), for over the earth is—according to medieval and modern-era understanding—heaven. However, from a Christian perspective such terminology is forbidden, as the word *ascension* is reserved exclusively for Mary and the saints. Therefore it is revealing that cultural descriptions of the witch talk of the air instead of heaven. After all, according to heathen concepts the air is inhabited by elemental ghosts such as fairies, who have been declared to be allies of the devil. Witches were accused of communicating with them.

Venus Kallipygos, she "with the pretty posterior," was the model for this young witch, who is being anointed for flight by her aged colleague. (Maleuvre, after Queredeau, *Tableau de l'incinstance*, 1612, Paris, Bibliothèque Nationale.)

clients from respectable circles seeking magical potions, books, skulls, frogs, and other "disgusting creatures," as well as the inevitable witches' cauldron, which has human legs jutting out of it, and so on.

The *Hexenküchen* of Frans Francken, who descended from a large dynasty of painters in Antwerp and whose craft and artistic reputation was carried on by his son, were created in the atmosphere of the Counter-Reformation. Fifteen years before Francken's birth the reformatory iconoclasts in Antwerp created a separation between the Catholic-influenced southern provinces of the Netherlands and the reformed northern ones. In 1585, four years after the birth of the painter, the battle for religious and political freedom dominated the atmosphere as Spanish troops militarily forced the people of Antwerp to accept the Catholic creed and sixty percent of the merchants and intellectuals moved to the north. But after 1595 these groups returned in large numbers to their hometown, drawn by sinking taxes and the twelve-year armistice between Spain and the united provinces of the Netherlands— which gave not only them but also their contemporaries who remained Catholic a strengthened sense of national consciousness. In this setting of close spiritual and denominational cooperation as well as Antwerp's commercial contacts with the lands of Spain and Portugal (both countries claimed Antwerp as a protectorate), more citizens could afford to commission artwork for their personal enjoyment. The scenes of the witches by Frans Francken must have been particularly popular, as he made countless replicas of the subject.[89]

It it important to recognize that one cannot necessarily ascertain the inner position of the artist based upon the image. Despite recurring witch trials, which afflicted certain regions and times with hysteria,[90] most artists could conceal their personal viewpoints behind their work and maintain a certain distance from the prevailing influences of the times, and from their clients and benefactors.

An example of this is Lucas Cranach the elder, from whom a drawing of witches flying on goats has been preserved.[91] Like his countryman the electoral prince Friedrich the Wise, who at first was a Catholic with a fervent reverence of images of saints and relics, early on in the struggle Cranach turned to the reformer Luther and created radical anti-Roman, antipapist "battle images" of the "new belief." Nevertheless, commissioned work existed at the same time; in other words, work was commissioned by Catholic clients and included Catholic content. Thus "old believers" such as Cardinal Albrecht von Brandenburg hired the studio of Lucas Cranach to paint for his so-called Roman Battlement—his residence in Halle—142 pictures of saints and passion plays, images that speak a language entirely different from that of Cranach's personal drawings, as they were aimed against the creed of Luther.[92]

---

[89] A validation of my thesis that the depiction of witches—which became an independent subject that was only tangentially built upon the picture of the witch as described by the Church—is found in the dissertation by Härting, 1983, whose historical delineation I follow here. With regard to Francken, Härting concedes at the very most the possibility that Francken knew the writings of a Jean Bodin about the "Demonology of Witches," which appeared in Antwerp in 1580 and 1593, or the text *De oculta philosophia* by Agrippa von Nettesheim, which had already been published in 1581.

[90] As this investigation of the witch has demonstrated, one must guard carefully against lumping things together. The witch trials occurred in waves that often correspondeded to social-historical times of crisis, and the effects varied greatly according to their time and place. For example, during a comparable period of time in the Swiss canton of Thurgau only two executions took place, while, according to Wolfgang Behringer (in van Dülmen, 1987: 162) in Vaud there were 3,371!

[91] This is a border drawing in the 1515 prayer book of Kaiser Maximilian I, which is stored in the Bavarian Staatsbibliotek in Munich.

[92] This subject matter was researched by Andreas Tacke, *Der katholische Cranach: Zu zwei Großaufträgen von Lucas Cranach d. Ä., Simon Frank und der Cranach Werkstatt (1520–1540)*, Berliner Schriften zur Kunst, vol. 2, Mainz: Phillip von Zabern, 1992.

This demonstrates not only the denominational independence of an artist such as Cranach during the first decades of the Reformation, but also that he—without heed to his personal religious persuasion—made no restrictions regarding denomination in his choice of clients and subject matter. On the other hand, we know that for Francisco de Goya, who had contact with intellectual circles during the Enlightenment, the witch—and not the witch craze—was an example of a backward world that had to be overcome. In his lithograph series he denounced the superstition and the narrow-mindedness of ecclesiastical dignitaries.

Artists repeatedly used certain clichés when depicting the witch, regardless of their personal spiritual belief systems. As independent and enlightened as these artists might have been, they were nonetheless bound to show allegiance to the Christian worldview. In this worldview only God can determine fate, health, life, disease, and death. Therefore any human who can show evidence of a magical ability to use the healing powers of nature must necessarily be viewed as an ally of demonic powers in cultures such as ours, which are shaped by Christianity. It was ironically their ability to help their fellow human beings—a truly Christian virtue—with their knowledge of plant medicine, the weather, and divination that led to the condemnation of witches. Their crime for imitating the Christ who healed the sick was to abrogate these powers decreed as the property of God alone. For this crime they suffered relentless persecution and were condemned to silence, a silence that was extended to all aspects of their craft and the great pagan tradition from which it had come—a silence that is only now beginning to lift.

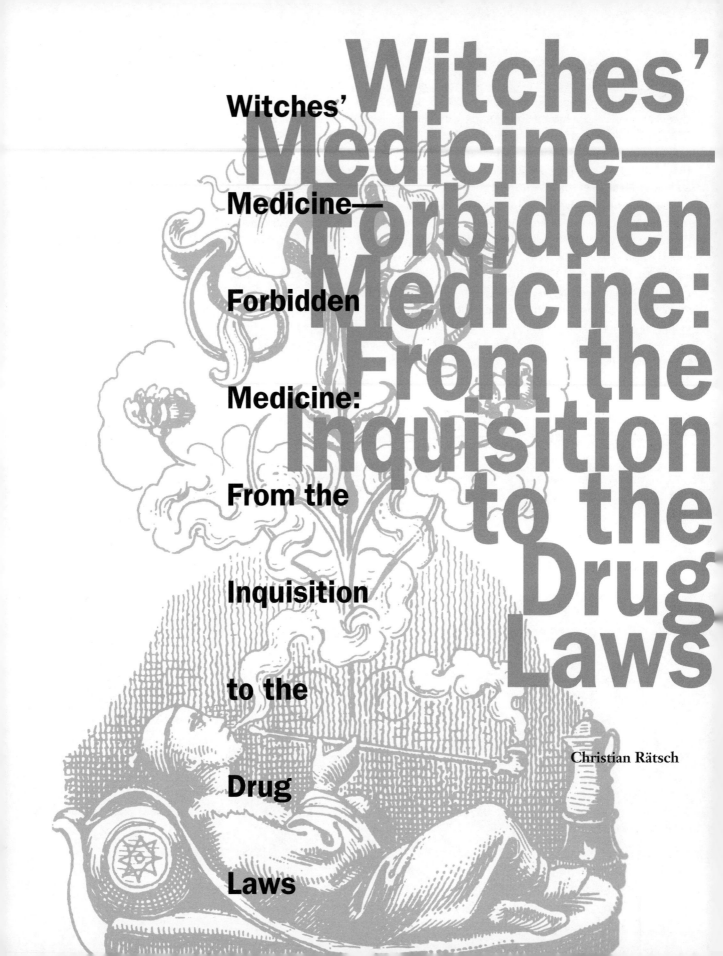

Witches' Medicine—Forbidden Medicine: From the Inquisition to the Drug Laws

Christian Rätsch

The current drug laws are like a modern version of the Hexenhammer (*Malleus Maleficarum*, or Hammer of the Witches). Just as the Hexenhammer paved the way for the murder of millions of people, drug laws have made it possible to place certain undesirable people within a society under surveillance and to suppress an individual's freedom to use healing remedies as he or she sees fit. Because of drug laws the sensible and medically valuable use of some of the best and most successful medicinal plants that humans have discovered has become a punishable offense. As the Bible forbade eating the fruit of the tree of knowledge, the Church forbade witches the use of their "traveling mediums"—and modern humans have been forbidden to use consciousness-altering substances (the so-called drugs[1]) in the same way. The organic chemist Jonathan Ott, in his own right a brilliant authority on psychoactive plants and substances, calls this the "pharmacratic Inquisition" (Ott, 1996). Even inebriation in and of itself—regardless of what caused it—has been repeatedly demonized.[2] At the same time, the desiring toward inebriation is one of the basic characteristics of our nervous system. It is possible that there is even an instinct that drives us to inebriation—similar to the instinct that pushes us to eat, drink, have sex, and survive.

If we cast our eyes back upon the history of the plants and plant constituents that have been forbidden by drug laws, the Western obsession with conducting witch trials against unpopular people becomes readily apparent. The egocentric and selfish Catholic religion was the driving force behind the witch trials. Brimming with Christian spirituality, the *Malleus Maleficarum*, the infamous Hammer of the Witches, struck a devastating blow to society. The current drug laws are filled with the same ideology. The arrogant presumptuousness of Christianity, that it has the one and only true God who "justifies" every legal and moral caprice, forms the spiritual foundation of the drug laws. It should also not be forgotten that modern drug laws were written mainly by Christian politicians and Church leaders. What Pope Innocent VIII began when he forbade the use of cannabis in his "witches' bull" of 1484 (Amrein, 1997) was set forth by a Dutch bishop:

> Within the framework of the First International Opium Agreement (IOA) of 23 January 1912 in The Hague (The Hague Agreement) and under the chairmanship of Bishop Brent, opium, cocaine, and morphine were outlawed and the foundation for drug prohibition in the twentieth century was laid (Körner, 1994: 3).

As a result of the Second Geneva Conference on Opium in 1925, the opium laws were introduced in 1929 in the German Reich. In 1949, after the Second World War, the laws were declared still valid by the Christian-Democrat regime.

When the American establishment, consisting mainly of puritanical and fundamentalist Christians, grew frightened and bewildered when faced with the germinating hippie movement, it reacted by instituting paranoid drug laws. The laws were used to legitimize the suppression of consciousness-expanding experiences and the

---

[1] "The term 'drug' includes, in addition to the chemical compounds of the prohibited plants (such as those occurring in cannabis plants, *Papaver orientale* and *Papaver somniferum* plants, and psilocybin mushrooms for example), the plant matter (such as coca leaves, and flowers, leaves, and stems of the cannabis plant), the plant constituents (for example the alkaloids contained in the opium poppy, morphine, thebaine, codeine, and ethyl morphine), the active properties contained in the coca leaves cocaine and ecgonin, the resin (hashish) from the cannabis leaves and the active compound THC (tetrahydrocannabinol), and the mescaline from the peyote cactus" (Körner, 1994: 66).

[2] For example: "The demons of drunkenness seek their sacrifice. The seductive poisons will make the inebriation immortal but as long as there are humans on this earth, there will always be hands that reach for it; hands which are curious, tired, and often trembling with excitement" (Graupner, 1966: 15).

"It is better to be infirm and sick than to be made healthy through magic. If you go to witches, you will have forsaken God the Father."

—GEILER VON KAYSERSBERG, *FASTENPREDIGT* [LENT SERMON] (1508)

Demon Intoxication: Drugs, Poisons, Alcohol was published in 1966, the same year that LSD was made illegal; with both of these acts pharmacologically induced intoxication was demonized.

creation of a new way of life. The drug laws also served as tools for persecuting social outcasts and undesirables.

Hippies were accused of the same things as witches before them: drug abuse, promiscuity, and immoral attitudes toward the Christian ethic (Golowin, 1977). The hippies were blamed for Satanism, which included Black Mass and ritual murder. As "proof," Charles Manson and his family were trotted out. Although this crazy man and his murderous band saw themselves as new Christians, and their followers worshiped Manson as Christ and savior, they were not hippies.[3] After all, liberation from Christian feelings of guilt and duty was part of the ideology of the hippies. Besides, they had eaten again from the tree of knowledge and discovered the Divine in and of itself—not in the words of a priest.

In 1971, because of an international treaty concerning psychotropic substances that was pushed through by the United States, the opium laws, which had been valid up to that point in West Germany, were amended and became the *Gesetz über den Verkehr mit Betaübungsmitteln* (Regulations of the Drug Trade). The establishment of an office in the German federal government read like a broadside from the time of the Inquisition:

> The misuse of intoxicating substances that are designated as drugs in the opium laws threatens to reach a dangerous level. This phenomenon can no longer be considered a passing trend and consequently dismissed. Like a plague it spreads more and more throughout the Federal Republic of Germany. In ever-broadening circles the citizens are caught in its current. The youth in particular are at risk, often already in danger by puberty. The number of young people who consummate their entrance into the drug world is increasing. At the same time it has been demonstrated that the average age at which the entrance occurs has lowered. Even the children have not been spared. The seriousness of the situation must be emphatically underscored by the incidents of death that have occurred in recent times, in particular among the youth. . . .
>
> One of the measures the [German] federal government is preparing is a cohesive plan of action in the fight against drug addiction. The law is in service of the goal to stop the drug trend in the Federal Republic of Germany and to avert great danger from the individual and the general public. It has to do with protecting the individual people, in particular the youth, from grave and often irreparable harm to their health and a disturbance of their personality, their freedom, and their existence. It has to do with protecting the families from the tragedy which threatens them when a member has fallen into the grips of drug addiction. It has to do with sparing the general public from falling victim to the high price of an unchecked wave of drug use. And finally, it has to do with not allowing it to affect the ability of society to function properly. . . .
>
> A particular sign of the drug wave has been the considerable increase in the use of the Indian hemp *(Cannabis sativa)* and the resin from it (hashish). In this regard we are talking about a hallucinogen that, according to the predominant opinion of medical science, with consistent use can cause a change in consciousness and lead to psychological addiction. . . . Apparently no withdrawal symptoms manifest with the drug and there is only a small tendency to increase the dose. The move to harder drugs is shown in particular among the younger people. With great probability it can be concluded that the drug serves an introductory function. In practical terms, the

---

[3] See the outsanding monograph by the Fugs musician Ed Sanders, *The Family: The Story of Charles Manson*, New York: E. P. Dutton, 1971.

youth complete their entrance into the world of drugs with hemp (BT-Drs 665/70, quoted from Körner, 1994: 5f.).

In this example the witches' salve of the Inquisition has been replaced by hemp, which had been thoroughly demonized by Pope Innocent VIII as well as by Henry Anslinger, the anti-marijuana crusader and original mastermind behind the war on drugs.[4] The motivation behind the government's drug laws are just as transparent as were the justifications for the witch hunts. Both stem from the imagination of the rulers. There is still an "inquisitor" employed by the current government; he is called a drug commissioner. It came as no surprise that when a Social Democrat politician presented a model for a pharmacy that would openly sell hashish and marijuana, the idea crumbled when it encountered the Christian Social Union (CSU) politician Eduard Lintner, who was backed by the likewise Christian-Socialist minister of health—in other words, the "chief inquisitor." It remains to be seen when they will set the funeral pyre for Heide Moser[5] on fire.

But, surprisingly, there are also government officials who want to bring the demonization of the hemp plant to an end. The Social Democratic senator Horst Bossung spoke in this regard:

> The drug problem . . . can be spoken of in terms of when someone has problems obtaining their preferred or medicinally necessary drugs. More precisely, they have drug problems when they have problems obtaining the drugs . . . For the hedonic consumers, in other words those who consume drugs for pleasure, this is highly irritating—for the sick who require cannabis for medical purposes, this is often extremely painful. For example some cancer patients, AIDS patients, and people with other illnesses, a permanent drug problem consists only of the fact that they are not able to get the medicinal cannabis that they need. These are the real, true drug problems (Bossung, 1995: 13).

These "true drug problems" are produced by the drug laws:

> The current problems that are connected to the illegal status of cannabis undoubtedly represent the biggest side-effects of the medicinal use of cannabinoids. There are many sedatives and remedies for sleep and pain with a far greater potential for addiction than cannabis that physicians are permitted to write a normal prescription for. The classification of cannabis as a prohibited drug is therefore no longer sensible today. A doctor should be able to prescribe cannabis preparations of defined quality like any other medicine (Grotenhermen and Huppertz, 1997: 9f.).

For more than six thousand years hemp has been used as a medicine everywhere it grows in the vicinity of humans. During my ethnomedicinal study *(Marijuana Medicine)* it came to light that the medicinal use of hemp is even more multifaceted than the possible uses of the entire plant. Over the course of history different cultures and various

---

[4] "In Europe the enjoyment of hemp at the time of the witch trials was a popular pastime, and the aphrodisiac activity of the hemp plant's compounds were commonly known. Not without reason did Hans Ulrich Megerle (1644–1709) rail against the "farmers who stuff themselves full with hemp as the Turks do with opium" (Lussi, 1996: 134).

[5] The Social Democrat Heide Moser has become famous with her pharmacy model for the controlled administration of cannabis products (c.f. Peter Raschke and Jens Kakle, *Cannabis in Apotheken*, Freiburn: Lambertus, 1997).

> ### Hildegard of Bingen (1098–1179) on Hemp
>
> "Hemp *(hanff)* is hot and grows when the air is neither very hot nor very cold, and its nature is similar. Its seed is salubrious and good as food for healthy people. It is gentle and profitable to the stomach, taking away a bit of its mucus. It is easy to digest, diminishes bad humors, and fortifies good humors. Nevertheless, if one who is weak in the head and has a vacant brain eats hemp it easily afflicts his head. It does not harm one who has a healthy head and full brain. If one is very ill, it even afflicts his stomach a bit. Eating it does not hurt one who is moderately ill.
>
> "Let one who has a cold stomach cook hemp in water and, when the water has been squeezed out, wrap it in a small cloth, and frequently place it, warm, on his stomach. This strengthens and renews that area. Also, a cloth made from hemp is good for binding ulcers and wounds, since the heat in it has been tempered" *(Physica,* chapter 11).

healing systems have used hemp to treat far more than a hundred indications. In other words, hemp is one of the most versatile medicinal plants of all! In the meantime its use in ethno- and folk medicine for numerous indications has been pharmacologically confirmed (see Rätsch, 1992; Grotenhermen and Huppertz, 1997). But like every good medicine, hemp is federally controlled: "Forbidden is the use of cannabis plants for the production of cannabis cigarettes, for making medications and cannabis tinctures (i.e., as a cough syrup, sleeping remedy, asthma and migraine medicine). Dealing with cannabis is forbidden and punishable, regardless if the cannabis plants and the cannabis products demonstrate enough THC contents for the consumer" (Körner, 1994: 56 f.).

Coca and Cocaine

After the establishment of the drug laws, coca plants (all species and varieties[6]) and the alkaloids found in them (cocaine, ecgonin) were made illegal, and to use them became punishable.

In the year 1630 on all church doors of the Peruvian kingdom an edict against astrologers, stargazers, and witches was hung. In it the witches[7] were accused of using "certain drinks, herbs, and roots, called *achuma*, *chamico* and coca, to numb their senses. The illusions and phantasms that take place are then reported as revelation or news" (Andritzky, 1989: 462). In those days people were already mixing up "consciousness expanding" with numbing. . . They saw their "opponent's allies" in the psychoactive plants (Andritzky, 1987: 550).

Achuma is the Native American name for a mescaline-containing cactus known in Ecuador and Peru as San Pedro *(Trichocereus pachanoi); chamico* is the ancient Native American name for the thorn apple *(Datura stramonium* ssp. *ferox).*

The use of coca—which has a tradition of about ten thousand years—was forbidden by colonial rulers and the inquisitors:

> The use of coca leaves was also a widespread tool of love magic. Doña Jana Sarabia, a young woman in Lima, knew "that when she used coca leaves to attract her lover

---

[6] These include *Erythroxylum coca* var. *coca, E. coca* var. *ipadu, E. novogranatense,* and *E. novogranatense* var. *truxillense.*

[7] "The witches of the colonial times were excellent healers. They knew the curative characteristics of the plants and possessed a great amount of knowledge about herbs, although this wisdom was buried beneath a mountain of superstitions and witchcraft practices. They commanded a respect so great that a Spanish doctor is said to have proclaimed that he had opposed the establishment of a professorship of medicine because the Indians heal better than the doctors" (MacLean Yestemos in Andritzky, 1987:549).

she found the same enjoyment and sinful pleasures as when he had actual sexual relations with her." . . . The use of coca leaves makes the precarious situation of the "colonial witches" before the tribunal particularly clear, that chewing coca leaves was a heathen worship of the "huacas, " the Indian sacred shrines. In a law of 18 October 1569, Philipp II urged the priests to beware of its use for witchcraft and superstitious practices, but confirmed the use of coca as medicine and stimulant for the heavy labor of the Indios. At this time there was a debate going on whether or not to completely forbid the use of coca because it was a hindrance to Christianization and to destroy the plants because the Indians were constantly reminded of their past because of them, or whether to allow them to be used on account of their quality as a food supplement. In addition to its widespread use as a medicine, the defenders added that the Indian mine workers refused to work when they didn't get their daily coca ration (Andritzky, 1987: 554).

In other words, when coca assists in the exploitation of the Indians, they are allowed to use it. (Strangely, coca is not allowed for Western workaholics.) Thus a number of "witches" and "warlocks" were accused because of their use of coca in combination with invocations, and were subsequently punished by the Inquisition (Andritzky, 1987: 554f.).

In the archives of the Spanish Inquisition in Peru an Indian love potion—distorted through the European witch-crazed eyeglasses—was documented. The case files state that Francisca Arias Rodríguez "took coca leaves, wax, and a woman's shoe in her hands. Then she would nail a scissors to the sole of the shoe, while invoking Satan, Barraba, and all the legions of demons. The invocation was closed with the following words: 'I bind you / with my heart I break you / your blood I drink / I call you to my love / come to me and stay / bound on hands and feet" (Millones, 1996: 44).

The Andean Indians handled countless problems and illnesses successfully with coca leaves in a variety of preparations: weakness, depression, painful hemorrhoids, nosebleeds, headaches, migraines, skin tumors, colic, stomachaches, diarrhea, itchy throat, fevers, coughs, colds, sinusitis, rheumatism, arthritis, ulcers, altitude sickness, and

The Nutritional Value of Coca Leaves[8]

Average amounts per 100 g dried leaves in comparison with the average amount in South American nutritional plants (per 100 g)

INGREDIENTS	COCA LEAVES	FOOD PLANTS
Protein	18.8 g	11.4. g
Fat	3.3 g	9.9 g
Carbohydrates	44.3 g	37.1 g
Fiber	13.3 g	3.2 g
Ash	6.3 g	2.0 g
Calcium	1,789 mg	99 mg
Phosphorus	637 mg	270 mg
Iron	26.8 mg	3.6 mg
Vitamin A (as beta-carotene)	10,000 IU	135 IU
Thiamin (vitamin B_1)	0.58 mg	0.38 mg
Riboflavin (vitamin B_2)	1.73 mg	1.73 mg
Vitamin C	1.4 mg	13 mg

[8] From James A. Duke, David Aulik, and Timothy Plowman, "Nutritional Value of Coca," *Botanical Museum Leaflets* 24(6): 113–19, 1975.

diabetes. Coca is therefore often called "aspirin of the Andes" (although it works better than the salicylic acid preparation). Native Americans regard coca as a food; indeed, the leaves have very high nutritional value (see box on page 202).

Poppy and Opium

"The light appeared in the darkness, and the darkness didn't know it."

—ROBERT ANTON WILSON, *MASKEN DER ILLUMINATEN* [MASKS OF THE ILLUMINATES] (1983)

The opium poppy (*Papaver somniferum* L. or *P. setigerum* L.), the Oriental poppy (*Papaver orientale* L. or *P. bracteatum)*, and the opium obtained from these plants, as well as the alkaloids found in them, have been forbidden by the drug laws, but doctors are still allowed to prescribe them (Körner, 1994: 164).

As early as the sixth century B.C.E. among the pre-Roman cultures in Daunia, Italy, the opium poppy enjoyed respect as the "tree of life" and a sacred plant (Leone, 1995). The poppy was *the* sacred plant of the great goddess Deo or Demeter (Kerényi, 1976 and 1991).

Opium is the best and most important pain remedy humans have ever discovered in nature. It was the only reliable narcotic for centuries or even millennia (Kuhlen, 1983). Opium has also been a beloved aphrodisiac and intoxicant since the Stone Age (Höfler, 1990: 92f.).

Although the poppy was considered a witches' plant, and despite the fact that both the poppy and opium are attributed as ingredients in witches' salves, the Inquisition could not put a stop to their use: it was too widespread. Opium was first forbidden during a period when synthetic opiates were taking over the market. So who benefits from the prohibition? Those who make money from it![9]

Mescaline and Psilocybin: The Forbidden Souls of the Gods

"Shall I perhaps persuade the men not to taste of the sweetest apple that the garden of our earthly paradise can produce?"

—GIORDANO BRUNO (1585) IN *ON THE HEROIC PASSIONS*, 1995

The peyote cactus (*Lophophora williamsii* [Lem. ex S. –D.] Coult., syn. *Anhalonium lewinii* Henn.) and the San Pedro Cactus (*Trichorcereus pachanoi* Britt. et Rose, syn. *Echinopsis pachanoi* [Br. et R.] Friedr. et G.D. Rowl.) are not expressly forbidden in the drug laws; however, their "soul," mescaline, is (Körner, 1994: 164).

The peyote cactus has been used by Native Americans and worshipped as a god since prehistoric times. Archaeological finds from the Pecos region of Texas pay witness to the fact that peyote was used as a ritual plant for more than seven thousand years (Boyd and Dering, 1996).

When the first Europeans started to crowd into the New World they encountered shamans, which they disparagingly referred to as witches,[10] sorcerers, or black magicians. Their gods or helping spirits were disparaged as idols and devil's workmanship; their sacred plants and drinks were defamed as witches' brews. In a letter of the Mexican Inquisition by Don Pedro Nabarre de Isla (enacted on June 29, 1620) it says:

What the introduction of the use of the herb or plant called peyote . . . for discovering thieves, foretelling other occurrences, and prophesying future events, has thus to do with superstition is to be condemned, for it is directed against the purity and perfection of our holy Catholic faith. That is certain, for neither this

---

[9] See the outstanding research in Hans-Georg Behr, *Weltmacht Droge: Das Geschäft mit der Sucht [Drugs as a World Power: The Business of Addiction]* (Vienna and Düsseldorf: Econ, 1980). See also Günter Amendt, *Sucht Profit Sucht*, Frankfurt A.M.: Zweitausandeins, 1984.

[10] In the year 1653 the Spanish missionary Father Bernabe Cobo (1580–1657) spoke very clearly: "With the name witch we cover all types of people who use superstition and illegal arts in order to perform wondrous things that exceed human capabilities, which they achieve through the invocations and the help of demons whose pact, implicit or explicit, touches on all their power and knowledge" (Andritzky, 1987: 544).

nor any other plant can possess the power or the intrinsic property of being able to bring forth the claimed effects, nor can they cause the mental images, fantasies, or hallucinations on which the divinations mentioned are based. In the latter the influences and interference of the devil are clearly recognizable, the true source of this vice, who first makes use of the Indians' natural gullibility and tendency toward idolatry, and then afflicts others who do not fear God enough and who did not possess enough faith.[11]

The Spanish missionary Hernando Ruiz de Alarcon left behind the most detailed reports of the late colonial times about the Native Americans' use of psychoactive magical plants—such as ololiuqui (*Turbina corymbosa* [L.] Raf.), peyote, and picietl (*Nicotiana rustica* L.). His writings were published in 1629 under the title *Treatise on the Heathen Superstitions that today live among the Indians Native to this New Spain*. This work became a kind of *Malleus Maleficarum*, the legal foundation for witch persecution in the New World. In this text the following is said about the use of peyote.

> Finally, whether it is the doctor himself or another person in his place, in order to drink this [ololiuqui] seed or one named peyote, which is another small root and to which they demonstrate the same trust as to the former, they close themselves in a room, which is normally a prayer room. No one is allowed to enter during the entire time of the questioning, which lasts as long as the questioner is not in his senses, for that is the amount of time in which, as they believe, will ololiuqui or peyote reveal that which was desired. As soon as the intoxication or the withdrawal of the power of judgement is over, the afflicted tells two thousand lies, among which the devil has usually strewn a few truths, so that he has completely confused or deceived them. . . . They also use the drink in order to find things that were lost [or] misplaced and to find out who took them or who stole them. . . . It should be precisely observed how much these poor people hide their superstitious beliefs in ololiuqui and peyote from us, and the reason for this is, as they admit, that he who questions them ordered them not to reveal it to us (Ruiz de Alarcon I: 6).

The prohibitionists of today would make a similar argument. But the question arises: Who is subservient to the "deception of the devil"?

Just as the use of peyote in Mexico was persecuted by the Inquisition, in Peru the medicinal and ritual use of the achuma, guachumar, or San Pedro cactus, which also contains mescaline, was forbidden and punished.

> [Circa 1730, in Cajamarca] two witches were discovered on a mountain. They had spread a colorful cloth out on the earth in front, on which they had placed mollusks, jugs, and various herbs, tobacco, and a number of small stones. Between the mollusks were two jugs, one on the fire with an herb which they call *guachumar*, the other empty . . . [The accused testified that] the stone with a hole in the middle was called San Pedro, and that he brings it to the sick in order to purify them [and that he] because of his idol worship took care to pray to Our Father, the Ave Maria and the Creed and in the middle of his tools he placed the image of the crucified Christ and later gripped the rattle, in order to dance and to sing in his language. [Then he said]

---

[11] Irving A. Leonard, "Peyote and the Mexican Inquisition 1620," *American Anthropologist* N. S. 44 (1942): 324–6.

that he constantly spoke with demons who appeared to him in the form of a man with a colorful dress, but that he sometimes did not appear although he called to him, which was a sign that he was not allowed to find the lost thing again (Andritzky, 1987: 558).

Despite colonial rule, the Inquisition, and state persecution these rituals (*mesas*) in northern Peru have been retained and today are an important element in the health of the people.

In ancient Mexico the magic mushroom (*Psilocybe* spp.) played a role similar to that of the peyote cactus. The mushrooms were ritually ingested in order to receive religious visions, to enter into contact with the gods, to bestow shamanic healing power, and to prophesy. The Indians were able to keep the use of the sacred mushroom secret through the colonial period and the Inquisition. The traditional use of the mushrooms was first discovered in the middle of the twentieth century by the Wassons (Wasson, 1986). The active components of the Mexican magic mushroom were first isolated by Albert Hofmann, the man who discovered LSD. At first the active ingredients were used—just like LSD—as an aid in psychotherapy (Ott, 1996). Today they are forbidden by the drug laws.

Ayahuasca: The Conquest Is Not Over

Ayahuasca is a preparation of at least two plants: from the ayahuasca liana (*Banisteriopsis caapi* [Spruce ex Griseb.] Morton, syn. *Banisteria caapi* Spruce) and the chacruna leaves (*Psychotria viridis* R. et P.). This drink represents the most significant shamanic medicine in the Amazons (Reichel-Dolmatoff, 1996). The actual active compound of the ayahuasca drink is *N,N*-Dimethyltryptamine (DMT), a substance that functions as a neurotransmitter. Because this substance is outlawed by the drug laws (Körner, 1994: 39), *every living person is illegal!*

During archaeological digs in Ecuador finds have been made that have been entered into the literature as "witches' jugs." Even scientists have fallen for this. The objects are actually very simple, large ceramic vessels that were used for making ayahuasca and are attributed to the Milagro Quvedo culture (500 B.C.E.–1500 C.E.) (Andritzky, 1989: 179).

Ayahuasca was never persecuted by the Inquisition; it is likely that the drink was overlooked within the abundance of Indian preparations. The use of ayahuasca was only forbidden as "devil's work" in the 1950s by a Swiss missionary (Andritzky, 1989: 133). The repression of the use of ayahuasca subsequently led to an uprooting and neglect of the culture.

The cultural inheritance of the Shipibo was also greatly destroyed by the modern missionaries. The Shipibo had a kind of writing that decoded and communicated certain experiences of the visionary world (ayahuasca patterns). "Earlier the designs were also drawn in books—presumably put together by the missionaries, the last of which was burned in 1978 by a man from Camito because it contained 'things of the devil'" (Andritzky 1989: 190).

When the chemistry and the pharmacology of ayahuasca were established by Western scientists (Bo Holmstedt, Dennis McKenna, James Callaway, Jonathan Ott, and so on), the amazement was great. The Amazon Indians have developed their own chemical science, one that is highly effective.

The active psychedelic substance *N,N*-Dimethyltryptamine, known as DMT for short, not only is made in the human body but is also present in countless plants and animals that are taken in as food. However, DMT does not go to the brain; before it gets there it is broken down by the enzyme monoamine oxidase, MAO for short. If the MAO fallout is prevented, then the DMT is able to pass through the blood-brain barrier without restriction, where it can then bind to the corresponding receptors and send the nervous system into an extraordinary state. This nervous system effect is expressed as lavish and overwhelming visions—and this is exactly what happens when one drinks ayahuasca. The beta carbolines harmaline and harmine are contained in liana; these are the MAO inhibitors that prevent the fallout of the monoamine oxidase. In this way the DMT found in the drink can penetrate the brain unhindered; there it releases an effect that lasts approximately one and a half hours. Ayahuasca represents a brilliant example of the "chemical engineering" of consciousness.

Now the American pharmaceutical companies want to have this for themselves. Patent number 5751 in the United States Marks and Patents Office, which was registered in June 1996 by the International Medicine Corporation (represented by Loren Miller), is rather perverse. In the patent the firm seeks to secure the chemical and pharmacological principles of ayahuasca as its trademark; in other words, it wants to monopolize the biochemistry of ayahuasca. If the patent is actually allowed, the native South Americans, the discoverers and guardians of the ayahuasca preparation, will be forbidden to cook their drink or it will only be permitted with a payment to the company as a licensing fee.

In an open letter to U.S. President Bill Clinton the chiefs of approximately four hundred Amazonian tribes protested this unsurpassed impudence. "To patent our medicine which we have inherited over many generations is an attack on the culture of our people and the entire humanity," declared Valerio Grefa, the speaker of the confederation of the Indian organization of the Amazon basin.[12]

Fortunately, the patent was rejected in 1999. But certainly the conquest is not over yet.

The "Drug" Business

The outstanding characteristic of the plants and substances that are banned by the drug laws is their powerful effectiveness. They are some of the best medicines ever discovered by humans. They are not inert junk, like the medicines that are shoved over the counter at the pharmacy for a lot of money. They are potent; in other words, they are effective. Opium is the best pain medication in the world. Hemp is probably the best antidepressive; coca is the only true tonic. But who makes money off healthy people—off the underlings who heal themselves with plants from their backyard or balcony gardens, the people who don't want to sacrifice their hard-earned money to doctors and pharmacists? Ineffective medicine is a more certain source of income, as is medicine such as Valium or Rohypnol, all of which pass the test of culturally acceptable addictions. Those who look into the question of whom the drug laws benefit will not believe their eyes, for it is the same people who want to withhold the enjoyment of sacred plants. The state needs tax-paying idiots, not free spirits. That is why Prozac (fluoxetine)[13] is legal but cannabis is still forbidden.

---

[12] See *Esotera*, 11/96, p. 4.

[13] Prozac, or fluoxetine, is considered among psychiatrists and users to be a "happy pill." The regular use of Prozac leads to the complete suppression of the symptoms of suffering but never to healing. It gives the illusion of a condition of happiness, much like the one Aldous Huxley described in his novel *Brave New World*. Prozac makes work-ready idiots out of psychiatric cases (cf. Peter D. Kramer, *Glück auf Rezept: Der unheimliche Erfolg der Glückspille Fluctin* [Happiness Prescription: The Amazing Success of the Happy-pill Fluctin], Munich: Kösel, 1995).

"The drinking of ayahuasca is fought by the linguists of the Summer Institute of Linguistics, the missionaries of all persuasions, and the Peruvian government."

—GERHARD BAER, "EINE AYAHUASCA–SITZUNG UNTER DEN PIRO (OSTPERU)" [AN AYAHUASCA SESSION AMONG THE PIRO (EAST PERU)], IN *SOCIÉTÉ SUISSE DES AMÉRICANISTES*, 1969

"We exist in a world where the fear of illusion is real."

—JEFF MARTIN AND THE TEA PARTY, "TEMPTATION" (ON *TRANSMISSION*, EMI RECORDS, 1997)

While on Prozac it is possible—even when plagued by the most profound spiritual pain and suffering—to fulfill one's role as a wheel in the business of the society, but cannabis encourages individual thinking. Yes, it is one's own thoughts that are threatening. They place the state and Christian order of things into question, and they correct them. The ban on the sacred heathen plants is the attempt to produce a dumb people who pay their taxes without any back talk. After all, dumb wheels turn too. The question remains: How long will this go on?

Those who sell the word of God also sell placebo medications. The demonization of a plant by the rulers serves the medical incapacitation of the underlings. The war against nature continues, indeed has even been intensified. But one thing is certain: Humans can never win against nature. They will always be her underlings, because in the end they are a part of her. We disappear into never-never land when Gaia shrugs her shoulders.

According to the New Age occult conception of Diana and Lucifer, the god of light, they were sister and brother. They were deeply in love with each other and produced a daughter named Aradia, or Herodias. Aradia was trained by her mother to be the first witch and was outfitted with a social-critical-anarchic consciousness. One day the witch goddess spoke this to her daughter.

> *True it is indeed, that you belong to the immortal*
> *But you were born so that you might become mortal*
> *You must climb onto the earth*
> *Be a teacher of the women and men*
> *Whose wish it is to learn the arts of the witches in your school . . .*
> *And you shall be the first among the witches;*
> *And your name should be the first in the whole world;*
> *And you should learn the art of poison-murder,*
> *To poison those who think of themselves as greater men than others,*
> *Yes, you should let them die in their palaces,*
> *And the soul of the oppressor you should bind with your strength!"* (Leland, 1979: 15).

News Update: Hemp Seeds Outlawed!

The New Inquisition strikes again. While hemp flowers and magic mushrooms are increasingly sold over the counter in Switzerland, the Christian federal government of Germany saw to it that as of December 19, 1997, hemp seeds were on the list as one of the illegal substances; thus they were outlawed (tenth amendment of the drug laws, as of February 2, 1998). With this the regime under chancellor Gerhard Schröder was the first to achieve making illegal a substance that is proved to have no psychoactive or otherwise mind-altering activity. The reasoning for this ruling is as follows.

> Therewith the widespread business of cannabis seeds procured by the individual for the planting of hemp for purposes of intoxication will be combated. Under the circumstances the seed is in particular determined for impermissible planting, when special seeds in counted amounts of kernels (for example 10 seed kernels for up to 150 DM), often in combination with lighting systems for the planting in living quarters and/or cellars with information about the tetrahydrocannibol (THC) contained in the harvested plant, is offered and therewith leads to a planting that is not allowed.

Once again candy-coated paragraphs can be used to push through a technical jurisdiction. No longer are products forbidden or regulated as drugs, but a hypothetically assumed intention that has neither occurred nor has in any way been performed is quoted as the basis for the seed prohibition. It heralds a kind of lawmaking that must eventually lead to a ban on the production and sale of kitchen knives because some crazy person might come up with the idea of cutting open the throat of one of the drug agents in the government. And so law succumbs more and more to regime-true ideology. Therewith the federal German government is moving closer to the conception of law in the Third Reich. It is high time for Germans to once again be ashamed to be German! The step to book burning is only a small one. Anyone who publishes a hemp-cultivating book would be better off tarred as a Roman. And the Inquisition says hello again.

Appendix

Plants Associated with Witches and Devils

(Following Ahrendt-Schulte, 1994; Aigremont, 1987; Arends, 1935; Carl, 1995; Gessmann, n.d.; Ludwig, 1982; Marzell, 1943–1977; Ott, 1996; Reinhard, 1993; Schoen, 1963, expanded)

European common name (English translation)	Botanical name (English common name) Pharmaceutical term
Blaue zauberwurz (blue magic herb)	*Erigeron alpinus* L. (fleabane)
Chapeau du diable (devil's hat)	*Petasites hybridus* (L.) Fl. Wett. (Butterbur) (syn. *Petasites officinalis* Moench)
Deifele (little devil)	*Thuja occidentalis* L. (thuja, red cedar) Pharmaceutical term: suppository
Drudenast (druid's knot)	*Viscum album* L. (mistletoe) ssp. *abietis* (Wiesb.) Abrom. (syn. *Viscum abietis* [Wiesb.] Fritsch) (parasitic growth on fir trees [*Abies*]) ssp. *album* (parasitic growth on deciduous trees) ssp. *austriacum* (Wiesb.) Vollm. (syn. *Viscum laxum* Boiss. et Reut.) (parasitic growth on pines [*Pinus*] and larches [*Larix*])
Drudenbätzlein (druid droppings)	*Lycopodium clavatum* L. (wolf's claw, common club moss)
Drudenbaum (druid's tree)	*Prunus padus* L. (bird cherry) (syn. *Cerasus padus* [L.] DC., *Padus avium* Mill.)
Drudenbeere (druid's berry)	*Vaccinium myrtillus* (bilberry, huckleberry, whortleberry)
Drudenbeutel (druid's sack)	*Lycoperdon* spp. (puffball)
Drudenblüh (druid's blossom)	*Prunus padus* L. (bird cherry) (syn. *Cerasus padus* [L.] DC., *Padus avium* Mill.)
Drudenblume (druid's bloom)	*Impatiens noli-tangere* L. (touch-me-not)
Drudeneier (druid's eggs)	*Lycoperdon* spp. (puffball)
Drudenfeder (druid's feather)	*Dryopteris filix-mas* (L.) Schott (male fern) (syn. *Aspidium filix-mas* L.)
Drudenfurz (druid's fart)	*Lycoperdon* spp. (puffball)
Drudenfuß [1] (druid's foot)	1. *Acer platanoides* L. (Norway maple) 2. *Antennaria dioica* (L.) Gaertn. (life everlasting, pussytoes) (syn. *Gnaphalium dioicum* L.) var. *borealis* A. Camus (wooly pussytoes) (syn. *Antennaria tomentosa* hort., *A. candida* hort.) var. *dioica* 3. *Lycopodium* spp. (club moss) *L. annotinum* L. (stiff club moss) *L. clavatum* L. (wolf's claw, common club moss) pharmaceutical term: wolf's claw herb, Herba Lycopodii 4. *Viscum album* L. (mistletoe)
Drudenfußchrut (druid's foot herb)	*Lycopodium clavatum* L. (wolf's claw) *Lycopodium* spp.
Drudengakelein (little druid's goblin)	*Lycopodium clavatum* L. (wolf's claw)
Drudengarn (druid's yarn)	*Cuscuta* spp. (dodder)
Drudengras (druid grass)	*Lycopodium clavatum* L. (wolf's claw)
Drudenhaxen (druid hocks)	*Lycopodium clavatum* L. (wolf's claw)
Drudenköbi (druid's vessel)	*Viscum album* L. (mistletoe)
Drudenkraut (druid's herb)	1. *Lycopodium clavatum* L. (wolf's claw) 2. *Nerium oleander* L. (oleander) 3. *Verbena officinalis* L. (vervain)
Drudenmehl (druid's meal)	*Lycopodium* spp. *L. clavatum* L. (wolf's claw) pharmaceutical term: wolf's claw spores
Drudenmilch (druid's milk)	1. *Chelidonium majus* L. (greater celandine) 2. *Euphorbia* spp. (spurge)
Drudennest (druid's nest)	*Viscum album* L. (mistletoe)
Drudenpfeifen (druid's pipes)	*Prunus padus* L. (bird cherry)
Drudenweide (druid's meadow)	*Prunus padus* L. (bird cherry)
Drudenzwiebel (druid's onion)	*Ornithogalum umbellatum* L. (star of Bethlehem)
Drudenzwirn (druid's twine)	*Lycium* spp. (wolfberry)
Druseltill (witch's dill)	*Potentilla erecta* (L.) Hampe (cinquefoil) (syn. *Potentilla tormentilla* Stokes, *P. sylvestris* Neck) pharmaceutical term: Rhizoma Tormentillae
Drutenfußmehl (druid's foot flour)	*Lycopodium* spp. (club moss) pharmaceutical term: wolf's claw spores
Dubelskörner (devil's grain)	1. *Anamirta cocculus* Wight et Arn. (fish berry) pharmaceutical term: Fructus Coccoli (cockle grain) 2. *Laurus nobilis* (bay laurel) pharmaceutical term: Fructus Lauri
Dübelspannkoken (devil's pancakes)	fungi (mushrooms in general)
Düwelsbeere (devil's berries)	*Atropa belladonna* L. (belladonna)
Düwelsgsichtli (little devil's face)	*Soldanella alpina* L. (alpine snowbells)

[1] Various fossils were included under the common classification of druid's foot (*Drudenfuß, Trudenfuß*). These fossils were ritually honored in pre-Christian times and were still used as amulets into the early modern era. Sea urchins and stones with holes in them are included in this category of popular wisdom. Magical stones such as these were used by farmers as protection of the milk in the milk barn. They were said to banish milk witches, who caused the milk to dry up or to go bad (c.f. Rätsch, 1997a, and Reinhardt, 1993).

Düwelsknobeli
(little devil's dumplings) — *Allium vineale* L. (field garlic)

Düwelstroad
(devil's stairway) — *Polytrichum commune* L. (ground moss)

Düwelssmer
(devil's grease) — *Rubus caesius* L. (dewberry)

Duvelsbete
(devil's prayer) — *Marrubium vulgare* L. (horehound)

Frühlingsteufelsauge
(spring devil's eye) — *Adonis vernalis* L. (yellow pheasant's eye)

Gottes Hand und Teufels Hinterbacken
(God's hand and devil's rear end) — *Orchis* spp. (orchid)

Häksepolwer
(witch's powder) — *Lycoperdon* spp. (puffball)

Herbe au diable
(devil's herb)
1. *Cynoglossum officinale* L. (hound's tongue)
2. *Potentilla erecta* (L.) Hampe (cinquefoil)
   pharmaceutical term: Rhizoma Tormentillae

Herbe aux sorciers
(sorcerer's herb) — *Datura stramonium* L. (thorn apple)

Herbe des démonaiques
(demon's herb) — *Datura stramonium* L. (thorn apple)

Hexachrut
(witch herb)
1. *Linaria vulgaris* Miller (toadflax)
   pharmaceutical term: Herba Linariae
2. *Scrophularia nodosa* L. (figwort)
   pharmaceutical term: Herba Scrophulariae

Hexe
(witch)
1. *Aconitum napellus* L. (monkshood)
2. *Dryas octopetala* (white mountain avens)
   spp. *octopetala*
   (= spp. *chamaedryfolia* [Crantz] Gams)
   var. *integrifolia* (Vahl) Hook f. (Arctic Dryad)
   (syn. *Dryas integrifolia* Vahl, *Dryas tenella* Pursh)
   f. *argentea* (Blytt) Hult.
   (= var. *argentea* Blytt, syn. *Dryas lanata* Stein ex Correv., *Dryas vestita* [Beck] hort.)
3. *Papaver rhoeas* L. (red poppy)
   (syn. *Papaver strigosum* [Boenn.] Schur)

Hexechrut
(witch herb) — *Actaea spicata* L. (baneberry, herb Christopher)
(syn. *Actaea nigra* [L.] Ph.)

Hexenanis
(witch's anise) — *Nigella sativa* L. (black cumin)
pharmaceutical term: Semen Nigellae

Hexenast
(witch's branch) — *Viscum album* L. (mistletoe)

Hexenauge
(witch's eye) — *Fritillaria imperialis* L. (crown imperial lily)

Hexenbaum
(witch's tree) — *Prunus padus* L. (bird cherry)
pharmaceutical term: Cortex Pruni padi

Hexenbeere
(witch's berries)
1. *Empetrum nigrum* L. (crowberry)
   ssp. *hermaphroditum* (Lange) Böcher
   (syn. *Empetrum hermaphroditum* [Lange] Hagerup)
   ssp. *nigrum*
2. *Viscum album* L. (mistletoe)

Hexenbesen
(witch's broom)
1. from *Taphrina* and *Melampsora* mushrooms, which grow on white pine, birch, and cherry trees
2. *Viscum album* L. (mistletoe)
3. *Pulsatilla alpina* (L.) Delabre (pasqueflower) (syn. Anemone alpina L.)
4. *Equisetum arvense* L. (horsetail)
5. *Conyza canadensis* (Canadian spikenard) (syn. *Erigeron canadensis* L.)
6. *Silene latifolia* Poir. ssp. *alba* (Mill.) Greuter et Burdet (catchfly) (syn. *Lychnis alba* Mill., *Lychnis vespertina* Sibth., *Melandrium album* [Mill.] Garcke, *Silene alba* [Mill.] E.H.L. Krause non Mühlenb. ex A. Gray, *Silene pratensis* [Rafn] Godr. et Gren.)
7. "Sleep apple": rose gall from *Rosa canina* L. (dog rose)

Hexenbeutel
(witch's purse) — *Lycoperdon* spp. (puffball)

Hexenbirke
(witch's birch) — *Betula pendula* Roth (white birch)
(syn. *Betula alba* L. sensu Coste, *Betula verrucosa* Ehrh.)

Hexenblume
(witch's flower)
1. *Anemone nemorosa* L. (wood anemone)
2. *Cardamine pratensis* L. (cuckooflower)
3. *Digitalis purpurea* L. (purple foxglove)
4. *Euphrasia rostkoviana* Hayne (eyebright) (syn. Euphrasia officinalis L.p.p.)
5. *Hypericum perforatum* L. (Saint John's wort)

Hexenbusch
(witch's bush) — *Viscum album* L. (mistletoe)

Hexendill
(witch's dill) — *Anethum graveolens* (dill)
spp. *graveolens* (field dill)
spp. *hortorum* (garden dill)

Hexendistel
(witch's thistle) — *Eryngium campestre* L. (snakeroot)

Hexendorn
(witch's thorn)
1. *Rhamnus catharticus* L. (buckthorn)
2. *Rosa canina* L. (dog rose)

Hexendreck
(witch's filth) — *Nostoc commune* Vauch. (blue-green algae, witch's butter)
(syn. *Tremella nostoc* L.)

Hexendreeg
(witch's waste) — *Nostoc commune* Vauch. (blue-green algae)
(syn. *Tremella nostoc* L.)

Hexenei
(witch egg)
1. *Phallus impudicus* L. ex Pers. (stinkhorn) (syn. *Ithyphallus impudicus* [L. ex Fr.] Pers. E. Fischer)
2. *Elaphomyces granulatus* Fr. (common deer truffle) (syn. Hypogaeum cervinum Pers.)
3. *Amanita muscaria* (L. ex Fr.) Pers. (fly agaric)
4. *Lycoperdon* spp. (puffball)

Hexenfelsen
(witch's cliffs) — *Lycoperdon* spp. (puffball)

Hexenfinger
(witch's finger) — *Clematis vitalba* L. (travelers' joy)

Hexenfittich
(witch's wing) — *Dryptoteris filix-mas* (L.) Schott (male fern)

Hexenflachs
(witch's flax) — *Eriophorum* spp. (wool grass)

Hexenfurzli
(little witch's fart)

Lycoperdon spp. (puffball)

Hexenfurz
(witch's fart)

1. various *Bovista* (puffball)
2. *Lycoperdon* spp. (puffball)
3. *Colchicum autumnale* L. (autumn crocus)

Hexengarn
(witch's yarn)

1. *Cuscuta* spp. (dodder)
2. *Galium aparine* L. (cleavers)

Hexengerste
(witch's barley)

Hordeum murinum L. (mouse barley)

Hexengespei
(witch's spittle)

Nostoc commune Vauch. (blue-green algae)
(syn. *Tremella nostoc* L.)

Hexengras
(witch's grass)

Eriophorum spp. (wool grass)

Hexenhaar
(witch's hair)

1. *Clematis vitalba* L. (travelers' joy)
2. *Cuscuta* spp. (dodder)
3. *Galium aparine* L. (catch-weed)

Hexenhasel
(witch hazel)

Hamamelis virginiana L. (witch hazel)

Hexenholz
(witch's wood)

Prunus padus L. (bird cherry)

Hexenkaas
(witch's cheese)

Nostoc commune Vauch. (blue-green algae)
(syn. *Tremella nostoc* L.)

Hexenkäse
(witch's cheese)

Nostoc commune Vauch. (blue-green algae)
(syn. *Tremella nostoc* L.)

Hexenkamm
(witch's comb)

Dipsacus sylvestris Huds. (teasel)
(syn. *Dipsacus fullonum* L.p.p.)

Hexenkirsche
(witch's cherry)

Lonicera alpigena L. (dwarf alpine
honeysuckle)

Hexenklee
(witch's clover)

Cuscuta epithymum (L.). L. (dodder)

Hexenkörner
(witch's grain)

Paeonia spp. (peony)
P. officinalis L. em. Gouan
P. peregrina Gremli non Mill.
P. corallina Retz.
pharmaceutical term: Semen Paeoniae

Hexenkohl
(witch's coal)

Heracleum sphondylium L. (cow parsnip)

Hexenkraut
(witch herb)

1. *Chelidonium majus* L. (greater celandine)
   pharmaceutical term: Herba Chelidonii
2. *Hypericum perforatum* L. (Saint John's wort)
   pharmaceutical term: Herba Hyperici
3. *Lycopodium clavatum* L. (wolf's claw)
   pharmaceutical term: Herba Lycopodii
4. *Valeriana officinalis* (valerian)
5. *Dryopteris filix-mas* (L.) Schott (male fern)
6. *Stachys* spp. (betony)
   S. annua L. (hedge nettle betony)
7. *Actaea spicata* L. (baneberry)
   (syn. *Actaea nigra* [L.] Ph. Gaertn.)
8. *Artemisia* spp.
   A. aboratanum L. (southernwood)
   A. cina O.C. Berg (wormseed)
   A. vulgaris L. (mugwort)
9. *Impatiens noli-tangere* L. (touch-me-not)
10. *Mentha pulegium* L. (poleo mint)
11. *Circaea lutetiana* L. (enchanter's
    nightshade)
12. *Atropa belladonna* (belladonna)
13. *Agrostemma githago* (corn cockle)

14. *Anethum graveolens* (dill)
15. *Datura stramonium* (thorn apple)
16. *Dictamnus albus* L. (burning bush)
    (syn. Dictamnus fraxinella Pers.)
    var. *albus*
    var. *caucasicus* (Fisch. et C.A. Mey.) Rouy
    (syn. *D. caucasicus* Fisch. et C.A. Mey.
    Fisch. ex Grossh.)
17. *Epilobium angustifolium* L. (rose bay)
    (syn. *Chamaenerion angustifolium* [L.]
    Scop., *Chamerion angustifolium* [L.]
    Holub)
18. *Euphorbia* spp. (spurge)
19. *Galinsoga parviflora* Cav. (gallant soldier)
20. *Heliotropium europaeum* L. (heliotrope)
21. *Huperzia selago* (L.) Bernh. ex Schrank et
    Mart. (fir club moss)
    (syn. *Lycopodium selago* L.; *Urostachys selago*
    [L.] Herter)
22. *Linaria vulgaris* Mill. (toadflax)
23. *Mandragora officinarum* L. (mandrake)
24. *Melampyrum nemorosum* L. (wood cow
    wheat)
25. *Najas marina* L. (spiny naiad)
26. *Nigella damascena* L. (love in a mist, devil
    in the bush)
27. *Origanum vulgare* L. (oregano) ssp. *viride*
    (Boiss.) Hayek
    (syn. *O. heracleoticum* L.p.p.) ssp. *vulgare*
28. *Reseda luteola* L. (grindelia)
29. *Ruta graveolens* L. (herb of grace, garden
    rue)
30. *Scrophularia nodosa* L. (figwort)
31. *Sedum* spp.
    S. acre L. (stonecrop)
    S. album L. (houseleek)
    ssp. *album*
    ssp. *teretifolium* (Lam.) Syme
    (= ssp. *micranthum* [Touss. Bast.] Syme,
    Sedum micranthum Touss. Bast.)
    S. telephium L. (life everlasting)
    ssp. *fabaria* (W.D.J. Koch) Kirschl.
    (syn. *S. fabaria* Koch, *S. vulgare* [Haw.]
    Link)
    ssp. *maximum* (L.) Krock.
    (syn. *S. maximum* [L.] Hoffm.)
    ssp. *telephium* L.
    (syn. *S. purpurascens* Koch, *S. purpureum*
    [L.] Schult.)
32. *Senecio vulgaris* L. (groundsel)
33. *Stratiotes aloides* L. (water soldier)
34. *Thesium* spp.:
    T. alpinum L. (Alpine bastard toadflax)
    T. pyrenaicum Pourr.
    (syn. Thesium pratense Ehrh.)
35. *Thymus serpyllum* L. (creeping thyme)
36. *Trifolium arvense* L. (rabbitfoot clover)
37. *Viscum album* L. (mistletoe)

Hexenküglein
(little witch's balls)

Euphorbia spp. (spurge)

Hexenkümmel
(witch's caraway)

Datura stramonium L. (thorn apple)

Hexenleiterchen
(little witch's ladder)
Dryopteris filix-mas (L.) Schott (male fern)

Hexenlichter
(witch's lights)
Taraxacum officinale Weber (dandelion)
(syn. *Leontodon taraxacum*)

Hexenmehl
(witch's meal)
1. *Lycopodium* spp./*L. clavatum* L.
(club moss/wolf's claw) spore dust
2. *Lycoperdon* spp. (puffball)
3. *Filipendula ulmaria* (L.) Maxim. (queen of
the meadow)
(syn. *Spiraea ulmaria* L.)

Hexenmehlkraut
(witch's flour herb)
Lycopodium clavatum L. (wolf's claw)
pharmaceutical term: Herba Lycopodium

Hexenmilch
(witch's milk)
1. *Chelidonium majus* L. (greater celandine)
2. *Euphorbia* spp. (spurge)
3. *Taraxacum officinale* Weber (dandelion)

Hexenmilchkraut
(witch's milk herb)
Chelidonium majus L. (greater celandine)

Hexemilchwurz
(witch's milk wort)
Valeriana officinalis (valerian)
pharmaceutical term: Rhizoma Valerianae

Hexenmoos
(witch's moss)
Lycopodium clavatum L. (wolf's claw)

Hexennägeli
(witch's little nails)
Dianthus carthusianorum L. (clusterhead pink)
ssp. *atrorubens* (All.) Hegi
ssp. *latifolius* (Griseb. et Schenk) Hegi
ssp. *tenuifolius* (Schur) F.N. Williams
ssp. *vaginatus* (Chaix) Rouy et Fouc.

Hexennest
(witch's nest)
Viscum album L. (mistletoe)

Hexennudel
(witch's noodle)
Berberis vulgaris L. (barberry)

Hexenparaplü
(witch's umbrella)
fungi (mushrooms in general)

Hexenpilz
(witch's mushroom)
1. *Lycoperdon* spp. (puffball)
2. *Boletus luridus* Schaeff.: Fr. (boletus)

Hexenpölsterlein
(little witch ghost)
rose gall on the *Rosa canina* L. (dog rose)

Hexenpüster
(witch's bellows)
Lycoperdon spp. (puffball)

Hexenpulver
(witch's powder)
pharmaceutical term: Pulv. pro equis.

Hexenpusters
(witch's pustule)
Lycoperdon spp. (puffball)

Hexenrauch
(witch's smoke)
Nigella sativa L. (black cumin)
olibanum (frankincense)
pharmaceutical term: asa foetida et Semen
Nigellae

Hexenrauchwurzel
(witch's smoke root)
Valeriana officinalis L. (valerian)
pharmaceutical term: Radix Valerian

Hexenring
(witch's ring)
ring-shaped growth form of mushrooms
(for example, *Amanita muscaria* [L.] Pers.
[fly agaric], *Agaricus campestris* [J.E.
Lange] Fr. [meadow mushroom],
Craterellus cornucopioides [L.] Pers.
[horn of plenty])

Hexen-Röhrling
(witch's pipes)
1. *Boletus luridus* Schaeff.: Fr. (lurid bolete)
2. *B. luridiformis* Rostk in Sturm
(dotted-stem bolete)
3. *B. lerythropus* (Fr.: Fr.) Pers.
4. *B. dupainii* Boud.
5. *B. torosus* Fr.
6. *B. rhodoxanthusus* (Krombh.) Kallenb.

Hexenscheiß
(witch's shit)
Corydalis cava (L.) Clairv. (hollow larkspur)
(syn. *Fumaria cava* [L.] Mill., *Fumaria bulbosa*
Mill. 1771 non L., *Corydalis bulbosa* [L.]
auct. non DC.)

Hexenschiß
(witch's shit)
Lycoperdon spp. (puffball)

Hexenschlotte
(witch's onion leaf)
Colchicum autumnale L. (autumn crocus)

Hexenschmalz
(witch's lard)
Fuligo septica L. (dog vomit, slime mold)

Hexenschmer
(witch's grease)
Rubus fructicosus L. (blackberry)

Hexenschwamm
(witch's sponge)
1. *Boletus luridus* Schaeff.: Fr.
2. *Lycoperdon* spp. (puffball)
3. *Nostoc commune* Vauch. (blue-green algae)

Hexenschwammerl
(witch's slime)
Nostoc commune Vauch. (blue-green algae)

Hexenseide
(witch's silk)
Cuscuta spp. (dodder)

Hexenseil
(witch's rope)
Clematis vitalba L. (travelers' joy)

Hexensessel
(witch's chair)
fungi (mushrooms in general)

Hexenspiritus
(witch's spirit)
Camphor Schnapps, Spiritus sap. Camph.

Hexenspitzel
(witch's point)
Elaphomyces granulatus Fr. (deer truffle)

Hexenspitzet
(witch's point)
Elaphomyces granulatus Fr. (deer truffle)
pharmaceutical term: Bolet. Cervinus

Hexenspon
(witch's spoon)
Leucanthemum vulgare (oxeye daisy)
(syn. *Chrysanthemum leucanthemum* L.)

Hexensporn
(witch's spur)
Bidens tripartitus L. (water agrimony)

Hexenstaub
(witch's dust)
1. *Lycopodium* spp. (club moss)
club moss spores
2. *L. clavatum* L. (wolf's claw)
3. *Lycoperdon* spp. (puffball)

Hexenstock
(witch's stick)
Viscum album L. (mistletoe)

Hexenstrang
(witch's cord)
1. *Clematis vitalba* L. (travelers' joy)
2. *C. recta* L. (upright virgin's bower)
3. *Lycium* spp. (wolfberry)

Hexenstrunk
(witch's drink)
Viscum album L. (mistletoe)

Hexenstrupp
(witch's shag)
Lycopodium clavatum L. (wolf's claw)
wolf's claw spores

Hexentanz
(witch's dance)
Lycopodium clavatum L. (wolf's claw)

Hexentreppen
(witch's steps)
Aloe variegata L. (aloe)

Hexenulme
(witch's elm)
1. *Ulmus* spp. (elms)
2. *U. glabra* Huds. Emend. Moss (Scotch
elm, wych elm)
(syn. *Ulmus campestris* L.p.p., *Ulmus
montana* With., *Ulmus scabra* Mill.)
3. *U. laevis* Pall.

Hexenveilchen
(little witch's violet)
Chelidonium majus L. (greater celandine)

Hexenwiderruf (witch's revocation)	1. *Polytrichum commune* L. (ground moss) 2. *Adiatum capillus veneris* L. (Venus hair) pharmaceutical term: Herba Adianti
Hexenwinde (witch's vine)	*Clematis vitalba* L. (travelers' joy)
Hexenwirbel (witch's whirl)	*Cuscuta* spp. (dodder)
Hexenwurzel (witch's root)	*Dryopteris filix-mas* (L.) Schott (male fern) pharmaceutical term: Rhizoma Filicis
Hexenzwiebel (witch's onion)	*Allium ursinum* L. (ransoms)
Hexenzwirn (witch's twine)	1. *Clematis vitalba* L. (travelers' joy) 2. *C. recta* L. (upright virgin's bower) 3. *Lonicera periclymeum* L. (English wild honeysuckle)
Hexli (little witch)	*Nigella damascena* L. (love in a mist)
Kleeteufel (clover devil)	1. *Cuscuta* spp. (dodder) 2. *Orobanche minor* Sm. (small broomrape)
Mors du Diable (devil's bit)	*Succisa pratensis* Moench (syn. *Scabiosa succisa* L.)
Perchtakraut (perchta herb)	1. *Chrysanthemum* spp. 2. *Tanacetum parthenium* (L.) Schultz Bip. (pellitory) (syn. *Matricaria parthenium* L., *Pyrethrum parthenium* Sm.)
Satanspilz (Satan's mushroom)	*Boletus satanas* Lenz (Satan's bolete)
Satansröhrling (Satan's little pipe)	1. *Boletus satanas* Lenz (Satan's bolete) 2. *B. splendidus* Martin ssp. *splendidus* Sing. et Kuthan 3. *B. splendidus* Martin ssp. moseri Sing. et Kuthan
Satanstaler (Satan's plate)	*Lunaria annua* L. (penny flower) (syn. *Lunaria biennis* Moench)
Satanswurz (Satan's sausage)	*Succisa pratensis* Moench (devil's bit)
Schwarze Teufelskralle (black devil's claw)	*Phyteuma nigrum* F.W. Schmidt (spiked rampion)
Speiteufel (spit devil)	1. *Russula emetica* (Schaeff.) Pers. (sickener) 2. various puffballs
St. Walpurgiskraut (Saint Walpurgis herb)	*Botrychium lunaria* (L.) Sw. (moonwort)
Talismann des Teufels (devil's talisman)	*Atropa belladonna* L. (belladonna)
Teiwelsoarsch (devil's arse)	*Orchis* spp. (orchid)
Teufel (devil)	1. *Trapa natans* L. (water chestnut) 2. *Lycoperdon* spp. (puffball)
Teufel im Busch (devil in the bush)	*Nigella damascena* L. (love in a mist, devil in the bush)
Teufel und engel (devil and angel)	*Orchis* spp. (orchid)
Teufelabbiß (devil's bit)	1. *Agrimonia eupatoria* L. (agrimony) 2. *Pulsatilla vernalis* (L.) Mill. (spring pasqueflower) (syn. *Jacea communis* Delabre) 3. *Centaurea jacea* L. (brown knapweed) (syn. *Jacea communis* Delabre)

	4. *Euphorbia* spp. (spurge) 5. *Euphrasia rostkoviana* Hayne (eyebright) 6. *Geranium* spp. (cranesbill) 7. *Geum urbanum* L. (avens root) 8. *Hypericum perforatum* L. (Saint John's wort) 9. *Knautia arvensis* (L.) Coult. (field scabious) (syn. *Scabiosa arvensis* L.) 10. *Ranunculus aconitifolius* L. (fair maids of France) 11. *Orobanche rapum-genistae* Thuill. 12. *Potentilla anserina* L. (silverweed) 13. *P. erecta* (L.) Hampe (cinquefoil) 14. *Geum montanum* L. (mountain avens) (syn. *Sieversia montana* [L.] Spreng., *Parageum montanum* [L.] Hara) 15. *Senecio vulgaris* L. (groundsel) 16. *Succisa pratensis* Moench (devil's bit) (syn. *Scabiosa succisa* L.)
Teufelafbitt (devil's bite)	*Succisa pratensis* Moench (devil's bit)
Teufelchen (little devil)	1. *Iberis* spp. (candytuft) 2. *Knautia arvensis* (L.) Coult. (field scabious) pharmaceutical term: Rotul. Menth. Pip.
Teufels pyß (devil's piss)	*Primula veris* L. (cowslip) (syn. *Primula officinalis* [L.] Hill)
Teufels Tabakbeutel (devil's tobacco bag)	*Lycoperdon* spp. (puffball)
Teufelsabbiß (devil's bite)	*Succisa pratensis* Moench (devil's bit)
Teufelsabbischrut (devil's bite herb)	*Succisa pratensis* Moench (devil's bit) pharmaceutical term: Herba scabiosae
Teufelsabbisswurzel (devil's bite root)	1. *Succisa pratensis* Moench (devil's bit) pharmaceutical term: Rad. Succisae, Radix Morsus diaboli 2. *Taraxacum officinale* Weber (dandelion) pharmaceutical term: Radix Taraxaci, Dandelion Root
Teufelsabwärtspulver (devil's drowning powder)	*Potentilla erecta* (L.) Hampe (cinquefoil) Pharmaceutical term: Rhizoma Tormentillae pulv.
Teufelsäpfel (devil's apple)	*Citrullus colocynthis* (L.) Schrad. (bitter apple) (syn. *Cucumis colocynthis* L., *Colocynthis vulgaris* Schrad.) pharmaceutical term: Fruct. Colocynth.
Teufelsäuglein (little devil's eye)	*Ophrys insectifera* L. emend. L. (fly orchid) (syn. *Ophrys muscifera* Huds.)
Teufelsanbiß (devil's bite)	1. *Daphne mezereum* L. (mezereon) 2. *Primula minima* L. (red Alpine primrose) 3. *Succisa pratensis* Moench (devil's bit)
Teufelsangesicht (devil's face)	*Orchis* spp. (orchid)
Teufelsantlitz (devil's face)	*Orphrys insectifera* L. emend. L. (fly orchid)
Teufelsapfel (devil's apple)	1. *Citrullus colocynthis* (L.) Schrad. (bitter apple) 2. *Datura stramonium* L. (thorn apple) 3. *Mandragora officinarum* L. (mandrake)
Teufelsarsch (devil's arse)	*Orchis* spp. (orchid) the elder of the two root balls
Teufelsasche (devil's ash)	*Lycoperdon* spp. (puffball)

Teufelsast
(devil's branch)

Viscum album L. (mistletoe)

Teufelsauge

1. *Paris quadrifolia* L. (one berry)
2. *Adonis vernalis* L. (yellow pheasant's eye)
   pharmaceutical term: Herba Andonidis
3. *Adonis aestivalis* L. (summer pheasant's eye)
4. *Agrostemma githago* L. (corn cockle)
5. *Potentilla palustris* (L.) Scop.
   (syn. *Comarum palustre* L.)
6. *Cyclamen purpurascens* Mill. (snowbread)
   (syn. *Cylcamen europaeum* auct. non L.)
7. *Geranium phaeum* L. (mourning widow)
8. *Hyoscyamus niger* L. (black henbane)
9. *Physalis alkekengi* L. (winter cherry)
10. *Ranunculus acris* L. (lesser celandine)
    (syn. *Ranunculus acer* auct.)
11. *Tagetes* spp. (marigold)
12. *Zinnia* spp. (zinnia)

Teufelsaugen
(devil's eyes)

Hyoscyamus niger L. (black henbane)

Teufelsband
(devil's band)

1. *Antirrhinum orontium* L. (small
   snapdragon)
2. *Lycopodium clavatum* L. (wolf's claw)

Teufelsbart
(devil's beard)

1. *Pulsatilla alpina* (L.) Delabre (Alpine
   pasqueflower)
2. *P. vulgaris* Mill. (pasqueflower)
3. *Sedum acre* L. (stonecrop)

Teufelsbaum
(devil's tree)

1. *Ficus religiosa* L. (pipul tree)
2. *Rhamnus frangula* L. (buckthorn)
   (syn. *Frangula alnus* Mill.)
3. *Sambucus nigra* L. (elder)

Teufelsbeere
(devil's berry)

1. *Atropa belladonna* (belladonna)
2. *Paris quadrifolia* (one berry)
3. *Solanum* spp. (nightshade)
4. *Bryonia* spp. (bryony)
5. *Agropyrum repens* Beauvais (couch grass)
6. *Actaea spicata* L. (baneberry)
7. *Cornus sanguinea* L. (blood-twig dogwood)
   (syn. *Thelycrania sanguinea* [L.] Fourr.,
   Swida sanguinea [L.] Opiz)
8. *Daphne mezereum* L. (mezereon)
9. *Rhamnus frangula* L. (buckthorn)
10. *Ligustrum vulgare* L. (black privet)
11. *Lonicera nigra* L. (black honeysuckle)
12. *L. xylosteum* L. (honeysuckle)
13. *Physalis alkekengi* L. (winter cherry)
14. *Polygonatum odoratum* (Mill.) Druce
    (Solomon's seal)
    (syn. *Convallaria polygonatum* L.,
    Polygonatum officinale All.)
    var. *odoratum*
    var. *thunbergii* (C. Morr. et Decne.) Hara
    (syn. *Polygonatum thunbergii* C. Morr. et
    Decne., *Polygonatum japonicum* C.
    Morr. et Decne.)
15. *Rubus caesius* L. (dewberry)
16. *Sambucus nigra* L. (elder)
17. *Solanum diflorum* Vell.
    (syn. *S. capsicastrum* Link et Schau)
18. *S. dulcamara* L. (bittersweet)
19. *Viburnum opulus* L. (cramp bark,
    highbush cranberry)

Teufelsbesen
(devil's broom)

1. *Genista tinctoria* L. (dyer's greenwood)
2. *Cytisus scoparius* (L.) Link (Scotch broom)
   (syn. *Sarothamnus scoparius* [L.] Wimm. ex
   W.D.J. Koch, *Genista scoparia* [L.] Lam)
3. *Viscum album* L. (mistletoe)

Teufelsbettstroh
(devil's bedstraw)

Dryopteris filix-mas (L.) Schott (male fern)

Teufelsbirnen
(devil's pears)

1. *Centaurea jacea* L. (brown knapweed)
2. *C. scabiosa* L. (greater knapweed)
   (syn. *Acrocentron scabiosa* [L.] A. et D. Löve)
3. *Knautia arvensis* (L.) Coult. (field scabious)
4. *Taraxacum officinale* Weber (dandelion)

Teufelsbiß
(devil's bite)

1. *Equisetum palustre* L. (horsetail)
2. *Geum urbanum* L. (avens root)
3. *Ranunculus sceleratus* L. (blister buttercup)
4. *Succisa pratensis* Moench (devil's bit)

Teufelsbißwurzel
(devil's bite root)

Succisa pratensis Moench (devil's bit)

Teufelsbitt
(devil's bite)

Succisa pratensis Moench (devil's bit)

Teufelsblume
(devil's flower)

1. *Adonis aestivalis* L. (summer pheasant's eye)
2. *Arnica montana* L. (arnica)
3. *Calceolaria* spp. (slipper flower)
4. *Capsella bursa-pastoris* (L.) Medik.
   (shepherd's purse)
5. *Chrysanthemum segetum* L. (corn marigold)
6. *Chrysosplenium alternifolium* L. (mouse-
   eared saxifrage)
7. *Euphorbia* spp. (spurge)
8. *Euphrasia rostkoviana* Hayne (eyebright)
9. *Geranium robertianum* L. (herb Robert)
10. *Idolum diabolicum* (praying mantis)
11. *Silene latifolia* Poir. spp. *alba* (Mill.)
    Greuter et Burdet (catchfly)
12. *Orchis* spp. (orchid)
13. *Papaver rhoeas* L. (red poppy)
14. *Plantago major* L. (plantain)
15. *Pulmonaria officinalis* L. (lungwort)
16. *Sedum telephium* L. (life everlasting)
17. *Solanum diflorum* Vell.
18. *Stellaria holostea* L. (greater stitchwort)
19. *Taraxacum officinale* Weber (dandelion)

Teufelsblut
(devil's blood)

Daemomorops draco (dragon's blood)
pharmaceutical term: Sang. Draconis

Teufelsbrot
(devil's bread)

1. *Amanita muscaria* (L. ex Fr.) Pers. (fly
   agaric)
2. *Colchicum autumnale* L. (autumn crocus)
3. *Luzula campestris* (L.) DC. (field wood rush)
4. *Polytrichum commune* L. (ground moss)

Teufelsbutterstange
(devil's butter pretzel)

Euphorbia helioscopia L. (sun spurge)

Teufelsdampf
(devil's steam)

Lycoperdon spp. (puffball)

Teufelsdarm
(devil's gut)

1. *Calystegia sepium* (L.) (hedge bindweed)
   (syn. *Convolvulus sepium* L.)
2. *Convolvulus arvensis* L. (field bindweed)
3. *Cuscuta* spp. (dodder)

Teufelsdill
(devil's dill)

Anethum graveolens L. (dill)

Teufelsdillsamen
(devil's dill seeds)

Anethum graveolens L. (dill)

Teufelsdorn (devil's thorn)	1. *Ononis spinosa* L. (restharrow) 2. *Tribulus terrestris* L. (puncture vine)	**Teufelsgeld** (devil's money)	1. *Rhinanthus alectrolophus* (Scop.) Poll. (syn. *Alectrolophus* Scop.) 2. *Briza media* L. (quaking grass)
Teufelsdose (devil's box)	*Lycoperdon* spp. (puffball)	**Teufelsgeldbeutel** (devil's wallet)	1. *Rhinanthus alectrolophus* (Scop.) Poll. 2. *Colchicum autumnale* L. (autumn crocus)
Teufelsdraht (devil's thread)	1. *Cuscuta* spp. (dodder) 2. *Galium aparine* L. (cleavers)	**Teufelsgeldsack** (devil's money bag)	*Lycoperdon* spp. (puffball)
Teufelsdreck (devil's filth)	*Euphorbia* spp. (spurge) 1. *E. pilulifera* L. (pill-bearing spurge) 2. *Ferula asa-foetida* L. (asafetida) 3. *Lycoperdon* spp. (puffball) 4. *Lycopodium clavatum* L. (wolf's claw) 5. *Nostoc commune* Vauch. (blue-green algae)	**Teufelsgeldsäcklein** (devil's little sack)	*Capsella bursa-pastoris* (L.) Medik. (shepherd's purse)
		Teufelsgesichtlein (devil's little face)	*Soldanella alpina* L. (alpine snowbells) *Veronica chamaedrys* L. (germander speedwell)
		Teufelsgestreide (devil's grain)	*Polytrichum commune* L. (ground moss)
Teufelsdroge (devil's drug)	*Cannabis sativa* L. (hemp)	**Teufelsginster** (devil's dyers' broom)	*Genista anglica* L. (English dyers' broom)
Teufelsduus (devil's can)	*Lycoperdon* spp. (puffball)	**Teufelsglocke** (devil's bells)	1. *Aquilegia vulgaris* L. (common columbine) 2. *Soldanella alpina* L. (alpine snowbell)
Teufelsdups (devil's can)	*Lycoperdon* spp. (puffball)	**Teufelsglotzen** (devil's stare)	1. *Adonis aestivalis* L. (pheasant's eye) 2. *Paris quadrifolia* L. (one berry)
Teufelsei (devil's egg)	*Phallus impudicus* (stinkhorn)	**Teufelsgras** (devil's grass)	1. *Euphorbia esula* L. (leafy spurge) 2. *Linaria vulgaris* Mill. (toadflax)
Teufelsfeder (devil's feather)	*Dryopteris filix-mas* (L.) Schott (male fern)	**Teufelsgückle** (devil's little look)	*Atropa belladonna* L. (belladonna)
Teufelsfinger (devil's finger)	*Lycopodium clavatum* L. (wolf's claw)	**Teufelshaar** (devil's hair)	1. *Clematis vitalba* L. (travelers' joy) 2. *Cuscuta* spp. (dodder) 3. *Plantago lanceolata* L. (rib grass) 4. *Cytisus scoparius* (L.) Link 5. *Stipa pennata* L.
Teufelsfleisch (devil's meat)	1. fungi (mushrooms in general) 2. *Trifolium repens* L. (white clover)[2] pharmaceutical term: Flos Trifolii albi		
Teufelsflucht (devil's flight)	*Hypericum perforatum* L. (Saint John's wort)	**Teufelshand** (devil's hand)	1. *Orchis* spp. (orchid) pharmaceutical term: Tubera Salep, healing herb 2. *Petasites* hybridus (L.) Fl. Wett. (butterbur)
Teufelsförke (devil's pitchfork)	*Bidens tripartitus* L. (water agrimony)		
Teufelsföte (devil's paw)	*Artemisia vulgaris* L. (mugwort)	**Teufelshändchen** (devil's little hands)	*Orchis* spp. (orchid)
Teufelsfüßchen (little devil's foot)	1. *Lathyrus pratensis* L. (meadow vetchling) 2. *Orchis* spp. (orchid)	**Teufelshaube** (devil's hood)	*Lycoperdon* spp. (puffball)
Teufelsfurz (devil's fart)	*Lycoperdon* spp. (puffball)	**Teufelshoden** (devil's sack)	*Mandragora officinarum* L. (mandrake)
Teufelsfuß (devil's foot)	1. *Bothriochloa ischaemum* (L.) Keng (yellow bluestem) (syn. *Andropogon ischaemum* L., *Dichanthium ischaemum* [L.] Roberty) 2. *Artemisia vulgaris* L. (mugwort) 3. *Tussilago farfara* L. (coltsfoot)[3]	**Teufelshörnle** (devil's little horn)	1. *Thuja* spp. (thuja) 2. *Trapa natans* L. (water chestnut)
		Teufelsholz (devil's wood)	1. *Cornus sanguinea* L. (dogberry) 2. *Lonicera xylosteum* L. (honeysuckle)
Teufelsgabel (devil's fork)	1. *Capsella bursa-pastoris* (L.) Medik. (shepherd's purse) 2. *Erodium cicutarium* (L.) L'Herit. ex Ait. (red-stemmed stork's bill)	**Teufelshorn** (devil's horn)	*Soldanella alpina* L. (alpine snowbell)
		Teufelshose (devil's pants)	algae (algae in general)
Teufelsgäschel (devil's scourge)	*Cichorium intybus* L. (chicory)	**Teufelshosenband** (devil's waistband)	1. *Clematis vitalba* L. (travelers' joy) 2. *Lycopodium* spp. L (club moss) 3. *L. clavatum* L. (wolf's claw)
Teufelsgarn (devil's yarn)	*Cuscuta* spp. (dodder)	**Teufelshütchen** (devil's little hat)	*Plantago major* L. (plantain) pharmaceutical term: Herba Plantag.
Teufelsgeißel (devil's scourge)	1. *Amaranthus caudatus* L. (love lies bleeding) 2. *Cichorium intybus* L. (chicory) 3. *Epilobium angustififolium* L. (rose bay)	**Teufelshut** (devil's hat)	1. *Digitalis purpurea* L. (purple foxglove) 2. *Petasites* hybridus (L.) Fl. Wett. (butterbur)

---

[2] Hartlieb (fifteenth century) wrote about clover (*trifolium*, which Hartlieb called "Triuolium"): "The same is used by the masters in necromancy. Other sorcerers also make great art with it" (*Kräuterbuch*, 100).

[3] "Coltsfoot is an Arcadian herb, and it has the action of all fillies and all fast mares gallop racing over the hills" (Theocritus, 2: *Eidyllion*).

Teufelsjaffel
(devil's waffle)
1. *Capsella bursa-pastoris* (L.) Medik. (shepherd's purse)
2. *Erodium cicutarium* (L.) L'Herit. ex Ait. (red-stemmed stork's bill)

Teufelsjohannitraube
(devil's currant)
Ribes nigrum L. (black currant)

Teufelskäse
(devil's cheese)
fungi (mushrooms in general)

Teufelskappe
(devil's cap)
1. *Aconitum napellus* L. (monkshood)
2. Cantharelles cibarius Fr. (chanterelle)
3. fungi (various mushrooms)

Teufelskerze
(devil's candle)
Verbascum spp. (mullein)

Teufelskirsche
(devil's cherry)
1. *Atropa belladonna* L. (belladonna)
2. *Byronia* spp. (byrony)
3. *Cornus sanguinea* L. (dogberry)
4. *Rhamnus frangula* L. (buckthorn)
5. *Lonicera xylosteum* L. (honeysuckle)
6. *Rosa canina* L. (dog rose)
7. *Solanum diflorum* Vell.
8. *S. nigrum* L. (nightshade)
9. *Sorbus aucuparia* L. (European mountain ash, rowan tree) (syn. *Pyrus aucuparia* [L.] Ehrh.)
10. *Viburnum opulus* (cramp bark, highbush cranberry)

Teufelskirschen
(devil's cherries)
Physalis alkekengi L. (winter cherry)

Teufelskläuchen
(little devil's claws)
Luzula campestris (L.) DC. (field wood rush)

Teufelskläuli
(little devil's claws)
Claviceps purpurea (Fries) Tulasne (ergot)

Teufelsklatten
(devil's claws)
Solanum dulcamara L. (bittersweet)

Teufelsklauden
(devil's claws)
Solanum dulcamara L. (bittersweet)

Teufelsklaue
(devil's claw)
1. *Alchemilla xanthochlora* Rothm. (lady's mantle) (syn. *A. vulgaris* auct. non L., *A. pratensis* auct. non Opiz)
2. *Arctium lappa* L. (burdock) (syn. *Lappa major* Gaertn.)
3. *Dryopteris filix-mas* (L.) Schott (male fern)
4. *Claviceps purpurea* (Fries) Tulasne (ergot)
5. *Galium aparine* L. (cleavers)
6. *Huperzia selago* (L.) Bernh. ex Schrank et Mart. (fir club moss)
7. *Lonicera alpigena* L. (dwarf alpine honeysuckle)
8. *Lycopodium clavatum* L. (wolf's claw)
9. *Diphasiastrum complanatum* (L.) Holub. (ground cedar) (syn. *Diphasium complanatum* [L.] Rothm., *Lycopodium complanatum* L.)
10. *Orchis* spp. (orchid)
11. *Stachys palustris* L. (hedge nettle)
12. *Tropaeolum majus* L. (nasturtium)

Teufelsklauenwurz
(devil's claw root)
Dryopteris filix-mas (L.) Schott (male fern)

Teufelsklee
(devil's clover)
1. *Huperzia selago* (L.) Bernh. ex Schrank et Mart. (fir club moss)
2. *Orobanche minor* Sm. (small broomrape)

Teufelskleppel
(devil's rattle)
Typha latifolia L. (cattail)

Teufelsknoblauch
(devil's garlic)
Allium ursinum L. (ransom)

Teufelsklogge
(devil's bell)
Lycopodium clavatum L. (wolf's claw)

Teufelsknoten
(devil's knots)
Sanguisorba officinalis L. (great burnet) (syn. *S. major* Gilib., *Poterium officinale* [L.] A. Gray)

Teufelsköpflein
(devil's little head)
Trapa natans L. (European water chestnut)

Teufelskohl
(devil's coal)
Euphorbia spp. (spurge)

Teufelskolben
(devil's cock)
Phyteuma spicatum L. (spiked rampion)

Teufelskopf
(devil's head)
1. *Bidens tripartitus* L. (bur marigold)
2. *Euryale ferox* Salisb. (prickly water lily)
3. *Knautia arvensis* [L.] Coult. (field scabious)
4. *Armeria maritima* L. (sea thrift) (syn. *Statice armeria* L.)

Teufelskot
(devil's excrement)
Ferula asa-foetida L. (asafetida)

Teufelskrähenmehl
(devil's crow meal)
Lycopodium clavatum L. (wolf's claw)

Teufelskralle
(devil's claws)
1. *Astragalus glycyphyllus* L. (astragalus)
2. *Lonicera clavatum* L. (honeysuckle)
3. *Lycopodium clavatum* L. (wolf's claw)
4. *Orchis* spp. (orchid)
5. *Phyteuma* spp. (rampion)
   P. hemisphaericum L.
   P. orbiculare L.
   P. spicatum L. (spiked rampion)
   P. betonicifolium Villars
   P. halleri Allioni
   (syn. *P. ovatum* Honckeny)
   P. nigrum Schmidt (black devil's claws)
6. *Taraxacum officinale* Weber (dandelion)

Teufelskrallen
(devil's claws)
Orchis mascula L. (early purple orchid)

Teufelskrallenmehl
(devil's claw meal)
1. *Lycopodium clavatum* L. (wolf's claw)
2. *Huperzia selago* (L.) Bernh. ex Schrank et Mart. (fir club moss)

Teufelskraut
(devil's herb)
1. *Achillea ptarmica* L. (sneezewort)
2. *Aconitum napellus* L. (monkshood)
3. *Aegopodium podagraria* L. (ground elder)
4. *Anethum graveolens* L. (dill)
5. *Chamaemelum nobile* (L.) All. (Roman chamomile) (syn. *Anthemis nobilis* L., *Ormenis nobilis* [L.] J. Gay ex coss. et Germ.)
6. *Dryopteris filix-mas* (L.) Schott (male fern)
7. *Atropa belladonna* L. (belladonna)
8. *Cannabis sativa* L. (hemp)
9. *Capsella bursa-pastoris* (L.) Medik. (shepherd's purse)
10. *Chaerophyllum hirsutum* L. (hairy chervil)
11. *Chelidonium majus* L. (greater celandine)

12. *Datura stramonium* L. (thorn apple)
13. *Eupatorium cannabinum* L. (water hemp)
14. *Euphorbia* spp. (spurge)
15. *Galinsoga parviflora* Cav. (gallant soldier)
16. *Helleborus foetidus* L. (bearsfoot)
17. *Himantoglossum hircinum* Spreng. (lizard orchid)
   (syn. *Satyrium hircinum* L., *Loroglossum hircinum* Rich.)
18. *Hyoscyamus niger* L. (black henbane)
19. *Hypericum perforatum* L. (Saint John's wort)
20. *Lathraea squamaria* L. (toothwort)
21. *Linaria vulgaris* Mill. (toadflax)
22. *Lycopodium clavatum* L. (wolf's claw)
23. *Orchis* spp. (orchid)
24. *Plantago major* L. (plantain)
25. *Polygonum persicaria* L. (lady's thumb)
26. *Ranunculus acris* L. (lesser celandine)
27. *Sedum telephium* L. (life everlasting)
28. *Senecio jacobaea* L. (tansy ragwort)
29. *Senecio vulgaris* L. (groundsel)
30. *Solanum nigrum* L. (black nightshade)
31. *Succisa pratensis* Moench (devil's bit)
32. *Taraxacum officinale* Weber (dandelion)
33. *Urtica dioica* L. (nettle)

Teufelskrautwurz
(devil's herb wort)
Aconitum napellus L. (monkshood)

Teufelsküche
(devil's kitchen)
Colchicum autumnale L. (autumn crocus)

Teufelsküchle
(devil's little kitchen)
fungi (mushrooms in general)

Teufelskürbis
(devil's nut)
Bryonia spp. (bryony)

Teufelskutsche
(devil's coach)
Aconitum napellus L. (monkshood)

Teufelslaterne
(devil's lantern)
Taraxacum officinále Weber (dandelion)

Teufelsleiter
(devil's ladder)
1. *Asperugo procumbens* L. (madwort)
2. *Dryopteris filix-mas* L. Schott (male fern)
3. *Polemonium caeruleum* L. (Jacob's ladder)
4. *Pteridium aquilinum* (L.) Kuhn (bracken fern)

Teufelslicht
(devil's light)
Taraxacum officinale Weber (dandelion)

Teufelslöffel
(devil's spoon)
Drosera rotundifolia L. (sundew)

Teufelslûs
(devil's light)
Ranunculus arvensis L.

Teufelsmarge
(devil's mark)
Claviceps purpurea (Fries) Tulasne (ergot)

Teufelsmarterholz
(devil's torture wood)
Lonicera xylosteum L. (honeysuckle)

Teufelsmartern
(devil's torture)
Cornus sanguinea L. (blood-twig dogwood)

Teufelsmatten
(devil's mattress)
Lonicera xylosteum L. (honeysuckle)

Teufelsmehlsack
(devil's flour sack)
Lycoperdon spp. (puffball)

Teufelsmettern
(devil's mattress)
Cornus sanguinea L. (blood-twig dogwood)

Teufelsmilch
(devil's milk)
1. *Chelidonium majus* L. (greater celandine)
2. *Euphorbia* spp. (spurge)
3. *Ornithogalum umbellatum* L. (star of Bethlehem)

Teufelsmilchkraut
(devil's milk herb)
Chelidonium majus L. (greater celandine)

Teufelsnadelkissen
(devil's pincushion)
1. *Ferocactus cylindraceus* (barrel cactus)
2. *Echinocactus wislizeni, Ferocactus acanthodes*
3. *Ferocactus wislizeni* (echinocactus)

Teufelsnähgarn
(devil's sewing thread)
1. *Calystegia sepium* (L.) R. Br. (hedge bindweed)
2. *Convolvulus arvensis* L. (field bindweed)
3. *Cuscuta* spp. (dodder)
4. *Erigeron* spp. (spikenard)
5. *Fallopia convolvulus* (L.) A. Löve (black bindweed)
6. *Vicia cracca* L. (Gerard vetch)
7. *V. sepium* L. (bush vetch)

Teufelsnase
(devil's nose)
1. *Acer* spp. (maple)
2. *Capsella bursa-pastoris* (L.) Medik. (shepherd's purse)

Teufelsrohr
(devil's pipe)
Capsella bursa-pastoris (L.) Medik. (shepherd's purse)

Teufelspeitsche
(devil's whip)
Silene acaulis (L.) Jacq. (moss campion)

Teufelspest
(devil's pest)
Tussilago farfara L. (coltsfoot)

Teufelspeterlein[chrut]
(devil's parsley)
Conium maculatum L. (poison hemlock)

Teufelspeterleinsamen
(devil's parsley seed)
Conium maculatum L. (poison hemlock)
pharmaceutical term: Fructus Conii

Teufelspeterling
(little devil's parsley)
Conium maculatum L. (poison hemlock)

Teufelspflanze
(devil's plant)
Dictamnus albus L. (burning bush)

Teufelspfoten
(devil's paws)
Orchis spp. (orchid)
pharmaceutical term: tuber root balls

Teufelspilz
(devil's mushroom)
Lycoperdon spp. (puffball)

Teufelspratzen
(devil's paw)
1. *Bothriochloa ischaemum* (L.) Keng (yellow bluestem)
2. *Cynodon dactylon* (L.) Pers. (Bermuda grass)
3. *Orchis* spp. (orchid)
pharmaceutical term: tuber root balls
4. *Digitaria sanguinalis* (L.) Scop. (hairy crabgrass)
(syn. *Panicum sanguinale* L.)
var. *esculenta* (Gaud.) Caldesi
var. *sanguinalis*

Teufelspuppen
(devil's puppets)
Physalis alkekengi L. (winter cherry)
pharmaceutical term: Fructus Alkekengi

Teufelsrädlein
(devil's little wheel)
Lonicera xylosteum L. (honeysuckle)

Teufelsranke
(devil's vine)
1. *Clematis vitalba* L. (travelers' joy)
2. *Lycopodium clavatum* L. (wolf's claw)

Teufelsraub
(devil's loot)
Hypericum perforatum L. (Saint John's wort)

Teufelsrebe(n)
(devil's vine[s])
1. *Clematis vitalba* L. (travelers' joy)
2. *C. recta* L. (upright virgin's bower)
pharmaceutical term: Herba Clematidis

Teufelsregenschirm
(devil's umbrella)
Geranium phaeum L. (mourning widow)

Teufelsrippen
(devil's ribs)
1. *Taraxacum officinale* Weber (dandelion)
   pharmaceutical term: Herba Taraxaci
2. *Dryopteris filix-mas* (L.) Schott (male fern)

Teufelsrohr
(devil's pipe)
Clematis vitalba L. (travelers' joy)

Teufelsrübe
(devil's root)
Bryonia dioica Jacq. (white bryony, English mandrake)
(syn. *Bryonia cretica* L. spp. *dioica* [Jacq.] Tutin)

Teufelssäcklein
(devil's little sack)
1. *Capsella bursa-pastoris* (L.) Medik. (shepherd's purse)
2. *Veratrum album* L. (white hellebore)

Teufelssamen
(devil's seeds)
1. *Hyoscyamus niger* L. (black henbane)
2. *Veratrum album* L. (white hellebore)

Teufelsschaufel
(devil's shovel)
Capsella bursa-pastoris (L.) Medik. (shepherd's purse)

Teufelschlüssel
(devil's key)
Botrychium lunaria (L.) Sw. (moonwort)

Teufelsschmer
(devil's grease)
Rubus caesius L. (dewberry)

Teufelsschnupftabak
(devil's snuff tobacco)
1. *Lycoperdon* spp. (puffball)
2. *Tragopogon* spp. (salsify)

Teufelsschutt
(devil's trash)
Lycopodium L. (wolf's claw)
pharmaceutical term: Herba Lycopodii

Teufelsschwamm
(devil's sponge)
1. *Boletus edulis* Bull.: Fr. (king bolete)
2. *Lycoperdon* spp. (puffball)
3. *Tuber aestivum* Vittadini (summer truffle)

Teufelsschwanz
(devil's tail)
Glechoma hederacea L. (ground ivy)
(syn. *Nepeta hederacea* [L.] Trev.)

Teufelsseckeli
(little devil's sack)
Capsella bursa-pastoris (L.) Medik. (shepherd's purse)

Teufelsseide
(devil's silk)
Cuscuta spp. (dodder)

Teufelssilber
(devil's silver)
Lunaria annua L. (penny flower)

Teufelsspigge
(devil's pickaxe)
Cardamine pratensis L. (cuckoo flower)

Teufelssporn
(devil's spur)
Orchis spp. (orchid)

Teufelsspucke
(devil's spit)
Cardamine pratensis L. (cuckooflower)

Teufelsstäuber
(devil's dust)
Lycoperdon spp. (puffball)

Teufelsstange
(devil's branch)
Typha latifolia L.

Teufelsstern
(devil's star)
Dianthus deltoides L. (maiden pink)

Teufelsstrick
(devil's yarn)
Clematis vitalba L. (travelers' joy)

Teufelsstrumpfband
(devil's sockband)
Lycopodium clavatum L. (wolf's claw)

Teufelsswet
(devil's sweat)
Clematis vitalba L. (travelers' joy)

Teufelstabak
(devil's tobacco)
1. *Clematis recta* L. (upright virgin's bower)
2. *Lycoperdon* spp. (puffball)
3. *Orobanche minor* Sm. (small broomrape)

Teufelstabakbeutel
(devil's tobacco pouch)
1. *Colchicum autumnale* L. (autumn crocus)
2. *Lycoperdon* spp. (puffball)

Teufelstabaksak
(devil's tobacco sack)
Lycoperdon spp. (puffball)

Teufelstrauben
(devil's grapes)
1. *Asparagus officinalis* L. (asparagus)
   pharmaceutical term: Rhizoma Asparagi
2. *Hypericum perforatum* L. (Saint John's wort)

Teufelsüberstreich
(devil's finish)
Parnassia palustris L. (marsh grass of Parnassus)

Teufelsverjagen
(chase-off-the-devil)
Hypericum perforatum L. (Saint John's wort)

Teufelswägelein
(little devil's path)
1. *Filipendula ulmaria* (L.) Maxim. (meadowsweet)
2. *Lonicera xylsteum* L. (honeysuckle)

Teufelswies
(devil's sign)
Silene acaulis (L.) Jacq. (moss campion)
ssp. *exscapa* (All.) Bran-Blanq.
(syn *Silene exscapa* All., var. *exscapa* [All.] DC.)

Teufelswurz
(devil's wort)
Succisa pratensis Moench (devil's bit)

Teufelswurzel
(devil's root)
1. *Aconitum napellus* L. (monkshood)
   pharmaceutical term: Tuber Aconiti
2. *A. vulparia* Rchb. ex Spreng. (yellow wolfsbane) (*A. lycoctonum* auct. non L.)
3. *Colchicum autumnale* L. (autumn crocus)
4. *Helleborus purpurascens* Waldst. et Kit.
5. *Hyoscyamus niger* L. (black henbane)
6. *Orobanche minor* Sm. (small broomrape)
7. *Rumex patientia* L. (patience dock)
8. *Sedum telephium* L. (life everlasting)

Teufelszahn
(devil's tooth)
1. *Knautia arvensis* (L.) Coult. (field scabious)
2. *Neottia nidus-avis* (L.) L.C. Rich (bird's-nest orchid)
3. *Orchis* spp. (orchid)
4. *Taraxacum officinale* Weber (dandelion)

Teufelszahnbiß
(devil's tooth bite)
Gnaphalium luteo-album L. (cudweed)

Teufelszahnwurz
(devil's tooth herb)
Potentilla erecta (L.) Hampe (cinquefoil)

Teufelszankkraut
(devil's tooth herb)
Lycopodium clavatum L. (wolf's claw)

Teufelszeltlein
(little devil's tent)
Malva sylvestris L. (blue mallow)
(syn. *Malva mauritiana* L.)

Teufelszeller
(devil's cellar)
Ranunculus repens L. (creeping buttercup)

Teufelszwick
(devil's gusset)
Cuscuta spp. (dodder)

Teufelszwirn
(devil's yarn)
1. *Lycium barbarum*
   (syn. *Lycium halimifolium* Mill., *Lycium vulgare* Dun.)
2. *Cuscuta* spp. (dodder)
   pharmaceutical term: Herba Cuscutae
3. *Vitex agnus-castus* L. (chaste berry)
   pharmaceutical term: Phenghawar Djambi
4. *Aruncus dioicus* (Walt.) Fern. (goat's-beard)
   (syn. *Aruncus sylvestris* Kostel., *Aruncus vulgaris* Raf., *Spiraea aruncus* L.)
   var. *astilboides* (Maxim.) Hara
   (syn. *Aruncus astilboides* Maxim.)
   var. *dioicus*
5. *Lonicera alpigena* L. (dwarf alpine honeysuckle)

	6. *Fallopia convolvulus* (L.) A. Löve (black bindweed) (syn. *Polygonum convolvulus* L., *Bilderdykia convolvulus* [L.] Dumort., *Fagopyrum convolvulus* [L.] H. Gross)
	7. *Solanum dulcamara* L. (bittersweet)

Teufel
(devil)
Luzula campestris (L.) DC. (field wood rush)

Teuflein
(little devil)
Juncus articulatus L. (jointed rush)
(syn. *Juncus lampocarpus* Ehrh. ex Hoffm.)

Teuflich
(devilish)
Russula spp.

Trudefuß
(druid's foot)
various puffballs

Trudenbeutel
(druid's bag)
various puffballs

Trudenmilch
(druid's milk)
Chelidonium majus L. (greater celandine)

Trudenkraut
(druid's herb)
Lycopodium L. (wolf's claw)

Tüfelsabbisswurz
(devil's bite herb)
Potentilla erecta (L.) Hampe (cinquefoil)
pharmaceutical term: Rhizoma Tormentillae

Tüfelsbeerichrut
(devil's berry herb)
Atropa belladonna L. (belladonna)
pharmaceutical term: Folium Belladonnae

Trudenbeutel
(druid's sack)
Taraxacum officinale Weber (dandelion)

Tüfelschnoblauch
(devil's garlic)
Allium ursinum L. (ransom)
pharmaceutical term: Herba Allii ursini

Tüfelsmilch
(devil's milk)
Chelidonium majus L. (greater celandine)

Tüfelssecklichrut
(little devil's sack herb)
Capsella bursa-pastoris (L.) Medik. (shepherd's purse)
pharmaceutical term: Herba Bursae pastoris

Tuifeln
(devils)
Viola tricolor L. (pansy)

Walpurgisblümlein
(little Walpurgis flower)
Caltha palustris L. (marsh marigold)
(syn. *Caltha holubyi* Beck, *Caltha polypetala* Hochst ex Lorent)

Walpurgiskörner
(Walpurgis kernels)
Corydalis cava (L.) Clairv. (hollow larkspur)

Walpurgiskraut
(Walpurgis herb)
1. *Botrychium lunaria* (L.) Sw. (moonwort)
2. *Circaea lutetania* L. (enchanter's nightshade)
3. *Corydalis cava* (L.) Clairv. (hollow larkspur)
4. *Hypericum perforatum* L. (Saint John's wort)

Walpurgismai
(Walpurgis May)
1. *Lonicera xylosteum* L. (honeysuckle)
2. *Rosa rubiginosa* (sweetbriar rose)
(syn. *Rosa eglanteria* L.p.p.)

Walpurgisstaberl
(little Walpurgis staff)
Dryopteris filix-mas (L.) Schott (male fern)

Walpurgisstrauch
(Walpurgis shrub)
Lonicera xylosteum L. (honeysuckle)

Weiße Teufelskralle
(white devil's claw)
Phyteuma spicatum L. (spiked rampion)

Witch Elme
(witch elm)
Ulmus laevis Pall.

Witch Hasell
(witch hazel)
Ulmus glabra Huds. (Scotch elm, witch elm)

Wildes Teufelskraut
(wild devil herb)
Linaria vulgaris Mill. (toadflax)

Wych Hasel
(witch hazel)
Carpinus betulus L. (European hornbeam)

Zauberglöckchen
(little magic bells)
Fuligo septica L. (dog vomit, slime mold)

Zauberbutter
(magic butter)
Abutilon pictum (Gill. ex Hook. et Arn.) Walp. (flowering maple)
(syn. *Abutilon striatum* Dicks. ex Lindl.)

Zauberhasel
(magic hazel)
Hamamelis virginiana L. (witch hazel)

Zauberkraut
(magic herb)
1. *Circaea lutetiana* L. (enchanter's nightshade)
2. *Epilobium hirsutum* L. (great hairy willow herb)
3. *Lamium* spp. (blind nettle)
4. *Medeola virginiana* L. (Indian cucumber)

Zauberwurz
(magic wort)
Mandragora officinarum L. (mandrake)

Zauberwurzel
(magic root)
1. *Mandragora officinarum* L. (mandrake)
pharmaceutical term: Radix Mandragorae
2. *Bryonia* spp. (bryony)
pharmaceutical term: Radix Byroniae

Bibliography

Classical Sources

There are many recent and older translations of these works available. They have been cited in the usual way.

Apollodorus, *Library*
Apollonius of Rhodius, *Argonautica*
Apuleius, *Metamorphoses*
————. *Apologia*
Cicero, *On Divination*
————. *On Law*
————. *The Nature of the Gods*
Clemens Alexandrinus, *Hortatory Address to the Greeks*
————. *Protrepticus*
Codex iustinianus
Diocles, *Rhizotomaka*
Diodorus Siculus
Dioscorides, *Materia medica*
Ebers Papyrus
Euripides, *Bacchae*
————. *Medea*
Galen, *Opera omnia*
Heraclitus, *Fragments*
Herodotus, *The Histories*
Hesiod, *Theogony*
Homer, *The Iliad*
————. *The Odyssey*
————. [attributed to], *The Homeric Hymns*
Horace, *Odes*
————. *Epodes*
————. *Satires*
Hyginus, *Myths*
Kallimachos, *Poems*
Lucan, *The Civil War*
————. *Pharsalia*
Lucian, *Dialogues of the Hetaerae*
Lucretius, *On Nature*
Marcellus, *De medicamentis*
Medicina antiqua
Nonnus, *Dionysiaca*
Orpheus, *Argonautica* (*Orphic Songs of the Argonauts*)
————. [attributed], *Hymns* (*Orphic Hymns*)
Ovid, *Art of Love*
————. *The Metamorphoses*
Papyri Graecae Magicae (The Greek Magical Papyri)
Papyros Ebers
Physiologus
Pausanias, *Itinerary of Greece*
Petronius, *The Satyricon*
Pindar, *Odes*
Pliny, *Natural History*
Polyainos, *Stratigimata*
Propertius, *Elegy*
Publius Cornelius Tacitus, *Germania*
Quintilianus, *Declamaciones*
Sappho, *Songs*
Seneca, *Medea*
Tertullian, *De anima*
Theophrastus, *On Plants*
Tibullus, *Elegies*
Virgil, *The Aeneid*
————. *Ecologues*

English-language Translation Sources for Classics

Apollonius, *The Argonautica*. Translated by R. C. Seaton, Loeb Library v 1, Cambridge: Harvard University Press, 1980.
Apuleius, *Apuleius: Metamorphoses*. Translated by J. Arthur Hanson. Cambridge: Harvard University Press, 1989.
Herodotus. *The Histories of Herodotus*. Translated by Aubrey de Sélincourt, rev. A. R. Burn. New York: Penguin, 1972.
Homer, *The Iliad*. Translated by Robert Fitzgerald. New York: Anchor Press/Doubleday, 1974.
————. *The Odyssey*. Translated by Robert Fitzgerald, New York: Farrar, Straus, and Giroux, 1998.
Hyginus. *The Myths of Hyginus*. Translated by Mary Grant. Lawrence: University of Kansas, 1960.
Lucian, *Dialogues of the Hetaerae* I. Translated by Fowler. Oxford: Clarendon Press, 1905.
Orpheus, *Orphic Hymns*. Translated by Apostolos N. Athanassakis. Missoula, Mont.: Scholars Press, 1977.
Petronius, *The Satyricon*. Translated by P. G. Walsh. Oxford: Clarendon Press, 1996.
Pliny, *Natural History* (books XXIV–XXVII). Translated by W. H. S. Jones. Loeb Library, Cambridge: Harvard University, 1952.
Pindar. Fourth Pythian Ode. Translated by Richard Lattimore, Chicago: University of Chicago Press, 1976.
Tibullus. *Tibullus: Elegie*. Translated by Guy Lee. Liverpool: Francis Cains, 1982.
Virgil, *The Aeneid*. Translated by Robert Fitzgerald. New York: Random House, 1983.

Medieval and Early Modern Era Sources

Athanasius
1987. *Vita Antonii*, ed. Adolf Gottfried. Graz, Vienna, Cologne: Stryria.
Agrippa von Nettesheim, Heinrich Cornelius
1982 *Die magischen Werke*. Wiesbaden: Fourier.
Bock, Hieronymus
1539, 1577. *New Kreütterbuch*. Straßburg: Josiam Rihel.
Brunfels, Otto
1532. *Contrafayt Kreüterbuch*. Straßburg: Hans Schotten.
Bruno, Giordano
1995. "Über Magie." In *Works*, edited by Elisabeth von Samsonow. Munich: Diederichs.
Das sechste und siebente Buch Mosis
1984. Annotated by Wolfgang Bauer. Berlin: Karin Kramer Verlag.
della Porta, Giambattista
1589. *Magia naturalis*. Original Latin edition: Lugduni.
1680. *Haus-Kunst- und Wunderbuch*. German edition.
1957. *Natural Magick*. New York: Basic Books. Annotated by Wolfgang Bauer.
Fuchs, Leonart
1543. *New Kreütterbuch*. Basel: Michael Isingrin.
Gart der Gesundheit
12th–13th century (see Schipperges 1990)
Gerard, John
1633. *The Herbal*. London: Norton & Whitakers. Reprint (republished New York: Dover Books, 1975).
Hartlieb, Johannes
1980. *Das Kräuterbuch des Johannes Hartlieb*. Graz: Akademische Druck- u. Verlagsanstalt.
1989a. *Das Buch aller verbotenen Künste*. Edited, translated, and with commentary by Falk Eisermann and Eckhard Graf.

Ahlerstedt: Param (Esoterik des Abendlandes, v 4).

1989b. *Das Buch aller verbotenen Künste*. Edited and translated by Frank Fürbeth. Frankfurt: Insel TB.

Hildegard of Bingen

12th century. *Physica* (see Müller 1982).

Lonicerus, Adamus

1679. *Kreüterbuch*. [Frankfurt]: Matthäus Wagner.

Matthiolus, Pierandrea

1626. *Kreütterbuch*. Frankfurt: Jacob Fischers Erben.

Medicina antiqua

13th century (see Zotter 1980, also Biedermann 1972).

Megenburg, Conrad von

14th century. *Buch der Nature*.

Paracelsus

1989. *Mikrocosmos und Makrocosmos: Occulte Schriften*. Edited by Helmut Werner. Munich: Diederichs.

Porta, Giambattista della

1589. *Magia naturalis* (Original Latin edition). Lugduni.

1680. *Haus-Kunst- und Wunderbuch* (German edition).

1957. *Natural Magick*. New York: Basic Books.

Praetorius, Johannes

1668. *Blocksberg Verrichtung*. Leipzig.

1979. *Hexen-, Zauber- und Spukgeschichten aus dem Blocksberg*. Frankfurt: Insel.

Pseudo-Apuleius

9th century. *Herbarium*. (see Hunger 1935).

Sibyllinische Sammlung

5th century (see Clemens 1985).

Sprenger, Jakob and Heinrich Institoris

1938. *Der Hexenhammer*. Translated and with commentary by J. W. R. Schmidt. Vienna: Amonesta-Verlag.

Stubbes, Phillip.

1583. *The Anatomy of Abuses*. London. (Reprinted 1882, London: New Shakespeare Society.)

Tabernaemontanus, Jacobus Theodorus

1731. *Neu vollkommen Kräuter-Buch* (Bauhin edition). Basel and Offenbach: Johann Ludwig König.

Tacuinum Sanitatis [Garden of Health]

12th century

Terry, Patricia.

1990. *Poems of the Elder Edda*. Philadelphia: University of Pennsylvania.

von Bingen, Hildegard

12th century. *Physica* (see Müller 1982). English-language translations based on *Hildegard of Bingen's Physica*. Translated by Priscilla Throop. Rochester, VT: Healing Arts Press, 1998.

von Megenberg, Conrad

14th century. *Buch der Nature*.

von Nettesheim, Agrippa and Heinrich Cornelius

1982. *Die magischen Werke*. Wiesbaden: Fourier.

Weyer, Johann [= Wyer, Weier]

1575. *Von den Teuffeln/Zaubrern/Schwarzkünstlern/Hexen*. Frankfurt.

New Literature

Abraham, Hartwig and Inge Thinnes

1995. *Hexenkraut und Zaubertrank*. Greifenberg: Urs Freund.

Ahrendt-Schulte, Ingrid

1994. *Weise Frauen—böse Weiber: Die Geschichte der Hexen in der Frühen Neuzeit*. Freiburg: Herder.

Aigremont, Dr.

1987. *Volkserotik und Pflanzenwelt* (two volumes in one edition). Berlin: Express Edition [VWB]. (Reprint, originally published from 1907–1910.)

Aliotta, Giovanni, Danielle Piomelli, and Antonio Pollio

1994. "Le Piante narcotiche e psicotrope in Plinio e Dioscoride" in *Annali dei Musei Civici de Revereto* 9 (1993).

Allegro, John M.

1970. *The Sacred Mushroom and the Cross*. London: Hodder and Stoughton Limited.

Amendt, Günter

2003. *No Drugs, No Future: Drogen im Zeitalter der Globalisierung*. Hamburg: Europaverlag.

Amrein, Josef

1997. "Verpöntes Medikament auf Schweizer Prüfständen." *Die Weltwoche* 15/10.4.97.

Anderson, William

1990. *Green Man: The Archetype of Our Oneness with the Earth*. London and San Francisco: HarperCollins.

Andritzky, Walter

1987. "Die Volksheiler in Peru während der spanisch-kolonialen Inquisition" *Anthropos* 82.

1989. *Schamanismus und rituelles Heilen im Alten Peru*. 2 vols. Berlin: Clemens Zerling.

1989. "Ethnopsychologische Betrachtung des Heilrituals mit Ayahuasca (*Banisteriopsis Caapi*) unter besonderrem Berücksichtigung der Piros (Ostperu)" *Anthropos* 84.

Arends, G.

1935. *Volkstümliche Namen der Arzneimittel, Drogen, Heilkräuter und Chemikalien*. Berlin: Springer.

Asche, Roswitha and Ernst-Detelef Schulze

1996. *Die Ragginer: 200 Jahre Volksmedizin in Südtirol*. Munich: Pfeil.

Asselmann, I.

1883. *Die Entwicklung der altgriechischen Heilkunde*. Berlin: Carl Habel.

Bächtold-Stäubli, Hanns

1987. *Handwörterbuch des deutschen Aberglaubens*. vols 1–9. Berlin: Walter de Gruyter.

Barnett, Bernard

1965. "Witchcraft, Psychopathology and Hallucinations" in *British Journal of Psychiatry* 3.

Barnheim, Friedrich

1962. *Erotik und Hexenwahn*. Stuttgart: Weltspiegel-Verlag.

Bataille, Christophe

1998. *Annam—Absinth*. Frankfurt: Fischer.

Bauereiss, Erwin

1994. *Blauer Eisenhut*. Bad Windsheim: Wurzel-Verlag.

1995 (ed.). *Heimische Pflanzen der Götter: Ein Handbuch für Hexen und Zauberer*. Markt Erlbach: Raymond Martin Verlag.

Baumann, Hellmut

1982. *Die griechische Pflanzenwelt in Mythos, Kunst und Literatur*. Munich: Hirmer.

Bechstein, Ludwig

1986. *Hexengeschichten*. Frankfurt: Insel.

Becker, Gabriele, et al.

1980. *Aus der Zeit der Verzweiflung: Zur Genese und Aktualität des Hexenbildes*. Frankfurt: Suhrkamp.

Beckmann, Dieter and Barbara Beckmann

1990. *Alraune, Beifuß und andere Hexenkräuter*. Frankfurt and New York: Campus.

Behling, Lottlisa

1957. *Die Pflanze in der mittelalterlichen Tafelmalerei*. Weimar: Hermann Böhlaus Nachfolger.

Behr, Hans-Georg

1995. *Von Hanf ist die Rede*. Frankfurt: Zweitausendeins.

Benesch, Kurt

1985. *Magie der Renaissance*. Vienna: Poseidon Press.

Berger, Markus

2003. *Stechapfel und Engelstrompete: Ein halluzinogenes Schwesternpaar*. Solothurn: Nachtschatten Verlag.

Beuchert, Marianne

1995. *Symbolik der Pflanzen*. Frankfurt: Insel Verlag.

Biedermann, Hans

1972. *Medicina Magica*. Graz: Akademische Druck-u. Verlaganstalt.

1974. *Hexen—Auf den Spuren eines Phänomens*. Graz: Verlag für Sammler.

1989. *Dämonen, Geister, dunkle Götter*. Graz: Leopold Stocker.

Birmann-Dähne, Gerhild
1996 *Bärlauch und Judenkirsche*. Heidelberg: Haug.

Binroth-Bank, Christine
1994. *Medea in den Metamorphosen Ovids*. Frankfurt: Peter Lang. (Europäische Hochschulschriften, v. 62).

Birmann-Dähne, Gerhild
1996. *Bärlauch und Judenkirsche*. Heidelberg: Haug.

Blauert, Andreas (ed.)
1990. *Ketzer, Zauberer, Hexen: Die Anfänge der europäischen Hexenverfolgung*. Frankfurt: Suhrkamp.

Böhme, Robert
1970. *Orpheus: Der Sänger und seine Zeit*. Bern and Munich: Francke.

Boland, Maureen and Bridget
1983. *Was die Kräuterhexen sagen: Ein Magisches Gartenbuch*. Munich: Deutscher Taschenbuch Verlag.

Borgeaud, Phillipe
1988. *The Cult of Pan in Ancient Greece*. Chicago and London: University of Chicago Press.

Bossung, Horst
1995. "Die Erfindung des Drogenproblems am Beispiel Hasch" in Ralph Cosack and Roberto Wenzel, eds., *Das Hanftagebuch*. Hamburg: Wendepunkt Verlag.

Botheroyd, Sylvia and Paul F.
1995. *Lexikon der keltischen Mythologie*. Munich: Diederichs.

Bourne, Lois
1995. *The Witch Among Us: The Autobiography of a Witch*. London: Robert Hale.

Boyd, Carolyn E. and J. Philip Dering
1996. "Medicinal and Hallucinogenic Plants Identified in the Sediments and Pictographs of the Lower Pecos, Texas Archaic" in *Antiquity* 70 (268).

Bremness, Lesley
1994. *Kräuter, Gewürze und Heilpflanzen*. Ravensburg: Ravensburger Buchverlag.

Bröckers, Mathias
2002. *Cannabis*. Aarau: AT Verlag/Solothurn: Nachtschatten Verlag.

Brøndegaard, V. J.
1972. "Artemisia in der gynäkologischen Volksmedizin" in *Ethnomedizin* 2 (1.2).

Brosse, Jacques
1990. *Mythologie der Bäume*. Olten and Freiburg: Walter-Verlag.
1992. *Magie der Pflanzen*. Olten: Walter-Verlag.

Bruno, Giordano
1995. *Giordano Bruno*, edited, collected, translated, and with commentary by Elisabeth von Samsonow. Munich: Diederichs.

Budge, E. A. Wallis
1996. *The Divine Origin of the Craft of the Herbalist*. New York: Dover. (Originally published in London, 1928).

Burkert, Walter
1962. "Goês—Zum griechischen 'Schamanismus'" in *Rheinisches Museum für Philologiee* 105: 36–55.
1990. *Antike Mysterien*. Munich: Beck.
1997. *Homo Necans: Interpretationen altgriechischer Opferriten und Mythen*. (2nd ed.). Berlin: de Gruyter.

Camilla, Gilberto
1995. "Le erbe del diavolo 1: Aspetti antropologici" in *Altrove* 2.

Campbell, Joseph
1969. *The Flight of the Wild Gander*. Chicago: Regnery Gateway.

Camporesi, Piero
1990. *Das Brot der Träume: Hunger und Halluzinationen im vorindustriellen Europa*. Frankfurt and New York: Campus.
1991 *Geheimnisse der Venus: Aphrodisiaka vergangener Zeiten*. Frankfurt and New York: Campus.

Carl, Helmut
1995. *Die deutschen Pflanzen- und Tiernamen: Deutung und sprachliche Ordnung*. Wiesbaden: Meyer Verlag.

Caro Baroja, Julio
1967. *Die Hexen und ihre Welt*. Stuttgart: Klett. (Originally published in Madrid, 1961.)

Castiglioni, Arturo
1982. "Der Teufel und die Magie" and "In Luzifers Krallen" in *Hexen und Hexenmeister*. Gütersloh: Moewig.

Christensen, Bodil and Samuel Martí
1979 *Witchcraft and Pre-Columbian Paper*. Mexico: Ediciones Euroamericanas.

Chetan, Anand and Diana Brueeuton
1994. *The Sacred Yew*. London: Penguin Arkana.

Christensen, Bodil and Samuel Martí
1979. *Witchcraft and Pre-Columbian Paper*. Mexico: Ediciones Euroamericanas.

Cipolletti, Maria Susana
1989. *Langsamer Abschied*. Frankfurt: Museum für Völkerkunde.

Clark, R. J.
1968. "A Note on Medea's Plant and the Mandrake" in *Folklore* 79.

Clarkson, Rosetta E.
1992. *Magic Gardens*. New York: Collier Books. (Originally published New York, 1939.)

Clemens, Richard
1985 *Die sibyllinischen Orakel*. Wiesbaden: Fourier.

Clifton, Chas. S. (ed.)
1994. *Witchcraft Today: Shamanism and Witchcraft*, vol. 3. St. Paul: Llewellyn.

Clemens, Richard
1985 *Die sibyllinischen Orakel*. Wiesbaden: Fourier.

Conrad, Barnaby, III
1988. *Absinthe: History in a Bottle*. San Francisco: Chronicle Books.

Daniélou, Alain
1992. *Gods of Love and Ecstasy: The Traditions of Shiva and Dionysus*. Rochester, Vt.: Inner Traditions International.

David
1997. "Hexensalben" in *grow!—Marijuana Magazine* 6/97.

David-Neel, Alexandra
1984. *Heilige und Hexer: Glaube und Aberglaube im Lande des Lamaismus*. Wiesbaden: F. A. Brockhaus.

Daxelmüller, Christoph
1996. *Aberglaube, Hexenzauber, Höllenängste*. Munich: Deutscher Taschenbuch Verlag.

de Vries, Herman
1986. "Über die sogenannten Hexensalben" in *Salix* 2 (2).
1989. *Natural Relations*. Nürnberg: Verlag für moderne Kunst.
1991. "Über die sogenannten Hexensalben" in *Integration* 1. Revised edition of de Vries, 1986.
1993. "Heilige bäume, bilsenkraut und bildzeitung" in C. Rätsch, ed., *Naturverehrung und Heilkunst*. Südergellersen: Verlag Bruno Martin.

Delany, Daniel
1994 *Der Hexentrank*. Munich: Ehrenwirth.

DeForest, Mary Margolies
1994. *Apollonius'* Argonautica: *A Callimachean Epic*. Leiden: Brill.

Delany, Daniel
1994. *Der Hexentrank*. Munich: Ehrenwirth.

Diederichs, Ulf
1995. *Who's Who im Märchen*. Munich: Deutscher Taschenbuch Verlag.

Diepgen, Paul
1958. "Über den Einfluß der autoritativen Theologie auf die Medizin des Mittelalters" in *Abhandlungen der Geistes- und Sozialwissenschaftlichen Klasse*, 1958, no. 1, vol. 1. Mainz: Akademie der Wissenschaften und Literatur.

Dierbach, Johann Heinrich
 1833. *Flora Mythologica oder Pflanzenkunde in Bezug auf Mythologie und Symbolik der Griechen und Römer*. Schaan/Liechtenstein: Sändig. Reprint 1981.
Dinzelbacher, Peter
 1995. *Heilige oder Hexen?* Zurich: Artemis & Winkler.
Döbler, Hannsferdinand
 1979. *Hexenwahn: Die Geschichte einer Verfolgung*. Bergisch-Gladbach: Bastei-Lübbe.
Donner-Grau, Florinda
 1997. *Die Lehren der Hexe: Eine Frau auf den Spuren schamanischer Heiler*. Waldfeucht: Hans-Nietsch-Verlag.
Dreikandt, Ulrich K. (ed.)
 1975. *Schwarze Messen: Dichtungen und Dokumente*. Munich: Deutscher Taschenbuch Verlag.
Dross, Annemarie
 1978. *Die erste Walpurgisnacht: Hexenverfolgung in Deutschland*. Reinbek: Rowohlt.
Drury, Nevill
 1989. *Der Schamane und der Magier: Reisen zwischen Welten*. Basel: Sphinx.
Duerr, Hans-Peter
 1976. "Können Hexen fliegen?" in *Unter dem Pflaster liegt der Strand* v. 3.
 1978. *Traumzeit*. Frankfurt: Syndikat.
 1987 (ed.). *Die Wilde Seele: Zur Ethnopsychoanalyse von Georges Devereux*. Frankfurt: Suhrkamp.
Ehrenreich, Barbara and Deidrke English
 1981. *Hexen, Hebammen und Krankenschwestern*. Munich: Frauenoffensive.
Eliade, Mircea
 1982. *Von Zalmoxis zu Dschingis-Khan*. Cologne: Hohenheim.
 1992. *Schamanen, Götter und Mysterien: Die Welt der alten Griechen*. Freiburg: Herder.
 1993. *Geschichte der religiösen Ideen I*. Freiburg: Herder.
Emboden, William A.
 1974. *Bizarre Plants*. New York: Macmillan.
Engel, Fritz-Martin
 1978. *Zauberpflanzen—Pflanzenzauber*. Hannover: Landbuch-Verlag.
 1982. *Die Giftküche der Natur*. Hannover: Landbuch-Verlag.
Evans, Arthur
 1978. *Witchcraft and the Gay Counterculture*. Boston: Fag Rag Books.
 1988. *The God of Ecstasy: Sex-Roles and the Madness of Dionysos*. New York: St. Martin's Press.
Evans-Pritchard, E. E.
 1988. *Hexerei, Orakel und Magie bei den Zande*. Frankfurt: Suhrkamp.
Evans-Wentz, W. Y.
 1994. *The Fairy Faith in Celtic Countries*. New York: Library of Mystic Arts/Citadel Press.
Fabich, Fred
 1991. *Bauernmedizin*. Rosenheim: Rosenheimer.
Fankhauser, Manfred
 2002. *Haschisch als Medikament: Zur Bedeutung von Cannabis sativa in der westlichen Medizin*. Liebefeld: SGGP/SSHP/Schweiz. Apothekerverein.
Favret-Saada, Jeanne
 1979. *Die Wörter, der Zauber, der Tod: Der Hexenglaube im Hainland von Westfrankreich*. Frankfurt: Suhrkamp.
Ferkel, Siegbert
 1954. " 'Hexensalben' und ihre Wirkung" in *Kosmos* 50.
Festi, Francesco
 1995. "Le erbe del diavolo. 2: Botanica, chimica e farmacologia" in *Altrove* 2.
Findeisen, Hans
 1956. *Das Tier als Gott, Dämon und Ahne*. Stuttgart: Kosmos.

Fink, Hans
 1983. *Verzaubertes Land: Volkskult und Ahnenbrauch in Südtirol*. Innsbruck, Vienna: Tyrolia.
Fischer, L.
 1917. "Ein 'Hexenrauch': Eine volkskundlich-liturgie-geschichtliche studie" in *Bayerische Hefte für Volkskunde* 4.
Fischer-Homberger, Esther
 1984. *Krankheit Frau: Zur Geschichte der Einbildungen*. Darmstadt: Luchterhand.
Font Quer, Pío
 2002. *Plantas medicinales: El Dioscórides renovado* (4th edition). Barcelona: Ediciones Pemínsula.
Foster, Steven and James A. Duke
 1990. *A Field Guide to Medicinal Plants*. Boston: Houghton Mifflin.
Fowden, Garth
 1993. *The Egyptian Hermes: A Historical Approach to the Late Pagan Mind*. Princeton: Princeton University Press.
Fraenger, Wilhelm
 1975. *Hieronymus Bosch*. Dresden: Verlag für Kunst.
 1985. *Von Bosch bis Beckmann: Ausgewählte Schriften*. Cologne: DuMont.
Frazer, James Georg
 1991. *Der Goldene Zweig*. Reinbek bei Hamburg: Rowohlt.
Frerichs, G., G. Arends, and H. Zörnig (eds.)
 1938. *Hagers Handbuch der pharmazeutischen Praxis* (3 vols.) Berlin: J. Springer.
Früh, Sigrid
 1986 (ed.). *Märchen von Hexen und weisen Frauen*. Frankfurt: Fischer.
 2000. *Rauhnächte: Märchen, Brauchtum, Aberglaube* (6th edition). Waiblingen: Verlag Stendel. First edition 1998.
Führer, Hermann
 1925. "Solanazeen als Berauschungsmittel: eine historisch-ethnologische Studie" in *Archiv für experimentelle Pathologie und Pharmakologie* 111.
 1943. *Medizinische Toxikologie*. Leipzig: Georg Thieme.
Gallwitz, Esther
 1992. *Kleiner Kräutergarten: Kräuter und Blumen bei den Alten Meistern im Städel*. Frankfurt: Insel.
Gardner, Gerald B.
 1965. *Ursprung und Wirklichkeit der Hexen*. Weilheim: O. W. Barth.
Gartz, Jochen (ed.)
 1999. *Halluzinogene in historischen Schriften: Eine Anthologie von 1913–1968*. Solothurn: Nachtschatten Verlag.
Gawlik, Willibald
 1994. *Götter, Zauber und Arznei*. Schäflarn: Barthel & Barthel.
Gélis, Jacques
 1989. *Die Geburt*. Munich: Diederichs.
Gessmann, Gustav W.
 1922. *Die Pflanze im Zauberglauben und in der spagyrischen (okkulten) Heilkunst. Katechismus der Zauberbotanik mit einem Anhang über Pflanzensymbolik*. Berlin: Siegismund.
 n.d. *Die Pflanze im Zauberglauben*. Den Haag: J. J. Couvreur [reprint].
Giebel, Marion
 1990. *Das Geheimnis der Mysterien: Antike Kulte in Griechenland, Rom, und Ägypten*. Zurich and Munich: Artemis.
Ginzburg, Carlo
 1980. *Die Benandanti: Feldkulte und Hexenwesen im 16. und 17. Jahrhundert*. Frankfurt: Syndikat.
 1990. *Hexensabbat: Entzifferung einer nächtlichen Geschichte*. Berlin: Wagenbach.
Görres, Josef von
 1948 *Das nachtländische Reich*. Villach: Mortiz Stadler.
Golowin, Sergius
 1970. *Hexer und Henker im Galgenfeld*. Bern: Benteli.
 1971. "Psychedelische Volkskunde" in *Antaios* 12.
 1973. *Die Magie der verbotenen Märchen*. Giftkendorf: Merlin.

1977. *Hexen, Hippies, Rosenkreuzer: 500 Jahre magische Morgenlandfahrt.* Hamburg: Merlin.

1982a. *Die weisen Frauen: Die Hexe und ihre Heilwissen.* Basel: Sphinx.

1982b (ed.). *Kult und Brauch der Kräuterpfeife in Europa.* Allmendingen: Verlag der Melusine.

1989. *Das Reich der Schamanen.* Munich: Goldmann.

1991. "Psycheadelische Volkskunde" in W. Bauer et al., eds., *Der Fliegenpilz.* Cologne: Wienand Verlag.

2003 (ed.). *Von Elfenpfeifen und Hexenbier: Magie um unsere Genussmittel.* Solothurn: Nachtschatten Verlag.

Golther, Wolfgang
1985. *Handbuch der germanischen Mythologie.* Stuttgart: Magnus.

Graf, Fritz
1996. *Gottesnähe und Schadenzauber: Die Magie in der griechisch-römischen Antike.* Munich: Beck.

Graupner, Heinz
1966. *Dämon Rausch: Drogen, Gifte, Alkohol.* Hamburg: Hapus-Verlag.

Grewenig, Meinrad Maria (ed.)
1996. *Mysterium Wein: Die Götter, der Wein und die Kunst.* Ostfildern-Ruit: Verlag Gerd Hatje.

Griggs, Barbara
1982. *Green Pharmacy.* New York: Viking Press.

Grimm, Jacob
1877. *Deutsche Mythologie,* vols. I–III. Reprinted 1981. Frankfurt: Ullstein.

Grotenhermen, Franjo and Renate Huppertz
1997. *Hanf als Medizin: Wiederentdeckung einer Heilpflanze.* Heidelberg: Haug.

Grünther, Ralph-Achim
1992. "Hexensalbe—Geschichte und Pharmakcologie" in *Jahrbuch des ECBS,* 1992.

Guyonvarc'h, Christian –J. and Françoise Le Roux
1996. *Die Druiden: Mythos, Magie und Wirklichkeit der Kelten.* Engerda: Arun-Verlag.

Haag, Stefan
2002. *Von Druidentrank und Hexenkraut: Heil- und Zauberpflanzen aus aller Welt.* Stuttgart: Kosmos.

Haage, Bernhard
1984. "Dichter, Drogen und Hexen im Hoch- und Spätmittel-alter" in *Würzburger medizinhistorische Mitteilungen* 4.

Haas, Ursula
1991. *Freispruch für Medea* (Roman). Frankfurt, Berlin: Ullstein.

Habinger-Tuczay, Christa
1992. *Magie und Magier im Mittelalter.* Munich: Diederichs.

Haerkötter Gerd and Marlene Haerkötter
1986. *Hexenfurz und Teufelsdreck.* Frankfurt: Eichborn.
1991. *Wuterich + Hexenmilch: Giftpflanzen.* Frankfurt: Eichborn.

Haerkötter Gerd and Thomas Lasinski
1989. *Das Geheimnis der Pimpernuß: Liebeskräuter aus Gottes Garten.* Frankfurt: Eichborn.

Haining, Peter
1977. *Hexen: Wahn und Wirklichkeit in Mittelalter und Gegenwart.* Oldenburg, Hamburg: Stalling.

Hajicek-Dobberstein, Scott
1995. "Soma Siddhas and Alchemical Enlightenment: Psychedelic Mushrooms in Buddhist Tradition" in *Journal of Ethnopharmacology* 48.

Halbey, Marianne
1987. *66 Hexen: Kult und Verdammung.* Dortmund: Harenberg.

Halifax, Joan
1981. *Die andere Wirklichkeit der Schamanen.* Freiburg: O. W. Barth im Scherz Verlag.

Hall, Angus and Jeremy Kingston
1979. *Hexerei und Schwarze Kunst.* Glarus: Christoph Columbus Verlag.

Hansemann, D. von
1905 *Der Aberglaube in der Medizin und seine Gefar für Gesundheit und Leben.* Leipzig: B. G. Teubner.

Hansen, Harold A.
1981. *Der Hexengarten.* Munich: Trikont-dianus.

Harner, Michael
1973. "The Role of the Hallucinogenic Plants in European Witchcraft" in Michael Harner, ed., *Hallucinogens and Shamanism.* London: University of Oxford Press.

Härting, Ursula Alice
1983. *Studien zur Kabinettmalerei des Frans Francken II (1581–1642): Ein repräsntativer Werkkatalog.* Hildesheim, Zürich, New York: Gerog Olms.

Hartlaub, Gustav E.
1947. *Das Paradiesgärtlein von einem oberrheinischer Meister um 1410.* Berlin: Gebr. Mann.

Hartlaub, Gustav F.
1961. *Hans Baldung Grien—Hexenbilder.* Stuttgart: Reclam.

Hartzell, Hal
1991. *The Yew Tree: A Thousand Whispers.* Eugene, Oreg.: Hulogosi Communications, Inc.

Hasenfratz, Hans-Peter
1992. *Die religiöse Welt der Germanen.* Freiburg: Herder.

Hauschild, Thomas
1981. "Hexen und Drogen" in *Rausch und Realität,* vol. 1.

Hauschild, Thomas, Heidi Staschen, and Regina Troschke
1979. *Hexen: Katalog zur Ausstellung.* Hamburg: Hochschule für bildende Künste.

Hecht, Ingeborg
1977. *In tausend Teufels Namen: Hexenwahn am Oberrhein.* Freiburg: Rombach.

Heiler, Friedrich
1962. *Die Religionen der Menschheit.* Stuttgart: Reclam.

Heinze, Theodor (ed.)
1997. *P. Ovidius Naso—Der XXI Heroidenbrief: Medea an Jason. Mit einer Beilage: Die Fragmente der Tragödoie Medea.* Leiden: Brill.

Heiser, Charles B.
1987. *The Fascinating World of the Nightshades.* New York: Dover.

Heller, Gerhard
1993. "Die Tiergeister als Heilgehilfen nepalischer Schamanen" in Christian Rätsch, ed., *Naturverehrung und Heilkunst.* Südergellersen: Bruno Martin.

Hesse, Hermann (ed.)
1986. *Spuk- und Hexengeschichten.* Frankfurt: Insel.

Heyne, Isolde
1994. *Hexenfeuer.* Ravensburg: Ravensburger.

Höfler, Max
1990 *Volksmedizinische Botanik der Germanen.* Berlin: VWB. (Reprint from 1908.)

Hoffmann, E. T. A.
1982. *Die Elixiere des Teufels.* Stuttgart: Reclam.

Höfler, Max
1990. *Volksmedizinische Botanik der Germanen.* Berlin: VWB. Originally published 1908.

Honegger, Claudia (ed.)
1978. *Die Hexen der Neuzeit: Studien zur Sozialgeschichte eines kultuterllen Deutungsmusters.* Frankfurt: Suhrkamp.

Horst, Georg Conrad
1979. *Zauber-Bibliothek oder von Zauberei, Theurgie und Mantik, Zauberern, Hexen und Hexenprocessen, Dämonen, Gespenstern und Geistererscheinungen* (7 vols). Freiburg: Aaurum. Originally published 1821–1826.

Howard, Michael
1994. "Flying Witches: The *Ungueeunti Sabbati* in Traditional Witchcraft" in Chas. S. Clifton, ed,. *Witchcraft and Shamanism (Witchcraft Today, Book III).* St. Paul: Llewellyn.

Hug, Ernst
1993. *Wolfzahn, Bilsenkraut & Dachsschmalz: Rückblick in ein Schwarzwalddorf*. St. Märgen: Selbstverlag Ernst Hug.
Hughes, Pennethorne
1965. *Witchcraft*. Harmonsworth: Penguin.
Hugonot, J.-C.
1992. "Ägyptische Gärten" in *Der Garten von der Antike bis zum Mittelalter*, M. Carroll-Spillecke (ed.). Mainz: Phillip von Zabern.
Hunger, F. W. T.
1935. *The Herbal of Pseudo-Apulei*. (From the ninth-century manuscript in the Abbey of Monte Cassino [Codex casinensis 97] together with the first printed edition of Joh. Phil. de Lignmaine, [first published in Rome, 1481], both in facsimile). Leyden: Brill.
Hunger, Herbert
1974. *Lexicon der griechischen und römischen Mythologie*. Reinbek: Rowohlt.
Huxley, Francis
1974. *The Way of the Sacred*. New York: Dell.
Hyslop, Jon and Paul Ratcliffe
1989. *A Folk Herbal*. Oxford: Radiation Publications.
Iatridis, Yanoukos
1986. *Blumen von Kreta*. Athen: Selbstverlag.
Illmaier, Thomas
1997. *Rauschzeit*. Berlin: VWB.
Jezler, Peter
1994. *Himmel, Hölle, Fegefeuer: Das Jenseits im Mittelalter*. Munich: Fink.
Jütte, Robert
1993 (ed.). *Geschichte der Abtreibung*. Munich: C. H. Beck.
1996. *Geschichte der Alternativen Medizin*. Munich: C. H. Beck.
Kalweit, Holger
1987. *Urheiler, Medizinleute und Schamanen*. Munich: Kösel.
Kapur, Sohaila
1983. *Witchcraft in Western India*. Bombay: Orient Longman.
Kasas, Savas and Reinhard Struckmann
1990. *Wichtige Heilstätten der Antike: Epidauros und Korinth—Als die Medizin noch göttlich war*. Athen: Verlag Kasas.
Kerényi, Karl
1966. *Die Mythologie der Griechen*. Munich: Deutscher Taschenbuch Verlag.
1976. *Dionysos: Archetypal Image of Indestructible Life*. London: Routledge & Kegan Paul.
1991. *Eleusis*. Princeton: Princeton University Press.
1996. *Hermes Guide of the Souls* (revised edition). Woodstock, Conn.: Spring Publications.
Kieckhefer, Richard
1995. *Magie im Mittelalter*. Munich: Deutscher Taschenbuch Verlag.
Kiesewetter, Carl
1895. *Geschichte des neueren Okkultismus*, (2 vols.). Leipzig: Wilhelm Friedrich.
1902. *Die Geheimwissenschaften* (2nd ed.). Leipzig: Wilhelm Friedrich.
1982. "Aus der Hexenbotanik" in Sergius Golowin, ed., *Kult und Brauch der Kräuterpfeife in Europa*. Allmendingen: Verlag der Melusine.
Kindscher, Kelly
1992. *Medical Wild Plants of the Prairie*. Lawrence, Kans.: University of Kansas Press.
King, Francis X.
1988. *Hexen und Dämonen*. Hamburg: Interbook.
Kingston, Jeremy
1987. *Hexenzauber—Hexenwerk*. Frankfurt: Ullstein.
Klaniczay, Gábor
1991. *Heilige, Hexen, Vampire: Vom Nutzen des Übernatürlichen*. Berlin: Wagenbach.

Klapper, Joseph
1936. *Der schlesische Berggeist Rübezahl*. Series: Schlesienbändchen, published by the Landstelle für Heimatpflege in Niederschlesien, Breslau: Flemmings Verlag.
1960. *Der Eerfurter Kartäuser Johannes Hagen* in *Reformtheologe des 15. Jahrhunderts*, 1. (Teil: Leben und Werk). 9 vols. Erfurt: Erfurter Theologische Studien.
Kluckhorn, Clyde
1967. *Navaho Witchcraft*. Boston: Beacon Press.
Kluge, Heidelore
1988. *Zaubertränke und Hexenküche: Ddie geheimen Rezepte und Tinkturen der weisen Frauen*. Munich: Heyne.
Knab, Timothy J.
1995. *A War of Witches: A Journey into the Underworld of the Contemporary Aztecs*. San Francisco: HarperSanFrancisco.
1997. *Der Weg der Curanderos: Eine Reise in die Geisteswelt Mexikos*. Munich: Goldmann
Kokrotsch, Karl and Ronald Rippchen
1997. *Die Deutsche Kakerlake: Ein Kakerlake Kompendium*. Löhrbach: Der Grüne Zweig.
Körner, Harald Hans
1994. *Beck'sche Kurz-Kommentare: Betäubungsmittelgesetz—Arzeneimittelgesetz* (4th revised edition). Munich: Beck.
Kraemer, Olaf
1997. *Luzifers Lichtgarten: Expiditionen ins Reich der Halluzinogene*. Munich: Sphinx.
Kraus, Theodor
1960. *Hekate: Studien zu Wesen und Bild der Göttin in Kleinasien und Griechenland*. Heidelberg: Carl Wink Verlag (Heidelberger kunstgeschichtliche Abbhandlungen).
Krauss, F. S.
1906. "Liebeszauber der Völker: eine Umfrage von William Godelück" in *Anthropophyteia* 3.
Kräutermann, Valentino
1725. *Der Curieuse und vernünfftige Zauber-Arzt*. Frankfurt and Leipzig: Niedt.
Kreuter, Marie-Luise
1982. *Wunderkräfte der Natur: Von Alraunen, Ginseng und anderen Wunderwurzeln*. Munich: Heyne.
Kronfeld, Moritz
1981. *Donnerwurz und Mäuseaugen* (reprint). Berlin: Zerling.
Krug, Antje
1993. *Heilkunst und Heilkult: Medizin in der Antike*. Munich: C. H. Beck.
Kuhlen, Franz-Joseph
1980. "Hexenwesen—Hexendrogen" in *Pharmaziegeschichtliche Rundschau* 9.
1983. *Zur Geschichte der Schmerz-, Schlaf- und Betäubungsmittel in Mittelalter und früher Neuzeit*. Stuttgart: Deutscher Apotheker Verlag.
1984. "Von Hexen und Drogenträumen" in *Deutsche Apotheker Zeitung* 124.
Kühn, Wolfgang
1948. "Grünewalds Isenheimer Altar als Darstellung mittelalterlicher Heilkräuter" in *Kosmos* 44.
Künkel, Inca Petra
1988. *Verzeih mir, wenn ich fliehe: Reden an die Göttin Hekate*. Bonn: Verlag Gisela Meussling.
Kuhlen, Franz-Joseph
1980 "Hexenwesen – Hexendrogen" in *Pharmaziegeschichtliche Rundschau* 9.
Kunze, Michael
1982. *Straße ins Feuer: Vom Leben und Sterben in der Zeit des Hexenwwahns*. Munich: Kindler.
La Vey, Anton Szandor
1998. *Satan Speaks!* Venice, Calif.: Feral House.

Labouvie, Eva
  1991. *Zauberei und Hexenwerk: Ländlicher Hexenglaube in der frühen Neuzeit*. Frankfurt: Fischer.
Langlotz, Ernst
  1954. *Aphrodite in den Gärten*. Heidelberg: Carl Winter.
Lehmann, Arthur C. and James I. Myers (eds.)
  1989. *Magic, Witchcraft, and Religion: An Anthropological Study of the Supernatural* (2nd edition). Mountain View, Calif.: Mayfield.
Leibrock-Plehn, Larissa
  1992. *Hexenkräuter oder Arznei: Die Abtreibungsmittel im 16. und 17. Jahrhundert*. Stuttgart: WVG.
  1993. "Frühe Neuzeit: Hebammen, Kräutermedizin und weltliche Justiz" in R. Jütte, ed., *Geschichte der Abtreibung*. Munich: Beck.
Leland, Charles G.
  1979. *Aradia—Die Lehre der Hexen*. Munich: Trikont.
Lenz, Harald Othmar
  1966. *Botanik der Griechen und Römer*. Vaduz: Sändig. (Reprint. Originally published 1859.)
Leone, Laura
  1995. "*Papaver somniferum*: La pianta sacra ai Ddauni delle stele" in *Bollettino Centro Camuno Studi Preistorici* 28.
Lessa, William and Evon Z. Vogt
  1965. *Reader in Comparative Religion*. New York: Harper & Row.
Leubuscher, Rud.
  1850. *Ueber die Wehrwölfe und Thierverwandlungen im Mittelalter*. Berlin: G. Reimer.
Levack, Brian P.
  1995. *Hexenjagden: Die Geschichte der Hexenverfolgungen in Europa*. Munich: C. H. Beck.
Lewis, Ioan M.
  1987. "Der Kochkessel der Kannibalen" in H. P. Duerr, ed., *Die Wilde Seele: Zur Ethnopsychoanalyse von Georges Devereaux*. Frankfurt: Suhrkamp.
  1989. *Schamanen, Hexer, Kannibalen: Die Realität des Religiösen*. Frankfurt: Athenäum.
Linzenich, Peter
  1983. *Substantia humana: Die Quelle der Wirklichkeit*. Frankfurt: R. G. Fischer.
Loux, Françoise
  1980. *Das Kind und sein Körper in der Volksmedizin*. Stuttgart: Klett-Cotta.
Lessa, William and Evon Z. Vogt
  1965. *Reader in Comparative Religion*. New York: Harper & Row.
Lucie-Smith, Edward
  1979. *Johanna von Orleans*. Bergisch-Gladbach: Bastei-Lübbe.
Luck, Georg
  1962. *Hexen und Zauberei in der römischen Dichtung*. Zurich: Artemis.
  1990. *Magie und andere Geheimlehren in der Antike*. Stuttgart: Kröner.
Ludwig, Otto
  1982. *Im Thüringer Kräutergarten: Von Heilkräutern, Hexen und Buckelapothekern*. Gütersloh: Prisma Verlag.
Lussi, Kurt
  n.d. *Merkwürdiges aus Buholz: Eine Spurensuche*. Willisau: Buchverlag Willisauer Bote.
  1992. *Himmel und Hölle*. Willisau: Buchverlag Willisauer Bote.
  1996. "Verbotene Lust: Nnächtliche Tänze und blühende Hanffelder im Luzerner Hexenwesen" in *Jahrbuch für Ethnomedizin und Bewußtseinsforschung* 4 (1995).
  1998. "Innerschweizer Liebestränke: Eine Sammlung 'vergessener' Rezepte" in *Jahrbuch für Ethnomedizin und Bewußtseinsforschung* 5 (1996).
  2002. *Im Reich der Geister und tanzenden Hexen: Jenseitsvorstellungen, Dämonen und Zauberglaube*. Aarau: AT Verlag.

Maass, Ernst
  1974. *Orpheus*. Munich: C. H. Beck. (New edition Aalen: Scientia Verlag, 1974.)
Madejsky, Margret
  1995. "Von Liebestränken, gallsüchtigen Weibern und Sonnenbräuten" in *Kraut & Rüben* 10/95.
  1997a. "Hexenpflanzen—oder: Über die Zauberkünste der weisen Frauen" in *Naturheilpraxis* 50 (10).
  1997b. "Schlangen in Mythos und Heilkunst" in *Naturheilpraxis* 50 (10).
Madejsky, Margret and Olaf Rippe
  1997. *Heilmittel der Sonne*. Munich: Verlag Peter Erd.
Magister Botanicus
  1995. *Magisches Kreutherkcompendium* (2nd ed.). Speyer: Die Sanduhr.
Mann, John
  1994. *Murder, Magic and Medicine*. Oxford, New York, and Tokyo: Oxford University Press.
Marwick, Max (ed.)
  1975. *Witchcraft & Sorcery*. Harmmondsworth: Penguin.
Marzell, Heinrich
  1922. *Die heimische Pflanzenwelt im Volksbrauch und Volksglauben*. Leipzig: Quelle and Meyer.
  1926. *Alte Heilkräuter*. Jena: Eugen Diederichs.
  1927. "Alraun" in *Handwörterbuch des Deutschen Aberglaubens*, vol. 1. Berlin: de Gruyter.
  1935. *Volksbotanik: Die Pflanze im Deutschen Brauchtum*. Berlin: Verlag Enckehaus.
  1943–1977. *Wörterbuch der deutschen Pflanzennamen*. Leipzig: S. Hirzel-Verlagsbuchhandlung.
  1964. *Zauberpflanzen—Hexentränke*. Stuttgart: Kosmos.
Meinhold, W. (ed.)
  n.d. *Maria Schweidler, die Bernsteinhexe*. Berlin: Weltgeist-Bücher.
Mercatante, Anthony
  1980. *Der magische Garten*. Zurich: Schweizer Verlagshaus.
Merchant, Carolyn
  1987. *Der Tod der Natur*. Munich: C. H. Beck.
Merrifield, Ralph
  1987. *The Archaeology of Ritual and Magic*. London: B. T. Batsford.
Mettke, Heinz (ed.)
  1979. *Älteste Deutsche Dichtung und Prosa*. Leipzig: Reclam.
Metzner, Ralph
  1993. "Die schwarze Göttin, der grüne Gott und der wilde Mensch" in C. Rätsch, ed., *Naturverehrung und Heilkunst*. Südergellersen: Bruno Martin.
  1994. *Der Brunnen der Erinnerung*. Braunschweig: Aurum.
Meyer, Carl
  1884. *Der Aberglaube des Mittelalters und der nächstfolgenden Jahrhunderte*. Stuttgart: Magnus (reprint).
Meyer, Elard Hugo
  1903. *Mythologie der Germanen*. Strassburg. New edition by Phaidon Verlag, Essen.
Meyer, Marvin and Paul Mirecki (ed.)
  1995. *Ancient Magic and Ritual Power*. Leiden: Brill.
Michelet, Jules
  1952 and 1956. *La Sorcière* (original edition, with annotations and text alteration by Lucien Refort), vols. 1 and 2. Paris: Librairie Marcel Didier.
  1977. *Die Hexe*. Berlin: Verlag Jacobsohn. Originally published 1863. (Reprint of the 1963 original.)
Millones, Luis
  1996. "Love Spells: Supernatural Powers and Love Relationships in the Peruvian Andes" in *Perú Mágico*.
Mitrovic, Alexander
  1907. "Mein Besuch bei einer Zauberfrau in Norddalmatien" in *Anthropophyteia* 4.
Mrisch, Wilhelm
  1978. "Erfahrungen mit Hexen und Hexensalben" in *Unter dem Pflaster liegt der Strand* 5.

Mühlmann, Wilhelm E.
1984. *Die Metamorphose der Frau: Weiblicher Schamanismus und Dichtung*. Berlin: Dietrich Reimer.
Müller, Irmgard
1982. *Die pflanzlichen Heilmittel bei Hildegard von Bingen*. Salzburg: Otto Müller.
Müller-Ebeling, Claudia
1987. "Die Alraune in der Bibelle" in Alfred Schlosser, *Die Sage vom Galgenmännlein im Volksglauben und in der Literatur*. Berlin: VWB, 1987. Originally published 1912.
n.d. "Die Alraune in der Bibelle" in Roland Ranke Rippchen, *Das Böse Bibel Buch*. Löhrbach: Werner Pieper's Medienexperimente.
1991. "Wolf und Bilsenkraut, Himmel und Hölle: Ein Beitrag zur Dämonisierung der Natur" in Susanne G. Seiler, ed., *Gaia—Das Erwachen der Göttin*. Braunschweig: Aurum.
1993. "Die Dämonisierung der Natur" in C. Rätsch, ed., *Natur-verehrung und Heilkunst*. Südergellersen: Bruno Martin.
1997. *Die "Versuchung des heiligen Antonius" als "Mikrobenepos." Eine motivgeschichtliche Studie zu den drei Lithographiefolgen Odilon Redons zu Gustave Flauberts Roman*. Berlin: VWB.
Müller-Ebeling, Claudia and Christian Rätsch
1986. *Isoldens Liebestrank*. Munich: Kindler.
Müller-Ebeling, Claudia, Christian Rätsch, and Surendra Bahadur Shahi
2000. *Schamanismus und Tantra in Nepal*. Aarau: AT Verlag.
Multhaupt, Tamara
1990. *Hexerei und Antihexerei in Afrika*. Munich: Trickster.
Murray, Margaret A.
1952. *The God of the Witches*. New York: Oxford University Press/London: Faber and Faber.
Naegele, Verena
1997. "Hexen—Kampf gegen das Naturprinzip" in *Natürlich* 17 (2).
Nauwald, Nana
2002. *Bärenkraft und Jaguarmedizin: Die bewusstseinsöffenenden Techniken der Schamanen*. Aarau: AT Verlag.
Needham, A. David
1986. *Masks, Transformation, and the Paradox*. Berkeley: University of California Press.
Nepali, Gopal Singh
1988. *The Newars*. Kathmandu: Madhab Lal Maharjan Himalayan Booksellers.
Ochsner, Patricia
1997. *Über Hexenkult, Flugsalben & Hexenkräuter*. Schönbühl: Mimeograph.
Opitz, Claudia (ed.)
1995. *Der Hexenstreit: Frauen in der frühneuzeitlichen Hexenverfolgung*. Freiburg: Herder.
Ott, Jonathan
1996. *Pharmacotheon*. Kennewick, Wash.: Natural Products.
Ott-Koptschalijski, Constance and Wolfgang Behringer (eds.)
1990. *Märchen und Mythen vom Fliegen*. Frankfurt: Fischer.
Pahlow, Mannfried
1993. *Das große Buch der Heilpflanzen*. Munich: Gräfe and Unzer.
Paris, Ginette
1991. *Pagan Grace: Dionysos, Hermes, and Goddess Memory in Daily Life*. Dallas: Spring Press.
Pendell, Dale
1995. *Pharmako/Poeia: Plant Powers, Poisons, and Herbcraft*. San Francisco: Mercury House.
Perez de Barradas, José
1957. *Plantas magicas americanas*. Madrid: Inst. Bernardino de Sahagún.
Perger, K. Ritter von
1864. *Deutsche Pflanzensagen*. Stuttgart and Oehringen: Schaber.
Petermann, Gerhard
1990. "Der Olymp: Sitz der Götter—Thron der Freiheit" in Karl Gratzl, ed., *Die heiligsten Berge der Welt*. Graz: Verlag für Sammler.

Peuckert, Will-Erich
1944. *Theophrastus Paracelsus*. Stuttgart, Berlin: Kohlhammer.
1951. *Geheimkulte*. Heidelberg: Carl Pfeffer Verlag. (Reprint by Hildesheim: Olms Verlag, 1988.)
1957. "Göttingen und die magische Hausväterliteratur" in *Zeitschrift für deutsche Philologie* 76.
1960. "Hexensalben" in *Medizinischer Monatsspiegel* 8.
1960. "Der Nacherlebte Hexensabbath: Zu Will Peukerts Selbstversuch mit Hexensalben" in *Forschungsfragen unserer Zeit* Paehl. Oberbayern 7.
Piomelli, Daniele and Antonio Pollio
1994 "*In upupa o strige*: A Study in Renaissance Psychotropic Plant Ointments" in *Hist. Phil. Life Sci.* 16.
Plotkin, Mark J.
1994. *Der Schatz der Wayana: Abenteuer bei den Schamanen im Amazonas-Regenwald*. Bern: Scherz.
Pörksen, Gunnhild (ed.)
1988 *Paracelsus—Frühe Schriften zur Heilmittellehre*. Frankfurt: Fischer.
Pohl, Friedrich Wilhelm and Christoph Türcke
1983. *Heilige Hure Vernunft: Luthers nachhaltiger Zauber*. Berlin: Wagenbach.
Pollio, Antonino, Giovanna Aliotta, and E. Giuiliano
1988. "Etnobotanica delle Solanaceae allucinogene europee" in *Atti del Congresso Internazionale di Storia della Farmacia*. Piacenza.
Pörksen, Gunnhild (ed.)
1988. *Paracelsus—Frühe Schriften zur Heilmittellehre*. Frankfurt: Fischer.
Przybyszewski, Stanislaw
1979. *Die Synagogue Satans*. Berlin: Zerling. Originally published 1900. (Reprint of the original edition from 1900.)
Quayle, Eric and Michael Foreman
1986. *The Magic Ointment and Other Cornish Legends*. London: Macmillan.
Rachleff, Owen S.
1990. *The Occult in Art*. London: Cromwell.
Rahner, Hugo
1957. *Griechische Mythen in christlicher Deutung*. Zurich: Rhein-Verlag.
Raiber, Hedwig
1986. *Wir werden was wir sind*. Dusslingen: Chiron.
Randolph, Pascal Beverly
1992. *Magia Sexualis: Die sexualmagischen Lehren der Bruderschaft von Eulis*. Wien: Edition Ananael.
Ranke-Graves, Robert von
1960. *Food for Centaurs*. New York: Doubleday.
1984. *Griechische Mythologie: Quellen und Deutung*. Reinbek: Rowohlt.
1985. *Die Weiße Göttin: Sprache des Mythos*. Reinbek: Rowohlt.
1992. *The Greek Myths* (complete edition). London: Penguin Books.
Rätsch, Christian
1987a. *Kinder des Regenwaldes*. Münster: Coppenrath.
1987b. "Der Rauch von Delphi: Eine ethnopharmrakologische Annäherung" in *Curare* 10(4).
1990. *Pflanzen der Liebe*. Bern: Hallwaeg.
1992. *Hanf als Heilmittel: Eine ethnomedizinsche Bestansaufnahme*. Löhrbach: Werner Pieper's MedienXperimente und Solothurn: Nachtschatten Verlag (Der Grüne Zweig 154).
1993 (ed.). *Naturverehrung und Heilkunst*. Südergellersen: Bruno Martin.
1994. "Die Alraune in der Antike" in *Annali dei Musei Civici dei Rovereto* 10.
1995. *Heilkräuter der Antike in Ägypten, Griechenland und Rom*. Munich: Diederichs Verlag (DG).
1996a. "'Die Grüne Fee': Absinth in der Schweiz" in *Jahrbuch für Ethnomedizin und Bewußtseinsforschung* 5 (1995).
1996b. *Urbock—Bier jenseits von Hopfen und Malz*. Aarau: AT Verlag.

1996c. *Räucherstoffe—Der Atem des Drachen*. Aarau: AT Verlag.
1997a. *Die Steine der Schamanen: Kristalle, Fossilien und die Landschaften des Bewußtseins*. Munich: Diederichs.
1997b. *Enzyklopädie der psychoaktiven Pflanzen*. Aarau: AT Verlag.
1997c. *Medizin aus dem Regenwald*. Neckarsulm: Hammp Verlag/ Natura Med.
1998a. *Enzyklopädie der psychoaktiven Pflanzen*. Aarau: AT Verlag.
1998b. "Das Hexensalbenrezept des Johannes Hartlieb" in Johannes Hartlieb, ed., *Das Buch der verbotenen Künste*. Munich: Diederichs.
1998c. "Paracelsus, der trunkene Heiler" in Roger Liggenstorfer, et al., eds., *Die berauschte Schweiz*. Solothurn: Nachtschatten Verlag.
1998d. "'Arcana, die Geheimmittel' des Paracelsus" in *Natur-heilpraxis* 51(5).
2001a. "Epilog: Geistbewegendes bei Paracelsus" in Olaf Rippe, et al., *Paracelsusmedizin: Altes Wissen in der Heilkunst von heute*. Aarau: AT Verlag.
2001b. "Heras Hexensalbe oder hexen@salbe" in *Hexenwelten*. Hamburg: Holos Verlag.
2002. *Schamanenpflanze Tabak. Band 1: Kultur und Geschichte des Tabaks in der Neuen Welt*. Solothurn: Nachtschatten Verlag.
2003. *Schamanenpflanze Tabak. Band II: Das Rauchkraut erobert die Alte Welt*. Solothurn: Nachtschatten Verlag.

Rätsch, Christian and Claudia Müller-Ebeling
2003. *Lexikon der Liebesmittel: Pflanzliche, mineralische, tierische und synthetische Aphrodisiaka*. Aarau: AT Verlag.

Rätsch, Christian and Jonathan Ott
2003. *Coca und Kokain: Ethnobotanik, Kunst und Chemie*. Aarau: AT Verlag.

Reichel-Dolmatoff, Gerardo
1996. *Das schamanische Universum: Schamanismus, Bewußtsein und Ökologie in Südamerika*. Munich: Diederichs.

Reinhardt, Kay (et al.)
1993. *Drudenfuss & Donnerkeil—"Hexenzauber" und seine Abwehr*. Schongau: Stadtmuseum.

Richter, E.
1960. "Der nacherlebte Hexensabbat" in *Forschungsfragen unserer Zeit* 7.

Riley, Judith Merkle
1994. *Die Hexe von Paris*. Bergisch-Gladbach: Bastei-Lübbe.

Rippe, Olaf, Margret Madejsky, Max Amann, Patricia Ochsner, and Christian Rätsch
2001. *Paracelsusmedizin: Altes Wissen in der Heilkunst von heute*, Aarau: AT Verlag.

Robbins, Rossell Hope
1959. *The Encyclopedia of Witchcraft and Demonology*. New York: Crown.

Robinson, D.
1994. "Plants and Vikings: Everyday Life in Viking Age Denmark" *Botanical Journal of Scotland* 46 (4).

Roth, Lutz, Max Daunderer, and Kurt Kormann
1994. *Giftpflanzen—Pflanzengifte*, 4th ed. Landsberg: ecomed.

Rother, Rea
1997. "Moderne Hexen, die auf Naturmedizin vertrauen" in *Die Weltwoche* 17 (24)NR 17/24.4.97.

Rothman, T.
1972. "De Laguna's Commentaries on Hallucinogenic Drugs and Witchcraft in Dioscorides' Materia Medica" in *Bulletin of the History of Medicine* 46.

Ruck, Carl A. P.
1975. "Euripides' Mother: Vegetables and the Phallos in Aristophanes" in *Arion* N. S. 2 (/1).
1981. "Mushrooms and Philosophers" in *Journal of Ethnopharmacology* 4.
1982. "The Wild and the Cultivated: Wine in Euripides' *Bacchae*" in *Journal of Ethnopharmacology* 5.
1983. "The Offerings from the Hyperboreans" in *Journal of Ethnopharmacology* 8.

Rueb, Franz
1996. *Hexenbrände: Die Schweizergeschichte des Teufelswahns*. Zurich: Weltwoche.

Ruiz de Alarcon, Hernando
1984. *Treatise on the Heathen Superstitions*. Norman, Okla.: University of Oklahoma Press.

Rust, Jürgen
1983. *Aberglaube und Hexenwahn in Schleswig-Holstein*. Garding: Cobra-Verlag.

Rüttner-Cova, Sonja
1988. *Frau Holle: Die gestürzte Göttin*. Basel: Sphinx.

Sallmann, Jean-Michel
1991. *Hexensabbat*. Ravensburg: Ravensburger. Originally published in Paris, 1987.

Samorini, Giorgio and Gilberto Camilla
1995. "Rappresentazioni fungine nell'arte greca" in *Annali dei Musei Civici di Roverto* 10(1994).

Schade, Sigrid
1983. *Schadenzauber und die Magie desr Körpers: Hexenbilder der frühen Neuzeit*. Worms: Werner'sche Verlagsgesellschaft.
1984. "Zur Genese des voyeuristischen Blicks: Das Erotische in den Hexenbildern Hans Baldung Griens" in C. Bischoff et al., eds., (Hg.), *Frauen—Kunst—Geschichte*. Gießen.
1987. "Kunsthexen—Hexenkünste. Hexen in der bildenden Kunst vom. 16. bis 20. Jahrhundert" in van Dülmen, 1987.

Schall, Paul
1965. *Zaubermedizin im Alten China?* Stuttgart: J. Fink Verlag.

Scheffler, Lilian
1983. *Magiá y brujería en México*. Mexico: Panorama Editorial.

Schenk, Gustav
1948. *Schatten der Nacht*. Hannover: Sponholtz.
1954. *Das Buch der Gifte*. Berlin: Safari.

Schipperges, Heinrich
1990. *Der Garten der Gesundheit: Medizin im Mittelalter*. Munich: Deutscher Taschenbuch Verlag.

Schlosser, Alfred
1987. *Die Sage vom Galgenmännlein im Volksglauben und in der Literatur*. Berlin: VWB. Originally published 1912.

Schmidt, Brian B.
1995. "The 'Witch' of En-dor, 1 Samuel 28, and Ancient Near Eastern Necromancy," in Marvin Meyer and Paul Mirecki (ed.) *Ancient Magic and Ritual Power*. Leiden: Brill.

Schmiedeberg, O.
1918. "Über die Pharmaka in der Illias und Odyssee" in *Schriften der wissenschaftlichen Gesellschaft* 36.

Schmitt, Jean-Claude
1993. *Heidenspaß und Höllenangst: Aberglaube im Mittelalter*. Frankfurt and New York: Campus.

Schmölders, Claudia
1983. *Vom Paradies und anderen Gärten*. Cologne: Diederichs.

Schober, Eduard
1984. *Blutbann, Wunderglaube und Hexenwahn*. Klagenfurt: Kärntner Druck- und Verlagsanstalt.

Schoen, Ernest
1963. *Nomina popularia plantarum medicinalium*. Zurich: Galenica.

Schöpf, Hans
1986. *Zauberkräuter*. Graz:. ADEVA Akademische Druck-u. Verlagsanstalt.
2001. *Volksmagie: Vom Beschwören, Heilen und Liebe zaubern*. Graz, Wien, Cologne: STYRIA.

Schröder, Ingo W.
1998. "'Deine Säfte bringen mich nach Phantasienn ...' (1) Die Rolle von Drogen in Neuen Hexenkulten" *Jahrbuch für Ethnomedizin und Bewußtseinsforschung* 5 (1996): Berlin: VWB.

Schultes, Richard E. and Albert Hofmann
1980. *The Botany and Chemistry of Hallucinogens*. Springfield, Ill.: Charles C. Thomas.
1995. *Pflanzen der Götter*. Aarau: AT Verlag.

Schurz, Josef
    1969. *Vom Bilsenkraut zum LSD*. Stuttgart: Kosmos.
Schwamm, Brigitte
    1988. *Atropa belladonna, eine antike Heilpflanze im modernen Arzneischatz*. Stuttgart: Deutscher Apotheker Verlag.
Sebald, Hans
    1990. *Hexen: Damals—und heute?* Frankfurt and Berlin: Ullstein.
Seligmann, Kurt
    n.d. *Das Weltreich der Magie: 5000 Jahre geheime Kunst*. Wiesbaden: Löwit. (Originally published in New York, 1948.)
    1982. "Hexensabbat" in *Hexen und Hexenmeister*. Gütersloh: Moewig.
    1996. *Die magischen Heil- und Schutzmittel*. Berlin: Reimer.
Seligmann, Siegfried
    1996. *Die magischen Heil- und Schutzmittel aus der belebten Natur: Das Pflanzenreich*. Berlin: Reimer.
    1999a. *Die magischen Heil- und Schutzmittel aus der belebten Natur: Das Tierreich*. Berlin: Reimer.
    1999b. *Die magischen Heil- und Schutzmittel aus der belebten Natur: Der Mensch*. Berlin: Reimer.
Sepulveda, Maria Teresa
    1983. *Magiaá, brujería y supersticiones en México*. Mexico: Editorial Everest Mexicana.
Shah, N. C. and M. C. Joshi
    1971. "An Ethnobotanical Study of the Kumaon Region of India" in *Economic Botany* 25.
Sigruna
    1996. "Freya, Walküren, Disen und die Erde" in Vicky Gabriel and Igor Warneck, *Hag & Hexe*, vol. 2. Bündigen.
Silva, Raymond
    1975. *Magie in der Medizin*. Geneva: Ariston.
Simmons, Marc
    1980. *Witchcraft in Southwest: Spanish and Indian Supernaturalism on the Rio Grande*. Lincoln and London: University of Nebraska Press (Bison Books).
Smith, Huston
    1970. "Psychedelic Theophanies and the Religious Life" in *Journal of Psychedelic Drugs* 3 (1).
Söhns, Franz
    1920. *Unsere Pflanzen: Ihre Namenserklärungen und ihre Stellung in der Mythologie und im Volksaberglauben* (6th edition). Leipzig and Berlin: Teubner.
Soldan-Heppe
    1911. *Geschichte der Hexenprozesse*. Revised by Max Bauer. Reprint: Hanau/M.: Müller & Kiepenheuer.
Spilmont, Jean-Pierre
    1984. *Magie*. Munich: Heyne.
Spretnak, Charlene
    1984. *Lost Goddesses of Early Greece*. Boston: Beacon Press.
Stannard, J.
    1962. "The Plant Called Moly." *Osiris* 14: 254–307.
Staschen, Heidi
    1983. "Hexenprozesse im Mittelalter und in der frühen Neuzeit" in *Ergebnisse* 16.
Stelzl, Ulrike
    1983. *Hexenwelt: Hexendarstellungen um 1900*. Berlin: Frölich & Kaufmann.
Stiles, Ezra
    1761. "Extracts from the Itineraries and Miscellanies of Ezra Stiles" in Virgil J. Vogel, *American Indian Medicine*. Norman, Okla.: University of Oklahoma Press.
Storch, Wolfgang (ed.)
    1997. *Mythos Orpeus*. Leipzig: Reclam.
Storl, Wolf-Dieter
    1988a. *Feuer und Asche—Dunkel und Licht: Schiva—Urbild des Menschen*. Freiburg: Bauer.
    1988b. "Hexenkräuter wirken wirklich" in *Esotera* 12 (88).
    1989. "Kosmisch Kochen" in *Esotera* 4 (89).
    1993a. "Die Werkzeuge der Wurzelgräber: Elemente archaischer Pflanzensammelrituale" in C. Rätsch, ed., *Naturverehrung und Heilkunst*. Südergellersen: Bruno Martin.
    1993b. *Von Heilkräutern und Pflanzengottheiten*. Braunschweig: Aurum.
    1996a. "Heilkräuter: Komplexität des Lebendigen" in *Natürlich* 16 (5).
    1996b. *Kräuterkunde*. Braunschweig: Aurum.
    1996c. *Heilkräuter und Zauberpflanzen zwischen Haustür und Gartentor*. Aarau: AT Verlag.
    1997a. *Pflanzendevas—Die Göttin und ihre Pflanzenengel*. Aarau: AT Verlag.
    1997b. "Ernährung, kulturelle Identität und Bewußtsein" in E. Diallo-Ginstl, ed., *Ernährung und Gesundheit*. Stuttgart/Neckarsulm: Natura Med/Hampp.
    2000a. "Die Werkzeuge der Wurzelgräber: Elemente archaischer Pflanzensammelrituale" in Franz-Theo Gottwald and Christian Rätsch, eds., *Rituale des Heilens: Ethnomedizin, Naturerkenntnis und Heilkraft*. Aarau: AT Verlag.
    2000b. *Pflanzen der Kelten*. Aarau: AT Verlag.
    2000c. *Götterpflanze Bilsenkraut*. Solothurn: Nachtschatten Verlag.
    2002. *Shiva, der wilde, gutige Gott*. Burgrain: KOHA.
Stramberg, Chr. Von, et al.
    1986. "Hexenfahrten" in Hermann Hesse, ed., *Spuk- und Hexengeschichten*. Frankfurt: Insel [originally appeared in *Rheinischen Antiquarius* v. II. 4, c. 1851]
Strassmann, René A.
    1994. *Baumheilkunde*. Aarau: AT Verlag.
Ström, Ake V. aund Haralds Biezais
    1975. *Germanische und Baltische Religion*. Stuttgart: Kohlhammer.
Sturm, Dieter and Klaus Völker (ed.)
    1994. *Von denen Vampiren*. Frankfurt: Suhrkamp.
Svoboda, Robert E.
    1993. *Aghora: At the Left Hand of God*. New Dehli: Rupa & Co.
Tabor, Edward
    1970. "Plant Poisons in Shakespeare" in *Economic Botany* 24 (1).
Tieck, Ludwig
    1988. *Hexen-Sabbat*. Frankfurt: Insel.
Tillford, Gregory L.
    1997. *Edible and Medicinal Plants of the Mountains West*. Missoula, Mont.: Mountain Press.
Tochtermann, Sibylle
    1992. *Der allegorisch gedeutete Kirke-Mythos*. Frankfurt: Peter Lang.
Traherne, Thomas
    1991. *Selected Poems and Prose*. Alan Bradford, ed. London: Penguin Books.
van Dülmen, Richard (ed.)
    1987. *Hexenwelten: Magie und Imagination*. Frankfurt: Fischer.
van Zuylen, Gabrielle
    1995. *The Garden: Visions of Paradise*. London: Thames and Hudson.
Vogel, Virgil
    1982. *American Indian Medicine*. Norman, Okla.: University of Oklahoma Press
Vogt, Donald
    1981. "Abisinthium: A Nineteenth-century Drug of Abuse" in *Journal of Ethnopharmacology* 4 (3).
Völker, Klaus (ed.)
    1977. *Von Werwölfen und anderen Tiermenschen*. Munich: Deutscher Taschenbuch Verlag.
vom Scheidt, Jürgen
    1984. "Hexensalben" in W. Schmidbauer and J. vom Scheidt, *Handbuch der Rauschdrogen*. Frankfurt: Fischer.
von Görres, Josef
    1948. *Das nachtländische Reich*. Villach: Mortiz Stadler.
von Hansemann, D.
    1905. *Der Aberglaube in der Medizin und seine Gefahr für Gesundheit und Leben*. Leipzig: B. G. Teubner.
von Perger, K. Ritter
    1864. *Deutsche Pflanzensagen*. Stuttgart and Oehringen: Schaber.

von Stramberg, Chr. et al.
    1986. "Hexenfahrten" in Hermann Hesse, ed., *Spuk- und Hexengeschichten* . Frankfurt: Insel. Originally appeared in *Rheinischen Antiquarius* v. 2 (4), c. 1851.
von Wlislocki, Heinrich
    1891. *Volksglaube und religiöser Brauch der Zigeuner*. Münster: Aschendorffsche Buchhandlung.
Vonarburg, Bruno
    1996. "Die Tollkirsche (1. Teil)" in *Natürlich* 10/96.
Vries, Herman de
    1986. "Über die sogenannten Hexensalben" in *Salix* 2(2).
    1989. *Natural relations*. Nürnberg: Verlag für moderne Kunst.
    1991. "Über die sogenannten Hexensalben" in *Integration* 1. [Revised edition by de Vries 1986.]
    1993. "Heilige bäume, bilsenkraut und bildzeitung" in C. Rätsch, ed., *Naturverehrung und Heilkunst*. Südergellersen: Verlag Bruno Martin.
Walker, Deward E., Jr. (ed.)
    1989. *Witchcraft and Sorcery of the American Native Peoples*. Moscow, Idaho: University of Idaho Press.
Waldvogel, Ruth
    1979. *Pharmakopsychologie der Hexensalben*. Zurich: Selbständige Arbeit am Psychologischen Institut der Universität Zurich, MS.
Wallbergen, Johann
    1988. [*Johann Wallbergens Sammlung*] *Natürlicher Zauberkünste* (1769). Leipzig and Weimar: Gustav Kiepenheuer Verlag.
Wallinger, Elisabeth
    1994. *Hekates Töchter: Hexen in dert römischen Antike*, Wien: Wiener Frauenverlag.
Wasson, R. Gordon
    1986. *Persephone's Quest: Entheogens and the Origins of Religion*. New Haven and London: Yale University Press.
Wasson, R. Gordon, Albert Hofmann, and Carl A. P. Ruck
    1984. *Der Weg nach Eleusis: Ddas Geheimnis der Mysterien*. Frankfurt: Insel.
    1998. *The Road To Eleusis: Unveiling the Secret of the Mysteries* (twentieth anniversary edition). Los Angeles: Hermes Press/Dailey.
Watts, Donald
    2000. *Elsevier's Dictionary of Plant Names and Their Origin*. Amsterdam: Elsevier.
Wedeck, Harry E.
    1966. *A Treasury of Witchcraft: A Source Book of the Magic Arts*. New York: The Citadel Press.
Weiss, Rudolf Fritz
    1991. *Lehrbuch der Phytotherapie*. Stuttgart: Hippokrates.

Werneck, Heinrich L. and Franz Speta
    1980. *Das Kräuterbuch des Johannes Hartlieb*. Graz: Akademische Druck- u. Verlagsanstalt. [= Hartlieb 1980]
Weustenfeld, Wilfried
    1995. *Zauberkräuter von A-Z: Heilende und mystische Wirkung*. Munich: Verlag Peter Erd.
    1997. *Die Rauschdrogen der Hexen und ihre Wirkungen*. Lübeck: Bohmeier Verlag.
Wheelwright, Edith Grey
    1974. *Medical Plants and Their History*. New York: Dover.
Wiemann-Michaels, Annette
    1994. *Die verhexte Speise: Eine ethnopsychosomatische Studie über das Depressive Syndrom in Nepal*. Frankfurt: Peter Lang (Medizin in Entwicklungsländern, 35).
Winkelman, Michael J.
    1992. *Shamans, Priests, and Witches: A Cross-Cultural Study of Magico-Religious Practitioners*. Tempe: Arizona State University.
Wippermann, Günther
    1959. *Aberglaube und Medizin*. Berlin: Verlag für Kunst Verlag Volk und Gesundheit.
Wlislocki, Heinrich von
    1891 *Volksglaube und religiöser Brauch der Zigeuner*. Münster: Aschendorffsche Buchhandlung.
Wohlberg, Joseph
    1990. "Haoma-Soma in the World of Ancient Greece" in *Journal of Psychoactive Drugs* 22 (3).
Wolf, Hans-Jürgen
    1980. *Hexenwahn und Exorzismus: Ein Beitrag zur Kulturgeschichte*. Kriftel: Historia Verlag.
    1994. *Hexenwahn: Hexen in Geschichte und Gegenwart*. Bindlach: Gondrom.
Yilmaz, Martina
    1985. *Zauberkräuter Hexengrün*. Berlin: Johanna Bohmeier.
York, Ute
    1997. *Mondmagie und Liebeszauber: Wunderkräuter, Hexensalben und magisches Wissen für Frauen*. Munich: Knauer.
Zahl, Peter-Paul
    1995. *Teufelsdroge Cannabis* (crime novel). Berlin: Verlag Das Neue Berlin.
Zotter, Hans
    1980. *Antike Medizin: Die medizinische Sammelhandschrift Cod. Vindobonensis 93 in lateinischer und deutscher Sprache*. Graz: Akademische Druck-u. Verlagsanstalt.
Zuylen, Gabrielle van
    1995 *The Garden: Visions of Paradise*. London: Thames and Hudson.

Acknowledgments

Although the three of us have brewed up a new magical potion, like three witches, the idea to write a book about witches' medicine came from our publishers and friends Urs Hunziker and Heinz Knieriemen.

We are particularly grateful to our dear friend and pharmacist Patricia Ochsner. Her ideas and her expertise were important ingredients.

More wonderful additives were provided by Anupama Grell and Roger Liggenstorfer, Wolfgang Kundrus and Janine Warmbier, Conny and Hartwig Kopp, Daniel Delany, Margret Madejsky and Olaf Rippe, Daniela Baumgartner, Andrew Sherrat, and Peter Linzenich.

For the English-language edition we appreciate the contributions of our translator, Annabel Lee, and our editors Susan Davidson, Robin Catalano, and Doris Troy.

Greatest thanks!
To your health. In the name of Hecate!

Index